PERSONNEL LAW

Kenneth L. Sovereign, J.D.

*Member of the Minnesota
and
American Bar Associations*

Reston Publishing Co., Inc.
A Prentice-Hall Company
Reston, Virginia

TO MY WIFE, JANET, WHO TOLERATES ME

Library of Congress Cataloging in Publication Data

Sovereign, Kenneth.
    Personnel law.

    Includes bibiographical references and index.
    1. Labor laws and legislation—United States.
I. Title.
KF3455.S68 1984   344.73′01   83-21267
ISBN 0-8359-5505-2   347.3041

Printed in the United States of America

TABLE OF CONTENTS

ACKNOWLEDGEMENTS

The author is deeply indebted to his many personnel and legal associates, too numerous to mention for their encouragement and suggestions in combining the law with the personnel function. To the approximately one thousand lawyers and personnel practitioners who were participants in seminars conducted by the author and sponsored by professional associations and adult educational facilities of colleges and universities, a special thanks for their practical suggestions when field-testing this relatively new subject of personnel law. However, it is only proper that I accept full responsibility for the conclusions, including errors, omissions, and other "goofs" that may occur.

Special recognition is given to Gary F. Overstreet and Michael W. Monk of the law firm of Finley, Kumble, Wagner, Heine, Underberg & Manley of Beverly Hills, CA, who gave competent legal assistance. John B. Salazar, a personnel practitioner in the San Francisco area, provided expertise in the personnel area. Warren W. McIntire of the College of St. Thomas, St. Paul, MN, made academic contributions to the material.

The use of the excellent library facilities of the State of Minnesota Law Library and the University of Minnesota Industrial Relations Reference Library and the cooperation from their component staffs made possible the necessary research and authoritative references contained in the book. A note of appreciation must be given to Debbie Napiorkowski, the author's former secretary, who placed the typing of the manuscript second only to bearing her first child.

FOREWORD

The personnel function has gone through revolutionary changes since the 1960s. Each of its many subfunctions has been affected drastically by new laws and government regulations. New goals and functions have been mandated. The personnel director's job and the manager's job have been altered substantially; past practice is not only obsolete but possibly illegal.

First, multiple yardsticks for personnel decisions are required *by law*. In 1960 a firm would "hire the best man" in terms of his potential contribution to the firm's profits. Today the term *men* would be changed to *person*; *social* goals (not those set out by the firm) might well take precedence over profits as the key criterion for decision. Indeed, the legally required employment decisions of today's personnel directors and managers might return *lower* profits than if they used the techniques and decision criteria of 1960. But today the personnel function *has no choice* except to blend profit and social welfare criteria in proper proportions.

Second, the personnel function operated in more of a *specialized* framework: employment decisions were employment decisions, promotion decisions were promotion decisions, compensation decisions were compensation decisions, and so on. Today planning, activating, and evaluating these component parts must be integrated into a cohesive whole. A decision to recruit must involve many complicated and highly interrelated legal considerations. A recruitment plan must involve not only how to get the recruit but *legal* selection criteria, *legal* training criteria, *legal* compensation criteria, *legal* promotion criteria, etc.

The manager who is to supervise the new recruit cannot simply exercise best judgment as to who would do the job best. Nor can the union simply exercise such authority.

On the other hand one cannot ignore such concepts as profits, labor productivity and costs, competitive wages and benefits, and other *economic* considerations. These are vital in employment decisions. If these economic objectives are not met satisfactorily, there simply will not be jobs (or sufficient jobs) to effectuate the social objectives and reduce the social turbulence underlying these new laws.

Obviously we must integrate and balance the legal (social) and economic objectives and programs. We must deliberately create a new, positive legal-personnel system in the employing organizations of America.

Current confusion, disarray, and poor practice in personnel and industrial relations are in large measure a result of feeble, piecemeal, and disjointed concepts and programs. They are also a result of fast-moving social and economic changes coupled with a plethora of new legal regulations. We need to improve our conceptual and operational personnel systems by renewed emphasis on general systems and better synthesis of our models at both the theoretical and practical levels. We must improve integration of firm (or organization) and social concepts and their execution in order to improve managerial and professional personnel practice.[1]

We must integrate and implement a whole new set of rights of employees and would-be employees. We are beginning to approach, but are still far from having, paradigm general systems in personnel. This book is an important contribution to that end because it seeks to relate, explain, and integrate two major and vital dimensions of human resource management—personnel and labor (employment) law—in toto, not just bits and pieces or isolated cases. This book is directed to, and oriented toward, the personnel and industrial relations practitioner (and student) with the aim of improving performance through preventive professional practice based on improved knowledge, understanding, and wisdom.

One of the great tragedies is the knowledge application gap. So few practitioners use the best available principles and practices. Ignorance is the most important single cause of generally weak managerial (and personnel and industrial relations) performance—and hence failures in organization performance. Although this is the *knowledge* economy (hopefully not just the *information* economy), we don't use the knowledge that we have. Fortunately, Ken Sovereign's book goes far in removing the barriers of ignorance in relationships between personnel and labor law in the United States.

This is a new and different kind of textbook. It appears at a significant time of crisis in unsatisfactory productivity, and managerial performance, both as a nation and in individual organizations. Institutional health and employment relations are vitally related at both macro and micro levels. This book is designed to show what to do, how to do it, when to do it, and why. Its emphasis is on the practical—what to do on the job, how best to combine personnel principles and practice with labor (and employment) laws and regulations, not just how to get out of trouble but how to keep from getting into trouble in employment relationships. We have turned the corner to preventive personnel management.

Quite a few groups can be helped greatly by this book: managers, personnel people, would-be managers, employees, unions, the public, legislators, and certainly students. This text is especially valuable for those working for organizations too small to have a formal personnel and

---

[1] Cf. Marc J. Wallace, Jr., "Methodology, Research Practice, and Progress in Personnel and Industrial Relations," *Academy of Management Review* 8, no. 1 (1983):6–13.

industrial relations department. Above all, this text will send the college student into the real world, where legal yardsticks are among the major criteria in managerial decision making.

Managers, by one definition, are those who obtain results through the use of others, their employees (their personnel). Judgment of a manager's success or failure should be measured, not by what that manager does, but by what the team (personnel) accomplishes. As Dale Yoder wrote almost half a century ago in the first edition of his classic and definitive personnel text, every manager, whether knowing it or not, or whether wanting to be or not, is a personnel manager.[2] Studies at M.I.T. and elsewhere in the 1940s showed that 15 percent of managerial failures resulted from technical (substantive) weaknesses; 85 percent were from human relations (personnel) failings.

Most managers have not had formal training in either personnel and industrial relations or labor law. Many business and engineering schools, for example, do not require completion of a single course in these subjects. (Although more schools are now requiring such courses.)

It is small wonder that so many managers are uninformed and lack understanding in these areas. It's not too surprising that they resent "government intrusion" into their "right" to manage. These managers seem singularly unaware of where these "rights" came from—there is not, to my knowledge, evidence that Moses descended from the Mount a second time with a Stone of Management Rights.

Social institutions are created by society (the public). There are socially approved and accepted behaviors and ways of doing things. To survive, institutions must meet the test of social efficiency: do they accomplish society's goals?

Employment relationships provide numerous examples of social institutions: labor movements, collective bargaining, unions, worker's compensation, especially forms of management (agency, participative, owner-management, etc.). Society (or the public) creates, approves, and regulates social institutions. The law is an institution, and perhaps a stronger and more durable form of institution than customs. Public regulation is from society. The public sometimes regulates in ignorance; much of labor law and regulation consists of corrective measures.

Few institutions have been as badly perceived as the American form of management. Trusts and cartels, marketing, environment, financial methods, etc., have all been regulated, especially in this century. In the field of personnel and industrial relations we have used unions and labor laws to regulate and improve managerial practice and improve employment conditions for employees. There is a school of thought, to which I subscribe, that management got unions because they deserved them. Society has broadened management (and the employer's) responsibilities

---

[2] Dale Yoder. *Personnel and Labor Relations* (New York: Prentice-Hall Inc., 1938).

to include heavy doses of social responsibility as well as traditional profit making, efficiency, etc. Few top managers would argue that all of a business' goals boil down to one word: *profits*. Thus, today's and tomorrow's managers need to learn new concepts and skills, not the least of which are personnel and labor law, the subject of this book.

Personnel and labor law is a complex and complicated subject. This book does much to explain, in simple but accurate terms, how it works—what one can and should do and what one cannot. It must be pointed out, as Sovereign does, that many laws outrun the theory and knowledge base. Indeed, the public (society) has been very derelict in its responsibilities by failing to provide objective and measurable employment relations goals. For example, the Declaration of Independence, Constitution, and Bill of Rights are silent on the subject of employment, labor rights, and all other major concepts of employment relationships. Today, rights, authorities, and laws are split among federal, state, and other agencies, seemingly without regard to their alignment. We have gaps, overlaps, and inconsistencies beyond belief in industrial jurisprudence.

Labor laws, labor regulations, labor agreements, etc., include not only written documents; they also include such disparate forms as legal interpretations, verbal agreements, and past practice. Indeed, many portions of a firm's industrial jurisprudence may have relevance to that plant only.

As an example of the confusion in personnel-labor law, it is possible for me to puruse an employment grievance by going to (1) the National Labor Relations Board, (2) the equal employment route, (3) the courts, or (4) arbitration. (The first three have a common legal system; arbitration does not share their system and in effect has its own.) I can pursue relief via any of these four routes or all four simultaneously. If I am turned down by one of these institutions, I can start with another.

Labor laws are most often specific to specific personnel functions, e.g., recruitment, selection, compensation, training, and labor relations. This book is organized around this concept but strongly stresses interrelationships between and among specific functions and laws (a systems approach). Generally these laws fit as if they were put together by a committee and prove (unnecessarily) difficult to comprehend and put into practice.

As the author says, one can't just turn all this mess over to a lawyer; it's too expensive and there aren't enough competent labor lawyers. (General lawyers, or nonlabor legal specialists, typically have difficulty in comprehending and practicing labor law.)

What happens to the personnel and industrial relations specialists in the firm or organization? Can't they be expected to handle most labor law problems?

Many cannot, because most personnel people haven't had sufficient training or experience in personnel or labor law. This book should be especially valuable for them and enable them to do much more in their area.

Equally important, most firms and organizations do not, and cannot, afford to have personnel specialists. As a rule of thumb, a firm usually has about 100 employees before it employs a personnel person. Far fewer than half of U.S. firms have this many employees; 25 employees constitutes a large firm in the Unites States.

Without a personnel specialist, line managers must take care of these functions. This book is a handy reference for line managers, as well as those about to enter the business world.

"Personnel is the people part of the organization." This is true. And people have emotions, personalities, individual differences, and other human qualities. Some labor laws, personnel rules, etc., reflect *procedural* as well as substantive considerations—and one shouldn't be surprised if employees, managers, union officials, and bureaucrats get excited in the processes of relating personnel and labor law.

It takes both experience and formal education to be a personnel professional. A book of this kind is best written by one who has studied, taught, and practiced *both* labor law and personnel and industrial relations. Relationships between personnel and labor law, nuances, understanding, and wisdom, as well as synthesis and system, are improved by one with such combined experience. The author of this book meets this requirement handsomely.

Finally, one of the most cogent questions is, "Is this book too tough for me to grasp, even if I have to study it by myself, without being a student in a formal course in personnel, labor law, or personnel and labor law?" Of course, the answer depends on the reader's aptitudes, abilities, and experience. Not everybody can handle this book, but most college students, managers, and those with more than clerical experience in personnel should manage. The author of this book deliberately employs a writing style and level to facilitate understanding and interest the reader. This book's problem-centered approach reads as if written by someone who has been there and who speaks the language of the plant. This approach enlivens and enriches the pages that follow.

H.G. Heneman, Jr.
Professor Emeritus
University of Minnesota
Industrial Relations Center

PREFACE

IN ALL THINGS, SUCCESS DEPENDS UPON PREVIOUS PREPARA-
TION, AND WITHOUT SUCH PREPARATION THERE IS SURE TO BE
FAILURE.

CONFUCIUS

In recent years the law has made an increasing attempt to resolve social problems. Since organizational success is largely dependent on a good relationship of the employee to the organization, this new area of the law has resulted in a new constraint on personnel management that has made it imperative for practitioners to have a working knowledge of legal permissible activities and possible trouble areas with employees. The importance of legal knowledge in personnel management is expanding so rapidly that students who become managers or personnel administrators must be aware of the law if they are to avoid obsolescence at the beginning of their careers. This book is designed to alert students and tomorrow's managers of the legal considerations when an employer-employee relationship is established or contemplated.

The text is also useful to personnel practitioners and managers who are experiencing frustrations with the law in carrying out their daily tasks. The book illustrates how personnel practices and procedures that were considered sound concepts by most textbooks and practitioners have been eroded by statutes and court decisions. The business organization must cope with this legal change by employing managers and personnel administrators who update the policies and practices and can endure the legal climate in order to survive. In the application of the law to the traditional concepts of personnel management, the text pays special attention to the legal pitfalls of accepted practices and policies.

The personnel function is no longer rated as to its effectiveness on such factors as employee motivation, attitude, and productivity. Corporate personnel departments are considered staff support for the profit centers. The possibilities of loss through legal infractions are alarming.

Failure to accept the new legal climate will mitigate the personnel function to the extent that it will lose the gains it has achieved in recent years as a major professional staff function.

This text shows how accepted personnel administration by top management is subject to an external audit by the newly acquired employee's rights, enforceable through regulatory agencies and court decisions. The text discusses the traditional personnel practices and concepts used by management and taught in the classrooms of most colleges and universities and then shows how recent legal developments have either made many of these practices obsolete or have drastically changed them. The resource materials in personnel management textbooks and the labor law textbooks are blended into a new concept of personnel management. The emphasis on the professional-practical approach will help the student make the transition from the academic climate to the practical climate of human relations.

The author's experience enables him to present the material from the viewpoint of a personnel administrator, a lawyer, and a classroom instructor. The author became a lawyer while a personnel executive. For 18 years he instituted programs and policies in a large multiplant corporation as a personnel executive with a legal background and for 10 years as corporate counsel with a personnel executive background.

This text is not intended to replace the legal counsel of a company but to enable the manager to determine when to seek legal advice, make more efficient and economical use of the counsel, and make better appraisals of the quality of legal service.

The book is the author's interpretation of the subjects covered. It is to the best of the author's knowledge and belief accurate and authoritative. The material offered is with the understanding that it is not to be interpreted as legal advice or as consulting services. The cases cited are the courts' interpretation of the law as reported to the best of the author's knowledge as of November 1, 1983. They are illustrative of legal principles developed by courts and should not be used as legal authority without further research.

CHAPTER I

INFLUENCE OF THE LAW ON THE PERSONNEL FUNCTION

Chapter Contents
*Introduction
*Evolution Of Personnel Function
*Merging Of The Law Into Personnel
  Function
*Federal Laws Most Frequently
  Encountered In Personnel
  Management
*Education Of Workers
  As To Their Rights
*Relationship Of Personnel Problems
  To Legal Problems
*Summary And Conclusions

INTRODUCTION

Since the 1960s the law has imposed more restraint on the employee-employer relationship than at any other time. This pressure from regulations has affected traditional personnel policies and practices in two ways. Some personnel practitioners have abandoned all their previous practices for fear of running afoul of the law and end up doing nothing. An example of this attitude is refusal of employers to

1

give reference checks on job applicants. This practice protects one from litigation but when the practice becomes universal, everybody is hired, including the rapist and the kleptomaniac.

Another school of personnel practitioners has reacted to law by changing nothing until the law says change and then either complies with it or challenges it. An example might be a policy of compulsory retirement. After a complaint is filed under the law that prevents compulsory retirement until age 70, a policy is changed. However, when it comes to promotion, no consideration is given to a qualified 58-year-old but a 35-year-old is promoted unless challenged.

Neither reaction to the merging of the law into the personnel func-tion is correct. Doing nothing is a disregard for the law that can result in increased employee costs. Waiting for the law to force change in policy will subsequently result in a costly change, one that neither the employer nor employee may like.

The law's moving into the personnel office has forced the personnel administrator to consider not only the traditional employee relations consequences but a new problem of legal implications when making an employment decision. This chapter describes how the merging of the law into the personnel function has changed the work day of the personnel practitioner and prepares the reader for a more detailed treatment of the various laws in subsequent chapters.

EVOLUTION OF PERSONNEL FUNCTION

The personnel function as a part of the organization developed from necessity. Somebody was needed to hire employees, process termination, expedite paperwork, administer employee insurance, and act as a liason between management and the employee. Personnel practitioners were originally semiprofessional do-gooders; as organizations became larger, the function grew from an administrative task to one that involved decision making. The personnel director took a place in the "management cabinet" and was largely responsi-ble for people problems. In this intermediate stage of development, personnel was basically a technical function. As more regulations were passed and human resources became more expensive and important to the organization, the personnel director was regarded as a practical but professionally result-oriented person. The director worked closely with the chief executive officer on the people aspects of the business. At this state of the development law began to merge with the personnel function.[1]

---

[1] For references on personnel function see William F. Glueck, *Personnel: A Diagnostic Approach* (Plano, TX: Business Publications, Inc., 1982); Wayne F. Cascio and

MERGING OF THE LAW INTO PERSONNEL FUNCTION

With the enactment of several laws dealing with employee relations in the 1960s and 1970s, the personnel function saw another stage of development, whereby the law must be considered in almost every decision made by the personnel practitioner. Employee relations laws have had a profound effect on policies and practices of both large and small organizations. These policies and practices are subject to an external audit by a government regulatory agency. In order to pass this external audit, personnel administration must be more objective and develop job-related policies.

The legislative history of the employee relations laws clearly shows that these laws are not contrary to organizational goals; however, improper administration may result in not only added costs of doing business but also the impediment of business growth and proper use of human resources. Employee relations laws are relatively new, and accordingly there are many gray areas. The legal process of their interpretation by the courts is slow and often subject to the social climate existing when the court has a case before it. For this reason the gray areas afford the opportunity to management either to comply or challenge the application of the law to a given set of facts.

The philosophy of top management or its belief of the reasonableness of the particular law often influences management's decision on whether the law should be challenged. Management in the decision-making process seeks legal counsel, but lawyers also differ on the application of the law to a given set of facts unless there is a well-settled principle of law involved. Since the legal mind is seldom trained to consider the employee relations consequences of a legal decision, the input of the personnel practitioner at this stage of the decision is highly important.

The practitioner must not only point out the employee relations consequences but also consider the extent of compliance in other companies in the labor market areas as well as what the companies selling the same product are doing to ensure cost comparability. This entry of the law into the personnel function does not mean that personnel administrators must be lawyers, but they must be aware of possible legal implications and permissible activities. Because contemporary

Elias Awad, *Human Resource Management* (Reston, VA: Reston Publishing Co.,Inc., 1981); Dale S. Beach, *The Management of People at Work* (New York: Macmillan, 1980); Herbert G. Heneman III, Donald P. Schwab, John A. Fossum and Lee D. Dyer, *Personnel Human Resource Management* (Homewood, IL: Richard D. Irwin, Inc., 1980); Wayne F. Cascio, *Applied Psychology* (Reston, VA: Reston Publishing Co., Inc., 1978).

personnel administration must consider the legal implications before action is taken, more knowledge of the law is required than in the past.

FEDERAL LAWS MOST FREQUENTLY ENCOUNTERED IN PERSONNEL MANAGEMENT

The merging of the laws into the personnel function was a gradual process, accelerated by enforcement of discrimination laws, federal control of pension plans and welfare problems, and safety regulations, all of which seemed to come into focus in the middle 1970s. Exhibit I-1 lists the laws most frequently encountered by personnel management. Such laws as the Lea Act (antifeatherbedding in the broadcasting industry), Bynes Act (transportation of strike breakers), and Portal to Portal Act (prohibiting payment for travel to and from the work site under Fair Labor Standards Act) have been eliminated from the table because of their limited application or their universally accepted and followed provisions.

EXHIBIT I-1

Date	Name	Description
1866	Civil Rights Act	All persons are protected by
1870	(Sect. 1981 U.S. Code)	same laws regardless of race.
1931	Davis-Bacon Act	Requires federal construction contractors to pay prevailing wage rates.
1932	Norris-LaGuardia Act	Cannot use injunction to prevent a strike.
1935	National Labor Relations Act	Government intervention in labor-management matters, encourages union growth.
1936	Walsh-Healy Act	Establishes minimum and overtime rates for government contractors.
1938	Fair Labor Standards Act as amended	Sets minimum and overtime rates and time and one-half after 40 hours for all employers in interstate commerce.

continued

EXHIBIT I-1

Date	Name	Description
1947	Taft-Hartley Act (amendment to National Labor Relations Act)	Permits states to pass right-to-work laws, promotes free choice in accepting or rejecting union membership.
1959	Labor Management Reporting and Disclosure Act (Landrum-Griffin Act, amendment to National Labor Relations Act)	Gives employees more rights against union leaders. Eliminates sweetheart contracts. Requires disclosure of union financial affairs.
1963	Equal Pay Act	Requires same pay for women as for men doing similar work under similar working conditions.
1964 1972	Civil Rights Act Amended (Title VII)	Prohibits job discrimination based on race, color, religion, sex, or national origin.
1967 1978	Age Discrimination in Employment Act Amended	No job discrimination based on age for persons between 40 to 70 years old.
1967	Veterans Reemployment Rights as amended (Military Selective Service Act)	Requires employer to grant leaves of absence for military duty.
1970	Executive Order 11246	Federal contractors or sub-contractors prohibited from job discrimination based on race, color, religion, or national origin.
1970	Consumer Credit Protection Act	Puts restrictions on discharge for garnishment of more than debt.
1970	Occupational Safety and Health Act	Employer in interstate commerce must comply with federal health and safety standards; permits state administration.
1973	Health Maintenance Organization	Requires employers to offer employees optional health insurance coverage where available as an alternative to company plan.

continued

EXHIBIT I-1

Date	Name	Description
1973	Vocation Rehabilitation Act	Government contractors must take affirmative action to employ and advance qualified handicapped workers.
1974	Employee Retirement Income Security Act (ERISA)	Requires vesting in pension plans, insures pension funds, and requires employee communication.
1974	Vietnam Veterans Readjustment Assistance Act	Government contractors shall take affirmative action to employ and advance qualified Vietnam-era veterans.
1978	Pregnancy Discrimination Amendment to Title VII	Requires equal treatment for all employment practices with respect to pregnancy, childbirth, or related medical conditions.
	State Worker's Compensation Laws	Requires employers to pay compensation for work-related injuries; amount varies from state to state.
	State Unemployment Compensation Laws	Gives financial assistance for persons unemployed through no fault of their own; federal government levies tax, returns part to states.
	State Fair Employment Practices Legislation	Can supplement federal law by being more strict in job discrimination requirements.
	Miscellaneous state employment laws	Covers garnishments, polygraph tests, disclosure of employment information, where federal government does not preempt.

The mention of the state laws is only to remind the reader that they exist; often they close the jurisdictional loopholes left by the federal laws.

EDUCATION OF WORKERS AS TO THEIR RIGHTS

The frequency of legal problems in the contemporary personnel practitioner's day is beyond the comprehension of the personnel administrator of two decades earlier. The change is not only caused by the existence of regulations and laws but also by the worker being better educated on rights and obligations. Most laws and regulations promote communication to the employee by requiring the employer to post official notices to employees of their rights and the employer's obligations under the specific law. Many states also have similar posting requirements where federal laws do not apply. Exhibit I-2 illustrates the posting notice requirements of the federal laws. Most statutes require the regulatory agency to impose a penalty or fine for failure to meet the posting requirements. The regulatory agency will usually supply the poster on request. Defacement or covering part of the notice is deemed unacceptable posting. Posting provisions generally require that the notice be posted in a conspicuous place so as to permit ready observance. For some laws both applicants and employees must be communicated to; accordingly, the employment or personnel office is logical place for the postings. The employer who posts by the time clock or at an exit complies with the requirements of a conspicuous place but the posting is seldom read. Communications to employees should be placed where the employee will take time to read; an entrance, exit, or a time clock is not usually one of those places.

EXHIBIT I-2

Federal Statute	Employers Required to Post
Fair Labor Standards Act	Employers engaged in interstate commerce.
Walsh-Healy Act	Establishments engaged on a government supply contract exceeding $10,000.
Davis-Bacon Act	Employers on public construction contracts exceeding $2,000.
Civil Rights Act of 1964 as amended Title VII*	Employers of 15 or more employees and engaged in interstate commerce.

continued

EXHIBIT I-2

Federal Statute	Employers Required to Post
Executive Order 11246*	Federal government contractors and subcontractors, contractors under federally assisted construction contracts.
Vocational Rehabilitation Act of 1973*	Establishments engaged on government procurement contract exceeding $2,500.
Vietnam Era Veterans Readjustment Act of 1974*	Establishments engaged on a government procurement contract exceeding $10,000.
Age Discrimination in Employment Act, as amended	Employers of 20 or more employees and engaged in interstate commerce.
Occupational Safety and Health Act (where there is no state plan)	Employers engaged in a business affecting commerce.

* EEO Poster #1420 is the appropriate notice for compliance with these federal requirements.

In addition to communication via government posters, the labor unions have publicized the workers' rights under the laws and regulations in their periodicals and at meetings. They also hold training seminars for their members and leaders on the law and give information on how to exercise their rights. Forty-one labor education centers on university campuses work with labor organizations to provide educational opportunities to union members. (Most of these universities also have management education centers.) These labor education centers have a full-time staff who work with an advisory committee of union leaders. They develop a curriculum and course material in a wide variety of subjects. The centers are usually supported in part by the university budget, the remainder coming from tuition. Exhibit I-3 illustrates subjects in labor education classes.

EXHIBIT I-3

Name	Course Content
Workplace Safety and Health	Teaches safety and health hazard recognition, avoidance, and prevention. OSHA law, abatement techniques.

continued

EXHIBIT I-3

Name	Course Content
Railroad Unionism	*Topics covered include the development of the railroads and railroad unions, the Railway Labor Act, collective bargaining and grievance handling in the railroad and airline industries.*
Worker's Compensation	*To advise the members on what benefits are available and what the member must do to obtain benefits.*
Arbitration	*Covers discipline, workers' rights.*
Your Work/Your Health	*Health hazard recognition, evaluation and control, access to records.*
Organizing Issues and Strategies	*Guidelines for unions during organizing campaigns and laws covering organizing. The class also covers decertification, deauthorization, and internal organizing.*
Advanced Grievance Handling	*Course concentrates on grievance handling.*
Labor Law	*Covers public and private sector laws dealing with unfair labor practices, discrimination, interference with employee rights, good faith bargaining, and other subjects.*
Frontline Survival: Strategies for Women at Work	*The class covers how to be more assertive, what to do if sexually harassed on the job, how to be a more powerful negotiator.*

Source: 1983–1984 Union Leadership Academy course information, Labor Education Service, University of Minnesota, Minneapolis, MN.

A function of labor education centers at universities is to communicate to the union membership to encourage participation. Each school year 200 to 300 members will attend these classes on a given campus.

The media, notice-posting requirements of the several states, labor education centers, and the high level of education among the workers have contributed to making contemporary employees well-educated on procedures and remedies when their rights are violated. An employee who knows these rights and obligations is more likely to use those rights against an employer than the less-educated employee of the past, although some of the statutes granting those rights have existed for many years.

RELATIONSHIP OF PERSONNEL PROBLEMS TO LEGAL PROBLEMS

Although the personnel practitioner may be aware of the legal consequences of an employment decision, often other members of management are not. Management is sometimes hostile to the changes necessary to comply with government regulations and interference with employment decisions. It becomes the duty of the personnel practitioner to make management aware of the consequences of the regulations and applicable laws, to assess policies and practices in relation to developments in the law, and to obtain legal counsel when necessary. As the personnel function of management attempts to solve legal problems, solutions must be weighed in light of employee relations consequences. The following hypothetical situations point out the dilemma of the personnel practitioner since the law has entered that office.

A Personnel Administrator's Day

Situation	*Personnel administrator interviews a white female applicant and tells her she has to work shifts. She says has to talk to her husband about that. She states that she may be pregnant. Later interviews a less qualified but acceptable black unmarried female applicant and hires her.*
Legal Considerations	*Here the personnel administrator is exposed legally to a possible charge of sex discrimination under Title VII because of refusal to hire due to possible pregnancy. Is she an applicant before she talks to her husband or is she merely inquiring about the working conditions?*
Employee Relations Considerations	*Employee relations consequence is whether a pregnant employee is only short-term before she takes a leave of absence. Is pregnancy a consideration as to qualifications? What about training time, turnover rate, etc.?*
Situation	*Wife of an employee is a qualified over-the-road driver and applies for an opening as a driving partner of a married over-the-road driver.*
Legal Considerations	*If one refuses to hire, what is job-related reason? Are moral considerations valid for disqualification under Title VII?*
Employee Relations Considerations	*This can cause domestic problems that will reflect on performance, and stability of employment of both male and female employees.*
Situation	*Employee has been off work and ill for 14 weeks (sick benefits expired) and returns with a doctor's slip stating that she can perform only "light work." Supervisor says he does not have light work and sends her to personnel office.*

continued

A Personnel Administrator's Day

Legal Considerations

Under most handicap laws (both state and federal), must make reasonable effort to accommodate. If there is no light work, what data are available as to the physical requirements of all the jobs? Can you transfer to make room for handicapped worker?

Employee Relations Considerations

Past practice is to give light work to employees with an industrial accident to avoid loss of time for safety record purposes and loss of income for insurance purposes. What is the medical definition of light work; what is the employer's definition?

Situation

White male employee who had a better performance appraisal rating than a black female wants to know why he was not promoted instead of the black female.

Legal Considerations

Affirmative action goals are being satisfied, but was white male discriminated against to the extent that there will be a reverse discrimination charge?

Employee Relations Considerations

How valid is the performance appraisal program? It is subject to legal scrutiny. It has been the criterion used for promotions in the past although never validated.

Situation

Former employee stops in and demands to see her personnel file. The telephone rings. A prospective employer is calling for reference about the person demanding to see her file, who was discharged for allegedly refusing sexual relations with her married supervisor.

Legal Considerations

What was put in the file as the reason for termination? Is it libelous? What legal rights has the former employee to see her file? Was there job-related cause for discharge?

Employee Relations Considerations

How valid is the supervisor's denial of the facts? What is the source of information that leads to the decision to discharge? Are there other similar incidents that the company has been aware of and failed to do anything about?

Situation

Chief executive officer calls and wants to know why his secretary must keep a record of her time worked to be paid overtime.

Legal Considerations

Does the secretary's job content meet the requirements of the Fair Labor Standards Act to make her exempt from overtime? Is the job description accurate?

Employee Relations Considerations

CEO's secretary has probably objected to keeping her time, wants to be part of the management team who are exempted from overtime, wants to be different from other secretaries. Also she is a key person when you want to see the boss or communicate to him when you cannot see him. She often influences the boss on people problems.

continued

A Personnel Administrator's Day

Situation	*Supervisor wants to promote a qualified female to a job similar to one that a male is performing but it would result in a six–salary-grade increase if female was paid same as male. Six–salary-grade increase is against wage and salary policy.*
Legal Considerations	*Equal pay law must be considered. If doing the same work, must be paid the same regardless of policy. If refused promotion, sex discrimination charge is possible.*
Employee Relations Considerations	*What about other employees who have been held to the salary increase policy? What other salary inequities will be created if the six–salary-step increase is granted?*
Situation	*Personnel practitioner attends meeting with office supervisor who wants to terminate an employee who was a leader in a meeting with other employees about the length of their coffee break periods, a salary increase policy (office is nonunion).*
Legal Considerations	*Is this kind of action protected by the National Labor Relations Act although no union? Can one employee act collectively without a union? Is one meeting collective action under the law?*
Employee Relations Considerations	*This is a disruptive incident. Employer must maintain order in the office, cannot have employees getting together every time they are dissatisfied. Leader could cause problems, even promote a union if demands are not met.*
Situation	*Personnel administrator attends a meeting with supervisor who is investigating a rule violation with an employee. Employee says he wants a union representative present but he will be out of town for one week so wants the meeting postponed until he returns.*
Legal Considerations	*What legal rights does employee have for union representation? If he does have such a right, must you postpone the meeting for one week? Time may be an important consideration. Can you permanently postpone the meeting?*
Employee Relations Considerations	*Are you giving the union-represented employee an advantage that a nonunion representative does not have? Is this going around the grievance procedure? Union representative will interfere with investigation process.*
Situation	*OSHA inspection is taking place. Company walk-around representative objects to inspector entering certain areas and wants to stop the inspection.*
Legal Considerations	*Can you refuse a portion of the inspection after you have consented to entry under the rule that you can initially demand a search warrant for entry?*

continued

A Personnel Administrator's Day

Employee Relations Consideration	*What does the company want to hide in these areas? Is there something unsafe about the area to cause employees to refuse to work there? Is there some secret information that inspection will reveal?*
Situation	*Supervisor inquires whether he can stop an employee from punching the time clock a half hour early and punching out half hour after end of shift.*
Legal Considerations	*What is the employee doing the half hour before and after work time? Working for the employer to claim later overtime? How would the Department of Labor interpret this under the Fair Labor Standards Act?*
Employee Relations Considerations	*Why not trust the employee? Maybe he/she is doing it for convenience, is never late for work, avoids traffic delays, rides in car pool, or takes spouse to work.*
Situation	*Personnel administrator receives a call from supervisor that National Guard reservist wants six-month leave to go to officer's training school for the National Guard reservist.*
Legal Considerations	*Must give leave of absence for military duty but is this a voluntary assignment for which a leave of absence can be denied? Not sure, no case on it.*
Employee Relations Consideration	*Too long a leave. Employee must be replaced by training a new person.*

Whether the solutions of these problems should be based on legal considerations or employee relations considerations depends on several factors:

1. Do the facts fit into a well-established principle of law or is this a gray area, where there is a choice?

2. Is the employee relations consequence so severe that it is worth the cost of challenging the law to get a court interpretation?

3. What are the indirect and direct costs of compliance as compared to challenging the law through the courts?

4. How necessary to the company are the employee relations consequences? What are the problems if the employer complied to an unsettled area of the law?

In the past, determinations in employment decisions were made on instinct and had no basis except a certainty by the decision maker that they were right. The above examples point out that such decisions can, and often do, have legal consequences. When such a decision was made in the past, only management reviewed it. The law has become the second party in the reviewing process.

These considerations are available only if there is uncertainty about the interpretation of the statute or regulation. Management is responsible for compliance where there is no doubt about interpretation. The reasonableness of the statute or regulation also affects top management's decision on whether to challenge the law. The personnel practitioner's opinion of whether the law can be lived with often has a bearing on the decision. The personnel practitioner in the 1980s must find solutions to such employee relations problems if obsolescence is to be avoided.

SUMMARY AND CONCLUSIONS

The personnel function grew from necessity for staff assistance in the hiring or terminating of an employee and performing the necessary administrative functions related to the employee-employer relationship.

When the law became a part of the personnel function, as with any merger, new problems were created. At the time of the merger employees were well-educated; for those who wanted more educational opportunities, the state-supported university labor education centers are available.

In considering the relationship of the legal requirements to the employee relations consequences, the personnel practitioner must factor in such elements as the extent of compliance in other companies using the same labor market and actions to keep costs in line with the competition.

Many organizations believe that growing legal requirements have increased the cost of doing business. They begrudge the changes. In reality, no law or court decision demands:

* hiring the marginal applicant or not hiring the best-qualified applicant,
* retaining the incompetent employee, or
* promoting the unqualified employee.

What the law does is prescribe the proper manner for administrating personnel practices and policies but does not decide what the policies should be. Contemporary personnel management must consistently consider legal implications before policies are implemented in order to avoid costly legal problems.

Company policies and practices traditionally have been subjected only to internal audit by those within the organization. However, the law, courts, and regulatory agencies constitute a new and increasingly forceful external audit. They are making personnel administration more objective and more accountable.

Management often resists interference with its own way of doing business, especially a change that inhibits time-tested practices and curtails alternatives. Today's personnel administrator must still find a way to communicate to operating management that it may not have a full range of choices about how it deals with employees but is not prevented from acting in the best interests of the business. The first step to overcome this resistance is for the practitioner to accept the change that started in the early 1970s and has intensified subsequently.

The force of laws and regulatory agency guidelines has prompted greater professionalism of personnel administration. Casual, subjective administrative decisions have had to give way to clearly written, defensible policies.

Practices such as administering unvalidated tests as a panacea in hiring or requiring a high-school education not really needed to perform a particular job, not stating the real reason for termination, writing job descriptions to justify a salary increase but really not describing the job that an employee is doing, were common personnel practices. However, they no longer fit into professional personnel management.

Not only is it an absolute business necessity to have written personnel policies that can be universally accepted by operating management and objectively applied; it is also imperative that the policies be reviewed regularly in light of changing laws and legal interpretations. Generally, any policy that has not been updated for five years is obsolete.

Another fact that the personnel administrator must recognize is that the law does not concern itself with consequences of employee relations nor does it consider some of the problems that may be created by its interpretations and enforcement. Personnel administrators are increasingly faced with correlating a number of seemingly conflicting legal and employee relations implications. Therefore, they must have enough knowledge of the law to be aware of the legal implications and when to seek legal counsel.

A vital part of personnel administration involves advising management of the consequences for failure to apply the law as interpreted by a regulatory agency. As new laws have been enacted and government agencies created to enforce them, gray areas have erupted.

Most uncertainties in the law have resulted from regulatory agencies issuing guidelines or interpretative bulletins that sometimes exceed the original intent of a law. Until there is a sufficient body of judicial interpretation of these guidelines and agency interpretations, an organization has the option to challenge them. The extent of compliance to new laws that are not yet judicially interpreted is a business decision. The personnel administrator with the assistance of legal counsel must advise management of the alternatives so that the company can make a sound business decision, comply, challenge, or wait for enforcement procedures of the regulatory agency.

CHAPTER II

ROLE OF LEGAL COUNSEL IN PERSONNEL FUNCTION

Chapter Contents
*Introduction
*What To Expect Of Legal Counsel
*Use Of Legal Counsel In Labor Relations
*Distinction Between Personnel And Legal Function
*Increase In Litigation
*Function Of In-House Counsel
*Risk Analysis In Considering Litigation
*Relationship Of Legal Counsel To Employees
*Obtaining Legal Opinions
*Explanation Of Pretrial Procedures
*Summary And Conclusions

INTRODUCTION

In the 1970s there was a growing dependency of the personnel function on the legal counsel. This was caused by the social legislation of the late 1960s and early 1970s whereby the law has become an external auditor of the personnel function. The contemporary personnel practitioner must have enough knowledge of the law to make a determination of when legal advice is necessary and to use legal counsel in the most economical way.

This chapter's objective is not only to assist the personnel administrator in the economic use of legal counsel but to give a better understanding of how the corporate law department or law firm functions when called on for advice in the personnel area. The practitioner must be exposed to some of the basic legal procedures used in a lawsuit and realize that often a legal procedure or identification of a legal issue is the solution to the problem.

WHAT TO EXPECT OF LEGAL COUNSEL

Legal counsel assigned to the personnel function must be thoroughly familiar with the operation and business activities of the organization. One of the advantages of having an assigned counsel or in-house law department is that the legal advisor is more likely to have a thorough knowledge of the operations. Legal counsel must be familiar with personnel policy in the abstract and must know the reason behind the policy and the considerations used to formulate that policy. The courts in the legal interpretation of a statute must research the legislative history to determine the intent of the legislative body that passed the law. Like the courts, legal counsel must know the purpose and objective of a policy if legal advice is to be meaningful. Immediate legal advice is often essential in preventing a legal problem from becoming a long court case. Sometimes the employee is in the next room and the personnel practitioner must have the answer before the employee leaves the room.

The personnel department asks legal counsel to participate in the decision-making process by giving legal input. Often advice is requested after it is too late to prevent a small problem from becoming a litigation mountain. One of the most common errors of managers and personnel staff is not seeking legal advice early enough in the decision-making process.

Legal counsel should be expected to give an uncompromised legal opinion, which may not satisfy the person seeking it. Some companies have an attorney reporting to the head of the personnel function. In this situation it is difficult to give uncompromised legal advice to one's own supervisor when such advice may be adverse to the supervisor's decision. An attorney is not performing a legal function if for political reasons giving advice that is not based on the proper interpretation of the law.

Legal counsel for the personnel function is expected to give practical, feasible advice to a particular problem based on knowledge of the business as well as the law. Often managers will say not to ask the law department as the answer will be no. If this is the situation, legal counsel is failing in its assigned tasks of advising management. Managers do not want to know what they cannot do but what they can do and still be legal. The question that the company lawyer should ask in the opening conversation is, "How can I help you do what you want to do?" Feasible legal alternatives should be given. Where there are no alternatives within the law, that should be so stated but only after every possible alternative is explored. If managers choose to act outside the law, or where there is exposure to litigation, that is an enforcement problem for top management, not a legal function. Corporate legal counsel is not an enforcement function but an advisory one.

Legal counsel for a corporation is expected to anticipate problems before they arise and suggest appropriate action. This requires keeping up to date on new laws and their interpretation and notifying the managers on new court decisions or recent legislation that affects their operations. When the personnel practitioner is to make a presentation of pension benefits or leave of absence, vacation rights, safety, or any other personnel policy that may have legal implications, the legal department should review the presentation and call the attention to any possible exposure to the law. Sometimes legal counsel will not give a legal opinion but will criticize, disagree, or express a personal view about the policy. Such an opinion should be distinguished from a legal opinion. Employee relations policy should not be made by legal counsel; that is a function of the personnel department and operating management.

USE OF LEGAL COUNSEL IN LABOR RELATIONS

One common area of a quasi-legal function is labor arbitration.[1] Should the law department participate, or is it a labor relations matter? Practices vary. Some companies use lawyers only when an issue may have legal consequences. An increasing number of companies never use lawyers while others use lawyers exclusively.

Practice depends on how legal the company feels labor relations should get. Before the law entered the personnel function to the current extent, many personnel practitioners with a legal education believed that it is better to keep labor relations as nonlegal as possible. The policy of keeping all personnel functions as nonlegal as possible is a valid policy, but it is getting difficult to follow due to the increasing number of laws and employees who are more willing to sue their employer. The problem with a legal approach to labor relations problems is that the law is nonpersonal and inflexible and the employee must be forced through the legal door even when it does not fit; and bad employee relations result. The law must be applied to the facts; although the facts may be the same, the person or persons

---

[1] Where the arbitration award is taken to court the court proceedings are legal and use of lawyers is essential. Enforcement of arbitration awards is discussed in Chapter XI.

involved are not the same. Wherever possible a nonlegal solution to their problems would be the best for both the employee and the company.

When making a determination on whether lawyers should be used in arbitration, the decision maker must consider what the adversary is doing. Most labor unions avoid the use of lawyers in arbitration simply because it is too expensive; further, an international union representative can become proficient in presenting arbitration cases without being a lawyer. As discussed in Chapter XI arbitration proceedings are nonlegal because the arbitrator is not bound by legal rules of evidence or procedures. When the labor union does not use an attorney to present the arbitration case, this should influence management when determining whether it should adopt the legal approach. Many companies feel that in the interest of employee relations they should not use lawyers in this situation. Other companies argue that the use of lawyers gives an advantage at the hearing, especially if the arbitrator is a lawyer. The validity of this position is questionable.

In proceedings before administrative agencies such as the National Labor Relations Board (NLRB), Occupational Safety and Health Administration (OSHA), and Equal Employment Opportunity Commission (EEOC), government representatives are usually lawyers. It is advisable for the company to be represented by counsel because the federal rules of evidence and procedure are fol-lowed by the administrative law judge, and it is difficult to keep the proceedings nonlegal. Also, the administrative law judge gives little consideration to employee relations consequences of their decisions and employee relations arguments are given little weight.

Recommendation On When To Use Legal Counsel

One approach to the problem of when to use legal counsel is a policy of waiting until the problem advances to a stage where legal proceedings are instituted before involving attorneys. An affirmative action problem is a personnel matter until a show-cause letter is received. A selection procedure is not a legal problem until a discrimination charge is filed with a regulatory agency. An OSHA citation is a safety problem unless management wants to contest. A labor relations matter does not become a legal problem until a complaint is filed with the National Labor Relations Board. Once it becomes a legal matter, no information should be released about the personnel problem unless by the attorneys as irreparable harm can result.

Arbitration is not a legal problem or a legal procedure but a failure of the grievance procedure that seldom can be settled by a legal approach. The arbitrator has a wide discretion on conducting the hearing. There are no accepted rules of procedure. Pre-hearing discovery or other proceedings are seldom used. The arbitrator is not bound by the decisions of other arbitrators (no stare decisis) and the award is usually a personal interpretation of the labor agreement.

An attempt to make an arbitration a legal proceeding creates more problems than solutions. Arbitration is a labor relations problem; labor relations practitioners working with union committees and union international representatives or business agents of the local union are in the best position to find a permanent solution to the problem. The use of the third party does not suddenly make the problem legal. When one party or the other must go to court to enforce the arbitration award, the problem becomes a legal matter.

Although personnel problems do not become legal problems until a legal proceeding is instituted, this does not mean that from time to time the personnel practitioner should not consult with legal counsel to determine the legal consequences of an employment decision. There is no better way to prevent a personnel problem from becoming a legal problem than to get input from legal counsel before an employment decision is made.

DISTINCTION BETWEEN PERSONNEL AND LEGAL FUNCTION

When the personnel function obtained top management status, it became exposed to an avalanche of government regulations that brought the lawyers into an area with which they were often unfamiliar. The lawyer looks at a personnel problem in a legal context; decisions are based solely upon what the lawyer believes the law says one must do or not do. The personnel director must consider the consequences of a decision and the conflicting considerations between a personnel decision and legal decision. For example, it is a legal determination that only those employees who filed a claim for disability pay due to pregnancy should be paid when the court determines that the state law is valid; it is an employee relations consideration whether to pay all employees who became disabled from pregnancy whether they filed a claim or not.

The legal counsel determines only what is required under the law while the personnel practitioner in considering the employee relations consequences may go beyond what the law requires. For example, the courts have stated that a safety inspector from the Department of Labor cannot enter an employer's premises without a search warrant unless the employer agrees.[2] It is a policy decision whether employer wants to require a warrant.

When the legal counsel makes

---

[2] Marshall v. Barlow's, Inc., 436 U.S. 307 (1978).

decisions that are not based on interpretation of the law but are based on a belief of what the policy should be, the personnel practitioner must recognize this and make an employee relations determination, as long as the law is not violated.

INCREASE IN LITIGATION

The entry of the law into the personnel function is not a phenomenon particular to personnel, but it is indicative of the growth of law in all business and social activities. Beginning in the early 1970s there was a growing concern of people to be protected legally from every problem, even from their own gullibility. Litigation is growing so fast that it is difficult to know the total number of pending cases on the dockets of the courts. The unfriendly stigma of a lawsuit is rapidly disappearing. Doctors are sued by patients, lawyers by clients, parents by their children: brothers sue brothers and sellers sue their customers. As the mother said to the father "If I make Johnny eat his spinach, he will sue us." Social legislation of the 1970s such as antidiscrimination laws, the Occupational Safety and Health Act, Employee Retirement Insurance Act, and various environmental laws has given added opportunities to individuals never before experienced in judicial history. The alphabet-group of government regulatory agencies creates a thriving climate for the litigation-happy individual. To illustrate how people are suing each other at an increasing rate, in 1960 there were 59,284 civil suits filed in U.S. District Courts. By 1982 this figure increased to 206,193. This is an increase of 200% in a period when population increased by 25%. In 1982 there were 8,602 cases filed in the Federal Appelate Courts of which 4,975 were waiting to be tried by the end of the year.[3]

Although suits by consumers against manufacturers for damages caused by defective products account for a large proportion of the increased litigation, suits by employees against employers are rising rapidly. In January 1979 EEOC and referral state agencies had a backlog exceeding 100,000 cases. Suits by employees against their union and their employer for health damage or hazardous working environments, the enforcement of National Labor Relations Board orders by the Department of Labor, suits under the Fair Labor Standards Act and similar statutes relating to wages and working conditions are all on the increase with no visible signs that the trend will change. Some social scientists fear that these lawsuits will destroy personal relationships and trust between individuals that have made our society so pleasant.

[3] 1982 Annual Report of Director of Administrative Office of U.S. Courts (Washington D.C.: U.S. Government Printing Office).

Growth Of
The Legal Profession

It is a debatable question whether the increase in attorneys caused the increase in litigation or the increase in litigation resulted in an increase of attorneys.[4] Whatever the cause, Exhibit II-1 shows the American Bar Association study of an almost unbelievable increase since 1958. In 1982 the American Bar Association reported that there are more than 600,000 lawyers in the United States. Based on the 1980 census this would mean 1 lawyer for every 366 persons.

FUNCTION OF IN-HOUSE COUNSEL

The growth in litigation and legal matters has become an economic concern of the employer who has been faced with large legal fees. This has caused many companies to hire their own attorneys.

The attorney employed full-time by a company has become known as an in-house counsel as compared to an outside counsel who is a practicing attorney hired by a company for specific cases or when legal advice is needed. Within the management structure of a company the in-house counsel job title compares to other staff job titles in the organizational table such as general counsel, associate counsel, or assistant counsel. Often the top legal position within a company is an officer of the company, and the position will have a title of vice president, general counsel, or general counsel and secretary.

The in-house counsel serves to reduce the legal fees for outside counsel but does not eliminate them entirely. Some companies with sales over a billion dollars have outside counsel fees of over $1 million, in spite of an in-house counsel staff of 26 to 40 attorneys.[5]

The corporate law department was established primarily because of economic necessity. However, there are many advantages of an in-house law department if it is used properly and all members of management understand the purpose of the law department and its function.

The function of the law department is to inform management of the legal implications of its action and to give legal input in the decision-making process. The law department is not the keeper of corporate conscience because corporations do not make decisions; individuals do. The law department has no enforcement powers, but it must give practical and feasible advice based on knowledge of the business. Legal opinions are most often given on request; however, the law department some-

---

[4] A story is told about one lawyer moving to a small town and starving for business. A second lawyer moved into town; they both got rich.

[5] *The Corporate Legal Function: A Management Survey* (Chicago: A.T. Kearney, Inc., 1978).

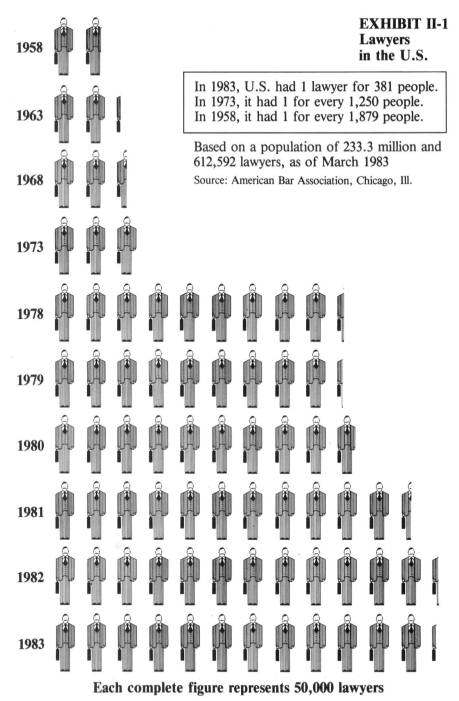

EXHIBIT II-1
Lawyers
in the U.S.

1958

1963

1968

1973

1978

1979

1980

1981

1982

1983

In 1983, U.S. had 1 lawyer for 381 people.
In 1973, it had 1 for every 1,250 people.
In 1958, it had 1 for every 1,879 people.

Based on a population of 233.3 million and
612,592 lawyers, as of March 1983

Source: American Bar Association, Chicago, Ill.

Each complete figure represents 50,000 lawyers

times renders opinions that are not requested. This is usually when the department wants to prevent legal problems in a known activity such as in product liability or antitrust matters or when there is a union organizational drive. For this reason the law department must keep up to date on changing concepts of regulatory agency policies, laws passed by Congress, and court interpretations.

The law department in a company is a legal problem-solving department that suggests appropriate action or alternatives to a particular problem or action. The in-house counsel must give the legal odds of winning or losing a case based on familiarity with the business and recognizing the desire of the management to reach a certain result. Because the law department is accessible to management, the solution to the problem is immediate as compared to the use of outside counsel. The in-house counsel is distinguished from the outside counsel by knowledge of the business and the personalities managing the business. The more readily accessible in-house counsel is the more apt to stop problems before they start through the practice of preventive law, and usually outside counsel does not perform the preventive law function.

The Outside Counsel

Companies who have attorneys employed full-time (in-house counsel) still use outside counsel for specialized services. The specialized services most widely used are in the areas of litigation, finance, antitrust, tax law, and personnel/labor law. Litigation is the most commonly required outside service by companies that have full-time lawyers.

The practice of most companies is that outside counsel is hired by the company law department or, if there is no law department, by a company executive. One of the tasks of the law department of a corporation is to assess the quality of the work of the outside counsel and determine the reasonableness of their fees; this is sometimes difficult to do by an executive who does not have in-house counsel available.

The law department determines when to use outside counsel and when to perform the tasks in-house. The determining factors vary from company to company. Some of the major considerations are availability of expertise in the law department, the workload, the jurisdiction where the problem arises, and the financial importance of the outcome compared to the cost of doing in-house versus outside use of counsel.

Selection Of Outside Counsel

In the selection of outside counsel the executive must remember that law is a personal service business. Although some law firms may have a larger percentage of good lawyers than others, the ultimate quality of the service depends on individuals within the law firm, not the name of the firm.

The executive or in-house counsel should look for a lawyer who will be vigorous in pursuing the issue but not one who takes a case without merit with the hope of becoming famous or satisfying an ego.

In the opening conference the executive or in-house counsel should assess the strengths and weaknesses of the attorney under consideration. This assessment is not necessarily about knowledge of the law, as this is difficult; but how well the attorney can deal with people, is the attorney motivated, will the attorney have time to work on the case or will it be assigned to another attorney in the firm with less experience. The attorney should always be asked whether the law firm has a conflict of interest in representing the opposing party at any time. The attorney should always be asked about the fees and an estimate of the cost of taking the case to various stages of litigation. Precaution in the selection of counsel at the outset prevents many problems as the case moves down the litigation path. The relationship with legal counsel must be developed in several areas:

1. There should be economic use of legal counsel in obtaining legal opinions whether written or oral.

2. Criteria in selection of counsel include vigorous pursuit of the case, motivation, ability to deal with people, and availability to work on the case.

3. Cost of legal counsel must be assessed along with a total assessment of the case as to chances of winning and consequences of winning or losing. Would compliance be less expensive and what are the consequences if one complies?

4. The relationship of legal counsel to employees must be clearly defined. The client is always the company. If an employee/client relationship is developed, the employee should hire a separate attorney. Information between employees and company attorney is confidential and should be treated as such.

5. The personnel executive should be familiar with the basic trial procedures such as interrogatories, depositions, summons and complaints, and subpoena as well as recognizing that the interpretation of the law varies in different judicial districts until the U.S. Supreme Court decides the issue.

RISK ANALYSIS IN CONSIDERING LITIGATION

When management is considering whether to challenge a law or to comply, it should have a conference with legal counsel and a number of risk considerations should be explored:

* Is the desired course of action likely to bring a lawsuit?

* Can the company financially risk the lawsuit or is compliance less expensive?

* What consequences may result from the desired course of action—in the marketplace, with corporate goodwill, on employee relations, on corporate objectives and priorities?

* Is the company in line with other companies in the industry?

The next consideration is the approximate cost of the case. In determining the cost it should be decided how far the company will appeal the case. Then one budgets for attorney's and witness cost at the first level of the hearing, the cost of appeal to next court until a final determination. When considering the attorney's cost, these cannot be exact figures; an attorney can only estimate the time involved. For example, in research sometimes an attorney can find a case that serves as authority for the client's position in an hour or two; at other times research may require half the day. Because all the attorney has to sell is time, a two-page opinion can cost $900 or $200 depending on the time for the research and drafting. When considering the cost of a case, the company should always ask the price per hour of attorney's time, and, if anybody else will be involved in the case, that person's hourly cost. Also when considering the cost, management time must be considered. Litigating a lawsuit involves the time of management personnel; cost as well as availability must be considered.

Once the cost of the case is determined, an assessment should be made of winning. There is never a sure case; the parties must look at the strengths and weaknesses of both the plaintiff and defendant and be prepared for a surprise decision. The role of the legal counsel in assessing the chances of winning is to consider the facts in light of research or expertise on the subject and advise the client; the final decision on whether to take the risk belongs to the client. Some companies are more adventurous than others.

Once it is decided to take the matter to court, a management representative should be assigned to the case and become involved as much as possible. A lot of the attorney's time can be saved by client availability. Another reason to be involved closely is that settlement is always a possibility at any stage of the proceedings and counsel cannot settle without consent of client. Sometimes settlement possibilities exist only for a short time; if the management representative is not available, that opportunity is lost.

When assessing whether to litigate or settle, the economic considerations must be weighed with the employee relations or operational consequences. Where a testing program is being challenged by EEOC and management is convinced that because of the low educational level of the local labor market, tests must be given in order to select qualified applicants, then the cost of litigation must be considered against the operational consequences if the test is eliminated as a selection tool.

RELATIONSHIP OF LEGAL COUNSEL TO EMPLOYEES

When there is an in-house counsel or a law firm that the company has designated as legal counsel, the relationship of counsel to the employees should be explained to the employee when the employee becomes involved in a legal problem. When an attorney is acting on behalf of a corporation on a legal matter involving an employee, the attorney-client relationship is between the attorney and the corporation. There is no attorney-client relationship with the employee unless the employee obtains a different attorney to represent his/her interests.

Information that an attorney obtains when acting for the corporation belongs to the corporation and is confidential to the corporation. The employee as an individual has no right to see the information or to use it. It is immaterial whether the employee gave the information to the attorney representing the corporation at the direction of a superior or obtained the information during the course of employment as long as the information was obtained while performing a function on behalf of the corporation and is relevant to the case.[6]

A corporation has a right to any information that the employee obtained in the course of employment and is job-related; the employee can be disciplined or discharged for refusing to disclose it. However, it is good employee relations to inform the employee fully how the information is being used. The employee has no constitutional right under the Fourth or Fifth Amendment to take immunity when the employer requests information.[7] Corporate counsel also can look at all the files concerning the employee; the employee has no remedy under the law to prevent it.

Often employees seek personal advice of the in-house counsel or company attorney. The corporation, as a matter of policy, must determine whether the attorneys should be used to give advice to employees when they have personal problems. Some personnel practitioners take the position that one hires the whole person; therefore employee's legal problems are company problems and the company should give them initial aid in the same manner that the company nurse does when an employee has a head cold.

Other employee relations practitioners take the position that getting too involved legally in an employee's personal problems can have an adverse effect if that ad-

---

[6] Diversified Industries v. Meredith, 572 F.2d 596 (8th Cir. 1977).

[7] U.S. v. Solomon, 509 F.2d 863 (2nd Cir. 1975).

vice is followed and the results are unfavorable to the employee. A policy followed by many companies is to refuse legal advice to employees on matters not related to their job duties. This may require an initial conference to determine whether the legal problem is job-related. If it is determined that it is not job-related, the employees are advised to seek their own lawyer. It is advisable to assess the merits of the case in this situation as the employee's lawyer may have different opinion.

Some companies will permit the in-house counsel to do so-called first echelon legal work. Legal counsel will look over a deed for an employee buying a house, for example, or give advice on an auto-mobile accident as to alternatives and the court procedure and assess and recommend a local attorney. Companies that use their in-house counsel in this manner believe that it is good employee relations as long as their counsel does not get involved in the employee's personal legal problems to the extent of representing the employee against the other party or giving advice for which the company may be responsible in the event of adverse consequences. This is the best policy for companies with in-house counsel if it is restricted to nonunion management personnel.

The benefit to the company outweighs the adverse results as long as discretion is used.[8]

OBTAINING LEGAL OPINIONS

The opinion of counsel can be valuable to the practitioner, depending on how it is obtained and used. An option should be requested before taking any questionable action that may result in legal implications.

The outside legal counsel or the law department should get the problem as early as possible. The more lead time before the legal opinion must be rendered, the more time for research and the more complete is the opinion. Often a considerable amount of research is necessary: a half-page memo or let-ter may be the result of eight hours of research.

Since opinions are expensive, when an opinion is requested the problem should be properly framed. Asking further questions takes time, which increases the cost of legal services. When requesting an opinion, the personnel executive should:

1. Give the attorney all known facts. Facts should not be condensed or digested. Do not be reluctant to disclose all the facts even those that are damaging.[9]

---

[8] Those benefits could include saving management time as the employee sees a lawyer or employee satisfaction. A troubled employee is often a poor producer.

[9] In this author's experience as in-house counsel failure to disclose damaging facts was a common practice among managers.

2. When giving the facts, be prepared to provide documents such as memos, letters, or other written support.

3. Always identify assumptions and state those separately from the facts.

4. Be prompt in returning information requested. When attorney must call twice for the same information, the company is usually charged for two telephone calls.

5. When calling for advice, have all the documents available and think out the questions beforehand.

Sometimes a person will receive two different legal opinions on the same issue or problem. There are several reasons why legal opinions differ:

1. A slight difference in the facts or circumstances may have a different legal result.

2. There may be some changes in the laws between the time the first opinion and second opinion are received.

3. Different lawyers may come to different conclusions when they weigh various facts and interpret statutes or court decisions. Experience, background, and personal beliefs often affect the interpretation of the law.

4. In gray areas of the law there are legal risks that cannot be avoided. Different attorneys may give different advice. Some will be more adventur- ous than others in assessing a legal problem.

Written Versus Oral Opinions

Because of the expediency of the situation, many practitioners will telephone legal counsel and ask for an immediate oral opinion. An oral opinion has many pitfalls and should not be used to solve important legal problems. This is especially true where legal counsel is not familiar with the subject matter. Even where the counsel is considered an expert, oral opinions can be misleading and should be used only when the problem is routine and an immediate answer is essential. The pitfalls of an oral opinion are that:

1. The attorney has to remember the facts and apply them to the law with little thought.

2. There is a danger that the recipient of the opinion may misunderstand it.

3. There is no record of the opinion. If the consequences are adverse, there is always a question of what facts were given and the content of the opinion.

4. Since oral opinions lack research, it may not reflect the most current law.

Written opinions take longer, are more costly, but have fewer misunderstandings and can be retained in the file for future reference. However, when using an opinion in another situation, care must be taken that the facts are the same.

Information that an attorney receives or gives a company employee is privileged information that cannot be used by a third party or subpoenaed.[10] It is important to identify that the information was received through the attorney as an employee of the company and to classify it as confidential in file. One way to do this is to mark all legal opinions confidential and received through an attorney-client relationship. An example of how documents should be marked when received from an attorney is shown in Exhibit II-2.

EXHIBIT II-2

The enclosed matters are communicated to you in confidence and constitute or contain legal services given to you by legal counsel. There are to be no duplications distributed or otherwise disclosed except through the attorney rendering them.

A statement similar to this should be marked on all documents from counsel. Usually the counsel will do so, but if not, then the person receiving them should do it.

Judicial District Differences

The court requirements involving evidence, methods of pleading, and court procedure often vary from state to state and in various judicial districts within a state. Sometimes judicial districts will disagree in the interpretation of the same statute. Where there is a difference between the various courts in the federal court system, the case often goes to the U.S. Supreme Court or in the case of a state statute to the state supreme court. The highest court will hear the case only if one of the parties to the lawsuit appeals the decision of the lower court and the court agrees to hear the appeal. With the U.S. Supreme Court a request is made in the form of writ of certiorari.

Sometimes this does not happen, and the law is enforced differently in one judicial district than in the other. For example, the U.S. Court of Appeals for the Fourth Circuit (Maryland, Virginia, West Virginia, North Carolina and South Carolina) has interpreted the National Labor Relations Act to mean that before the National Labor Relations Board can order an election where an unfair labor practice is found, the union must show that the majority of the employees have authorized the union to represent them.[11] The U.S. Court of Appeals for the Third Circuit (New Jersey, Pennsylvania, Delaware, and Virgin Islands) has said that the union needs only 30 percent of

---

[10] Upjohn v. U.S., 101 Sup.Ct. 677 (1981).

[11] NLRB v. S.S. Logan Packing, 386 F.2d 562 (4th Cir. 1967).

the employees before the board can order an election.[12]

If a case arose in state of Virginia, the board could not certify a union without an election when an unfair labor practice exists unless the union showed that it represented a majority of the employees. If the case came up in Pennsylvania, the union would need only 30 percent to be certified without an election. When the U.S. Supreme Court has not decided a legal issue, whatever the highest court in that state or judicial district decides is the law for that district.

EXPLANATION OF PRETRIAL PROCEDURES

The personnel executive should become familiar with the basics of pretrial procedures because often the servicing of court proceedings against the company is made to the persons in the personnel office when the matter involves employees. Most legal documents have a time limit in which they have to be acted on; it is highly important that the documents are expedited promptly. Failure to act within the time limits can result in liability by default or other serious legal consequences. In most legal documents the time limits are clearly stated, and the court serving the papers and the attorneys involved are clearly stated on the documents.

Pretrial Discovery Procedures

Interrogatories are a set or series of written questions served on one party in a proceeding for the purpose of a factual examination of a prospective witness. They are used mostly in pretrial discovery to obtain information to aid the attorney in preparing the case and selecting witnesses.

The personnel practitioner will sometimes receive the interrogatories from an opposing attorney to obtain information about employees. An attorney should always review the information before it is mailed. Answers to interrogatory questions are not done under oath but are often used as a basis for questions that are answered under oath. Answers can also determine how the attorney will try the case. The request for interrogatories comes directly from the attorney requesting them; they do not need court approval.

Exhibit II-3 is an interrogatory served on a company where the personnel department would supply the answers. In the interest of brevity, only enough questions are included to show a typical interrogatory.

---

[12] United Dairy Farmers Co-op Assn. v. NLRB, 633 F.2d 1054 (3rd Cir. 1980).

EXHIBIT II-3

STATE OF _____   DISTRICT COURT

COUNTY OF _____   SECOND JUDICIAL DISTRICT

LEO SMITH,	)	
	)	
Plaintiff,	)	
	)	
v.	)	INTERROGATORIES
	)	
ABC COMPANY	)	
	)	
Defendant.	)	

TO: DEFENDANT ABC COMPANY AND ITS ATTORNEY JOHN ROE,
   (ATTORNEY'S ADDRESS)

     PLEASE TAKE NOTICE that Plaintiff, Leo Smith, requests, pursuant to Rule 33 of the Rules of Civil Procedure, that the Defendant ABC Company answer the following Interrogatories within the time prescribed by law. These Interrogatories shall be deemed continuing in nature and should the answers require modification or supplementation it is demanded that you so advise Plaintiff and his attorney.

DEFINITIONS

     Unless conclusively altered by the context of a specific Interrogatory, the following definitions are to be considered to apply to all the Interrogatories contained herein.

    A.   You and Your means ABC Company, present and former directors, officers, employees, attorneys, agents, representatives, and any and all other persons, firms, corporations or entities acting or purporting to act on behalf of ABC Company.

    B.   Identify or Identification

        1.   When used in reference to a person, means her or his:

            a.   Full name

            b.   Present or last known residence address

            c.   Position and job description at the time in question.

INTERROGATORIES

1.   Describe the nature of the supervision of your premises employed to maintain control over employees on the job, in the cafeterias, and in any other areas of the premises to which the employees have access.

2.   Had you received any complaints in 1975 by nonunion workers that they were being harassed by union workers?

3.   If the answer to interrogatory No. 2 is yes, identify all persons who made such complaints?

4.   Did any security unit, the foreman or any other of your employees investigate such complaints?

continued

EXHIBIT II-3

LAW OFFICES OF RICHARD ANDERSON

By _____
Richard Anderson
(Address)
Dated _____   (Telephone)

DEPOSITION

The deposition is a pretrial discovery procedure whereby the testimony of a witness is taken outside open court, pursuant to permission by the court to take testimony from a witness. Most questions are based on, but not restricted to, the interrogatories.

A deposition in the court proceeding becomes a written declaration of the witness under oath made on notice to the adverse party for the purpose of enabling the witness's attorney to attend the hearing and cross examine if necessary. A deposition differs from interrogatories in that it is under oath and it is used under certain conditions in court proceedings for questioning the witness. When a deposition is taken, it is contemplated that the person will be a witness in the trial, but this is not always the case.

When an employee is requested to give a deposition, often there is a sense of insecurity; although the other attorneys may be present, the employee requests the legal counsel from the company to be present. This is a policy matter for management and legal counsel to determine. Some companies consider it good employee relations to give legal security to an employee when giving a deposition; others feel that the presence of one attorney representing the employee's interest is enough.

SUBPOENA

The subpoena is an order directed to a person to testify as a witness at a particular time and place.[13] The most common subpoena in the personnel department is to appear and bring all documents and written materials related to the subject matter of the case. This is called a subpoena duces tecum. Often the records are all that the attorney wants, and production of the records satisfies the subpoena; it is not necessary for the person in charge of the records to testify. However, permission from the attorney signing

---

[13] *Black's Law Dictionary,* 5th ed., (St. Paul, MN: West Publishing Co., 1979).

EXHIBIT II-4

No. 3073—Subpoena Duces Tecum. (Rev. 1963)

State of Minnesota,

County of _____Smithson_____

DISTRICT COURT

_____1st_____ _Judicial District_

_____John Doe_____

_____

_vs._   _Plaintiff_____

_____Homer Smith_____

_____

_Defendant_____

SUBPOENA
DUCES TECUM

THE STATE OF MINNESOTA TO_____ ABC Corp., Milltown, Minnesota _____:

You are hereby commanded to appear in the above named court at the Court House, in the

County _____of_____ Smithson _____, on the _____22nd_____

day of _____August_____, 19_82_, at _____9:00_____ o'clock_____ fore _____noon, then and

there to testify on behalf of _____John Doe_____ in

above entitled proceeding.

You are further directed and commanded to bring with you the following papers and documents

now in your possession or under your control, viz.:

> All Personnel Records, including wages paid during the last two years,
> days absent during said period, all medical records and work performance
> records and appraisals.

WITNESS, The Honorable_____ RONALD E. HACH _____Judge of said

Court, and the seal thereof this _____2nd_____ day of _____July_____, 19 _82_

HAZEL G. ART

_____ _Clerk_

By _~Wallace Meadow~_ _____

Deputy

State of Minnesota,

County of_____Smithson_____

I hereby certify and return that I served the within Subpoena on the within named

_____Personnel Director_____

_____by reading the same to him and delivering to him

a true copy thereof, at_____ ABC Corp., 415 Jones St., Milltown, Minnesota _____

in said County and State, on this_____15_____ day of_____Aug._____, 19 _82_

SHERIFF'S FEES:

Arnold Anderson

Sheriff of said County

Service, _____15.00_____

Mileage, - $ _____12.00_____

By _~M. Johnson~_ _____

(All names and places are fictitious)

the subpoena not to appear is required. When receiving a subpoena duces tecum, the attorney requesting the documents should always be asked whether only the records are wanted or the person subpoenaed must testify. A lot of time will be saved if documents only must be produced. Also, it is not advisable for the personnel practitioner to appear in the courtroom and be called as a witness subject to cross examination. Any personnel document marked confidential, as between company counsel and the employee, need not be produced.

Exhibit II-4 is a typical subpoena duces tecum, often received in worker compensation, divorce and other civil suits, and government proceedings. Subpoena duces tecum is also used in criminal proceedings.

SUMMONS

A summons is a document served on the defendant to appear in court and to give an answer within a specified time to the suit that has begun against the person. The nature of the lawsuit is stated in the complaint.

It is important to note the time and date when the summons is received as the answer must be within specified time, usually 20 or 30 days. As soon as a summons is received, legal counsel should be notified. Exhibit II-5 is an example of a summons used in a civil case.

EXHIBIT II-5

STATE OF _____   DISTRICT COURT

COUNTY OF _____   SECOND JUDICIAL DISTRICT

LEO SMITH,   )
)
                    Plaintiff,   )
)
         v.   )   SUMMONS
)
ABC COMPANY   )
)
                    Defendant.   )

THE STATE OF MINNESOTA TO THE ABOVE-NAMED DEFENDANT:
    You are hereby summoned and required to serve upon Plaintiff's Attorney an Answer to the Complaint which is herewith served upon you within twenty (20) days after the service of this Summons upon you, exclusive of the day of such service. If you fail to do so, judgment by default will be taken against you for the relief demanded in the Complaint.

                              John Roe
                              Attorney for Plaintiff
                              (Address)
                              (Telephone)

COMPLAINT

A complaint in a civil proceeding is the first or initial pleading by the plaintiff. It asks the court for legal redress of an alleged wrong. The complaint is usually received with the summons. Under the rules of civil procedure of the courts it must contain certain information about the case such as the names of the parties, county and name of the court where the action is brought, and relief sought. When a complaint is received, it should be immediately turned over to legal counsel because this is legal notice that the plaintiff has started a lawsuit against the defendant. The complaint also states why the defendant is being sued.

Exhibit II-6 is an example of a complaint. It was filed by a person owning a semitrailer who is suing for injuries caused by improper loading of the trailer by employees of the defendant. The personnel department should not in any way respond to a complaint but refer it to legal counsel. For the purposes of brevity, only the essential elements of the complaints are shown in Exhibit II-6.

EXHIBIT II-6

STATE OF _____   DISTRICT COURT

COUNTY OF _____   SECOND JUDICIAL DISTRICT

LEO SMITH,   )
)
             Plaintiff,   )
)
        v.   )   COMPLAINT
)
ABC COMPANY,   )
)
             Defendant.   )

Plaintiff, for his cause of action against the above Defendant, alleges as follows:

I.

That some time prior to May 25, 1976, Plaintiff, Leo Smith, at that time an independent trucker, pursuant to a Contract of Employment, picked up a semitrailer at the business place of Defendant at 2334 Oakdale Avenue, Milltown, Mill County, Minnesota, which trailer had been loaded by Defendant's agents, servants, or employees, with large rolls of foil for transport to Defendant's facility in Chicago, Illinois.

II.

That at said time and place, Defendant, through its agents, servants, or employees, acted in a careless, negligent, and unlawful manner by failing to secure properly, block, or insure otherwise that said rolls of foil, when loaded in said trailer, could not come loose and roll off said trailer and injure persons in the vicinity thereof.

continued

EXHIBIT II-6

III.

On May 25, 1976, at Defendant's facility in Chicago, Illinois, while said trailer was being unloaded by Defendant's agents, servants, or employees, a roll of foil fell on Plaintiff, thereby crushing his body.

IV.

That said injuries were as a direct result of the negligence, carelessness, and unlawful behavior by Defendant, through its agents, servants or employees, in failing to secure properly or block said rolls and thereby preventing them from rolling off the trailer.

V.

WHEREFORE, Plaintiff demands judgment against the Defendant in the amount of One Million Dollars ($1,000,000), together with costs and disbursements herein.

John Roe
Attorney for Plaintiff
(Address)
(Telephone)

The essential elements of the complaint should be noted. Paragraph I tells what the defendant did. Paragraph II describes the wrong committed by the defendant. Paragraphs III and IV state the result of that wrong, and paragraph V states the relief or remedy requested by the plaintiff.

SUMMARY AND CONCLUSIONS

Legal counsel, whether inhouse or outside counsel, is expected to give an uncompromised legal opinion on how the personnel executive can carry out duties as desired and still be legal. The distinction between the legal and personnel function must be kept separate when opinions are made to the personnel executive.

Although it is common practice to use attorneys in arbitration, labor relations should be kept as nonlegal as possible. Accordingly, attorneys should not be used in arbitration except in rare instances. Arbitration is a nonlegal process. An attempt to make it legal defeats its purpose of resolving disagreements over interpretation of a labor contract.

Statistics show that society is litigation-happy; everybody is suing and there is no end in sight. The increase in litigation of all types including employee relations cases means that legal implications of employment decisions will not go away and the personnel executive must adopt a relationship with legal counsel to cope with it.

If the personnel executive develops policies and procedures that considers legal implications, the marriage of the law with the personnel function will not be a costly one. The most economical relationship will allow the organization to continue to function without having to restrict legal advice in areas where it is needed and can prevent exposure to lawsuits.

CHAPTER III

AN OVERVIEW OF DISCRIMINATION LAWS AND THEIR APPLICATION TO PERSONNEL MANAGEMENT

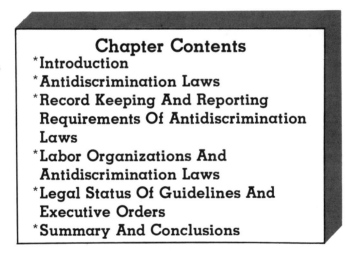

Chapter Contents
*Introduction
*Antidiscrimination Laws
*Record Keeping And Reporting Requirements Of Antidiscrimination Laws
*Labor Organizations And Antidiscrimination Laws
*Legal Status Of Guidelines And Executive Orders
*Summary And Conclusions

INTRODUCTION

Chapter I described how the law moved into the personnel function and drastically changed personnel management. Employment practices had been a matter of individual choice for each organization. Whatever was accepted by management became the policy and was continued without interference from an outside source. For the most part the practices adopted were in accord with the attitudes and beliefs common in the business, the geographic region, the social, religious, political or ethnic society in which management operated. Frequently they were transmitted by word-of-mouth rather than by writing.

These well-accepted practices and policies are no longer advisable. A key reason has been the impact of antidiscrimination legislation that outlaws policies and practices that result in disparate treatment of any protected class of applicants or employees.

State and federal antidiscrimination statutes affect all phases of the employment process, from initial advertising of a job vacancy through hiring, promotion, discipline, discharge, and retirement of the employee. These statutes prevent the employer from treating job applicants or employees differently on the basis of race, color, religion, sex, age, national origin, or handicap. The employer is not only prevented from treating employees differently but must afford equal opportunities for all classes of employees and applicants. The various antidiscrimination laws protect the individual in the given right to take and hold a job and to be promoted free of discrimination because of race, color, religion, sex, national origin, or age.

A physically disabled person is also protected from discrimination in federal employment and by most state laws. Government contractors and institutions receiving public assistance must have affirmative action programs for hiring the handicapped. Disabled veterans and veterans of the Vietnam era are also protected as to employment by the federal government or by firms doing business with the federal government (many states have similar laws).

When there is a determination, either by a regulatory agency or court, that discrimination has occurred, the employer has an affirmative duty to correct the practice and to restore the individual to the rightful place in the employment relationship, including making whole for any monetary losses.

This chapter provides an overview of the antidiscrimination laws that are the authority for government enforcement regulations. The chapter also familiarizes the reader with useful terms and definitions, with in-depth treatment of laws and terms in subsequent chapters.

ANTIDISCRIMINATION LAWS

Title VII Civil Rights Act Of 1964 (42 USC-2000e)

The broadest antidiscrimination statute is the 1964 Civil Rights Act (commonly called Title VII). It is the principal source of antibias rules for employment practices. The act prohibits discrimination in all employment decisions on the basis of race, color, religion, national origin, or sex, including pregnancy, childbirth, or abortion. Title VII applies to employer, labor unions, apprenticeship committees, employment agencies, and state and local governments. It covers all employees from the part-time office boy to the chief executive officer. Before a business is subject to the act, it must affect interstate commerce and employ 15 or more individuals for at least 20 weeks during the current or preceding calendar year. Title VII originally excluded private institutions that accepted federal funds. In 1972 Congress amended Title VII with Title IX. However, the amendment is concerned only with sex discrimination and cuts off federal assistance where the institution doesn't comply.[1]

The Equal Employment Opportunity Commission enforces the objectives of the act. All charges under Title VII must begin with the EEOC or a state referral agency, whose decision is not binding on the EEOC.

Definition Of Race, Color, Religion, Sex, And National Origin Under Title VII

Race under Title VII is usually referred to as members of racial minorities, but protection of members of majority races is also covered. For the purposes of determining whether an individual is a member of a protected class, the EEOC allows racial classification by minority groups through visual surveys or direct personal inquiry where other methods are not practical.

Color is related to racial discrimination in that the color of an individual's skin should not be used as a basis for an employment decision. It has little application where color of skin would place an individual as a member of race, except that within the race group there could be discrimination. This would occur when one of two black employees is selected because of lighter complexion and more distinct Caucasian features. Since color is so closely related to race, it is seldom used as a single basis for discrimination.

Religious freedom has its basis in the Constitution but the Constitutional provision was not applied to the employment situation. As used in Title VII, it is unlawful to discriminate because of any religious activity. Where there is interference through the employment relationship such as being scheduled to work on a religious holiday, there is a duty to make an effort to accommodate.[2] One frequent problem with religion is when religious beliefs interfere with a labor union membership.

---

[1] If an employer is not covered by federal law, state or municipal laws fill in the void. Employers should not seek jurisdictional shelter under federal law because some other law will cover them.

[2] Duty to accommodate will be discussed in Chapter V.

Generally an employee does not have to join a labor union or pay dues if it is against one's beliefs but must pay the amount, equal to the dues, to charity.[3]

Sex discrimination under Title VII was added after the bill was reported out of the committee to the floor of the House of Representatives. Therefore it is impossible to determine legislative intent from committee hearings as in other protective classes.[4] Most disputes arise under sex because of stereotyped characterizations of the sexes and as a result one is favored over the other. The statutory definition of sex discrimination was amended in 1978 to include pregnancy, childbirth, or related medical conditions. The effect of the statute is that one must treat pregnancy like any illness as to benefits and other personnel policies.

Transsexuality or a change in sex by surgical or other means is not covered by the statute,[5] according to one court of appeals.

Unlawful discrimination based on national origin usually occurs in areas where the employer requires English to be spoken but the requirement is not necessary for performance of the job. National-origin-related appearance, including dress and grooming traits, may be an unlawful basis of discrimination if not justified by requirements of the job.

Title VII has not excluded aliens as they would be entitled to the Equal Protection Clause of the Fourteenth Amendment. However, an employer may refuse employment to noncitizens if such a policy does not have the purpose or results in discrimination on the basis of national origin.

Civil Rights Act Of 1866

This statute was passed after the adoption of the Thirteenth Amendment to the Constitution after the Civil War. It was intended to protect the rights of racial minorities. The right of white citizens to contract, to sue, to participate in legal proceedings, and to enjoy full and equal benefit of all the laws was extended to all other persons under this act. It does not apply to sex discrimination. It was not until after the passage of Title VII that the act was applied to employment. The courts adopting the social climate of the times found in 1967 that because the employment relationship was a contract, the 1866 statute would apply. The courts also found that because the statute granted all citizens the same property rights, and that continued employment is viewed as a legally recognizable property right, therefore the statute applies to all employment situations, not just contractual rights. This statute is

---

[3] Tooley v. Martin-Marietta Corp., 648 F.2d 1239 (9th Cir. 1981).

[4] When other phases of Title VII were being argued on the floor of the House of Representatives, Congressman Howard Smith from Virginia, in an attempt to block the bill, stated that the bill was so unreasonable that one might as well include sex, so Congress did.

[5] Holloway v. Arthur Andersen & Co., 566 F.2d 659 (9th Cir. 1977).

widely used in present discrimination lawsuits.

Civil Rights Act Of 1871

This is another law that seeks to restore rights to former slaves after the Civil War. The law was intended to plug loopholes in the 1866 statute, where discrimination because of race would occur as a result of a state law, usage, custom, or conspiracy between two or more persons. It applies to both private and public employers as well as private individuals who are found conspirators under the act. The statute is not widely used by the persons whom it was designed to protect, primarily because other laws afford the same relief, with the exception of racial conspiracy by individuals, or co-workers. It is often difficult to prove and even more difficult to recover damages or receive any other type of relief when the violation is by individuals.

Title I Civil Rights Act Of 1968 (18 USC 245)

This statute imposes criminal penalties for interference with a person's civil rights, including employment rights. The law applies to anyone who by force or threat of force willfully injures, intimidates, or interferes with a person because of race, color, religion, or national origin. Activities prohibited by statute include interference with applying for or enjoying employment or related privileges in either public or private sector.[6] As with the 1871 statute, Title I applies to disputes between individuals usually not involving the employer but arising in an employment situation. The remedy or damages are not readily available, except in rare instances, from an individual in same manner as if an employer were involved. It appears that a charge of sexual harassment against a co-worker could be brought under this statute.[7]

Equal Pay Act Of 1963

Although discrimination in employment on the basis of sex is forbidden in Title VII, the paying of workers of one sex at a rate different from that paid the other sex for the same work is specifically unlawful under the Equal Pay Act of 1963 (an amendment to the Fair Labor Standards Act). In order for the work to be considered the same the jobs must involve equal skill, equal effort, and equal responsibility and be performed under similar working conditions in the same establishment. The law applies to all employees of any enterprise that has two or more employees engaged in interstate commerce or otherwise affects interstate commerce and has a gross volume of at least $250,000. The act also applies to government workers but does not apply to labor unions because they do not set wages and because

---

[6] *Public sector* as used in this book refers to government employees in all federal, state, and municipal governments as well as public education institutions; the private sector includes all other employees.

[7] See Chapter VIII for a discussion of sexual harassment.

pressure on the employer to set wages is not a violation.[8]

An employee who brings a complaint under this act is entitled to jury trial and may be awarded double damages as liquidated damages if the violation is willful. Compliance to the act does not permit the employer to lower the wages of the opposite sex but compels raising the wages of those individuals against whom the employer discriminated. The enforcement of Title VII using Equal Pay Act defenses has been a matter of litigation for several years and has resulted in the adoption of the comparable wage theory by EEOC, with Title VII as authority that goes beyond the Equal Pay Act. Whether Title VII will replace lawsuits under the Equal Pay Act is yet to be determined by the courts. (This is further discussed in Chapter XIII.)

Age Discrimination In Employment Act Of 1967

This statute makes it unlawful to discriminate against employees or job applicants on account of age when they are between the ages of 40 and 70. The employer of 20 or more workers a year is subject to the act. Labor unions with 25 members, employment agencies, and apprenticeship programs that operate as referral services for employers in interstate commerce are also included. The act requires all employment decisions to be based on a factor other than age. An employee may be forced to retire before 70 years of age if shown unable to perform the duties of the job. Otherwise it is the employee's, not the employer's, decision when to retire. Employees who will receive at least $27,000 annual pension benefits are excluded and may be retired regardless of age. Senior policy makers or bona fide executives may be retired at 65. Federal employees may continue their employment indefinitely as there is no upper-age limit. Some states have a similar rule for state employees.

Rehabilitation Act Of 1973

This act applies only to businesses performing federal contract work and recipients of federal assistance programs of over $2,500. The act simply says that employment discrimination against a handicapped individual is prohibited. It requires the employer and institutions receiving federal assistance to take affirmative action to hire or advance qualified handicapped individuals and to accommodate their needs reasonably. There is no federal protection of the handicapped unless the employer is a government contractor or, as in the case of an educational institution, that receives federal aid. In this respect the act differs from Title VII, which covers all employers and does not include handicapped workers as a protected class.

The employer should be cautioned, however, that this is one area where the state laws have filled the void. Many states treat the handicapped as a protected class the same as race, sex, religion, and

---

[8] Brennan v. Emerald Renovators, Inc., 410 F.Supp. 1057 (SD NY 1975).

national origin. Further discussion of state laws for the handicapped is treated in Chapter VI. Because this is a federal contract compliance statute, the enforcement is with the Department of Labor. However, where federal assistance programs are involved under Section 504, the Department of Health and Human Services enforces the statute. If it decides not to proceed, the Office of Contract Compliance Programs may do so, cancel government contracts, or bar the employer from doing business with the federal government.

Executive Order 11246

In 1941 the executive branch of the federal government required defense contractors to provide equal employment opportunity for all their employees. In 1967 Executive Order 11246 was issued; it extended equal employment opportunity and affirmative action to all contractors and subcontractors do-

ing business with the federal government. Any contractor that does $50,000 worth of business in any given year and has 50 or more employees must have a written affirmative action program and file it with the Office of Federal Contract Compliance.

The order has enforcement powers by the cancellation, termination, or suspension of contracts for failure to comply. Also failure to comply with Title VII by a contractor, subcontractor, or a union can cause the Department of Labor to recommend the EEOC to institute proceedings. Compliance and reporting provisions of Executive Order 11246 have provoked extensive controversy among civil rights advocates and employers. Further consideration of affirmative action and recommendations for compliance within a positive personnel administration program are found in Chapter V.

RECORD KEEPING AND REPORTING REQUIREMENTS OF ANTIDISCRIMINATION LAWS

Regulations promulgated by the agencies responsible for enforcing antidiscrimination statutes have established record-keeping retention policies. Although compliance is not a statutory wrong but a violation of a rule, the employer should comply because the records may become the proof that an employment decision was made on a nondiscriminatory basis.

Under Title VII, job applications, resumes, payroll records and employee personnel files must be kept for a minimum of six months or until disposition of any personnel action involved under Title VII, whichever is later. Employers of 100 or more employees are required to file the EEO-1 report annually; this gives an inventory of employees by race, ethnic group, sex, job category, and salary. Unions with 100 or more members must file an EEO-3 report, and records must be kept for one year after the report. Private employment agencies have not been subject to the Title VII record-keeping or reporting requirement except in their capacity as employers.

Government contractors under Executive Order 11246 do not have a specific record-keeping requirement except to make all their records available for compliance review. Under the Rehabilitation Act of 1973 contractors and subcontractors must retain complaints or action taken for one year. The same rule applies for contractors under the Vietnam Era Veterans Readjustment Act of 1974.

The Equal Pay Act of 1963 requires that employees' records concerning wages, hours of work, and other terms of employment (including exempt-status employees) be kept for three years, although records supporting employment decisions under the act must be kept only for two years.

The Age Discrimination in Employment Act of 1967 rules requires that employment records including the employee's personnel file must be kept for one year. However, payroll information and information relating to name, address, birth date, and job category must be kept for three years.

LABOR ORGANIZATIONS AND ANTIDISCRIMINATION LAWS

A labor organization is defined, for coverage purposes under Title VII, as any organization, agency, or employee representation committee that exists to deal with the employer as to grievances, labor disputes, and conditions of employment. Any conference or joint board that is subordinate to a national or international labor organization is also subject to the act. The Age Discrimination in Employment Act (ADEA) defines a labor organization in the same way as Title VII. The labor organization must be have at least 15 members in the case of Title VII and 25

members to be under ADEA. The labor organization cannot exclude from membership or otherwise discriminate against members because of race, color, religion, sex, or national origin, or age, nor can it cause the employer to discriminate against an individual. It cannot maintain segregated locals or discriminate as to referrals or apprenticeship training programs.

Labor unions have a special duty under Title VII and the ADEA to represent fairly all employees apart from the requirements of the National Labor Relations Act. They must attempt to eradicate any discriminatory practices and process grievances within the scope of its bargaining agreement or power to negotiate a change.

Adverse Impact As Evidence Of Discrimination

Antidiscrimination laws or regulations promulgated under those laws did not define discrimination. The first task of the courts was to define discrimination. If an employment policy treated one class of employees or individuals within the class differently than another class or had the effect of eliminating employment opportunities of a protected class, the courts defined this as a disparate treatment that was unlawful unless a business necessity could be shown. In order for an employer to determine whether employment practices would result in an adverse impact on a member of the protected class the EEOC issued guidelines that would enable the employer to determine mathematically whether an adverse impact on a certain class of employees existed. This formula is not a legal

definition of a violation but only evidence of violation. When an adverse impact is found, the employer must give a nondiscriminatory reason why it exists. Exhibit III-1 illustrates how an employer can determine whether an adverse impact exists.

If the selection rate for minorities is less than 80 percent of the selection rate for the remaining applicants, an adverse impact is demonstrated. To make this computation, divide the selection rate for the minorities (or covered group) by the selection rate for the remaining applicants and compare the result to 80 percent. If the selection rate for minorities is less than 80 percent of the selection rate for the remaining applicants, an adverse impact is demonstrated. In this example 67 percent is below 80 percent; therefore an adverse impact would exist.

Legal Requirements To Sustain A Discrimination Lawsuit

It is a legal principle that before a person can go to court, it

EXHIBIT III-1		
Applicants	*Number of Minority Rejected*	*Number of Nonminority Rejected*
100	*53*	*30*

Rate of selection = 100 − rate of rejection

$$\frac{\textit{Selection rate for minorities (47\%)}}{\textit{Selection rate for nonminorities (70\%)}} = 67\%$$

must be shown that a wrong has been committed by stating certain facts. In discrimination lawsuits this is called a prima facie case (will establish a fact until rebutted). In alleging discrimination in employment the Supreme Court said that the charging party must establish a prima facie case by showing the following:[9]

1. The applicant is a member of a class protected by the statute alleged to be violated (sex, race, national origin, age, etc.).

2. The applicant applied for the vacancy and is qualified to perform the job. (Where the employer requested specific questions be answered in a resume and the applicant refused to answer those questions, the court held that the plaintiff had not completed the application process and therefore was not an applicant and failed to establish a prima facie case.)[10]

3. Although qualified the applicant was rejected.

4. After rejection, the job vacancy remained open and the employer continued to seek application from persons of equal qualifications. (If the employer rejects a minority but hires another equally qualified minority, this is not a defense to rebut the requirement that there was no rejection of the first applicant.)[11]

Requirements to establish a prima facie case have been applied to all employment situations including the ADEA.

If underutilization of a protected class can be shown, this is a strong evidence of discriminatory practice and will establish a prima facie case but can be rebutted by the employer by showing a nondiscriminatory reason.[12] Other defenses to a prima facie case are given in Chapter IX.

LEGAL STATUS OF GUIDELINES AND EXECUTIVE ORDERS

Before considering the EEOC guidelines in detail, a distinction must be made between statutes, rules, and regulations. Statutes are laws passed by a legislative body on a particular subject. The courts

---

[9] McDonnell Douglas Corp. v. Green, 411 U.S. 792 (1973).

[10] Tagupa v. Board of Directors Research Corp., U. of Hawaii, 633 F.2d 1309 (9th Cir. 1980).

[11] Connecticut v. Teal, 102 Sup. Ct. 2525 (1982).

[12] In Perryman v. Johnson Products Co., 698 F.2d 1138 (11th Cir. 1983) the court stated that rebuttal to a *prima facie* case may be "exceedingly light" and plaintiff by direct evidence must show discrimination.

do not challenge legislative authority other than to interpret the intent or desire of the legislative body in the administration of the law. If a statute exceeds the authority granted under the Constitution, then the authority of the legislative body will be challenged. The interpretation of the statutes by the courts along with the statute becomes law within that court's jurisdiction.

Guidelines are the formal statement of policy of the regulatory agency issuing them and have only the legal stature that the courts want to give them. They have no statutory basis. Guidelines must be distinguished from rules and regulations that are promulgated under the authority of a statute. Rules and regulations are enforceable in the courts if properly promulgated and if statutory authority exists.

The first judicial treatment of the guidelines within the context of discrimination laws was in Griggs v. Duke Power Co., 401 U.S. 424 (1971), where the court said as to guidelines:

Since the Act and its legislative history support the commission's construction, this affords good reason to treat guidelines as expressing the will of Congress.

This statement was reaffirmed in Albemarle Paper Co. v. Moody, 422 U.S. 405 (1975), where the court said as to guidelines:

They do constitute the administrative interpretation of the Act by the enforcing agency and consequently are given great deference.

After these two decisions, most legal observers of antidiscrimination law concluded that guidelines would have the force of law. One year after Albemarle the Supreme Court held contrary to the guidelines in Gilbert v. General Electric, 429 U.S. 125 (1976), and said that the guidelines should be given only consideration. In International Brotherhood of Teamsters v. U.S., 431 U.S. 324 (1977), the court held contrary to the guidelines as to seniority systems; it took the minority opinion to remind the court that it ignored the guidelines completely and was contrary to the Griggs and Albemarle cases.

The courts' decisions and problems in enforcement caused EEOC to make major revisions in its guidelines. The guidelines were adopted by all the federal government enforcement agencies before being issued. The Uniform Guidelines on Employee Selection Procedures, which became effective on September 25, 1978, considered the judicial scrutiny of the previous guidelines and as a result contain several of the Supreme Court interpretations of the law in the definitions and statement of policy. EEOC recognized that if future guidelines are to have judicial recognition, the commission must take court interpretations of the act into account and make the guidelines less policy and more law.

The fundamental principle of the guidelines is that where the employers' policies and practices have an adverse impact on employment or promotion opportunity of any race, sex or ethnic group, they are in violation of Title VII unless business necessity can be shown. If an adverse impact in policies or practices does not exist, the guidelines do not apply.

Executive orders pertain to the position of the executive branch of the government on a particular subject. The enforcement within the governmental departments is through the power of the executive branch. Enforcement in the private sector is to instruct governmental agencies not to do business with an enterprise that does not comply with the executive order. If refused business, the contractor has a right to a hearing and the government must show that it acted in a reasonable manner. However, the final decision is left up to the agency. Where the agency's action is arbitrary and capricious, this would be subject to judicial review.

The most widely used executive order is Executive Order 11246, which concerns discrimination in the private sector. The Supreme Court has not determined whether this executive order or others like it violates the Constitution or usurps the power of the executive branch of the federal government. The basic principles of all guidelines and executive orders are to correct past discrimination policies and to change employment policies that have an adverse impact. The purpose of regulations is to obtain a certain result through enforcement of a statute.

SUMMARY AND CONCLUSIONS

The discrimination laws reviewed in this chapter state one main theme to employers. When making an employment decision, the employer must be prepared to give a nondiscriminatory business reason for the decison, if that decision has an adverse impact or results in adverse treatment of a member of the protected class. The belief that a man who has a family to support should be preferred for a job opportunity exposes the employer to an indefensible lawsuit if a more qualified woman is not considered. Many women are seeking the same job satisfaction, promotions, and salary level as men.

Some employers feel that antidiscrimination laws have limited their ability to manage their employees. No employer should cease making employment decisions that it believes are in the best interest of the organization from fear of legal problems caused by antidiscrimination laws. These laws do not interfere with legitimate business purposes. What the employer should do is to build the record that shows the business reason for the decision. If no business reason can be found, it is questionable whether the decision is in the best interests of the business.

Enforcement of guidelines and executive orders sometimes go beyond what the law requires. When they do, it is important to challenge them, if compliance interferes with the employer's ability to manage the business. However, there may be an alternative way to achieve the same result without interrupting a personnel practice or policy. Guidelines and executive orders are result-oriented and are flexible as to methods to reach those results.

CHAPTER IV

STATUTORY RESTRICTIONS OF RECRUITING AND SELECTION

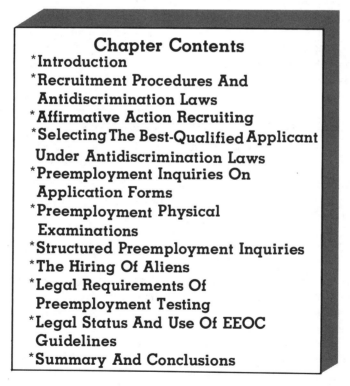

Chapter Contents
*Introduction
*Recruitment Procedures And
  Antidiscrimination Laws
*Affirmative Action Recruiting
*Selecting The Best-Qualified Applicant
  Under Antidiscrimination Laws
*Preemployment Inquiries On
  Application Forms
*Preemployment Physical
  Examinations
*Structured Preemployment Inquiries
*The Hiring Of Aliens
*Legal Requirements Of
  Preemployment Testing
*Legal Status And Use Of EEOC
  Guidelines
*Summary And Conclusions

INTRODUCTION

The antidiscrimination laws described in Chapter III have considerable impact on the entire personnel management function. One of personnel's major areas of activity is the recruitment and selection of qualified applicants. These areas were especially affected by antidiscrimination laws. The selection process deeply involves all members of management who interview job candidates and make decisions on selection. Members of management must be aware of the exposure to costly and time-consuming charges of discrimination even though they may be acting in good faith.

This chapter is designed to alert every person in the organization to the problems caused by antidiscrimination laws in the selection of the most qualified person for the job. What are the requirements of the antidiscrimination laws as to recruiting procedures, preemployment inquiries, interviewing, testing, and application forms? What is the best way to select the best-qualified candidate and still comply with antidiscrimination statutes? This chapter is concerned with federal law only. However, state fair employment practice laws can never lessen equal employment obligations of the employer and frequently increase them. An employer should always check both state and federal laws before making an employment policy decision. The antidiscrimination statutes do not specifically state what type of recruitment or selection is in compliance. We must look to court decisions, policies, and agency guidelines for direction.

RECRUITMENT PROCEDURES AND ANTIDISCRIMINATION LAWS

The recruitment procedure is the preliminary step to the selection procedure; unless designed properly, it will have a devastating effect on the selection of qualified applicants. The place to prevent adverse impact in selection is in the recruitment procedure. Some employers have said that it is not possible to select a qualified candidate because of the restrictions of antidiscrimination laws. This statement simply is not true. The supervisor who says, "Don't send me a minority or a female because I cannot refuse to hire them," does not understand the purpose and objective of the antidiscrimination laws.

Recruitment is a two-step process. First, the employer must announce a job opening to a labor market area that contains applicants capable of responding. Second, those capable of responding must become aware of and answer the announcement. The traditional methods used by employers in announcing a job opening are as follows:

1. newspaper ads

2. listing vacancies with state employment and private employment agencies

3. word-of-mouth or employee referrals

4. walk-ins or unsolicited applications by mail

5. college or institution recruiting

6. trade association publications

State and federal enforcement agencies have in specific incidents attacked all these methods as either having an adverse impact or failure to achieve proper applicant flow. (This is common when one or two sources of recruitment are relied on and others are not used.) It is imperative that a broad recruiting base be developed. Newspaper ads are a common method of recruiting; before antidiscrimination laws, these were subject to editing only by the publisher. Courts and regulatory agencies say that one should not use public notices or advertisements that discourage or limit employment opportunities of groups on the basis of sex, race, religion, ethnic origin, or physical handicap. Wording alone does not make an advertisement wrong. The key question is whether the phrasing limits the non-job-related characteristics of persons who may apply.[1] Non-job-related characteristics are illustrated in the following ad.

Help Wanted

Female, age 26–40, needed for Customer Service Department. Must have high school diploma and good credit rating. Call Mr. Jones at T.C. Mfg. Co. 666-4444.

This ad limits persons applying for the job opening; such limitations don't appear necessary for successful performance of the job. Certainly a male can perform the job as well as a female. Is a high school education really needed for the job? What does a good credit rating have to do with job performance?[2]

Any advertisement that limits the persons applying for non-job-related reasons is not serving the legitimate business purpose of seeking the best-qualified persons available. Disregarding the legal restrictions, this is not a sound recruitment practice. Most want ad violations can be avoided by changing the wording. Describing a preferred applicant as *attractive* could lead to objections that might be avoided by changing to *well-groomed* and *presentable*, terms that cover both male and female categories. A similar approach can be used to eliminate problems of race, age, and other discriminatory wording.

Another common recruiting method is word of mouth (sometimes called an informal contact or employee referrals). Many employment managers believe this the best source of qualified applicants. Courts closely examine this procedure because experience indicates that one worker will rarely refer another of a different race,

---

[1] Brennan v. Approved Personnel Service, Inc., 529 F.2d 760 (4th Cir. 1975).

[2] It is recognized that what the employment manager was trying to eliminate in requiring a good credit rating was an unstable applicant who may be subject to garnishments, but since a high percentage of minorities have poor credit rating, the employer would have to show that the persons with poor credit rating are poor performers.

nationality, religion, etc. As a result, a "built in headwind" limits the hiring of minorities if this is the sole source of applicants.[3] If the employee referral approach to recruiting is accompanied by an affirmative action program to encourage minorities and females to apply, the package would be perfectly acceptable to the courts.[4]

An affirmative action program to encourage minorities and females to apply would be to seek applicants actively from such sources as the Urban League, minority oriented media, local Spanish-American organizations, women's organizations, and schools with large minority populations. Some companies have made special efforts to broaden their recruiting programs. Exhibit IV-1 shows a survey of affirmative action recruiting programs for minority and females.

This survey shows that most companies have had special recruiting programs although they are slightly more common in large companies. Companies' surveys further stated that community agencies such as NAACP, Urban League, and churches are considered a good source of minority job applicants.

Where such recruiting is not being carried out, the courts, when finding discriminatory hiring, will force the company to correct the applicant flow by affirmative action. One court required a company to conduct recruitment visits in such a manner as to achieve maximum nondiscriminatory coverage and to maintain appropriate records to ensure compliance.[5] In another situation a company was required to recruit predominately in black colleges.[6] The Georgia Power case also stands for the rule that word-of-mouth recruiting or employee referral in an all-white work force was unlawful even though the method was neutral on its face (no intent to discriminate).

Recruitment procedures that require listing all new job openings with state employment agencies and advertising in media with an adequate minority and female audience will have little or no chance of EEOC investigations. When the employer chooses word-of-mouth or walk-in as the sole method of recruiting or any other single method of recruitment, the procedure will not be questioned unless the work force has a statistical imbalance. Only when there is an imbalance in the work force and there is evidence of adverse impact in the selection process, is a recruitment procedure questioned by the courts and regulatory agencies.

The traditional methods of recruiting should not be eliminated because of antidiscrimination laws;

---

[3] In EEOC v. Detroit Edison Co., 512 F.2d 301 (6th Cir. 1975) the court concluded that employee referrals would perpetually imbalance the work force in favor of white males that already existed at the facility.

[4] Diggs v. Western Electric, 587 F.2d 1070 (10th Cir. 1978); United States v. Georgia Power Co., 474 F.2d 906 (5th Cir. 1973).

[5] Morrow v. Crisler, 491 F.2d 1053 (5th Cir. 1974).

[6] U.S. v. Georgia Power, 474 F.2d 906 (4th Cir. 1973).

EXHIBIT IV-1

Affirmative Action Recruiting

	% of Companies						
	By Industry			By Size		All Companies	1976 Figures
	Mfg.	Nonmfg.	Nonbus.	Large	Small		
Company has a formal EEO program	89	75	88	90	80	84	86
Program includes an affirmative action plan	83	69	71	85	70	76	n.a.
Company has programs specifically for: Recruiting minority workers	71	63	69	78	61	68	69
Recruiting minorities for professional/managerial positions	59	58	62	71	52	59	58
Recruiting women for traditionally male jobs	64	54	55	67	54	59	61
Recruiting women for professional/managerial positions	56	56	62	65	52	57	57
Recruiting handicapped workers	44	36	60	55	37	45	n.a.

Reprinted by permission from *BNA's Personnel Policies Forum Survey*, copyright 1979 by The Bureau of National Affairs, Inc., Washington, D.C.

the same resources should be used for protected classes in the same manner as other employees. However, the employer should be alert to possible adverse impact. Exhibit VI-2 shows that when traditional sources are used, an adverse impact is likely if only a few sources such as walk-ins and college recruiting are used. The use of local community agencies is the most successful resource and alone would probably prevent an adverse impact. However, if all the sources are used, an adverse impact would be unlikely.

AFFIRMATIVE ACTION RECRUITING

EXHIBIT IV-2

Most Effective Recruiting Sources for Special Groups***

	Groups		
	*Minority Workers**	*Women**	*Handicapped***
Source			
Local community agencies	*33*	*18*	*60*
Advertising	*19*	*39*	*8*
Walk-ins	*9*	*10*	*3*
Employee referrals	*30*	*27*	*11*
College recruiting	*11*	*17*	*6*
Employment agencies	*20*	*21*	*5*

Note: Figures are percentages of all companies.

*Figures add to more than 100 percent because of multiple responses.

**Figures add to less than 100 percent because of nonresponses.

***Reprinted by permission from *BNA's Personnel Policies Forum Survey,* copyright 1979 by the Bureau of National Affairs, Inc., Washington, D.C.

SELECTING THE BEST-QUALIFIED APPLICANT UNDER ANTIDISCRIMINATION LAWS

The advent of Title VII caused changes in the selection of applicants for many organizations. The key new element was that the evaluation of the applicant must be objective. The practice of selecting candidates by the instincts of the supervisor, prejudices—often based on a single experience—or other subjective criteria will no longer withstand judicial scrutiny. It is questionable whether these subjective methods were effective in selecting the best-qualified person. (The author knew a supervisor who would not accept applicants from Wisconsin because he believed that they were all lazy!) The day of the supervisor who said that he could determine the physical strength of applicants by looking at the applicant is over. As one court said, an "eyeball test" is not valid for determining strength of an applicant.[7] These may be extreme examples but many other equally ridiculous ones could be given by employment managers.

[7] EEOC v. Spokane Concrete Products, 534 F.Supp. 518 (E. D. Wash. 1982).

PREEMPLOYMENT INQUIRIES ON APPLICATION FORMS

There is nothing in the federal statutes, guidelines, or court decisions that prevents making preemployment inquiries either on the application forms or orally except for garnishments or arrests. Such inquiries are required to have a job-related purpose and the information must not be used for discriminatory purposes. Where apprenticeship applications were asked for race and no Mexican-Americans were considered, the court held the inquiry was used for discriminatory purposes.[8]

If the application form has an adverse impact upon the hiring process, then it will be considered wrongful and will be challenged. These challenges will be indefensible where it can be shown that few applicants are placed after information is received and such information does not have a real business purpose in selecting qualified employees, as was the situation in Inspiration Consolidated Copper Co. case.

Unstructured preemployment inquiries such as "What do you expect in salary in five years?" present the greatest exposure to liability in the selection process.[9] Unless such inquiries have a purpose, the regulatory agencies or the courts may require the employer to show that no discriminatory purpose exists. The absence of a business purpose is taken as an indication of discriminatory intent. Specific areas where questions may lead to liability include:

Arrest and conviction. One Court held that questions about arrest are absolutely barred.[10] Questions about conviction should include a statement that the organization will consider the nature of the conviction, offense, age committed, and the like.

Age. Questions are not illegal per se but one should be prepared to give a good reason for asking.

Height and weight. It is claimed that this tends to screen out females and Americans of Asian and Spanish descent. This is difficult to defend if adverse impact is found unless height and weight are specific requirements of the job, e.g., police and prison guards.[11]

Marital status. This is illegal per se if asked only of women. (Unless prohibited by state law, some states such as Minnesota and California make married persons a protected group.) If asked of both sexes, this is probably okay if there

---

[8] U.S. v Inspiration Consolidated Copper Co., 6 CCH Employment Practices Decisions, para 8918 (DC, Ariz, 1973).

[9] Author once knew of a manager who would ask when "the War of 1812 was fought?" If the applicant didn't know, he would reject the applicant.

[10] Gregory v. Litton Systems, 472 F.2d 671 (9th Cir. 1972).

[11] Dothard v. Rawlinson, 433 U.S. 321 (1977).

is a no-spouse hiring rule, which is permissible under federal law.[12]

Husband's or wife's occupation. Is this related to job performance? EEOC will challenge on the basis that the employer is really trying to determine who is the principal wage earner with the idea that the secondary wage earner will work for less. This is not a good argument—just troublesome.

Length of time at present address. It may be designed to determine stability; it might be suspected as discriminatory against minorities who have a high incidence of changing addresses. If this were the sole criterion for selection and it could be shown that there is a statistical difference in rejections between minorities and nonminorities, the inquiry would have to be justified by a business reason.

Physical characteristics. When asking about physical characteristics of the applicant, it must be factually determined what physical requirements are necessary for the job. If similar positions have different requirements, it is questionable whether the physical requirements are job-related. Where females could not wear glasses but males could and jobs were similar, this is held an unlawful requirement.[13]

Although the application form may comply with federal law, more stringent state laws often could make the application form illegal. For this reason companies operating in several states find it difficult to develop one form that can be used nationally.

Sometimes companies ignore state laws. Unless the state has an active enforcement agency, the violation goes unnoticed. For example, an Ohio statute states that it is illegal to ask questions pertaining to applicants' sex or race unless the Ohio Civil Rights Commission has certified the question as representing a bona fide occupational qualification (BFOQ).[14]

In Minnesota it is illegal to ask marital status while in other states this may be perfectly legal if the inquiry has a nondiscriminatory purpose.[15]

Employers should always check state laws before being comfortable that their application form is legally sound.

PREEMPLOYMENT PHYSICAL EXAMINATIONS

Questions about physical requirements can lead into questions about medical history and a preemployment physical examination. Many preemployment physical examinations given by employers

---

[12] Harper v. TWA, 525 F.2d 409 (8th Cir. 1975).

[13] Laffey v. Northwest Airlines, 567 F.2d 429 (D.C. Cir 1976) Cert.den. 434 U.S. 1086 (1978).

[14] Ohio Revised Code Sect. 4112.02(E).

[15] Minnesota Statutes Annotated 363.03(1).

are not related to job performance. In a study by the Johns Hopkins Center for Metro Planning & Research Institute it was found that tasks actually performed by women had little relationship to the physical tests used to determine job qualifications.

An audit of company preemployment physical examinations is advisable in light of the requirement that any prerequisite to hiring must be job-related. The first step in determining an applicant's physical condition is to ask. Asking the applicant about physical conditions should be the starting point of determining whether the applicant can perform the job applied for. This can be done formally by a premedical questionnaire designed by the company physician. A form similiar to Exhibit IV-3 would determine the type of preemployment physical examination to be given or whether an examination is needed at all. Exhibit IV-3 is quite detailed; a less detailed questionnaire should be considered if there is concern about creating adverse applicant behavior as the job being applied for may have few physical requirements.

EXHIBIT IV-3

Date _____

Preemployment Medical History

Full name _____

Address _____

Date of birth _____ Social Security no. _____

Date of last doctor visit _____ Doctor's name and address

_____

Name and address of family physician if not same as above

_____

Circle illnesses or conditions that you have had and give approximate year of diagnosis and recovery date:

Diabetes	Glaucoma	Heart trouble
Cancer	Asthma	Jaundice
Tuberculosis	Alcoholism	Kidney disease
Venereal disease	Rheumatic fever	Vein trouble
Allergy	High blood pressure	Bleeding tendency (internal or external)
Drug addiction	Nervous disorder	

continued

EXHIBIT IV-3

Other illnesses or physical conditions not mentioned above (give year of diagnosis and

recovery date) _____

_____

_____

_____

Are you allergic or sensitive to any medicines or other substances? _____

Please describe. _____

_____

List operations that you have had, giving approximate dates, hospitals, and names and

addresses of surgeons. _____

_____

_____

List any permanent disability as result of injuries or illnesses. _____

_____

Name or otherwise identify medicines that you are now using or have used within the

last six months. _____

The questions in Exhibit IV-3 should be adapted to the particular operations and job categories. It may not be job-related to ask about diabetes unless diabetes is related to job performance. In many cases diabetes can be treated so it will not interfere with the job. Some of the questions may not relate to the job but would be important information for emergency treatment at the job site by a company nurse or first-aid specialist. These considerations should be carefully determined by the company physician and the personnel practitioner before the questionnaire is drafted.

One might wonder if the applicant would tend to falsify the information. This tendency always exists, but there is less likelihood from falsification when a written form is provided than if it is an oral, unstructured inquiry of the applicant's physical condition. Further the courts will almost always support discharge for falsifying information when applying for work.[16]

---

[16] In Jimerson v. Kisco Co., Inc., 404 F.Supp. 338, aff'd 542 F.2d 1008 (8th Cir. 1976) the court justified a discharge for falsifying an arrest record and not because of the arrest record or because an unlawful question was asked.

The next important step in making a preemployment physical job-related is to be assured that the doctor has knowledge of the physical requirements of the job. Often this is difficult as the doctor either does not want to take the time to study the job or the job content changes so rapidly that it makes the study obsolete in a short time. It is best for the doctor to observe the various jobs. If this is not possible, a good job description will be sufficient. In the job description the physical requirements of the job should be noted; when the job is changed, the job description should be updated and communicated to the doctor. Preemployment inquiries as to applicant's physical condition can be justified in determining job placement or, if the applicant is handicapped, in meeting the employer's obligation to accommodate through job placement.[17]

Although questions about medical history and physical or mental disabilities are not specifically prohibited by the law, they are hazardous unless a specific business purpose can be shown. Often the same information can be obtained without a discriminatory emphasis that may trigger an investigation or a complaint. For example, instead of asking whether an applicant has any disabilities, one should ask whether any disabilities would interfere with the ability to perform the job for which application is being made. If an applicant does not know, further inquiry as to the physical condition is justified.

It is advisable for the employer to audit the application form and other preemployment inquiries and ask, For what purpose is this question being asked? Can it be shown to be job-related? Does the urgency of the question justify the exposure to EEOC investigation and the time and monetary expenditure that go along with the investigation? If all these questions can be answered in the affirmative, then one should continue to make inquiries on the application form. If there is no real reason, it is advisable to eliminate those questions.

To assure that interviewers do not use answers to questions for discriminatory purposes, it is recommended to put a statement on the application form as follows: "Information obtained from questions asked on this form or orally will not be used for discriminatory purposes." Application forms have contained many questions unnecessary to the selection of qualified applicants; personnel practitioners seldom audited the application form. Antidiscrimination laws have caused a substantial improvement of the application form in that they relate the questions to the requirements of the job.[18]

---

[17] Treatment of handicapped workers is found in Chapter VI.

[18] See Joseph J. Famularo, *Handbook of Personnel Forms, Records, and Reports* (New York: McGraw Hill, 1982).

STRUCTURED PREEMPLOYMENT INQUIRIES

This discussion on preemployment inquiries has been directed to the employment manager or other personnel practitioners; however, as a practical matter interviews are conducted on all levels of management. To avoid exposure to discrimination and elimination of prejudice by management personnel, those who interview should not be allowed the discretion of the past. Written guidelines to standardize preemployment inquiries are helpful. All preemployment inquiries should have the specific purpose of determining the qualifications of the individual applicant as required by the job and not what the interviewer believes will make a good employee.

If the selection procedure is to fulfill its major objective of hiring qualified applicants, it is necessary to establish appropriate job specifications[19] and structure at least part of the interview. Before antidiscrimination laws, employers were not required to establish job specifications. If they did, their validity or accuracy was never questioned by anyone except internal management, which often aided in drafting them. Under antidiscrimination laws the selection procedure is subject to the EEOC Employment Guidelines, enforcement agencies, and scrutiny of the courts and must be modified to eliminate exposure, but still to be effective in selection of the best-qualified applicant.

One of the problems in the application form is that all questions are not job-related to all job categories. For this reason an application blank should be flexible to apply to several job categories. In order to accomplish this, the applicant should be asked to answer only those questions that apply to job being considered. This type of an application form will eliminate asking questions that are not job-related and may be implied to have a discriminatory purpose. Exhibit IV-4 is an example of an application form that eliminates questions that are not job-related for certain jobs, but are for others, and will also serve to select the best-qualified applicant.

THE HIRING OF ALIENS

Many employers require that an applicant be a U.S. citizen before eligibility for employment while other employers will hire aliens without inquiring as to whether they entered the country illegally or whether they have a work permit. Some often have ac-

---

[19] The term *job specifications* is usually a statement of duties, responsibilities, and what is expected of the employees.

EXHIBIT IV-4

Protection of Information on Application Forms
from Being Interpreted as Discriminatory

After general information is requested and there is need for special information the following section could be inserted.

The information requested below is needed for certain job assignment or for other nondiscriminatory reasons. Since this information is necessary only for certain jobs, answer only those questions where the box is checked. The remaining questions do not apply to the job(s) you are applying for.

| | Marital status   Date of marriage or divorce if any
| | What was your previous address?
| | How long have you lived at your previous address?
| | How long at your present address?
| | Weight
| | Height
| | Age
| | Have you been convicted of a crime in the last 10 years?
| | Names of all relatives working here.
| | Do you have any defects that will prevent you from performing the job(s) you are applying for? If yes, describe. _____
| | Occupation of father
| | Method of transporation to get to work

(Questions included above should be referenced to the requirements of at least one job.)

---

tual knowledge that the applicant entered the country illegally. All are acceptable under present statutes. The citizenship requirement is not considered a violation of antidiscrimination laws. There is no penalty for an employer who hires an illegal alien nor is there an obligation to inquire whether the applicant illegally entered the United States.[20] The employer's interest in determining whether an applicant is an alien is in preventing deportation to avoid losing the skill.

On the other hand the employer who uses the deportation avenue to get rid of employees may become involved in discrimination or other unfair employment practices. When an employer reported aliens to the Immigration Service because they were union activists and were thus deported, the court enforced an order of the National Labor Relations Board to reinstate the employees as this was discriminatory against union activity. Because they were already deported and reinstatement was not possible, the

---

[20]U.S. Code Sect. 1324. However, some states prevent an employer from hiring an illegal alien, in which case there is an obligation to require immigration papers, if not born in the United States. Legislation is pending in the 98th (1983) Congress to make unlawful hiring illegal aliens (S.F. #525).

Board ordered six months' back pay for each alien.[21] The Supreme Court has agreed to review this decision.

An employer can obtain a labor certificate if it can be shown that the alien can fulfill a needed skill or service that cannot be obtained in the United States. However, in some labor market areas it is difficult to get certificates, while in others it is relatively simple. Sometimes church organizations are willing to sponsor an alien. If employer knows of a rare skill that an alien possesses, requesting a church to be a sponsor is sometimes more effective and speedier than applying for a labor certificate. A personnel recruiter may benefit more by going to church than going to the labor or immigration offices.

Under the Immigration and Nationality Act of 1977 the Attorney General can discretely prescribe that an alien can be lawfully admitted for a permanent residence regardless of immigration quotas. The alien must make application for admittance under the Act and must further show eligibility to receive an immigrant visa ex-cept for immigration quotas. After the application is filed, the alien can receive specific authorization for employment from the immigration service.

Under present court decisions legal aliens have the same rights as citizens; however, there are exceptions in certain job categories. Where a school board denied tenure to alien teachers, the Supreme Court upheld the denial, stating that the teachers should set an example for students.[22] Present cases indicate that aliens are protected under antidiscrimination laws but to date the Supreme Court has not considered the issue. If an illegal alien would seek protection, deportation proceedings would probably preempt the discrimination complaint. The employer should inquire as to whether an applicant is an alien, not for any legal reasons but to determine whether the applicant is subject to deportation. This determination is important as to job assignments, training, and exposure to turnover, etc. If applicant has a rare skill that the employer desperately needs, the exposure to turnover may be worth it.

LEGAL REQUIREMENTS OF PREEMPLOYMENT TESTING

The most significant change in the selection process as a result of antidiscrimination laws is in the area of preemployment testing.[23] The field of industrial testing grew substantially after World War II

---

[21] NLRB v. Sure Tan, 672 F.2d 592 (7th Cir. 1982), Cert Granted 103 Supt. Ct. 2118 (1983).

[22] Ambach v. Norwich, 441 U.S. 68 (1979).

[23] For additional information on legal aspects of testing, see Richard D. Arvey, *Fairness in Selecting Employees* (Reading, MA: Addison Wesley Publishing Co, Inc., 1979).

to the extent that it was considered by many personnel practitioners a necessity in the selection process. The increased use of tests was often without an indication that it was an effective selection tool except that the personnel manager was not in vogue unless tests were used. Most testing programs were based on professional advice with little or no knowledge of the jobs for which the selection tests were given. Often the tests determined only whether the applicant was an average American. Testing programs, whether valid or invalid, became popular because they afforded a crutch for the selection of an applicant. It was an easy way for the nonprofessional interviewer to screen and select applicants.

For more than three decades professors were advising their students not to use a test as a selection tool unless it was validated as to determine whether the test could predict job performance;[24] this pseudo-psychological method of selecting applicants continued with increasing popularity. The failure of personnel practitioners to validate tests was contrary to sound selection practice and was doomed to fall under the axe of antidiscrimination laws. When the axe did fall, many employers abandoned tests altogether.[25] This result was unfortunate because a properly validated test is one of the least discriminatory means of selecting employees. It reduces the need to rely on the unconscious, illegal, subjective judgment of the interviewer.

Judicial requirements for valid testing can be found in two of the leading and most-quoted cases in antidiscrimination law. The first is Griggs v. Duke Power Co., 401 U.S. 424, decided by the Supreme Court in 1971. The selection test used by Duke Power Co. was the Purdue Vocational Test form B for initial testing and form A for retesting purposes. The time limits were disregarded, and it was considered a work test. Applicants protected by Title VII were affected adversely as shown in Exhibit IV-5.

Fifty-two percent of Caucasians tested were enrolled in a training program, but only 32 percent of blacks and 29 percent

EXHIBIT IV-5

Number Tested	Mean Score	Race	Enrolled in Training School
108	38.75	Caucasian	52
41	24.92	Negro	13
1	—	Oriental	1
1	—	American Indian	0
14	29.53	Spanish-American	5

Source: Court records, Griggs v. Duke Power, 401 U.S. 424 (1971).

[24] D. Yoder, *Personnel and Labor Relations* (Englewood Cliffs, NJ: Prentice-Hall, 1938).

[25] In survey in 1963, 90 percent of employers were using tests; in 1971 only 55 percent used tests of one kind or another. ASPA-BNA Survey #12 "Personnel Testing," *Bulletin to Management* (Washington, DC: Bureau of National Affairs, 1971).

Spanish-Americans. The test was not validated under EEOC guidelines. The court said that the guidelines stated the express intent of Congress. The Griggs case stands for the following principles in preemployment testing:

1. A test must be job-related. If verbal ability is not required to perform functions of the job, one should not test for it.
2. An employer's intent not to discriminate is irrelevant. This is applicable only to Title VII; other statutes require intent.
3. If a practice is fair in form but discriminatory in operation, it will not be upheld.
4. The key to any existing program that has adverse impact is *business necessity*. Business necessity was not defined by the court; it is discussed in Chapter IX.
5. Title VII does not forbid testing, only tests that do not measure job performance.
6. The test must measure the person for the job and not the person in the abstract.
7. Less-qualified applicants should not be hired over those better-qualified because of minority origins. There is no requirement to hire unqualified persons.

Validation Of Tests

If a test has an adverse impact on the selection process, it must be validated as to whether it is:

1. job-related,

2. predictive of performance, or
3. necessary because no less discriminatory methods are available; then business necessity is required.

Good faith effort or neutrality in placing applicants is irrelevant if an adverse impact results. The Court in Griggs did not say how the test should be validated, but at the time of the Grigg's decision Albemarle Paper Co. v. Moody, 422 U.S. 405, was working its way through the lower courts. In June 1975 the Supreme Court put to rest the question of what constituted the proper validation of a preemployment test as well as the back pay issue.

In 1963 Albemarle Paper Co. adopted the Wonderlic Test A and B series as a screening program for selection of employees. General population norms were used to set cutoff scores until the Griggs decision; after that Albemarle hired an expert in industrial psychology to validate the test. Ratings of job performance from three different supervisors were correlated with test scores. After the validation 96 percent of the white applicants passed the test and 64 percent of the blacks. The test scores were primarily used to select and place employees in 11 separate departments where 17 training lines of progression were established.

Exhibit IV-6 illustrates lines of progression in two separate departments. The term *lines of progression* is used in industry to define an on-the-job training method whereby the employee must be trained in the lower skilled

EXHIBIT IV-6

WOOD YARD DEPARTMENT

Yard Crew

Crane Operator
(Large)
↑
Long Log Operator
↑
Log Stacker Operator
↑
Small Equipment
Operator
↑
Oiler ←———
↑
Chip Unloader
↑
Chain Operator
(Start)
↑
Bulldozer
Operator
↑

Service Crew

Dempster-Dumpster
Operator
↑
Winch Truck Operator
↑
Truck Operator
↑
Winch Truck
Operator Helper
↑
Laborer
(Start)

(Note 1: Should the bulldozer operator job be discontinued the employee may move back down the line of progression according to seniority only in jobs he actually worked previously in moving up the line.)

(Note 2: The Knife Grinder is in the Wood Yard Department, but not in a line of progression.)

A PAPER MILL DEPARTMENT

Paper Machine
Line of Progression

Machine Tender No. 1
↑
Machine Tender No. 2
↑
Back Tender No. 1
↑
Back Tender No. 2
↑
Third Hand No. 1
↑
Third Hand No. 2
↑
Fourth Hand No. 1
↑
Fourth Hand No. 2
↑
Front Plugger No. 1
↑
Back Plugger No. 1
↑
Back Plugger No. 2
(Start)

Beater Room
Line of Progression

Beaterman
↑
1st Helper
(Start)

Brakeman
↑
Laborer
(Start)

Dead End Job—Janitor

Source: **Appendix to brief of employers,** *Albemarle Paper Co. v. Moody,* **No. 74-389.**

job before advancement to higher skilled job. Only job vacancies for the unskilled or beginning jobs are communicated or posted; promotion thereafter is automatic after training is completed, a vacancy occurs, and seniority permits.

The adverse impact as a result of the testing and selection program is illustrated by the Exhibits IV-7 and IV-8. Relatively few blacks were performing the higher skilled jobs, as shown in Exhibit IV-7.[26] Although the wood yard is an unskilled line of progression, the higher skilled jobs were performed by whites.

The paper mill department is considered a skilled line of progression. Exhibit IV-8 shows that as a result of the selection procedure few blacks were performing the skilled jobs except the bottom jobs, which are considered unskilled.

The court in Albemarle said that because the tests had an adverse impact on "hiring," the company must valid the tests. The validation of the tests by Albemarle was improper to show business necessity because:

1. The validation process used was not related to the job be-

EXHIBIT IV-7		
A. *Wood Yard Department*	*Negro*	*White*
Yard Crew		
Crane Operator (Large)	*0*	*9*
Long Log Operator	*0*	*4*
Log Stacker Operator	*0*	*4*
Small Equipment Operator	*0*	*4*
Bulldozer Operator	*0*	*1*
Oiler	*0*	*4*
Chip Unloader	*1*	*3*
Chain Operator	*0*	*4*
Chipper Operator No. 2		
Chipper Operator No. 1	*4*	*0*
Tractor Operator	*5*	*0*
Chip Bin Operator	*4*	*0*
Laborers	*12*	*0*
*Knife Grinder	*0*	*1*
Service Crew		
Dempster-Dumpster	*1*	*0*
Winch Truck Operator	*3*	*0*
Winch Truck Operator Helper	*1*	*0*
Laborer	*6*	*0*
Source: **Appendix to brief of employers,** *Albemarle Paper* **v.** *Moody,* **No. 74-389.**		

---

[26] Term used in Appendix of Albemarle Paper v. Moody, No. 74-389, is "negro." It is used in the Exhibits IV-7 and IV-8 refering to that case in its historic context. The term is now considered improper in antidiscrimination documents. The preferred term now is "blacks."

ing applied for. Subjective supervisors' ratings were compared to test scores. The study focused on experienced employees in upper level jobs; high scores of that group are not predictive of qualifications for new workers to perform lower level jobs.

2. The supervisors rated older whites and experienced workers, whereas tests were given to job applicants who were younger, unexperienced, and nonwhite.

Particular attention has been paid to these two cases because a substantial part of the 1978 EEOC Employee Selection Procedures Guidelines as related to testing had their origin in the Griggs and Albemarle cases.

Where a test has an adverse impact but the selection process does not, and accordingly the hiring was not disproportionate to the area population, the Court held that the selection process, including the selection test, does not violate the Due Process Clause of the *Fifth Amendment.*[27] Although the Griggs and Albemarle cases were brought under Title VII, it can be concluded from the decision in the Washington case that if a proportionate number of blacks had been selected, the tests would be acceptable. It is not the process that is being challenged by the courts but the results of the process. In the Washington case, 41 percent of new police hires were blacks, which was proportionate to the number of blacks in the total recruiting area. The test had an

EXHIBIT IV-8		
C. A Paper Mill Department	Negro	White
Paper Machine Line of Progression		
Machine Tender No. 1	0	4
Machine Tender No. 2	0	4
Back Tender No. 1	0	4
Third Hand No. 1	0	4
Third Hand No. 2	0	4
Fourth Hand No. 1	0	4
Fourth Hand No. 2	0	4
Front Plugger No. 1	0	4
Back Plugger No. 1	1	4
Back Plugger No. 2	0	4
Beaterman	0	4
1st Helper	0	4
Brokeman	4	0
Stock Puller	0	0
Laborer	1	0

Source: **Appendix to employer's brief,** *Albemarle Paper* **v.** *Moody,* **No. 74-389.**

[27] Washington v. Davis, 426 U.S. 229 (1976).

adverse impact when a higher percentage of blacks than whites failed the test and the test was shown to have had no relationship to job performance. The Court determined that adverse impact of the test did not affect the affirmative hiring of minority applicants and the selection procedure was therefore legal.

The employer or any user of selection procedures must determine whether there is an adverse impact; if one is found, it must be corrected or show business necessity. Records must be kept for two additional years on corrective activity. If adverse impact is not found, as in the case of skill tests that do not screen out minorities in disproportionate numbers, then no records need to be kept because guidelines do not apply.

Validation Procedures

Three types of validation procedures are defined in Section 14 of the guidelines. In the Griggs case the Supreme Court used the term *business necessity* as a justification for a procedure that discriminates. The term has not been defined by the courts except in the context of a factual situation. Generally it means a procedure necessary to the safe and efficient operation of the enterprise or where the procedure interferes with privacy.

Where an adverse impact is a result of an employment procedure, business necessity must be shown. Business necessity can be shown by validation of that procedure according to the guidelines.

1. *Criterion-related validity.* This is a collection of data that measure job performance and establish statistical relationships between measures of job performance and test scores. When job performance measures such as supervisor's ratings are correlated with test scores, this is predictive measurement of job performance. This is the traditional method of validation of preemployment tests, which has been used for more than 30 years. Supervisor ratings must be objective or will fail to meet the criteria in the Albemarle case.

2. *Content validity.* This correlates certain aspects of the job performance with test scores to measure job performance. This differs from the criterion validation in that the job performance is measured in the specific job for which applicant is being tested. This method of validation relies heavily on job analysis methods alluded to by the court in the Albemarle case.[28]

3. *Construct validation.* This is a psychological method of validation based on research whereby a psychological trait is identified as essential to the successful performance of

---

[28] Job analysis as used by the Court is a statement that provides basic information about job requirements and characteristics of persons who can succesfully perform the job.

the job and develops a selection procedure to measure the presence and degree of that trait. Examples of a trait would be leadership ability, ability to work under pressure, etc.

In determining whether the procedure has an adverse impact, statistical evidence should be considered; however, a statistically unbalanced workforce (disproportionate number of nonminorities or females) does not necessarily mean that the selection procedure is in violation. The reason for the condition may not be the selection procedure but a characteristic of the labor market. In Furnco Construction Corp. v. Waters, 438 U.S. 567 (1978), the Supreme Court in reversing the Seventh Circuit Court of Appeals, which relied on statistical evidence, stated:

It is clear beyond cavil that the obligation imposed by Title VII is to provide an equal opportunity for each applicant regardless of race, without regard to whether members of the applicants race are already proportionately represented in the workforce.[29]

It becomes apparent from this statement that the Court is not concerned so much with a statistical unbalanced work force as it is with the treatment of a single applicant. In the Furnco case the Court allowed the employer to demonstrate the reason for statistical unbalance; if proven a "business necessity," it would be valid.

Another important requirement of the guidelines is found in Section 5(I), where it is stated that procedures to select for a higher skilled job than the original job of the applicant would not be appropriate if three conditions existed:

1. The majority of the applicants selected do not progress to a higher level job within a short time after being placed on lower level job.[30]

2. There is no real distinction between the jobs in the lines of progression or if selection procedures measure skills necessary to perform the job.

3. Knowledge could be acquired on the higher job without being trained on the lower level job.

LEGAL STATUS AND USE OF EEOC GUIDELINES

It may be several years before courts completely accept 1978 guidelines; however, that part of the guidelines incorporating judicial

---

[29] 438 U.S. at p. 579.

[30] Five years would be considered too long until it is tested in the courts; a short period is a matter of judgment of the enforcement agency. The length of time would be somewhat related to the degree of skill required.

decisions is almost certain to be accepted by the courts. For this reason, selection procedures should be reviewed to determine whether they have an adverse impact as defined by the guidelines. If so, personnel administrators should consider corrective measures short of hiring or promoting unqualified persons.

The guidelines can be helpful in selecting or promoting qualified persons. However, where the procedure results in an adverse impact, the personnel practitioner should be prepared to validate the procedure. A valid procedure does not prevent the selection of qualified applicants although an adverse impact exists. Because the primary requirement of a selection procedure is to select qualified applicants, it should not be compromised. The guidelines should be used as a management tool in the selection of qualified applicants and not as an absolute selection procedure regardless of the results. Court decisions have always protected the employer's right to select qualified applicants.

SUMMARY AND CONCLUSIONS

Recruiting and selection have undergone major changes in recent years as a result of the antidiscrimination laws and the court's interpretation of those laws.

Recruitment is a procedure that is the beginning of the employment process. Unless this procedure complies with antidiscrimination laws, other employment activities will have a difficult time doing so. Many of the traditional methods of recruitment have been challenged by the courts. Courts have held violations where the recruiting base is limited to one or two sources or where recruiting tends to perpetuate an unbalanced work force.

In order for the selection procedure to withstand the external audit of antidiscrimination laws, inquiries of the applicant must have a job-related purpose and the information must not be for a discriminatory purpose. Accordingly, the application form must contain questions that aid in hiring the most qualified applicant according to the specifications for that job. Questions on the application form that cannot be shown to be job-related are a suspect of discriminatory motives.

It is not a violation of discrimination laws to require U.S. citizenship for employment. On the other hand it is not a violation of any federal law (except in some states) to knowingly to employ an illegal alien, although turnover by deportation must be considered. Aliens can enter this country under the Immigration and Nationality Act of 1977 outside of quotas if approved by the Attorney General. Aliens so approved are authorized to work in the United States. An alien with a rare skill can be admitted on an employer's request to the Department of Labor if it can be shown that the skill is not available in the United States or that training is impractical.

Aliens have the same rights as citizens although in certain situations these rights can be denied. It appears that legal aliens will be protected by antidiscrimination laws although the Supreme Court has not said so.

A major change has taken place in preemployment testing as a result of the antidiscrimination laws. Where test scores of minorities or females show adverse impact, business necessity must be shown by the validation process, provided that the test is substantially relied upon for selection purposes.[31]

The validation process must show that it is job-related and predictive of performance. If the selection practice is fair in form but discriminatory in operation, it will be struck down by the courts.

The Uniform Employee Selection Procedure Guidelines published by EEOC describe the position of the EEOC on how employers should conduct their recruiting, selection, and test validation procedures. Because the present guidelines contain the position of the

courts in several areas, it can be expected that the guidelines will be given more stature by the courts than past guidelines.

Certain positive procedures in the selection process will reduce exposure to litigation.

1. Screening interviews should determine qualifications as much as possible.

2. If applicants do not pass the screening evaluation, they should not be sent for a second interview. The concept that the primary interview is not the final selection and therefore a wide variety of applicants who have not been objectively evaluated should be sent for operational interviews is not a legally sound personnel practice today.

Adverse impact of a procedure does not mean that the employer must abandon the procedure but does mean that justification of its use may be required by the courts, as the U.S. Supreme Court said in Furnco Construction case at 438 U.S. 567 at 578. "Courts are generally less competent than employers to restructure business practices and ... should not attempt it."

---

[31] Further discussion of legal ramifications of testing can be found in Kenneth J. McCulloch, *Selecting Employees Safely Under the Law* (Englewood Cliffs, NJ: Prentice-Hall, 1981).

CHAPTER V

AFFIRMATIVE ACTION REQUIREMENTS AND PROMOTION POLICIES

Chapter Contents

*Introduction
*Scope And Purpose Of Affirmative Action
*Basic Elements Of An Affirmative Action Program
*Reverse Discrimination And Affirmative Action Plans
*Recommendations For Affirmative Action Plans
*Use Of Performance Appraisals In Promotion
*Judicial Review Of Performance Appraisals
*Validation Of Performance Appraisals
*Seniority And Antidiscrimination Laws
*Communication Of Promotional Opportunities
*Summary And Conclusions

INTRODUCTION

In the 1960s President Lyndon Johnson issued Executive Order 11246, which was an amendment to a series of unenforced executive orders issued by Franklin Delano Roosevelt in the early 1940s. In 1967 Executive Order 11246 was amended to conform with Title VII by including sex.[1] The basic theory of all executive orders is that it is a privilege to do business with the federal government and therefore certain conditions can be imposed on doing business with the government.

The conditions imposed by order 11246 is that a contractor or subcontractor cannot discriminate in employment because of race, sex, creed, color or national origin. The distinction between Executive Order 11246 and previous executive orders is that an Office of Federal Contract Compliance (OFCC) was established in the Department of Labor to enforce it. The executive orders include not only the hiring of applicants but the promotion of employees within an organization or governmental agency. Many employers took Executive Order 11246 more seriously than Title VII probably because under Title VII a charge had to be filed and a long period of contestation resulted and under 11246 the matter was immediate; one complied or lost a million-dollar contract. This quid pro quo (something for something) approach used by the OFCC in some instances caused many employers to overreact to Executive Order 11246 to the point where time-proven effective personnel principles were compromised or eliminated by the affirmative action program.

This chapter puts affirmative action programs in perspective and shows how hiring and promotion considerations were affected by 11246, as well as by antidiscrimination laws.

SCOPE AND PURPOSE OF AFFIRMATIVE ACTION

Approximately 75 percent of the work force is covered under Title VII, the Age in Discrimination and Equal Pay Act.[2] State and federal equal employment opportunity legislation extends to all but the smallest employer. The employer who has 1 or 100 employees cannot

---

[1] Executive Order 11375 (amending Executive Order 11246, relating to equal employment opportunity), *Federal Register* 32, (1967): 1403–04.

[2] *Employment and Earnings*, Bureau of Labor Statistics, Vol. 30, No. 1 (Washington, DC: Bureau of Labor Statistics, January, 1983). This publication reports a total civilian labor force of 110,204,000 in 1982 of which 77,908,000 are in protected classes as compiled from employment status tables by sex, age and race.

afford to disregard the national, state, or local policy that every person shall have a right to employment without regard to race, color, religion, sex, national origin, or age. It is a good personnel policy to have an affirmative action program; whether it is voluntary or forced on the employer by the government should not be a factor in adopting a policy. If the employer is to select and train the best-qualified applicants available, 75 percent of the labor force cannot be ignored. It is also difficult for the personnel director to explain to the sales manager why a government contract was lost because of the failure to adopt an affirmative action program that is neither a cost consideration nor impossible to institute.

The lack of affirmative action policies for minorities, female, and handicapped also has legal implications when a discrimination charge is filed against the employer, and the regulatory agency discovers that the employer did not have an affirmative action program. The employer's defense to a discrimination charge is badly shattered when the absence of an affirmative action program is discovered at some point in the proceedings. Usually the plaintiff's attorney will do so when cross examining the employer's witness.

All employers should have an affirmative action program whether or not they are a government contractor or subcontractor or whether they are a large or small employer.[3] It is uncertain when the employer will become a government contractor or subcontractor and will be required to have a program as a prerequisite to bidding on a purchase request. An additional reason is the possibility of receiving a discrimination charge. When this happens, it is too late to establish an affirmative action policy as a defense.

The scope of affirmative action is as broad as making the first sale and hiring the first person. The concept of affirmative action is a remedial concept that requests employers and labor unions to take positive steps voluntarily to improve the work opportunities of women, racial and ethnic minorities, handicapped workers, and Vietnam veterans who have been deprived of job opportunities. If the employer chooses not to have a program, the government may choose not to do business with that employer. There is nothing in Executive Order 11246 that demands the employer to hire or promote a person who is not the best-qualified for the job but just make a good faith effort to find qualified applicants among the members of the protected groups.

Although affirmative action has its purpose to encourage the employer to improve job opportunities for the protected classes, the OFCC is not prevented from

---

[3] Under Executive Order 11246, contracts under $10,000 and firms with less than 50 employees are exempted; in the case of handicapped workers all contractors or subcontractors are exempted if the contract is less than $2,500.

reporting any violations of Title VII to the Justice Department or EEOC for enforcement under Title VII of a discriminatory practice.

The objective of an affirmative action program has been accomplished if there is a measurable improvement in hiring, training, and promoting minorities or females in those job categories where job opportunities had been denied previously.

BASIC ELEMENTS OF AN AFFIRMATIVE ACTION PROGRAM

An affirmative action program has three basic elements: first, to identify those job categories where job opportunities have been denied; second, to develop programs that will correct underutilization of the protected classes; and third, to audit the programs as to their effectiveness. The first step in determining whether one can improve employment opportunities is to determine whether there will be any employment or promotion opportunities in a given period on which to improve.

To determine job opportunities, turnover and vacancies, future business needs must be ascertained. This is merely a work force planning procedure. If no vacancies or new jobs are anticipated, there can be no affirmative action for those job opportunities. The next step is to determine whether there has been a denial of job opportunities or there is another reason why there are no minorities or females in that job category. If there is a possibility to improve a job category as to employment or promotion of a member of the protected class, then it is considered an underutilized job category that can be improved on, and an affirmative action objective can be established. Affirmative action does not demand that underutilization be corrected but that a good faith effort be made to improve the number of minorities and females in a certain job category.

When determining the goal or objective to improve on, the possibility to do so should be considered. What is available in the community or in the labor market? What opportunities exist for hiring minority, female, or handicapped workers? It has been judicially determined that a labor market is defined for purposes of compliance to Title VII as an area where the employer has been recruiting.[4] However, new areas should be considered in affirmative action recruiting if the old method is not bringing results.

The implementation of an affirmative action program to increase job opportunities where they have been denied overlaps

---

[4] Hazelwood School District v. United States, 433 U.S. 299 (1977).

with the requirements of Title VII in the recruitment and selection process. A good affirmative action program will comply with requirements of Title VII when a charge is filed for discrimination in hiring.[5]

In order for the program to be effective it must be written and include a strong statement from top management that it will be enforced with vigor.[6] Without a top management statement it is difficult to show that there is a good faith effort to improve job opportunities. Additional evidence of good faith efforts are a broad recruiting source, participation in training programs, effective communication of the antidiscrimination policy within and without the organization, and the development of on-the-job training programs for minorities and females. A progress report to top management and a monitoring system to determine whether the good faith effort is being implemented are also essential to show that program is being enforced.

Employer Posture In A Compliance Review

If the employer is a government contractor of $10,000 or more, it is likely that a compliance review will be conducted to determine adequacy and implementation of an affirmative action policy. If in the opinion of the compliance officer the program is not effective, then recommendations are made to change it. If the employer refuses the changes, the compliance review officer can recommend cancellation of an existing contract or bar future contracts. Contract bar is effective only after a hearing. The final decision is made by the OFCC, subject to judicial review. When the agency cancelled a contract and issued a bar to future contracts and the employer appealed, the court held that the action was unreasonable because the affirmative action program was adequate.[7]

In order to avoid a dispute over the affirmative action program, the employer, after receiving notice from the review agency, should make preparation for compliance reviews. Proper preparation will enable the review officer to obtain all the pertinent facts about the program in the shortest possible time. It will also show an attitude of cooperation. Records such as applicant flow data, hiring records, and criteria used in testing, wage information, and number of promotions and demotions should be readily available. Employees are

---

[5] The distinction between enforcement of Title VII and Executive Order 11246 is that Title VII deals with individual or affected class complaints alleging that discrimination has taken place. Order 11246 is concerned with programs to correct past discrimination without reference to any specific complaint by an individual.

[6] Executive Order 11246 does not require a written statement unless the contract exceeds $50,000 in a 12-month period and employer has 50 or more employees. In the case of handicapped workers, the contractor must have contracts in excess of $2,500.

[7] Firestone Synthetic Rubber Co., v. Marshall, 507 F.Supp. 1330 (DC Tx. 1981).

often interviewed so it is advisable to have some names in mind if asked by the compliance officer what employees that employer would like to be interviewed. One should be prepared to give a business reason for underutilization categories and other implications of discrimination or lack of good faith effort.

Cooperation with the compliance officer is advisable, but it should not extend to those areas where the employer feels the compliance officer is on a fishing expedition, which may unreasonably burden the company to supply data or keep records that are irrelevant to the affirmative action program.

REVERSE DISCRIMINATION AND AFFIRMATIVE ACTION PLANS

Affirmative action is not a preference for a protected class if another class of employees is denied job opportunities. The showing of preference for the protected class over the other nonprotected groups (white males), regardless of qualifications, is referred to as reverse discrimination. (This is common usage. Technically it should be referred to only as discrimination since the statute only refers to race.) Reverse discrimination is unlawful because the protection given employees and applicants by Title VII and the 1866 Civil Rights Act does not refer to a particular race or one sex but refers to any race or any sex. Where white and black employees misappropriated antifreeze from an employer and only the white employees were discharged, the Supreme Court said that the basis of discharge was racial discrimina-

tion and not the crime since the black employees were not discharged.[8]

In one of the most publicized cases concerning reverse discrimination, the Supreme Court in Regents of the University of California v. Bakke, 438 U.S. 265 (1978) made it clear that where schools make race the determining factor in the admissions process, it is a violation of the Equal Protection Clause of the Fourteenth Amendment of the U.S. Constitution and Title VI of the Civil Rights Act of 1964.[9] The Court said that race could be one factor in devising affirmative action to help blacks and minority groups overcome the effects of past discrimination, but not the only consideration. In Bakke there were strict numerical quotas based solely on race; although the program sought to correct "socialite discrimina-

---

[8] McDonald v. Santa Fe Trail Trans. Co., 427 U.S. 273 (1976).

[9] The University of California had a special admissions program; minority candidates were rated only against each other and 16 of 100 places were reserved for qualified candidates within the minority group.

tion," such action is in violation of the Fourteenth Amendment.

The case was brought under the Fourteenth Amendment against a public employer who received federal funding, and was not an employment or promotion situation, however it answered a few questions for all employers, both public and private. The opinion was at times confusing in many respects, but it made it clear that the concept of affirmative action means that race and ethnic background can be given some but not total weight in the consideration of an applicant's qualifications for admission to a medical school. The Court never said what kind of affirmative action may be adopted by private employers; because it struck down numerical quotas, there is considerable doubt whether these are legal.[10]

This doubt was somewhat cleared up in the subsequent Supreme Court decision of Kaiser Aluminum & Chemical Corporation v. Weber, 443 U.S. 193 (1979), decided exactly one year after the Bakke case. In this situation the union and employer entered into a voluntary agreement of an affirmative action program designed to eliminate racial imbalances in the maintenance department, which was all white. The plan was to reserve 50 percent of the openings in the plant training programs for black employees until the number of black craft workers is commensurate with the percentage of blacks in the local labor force.

Weber alleged that because of the affirmative action program junior black employees were given training in preference to more senior white employees. The Supreme Court said that Title VII of the Civil Rights Act, although it literally forbids discrimination because of race, does not prohibit all private, voluntary, race-conscious affirmative action plans. Where through the collective bargaining process training spaces were preserved until a balance was achieved, it is lawful under Title VII. From this decision one can conclude that where an affirmative action plan voluntarily entered into between the union and company has as its objective to correct temporarily a racial imbalance and where racial differences are given equal quotas, it is a legal program.

Although the Court reiterated that reverse discrimination is still a violable cause of action, court decisions immediately after Weber show a reluctance to find reverse discrimination and cite Weber as authority.[11] EEOC guidelines issued in 1979 after Bakke[12] set out procedures that the employers can use in determining what type of action is needed and take reasonable steps to improve job opportunities

---

[10] In February 1979 EEOC published guidelines that specifically stated that racial ratios and numerical quotas had been eliminated in order to make it clear that any numerical objective is subject to availability of qualified applicants.

[11] Detroit Police Officers Assn. v. Young, 608 F.2d 671 (6th Cir. 1979).

[12] EEOC Guidelines on Affirmative Action, 29 CFR 1608 issued February 1979.

without reverse discrimination. To ease the employer's concern about exposure to reverse discrimination suits in affirmative action plans, EEOC will issue a statement on reverse discrimination that can be used as a defense in a court of law.[13] EEOC regulations say little about reverse discrimination; although an opinion from EEOC may be helpful in a reverse discrimination suit, it will not prevent the lawsuit nor necessarily be a complete defense for the employer. It is therefore advisable that the employer put a statement in the affirmative action plan that no member of any race will be favored in the selection to correct under-utilized categories.

Numerical quotas or race preference is not prohibited to correct discrimination where it has been judicially determined that discriminatory practices have existed. It is a well-established principle in discrimination law that a court can order racial preference as a remedy to correct past discrimination.[14]

Also, Congress by statute under certain conditions can constitutionally favor one race over another to correct discrimination.[15] Other than the court's authority to correct past discrimination and that of the Congress, any attempt to correct past discrimination by racial preference will probably be unlawful unless the program contains the elements found in Weber. (Voluntary, temporary, equal quotas that do not displace non-minorities.)

RECOMMENDATIONS FOR AFFIRMATIVE ACTION PLANS

The employers that do not have an affirmative action plan leave themselves wide open to cancellation of governmental contracts or refusal by the government to do business. Those employers that did not intend to do business with the government have defense problems if faced with a discrimination lawsuit. For these reasons it is recommended that:

1. All employers should have an affirmative action plan.

2. The plan should follow EEOC guidelines; where it deviates, a good business reason should be given. The plan cannot be declared in noncompliance if guidelines are followed. However, under no circumstances should the plan prevent the hiring or promotion of the best-qualified person available.

3. No plan should be designed

---

[13] EEOC Procedural Rules, 29 CFR 1601.33.

[14] Contractor's Assn. of Eastern Pa. v. Secy of Labor, 442 F.2d 159 (3rd Cir. 1971).

[15] Fullilove v. Klutznick, 444 U.S. 448 (1980).

to give preference of one class over the other, but it should be designed to seek qualified persons in the protected classes.

4. A definite statement should be made in the plan that preference of one group over another will not be given. Although reverse discrimination exposure has been greatly reduced since the Weber case, the exposure still exists.

5. Employment decisions should not deviate from the plan. If the plan causes bad employment decisions such as hiring of marginally qualified applicants, one should change the plan.

6. Personnel records should be reviewed periodically to determine whether the plan has in any way adversely affected the employment, training, or promotion of qualified candidates.

Promotion And Equal Employment Opportunity

The proper determination of whom to promote is a keystone in the successful management of any organization. It is a commonly accepted personnel doctrine that one determines promotion on the basis of ability to perform the job. No other criteria should be used with the exception of seniority, which is a determining factor only after candidates are in every other respect equally qualified to perform the job. An effective promotion program is easily defined but is much more difficult to implement. In the past, employee preferences, restrictive union contracts clauses, subjective recommendations of the supervisor, and invalid performance appraisals were all too often used as the basis for promotion. Antidiscrimination laws and their interpretation by the courts make it essential that promotion procedures and performance appraisals be reviewed. Most performance programs would not stand judicial scrutiny.

USE OF PERFORMANCE APPRAISALS IN PROMOTION

It is common practice to base promotions within a company on seniority or performance appraisals. A Bureau of National Affairs survey shows that 90 percent of 139 companies surveyed used performance appraisals as a basis for promotions.[16] Most of the performance appraisals used in industry rate personal traits rather than behavior on the job. This is the major cause of performance appraisals running afoul of the law.

Exhibit V-1 shows the factors

---

[16] Bureau of National Affairs, *Managerial Performance Appraisal Programs*, (Washington D.C.: 1974), pp. 4–5.

commonly used to appraise employees in industry and state government. Note the absence of behavior characteristics and predominance of trait characteristics.

The situation becomes more serious when one considers the extent that performance appraisals are used as a basis for personnel decisions, as shown in Exhibit V-2.

The survey that resulted in this exhibit relates only to formal rating systems. In other organizations the performance of employees and other factors related to their job performance is being rated informally. Whether the process is formal or informal, it is occurring and is subject to the external audit of antidiscrimination laws.[17]

	EXHIBIT V-1		
	Percentage of Employers Using Selected Factors in Appraising Employee Performance		
Factor	*Private Industry* *Mfg.*[a]	*Nonmfg.*[b]	*State Government*[c]
Managerial skills (knowledge, experience, ability to organize, etc.)	*80*	*87*	*74*
Achievement of goals (completion of programs, costs, production, etc.)	*81*	*87*	*26*
Job behaviors (as related to job duties)	*64*	*65*	*80*
Personal traits (attitudes, intelligence, dependability, etc.)	*61*	*65*	*80*
Potential (capacity to develop and advance, etc.)	*58*	*61*	*8*

Source: **W.H. Holley & H.S. Feild, "Performance Appraisal and Law,"** *Labor Law Journal,* **Chicago, Ill.: Commerce Clearing House, July 1975.**

[a]Based on a study of 166 firms by the National Industrial Conference Board, "Personnel Practices in Factory and Office: Manufacturing," *Studies in Personnel Policy,* No. 194, 1964, p. 17.

[b]Based on a study of 139 firms by the Bureau of National Affairs, *Managerial Performance Appraisal Programs,* Washington, D.C., 1974, pp. 4–5.

[c]Based on a study of 24 systems by H.S. Feild and W.H. Holley, "Performance Appraisal in Public Employment: An Analysis of State-Wide Practices," *Public Personnel Management,* 1975.

---

[17] For analysis of promotion systems, see Richard D. Conner and Robert L. Fjerstad, "Internal Personnel Maintenance," Chapter 4.6 in *ASPA Handbook of Personnel and Industrial Relations,* Dale Yoder and Herbert J. Heneman, eds. (Washington DC: Bureau of National Affairs, 1979).

EXHIBIT V-2

Percentage of Employers Using Performance Appraisal
Systems for Selected Purposes

Factor	Private Industry	State Government
Promotion	73	
Layoffs	27	58[a]
Discharge	46	
Wage and salary decisions	69	39
Training and development	61	38
Manpower planning and utilization	b	46

Source: **W.H. Holley & H.S. Feild, "Performance Appraisal and Law,"** *Labor Law Journal,* **Chicago, Ill.: Commerce Clearing House, July 1975.**

[a] The categories of promotion, layoffs, and discharge were combined in the survey of state governments.

[b] Not reported.

JUDICIAL REVIEW OF PERFORMANCE APPRAISALS

The performance appraisal and identification of promotable employees have been subject to bias for many years. In most organizations, norms have been consciously or unconsciously based on personality characteristics of white males.

The personnel professional has heard the adage, "Women are emotional, men are cool and discrete," or "Men are aggressive but women are pushy." This type of thinking often enters into promotion decisions, but Title VII, other antidiscrimination laws, and court decisions could change the adage to "the best man for the job may be a woman."

One of the first appellate courts to scrutinize performance appraisals was the Fifth Circuit in New Orleans. The employer's appraisal methods did not relate to performance on the job but, as shown in Exhibit V-1, to trait characteristics. The court said that where the appraisal is used to make an employment decision or an adverse impact is shown, the appraisal methods must be validated with performance.[18] In this case,

---

[18] Rowe v. General Motors, 457 F.2d 348 (5th Cir. 1972).

transfers were dependent almost entirely on favorable recommendation of the immediate supervisor, who used subjective evaluations of job performance as a basis for promotion. Subjective evaluations permitted the supervisor to exercise race discrimination in the promotion process.

One year later another court, in Brito et al. v. Zia Company, 428 F.2d 1200 (10th Cir. 1973), held that the Zia Company discriminated against Spanish-American workers when it used an invalid performance appraisal for promotion purposes. In that case the court said that the Zia Company failed to validate the test according to EEOC guidelines because the test was correlated with an invalid performance appraisal. The promotion procedure was invalid as a result. At Zia Company only a few evaluators kept any records. Some supervisors evaluated employees not directly under their supervision while other evaluators were present in the plant only half of the time; in some instances evaluation was done when the evaluator had not been in the plant for months.

It was clear that the evaluations were based on best judgments and opinions, with no evidence of identifiable criteria of job performance. In the Zia case the court relied heavily on EEOC guidelines. The decision followed the Griggs v. Duke Power case

cited in Chapter IV where the Court said that "the employer has the burden of showing that the procedure used manifests a relationship to the job in question."

Subjective selection procedures were struck down in the Griggs case. The courts are now quick to reject appraisal systems that are subjective and not related to job performance.[19] A subjective appraisal by its nature uses different criteria for different job categories and for different persons and therefore, gets the attention of the courts, just as other subjective decisions.

In one case the court said that unless there are written guidelines for the raters and they are otherwise trained in the standardized method of appraisal, the process is invalid.[20] Although the courts said that it is unlawful in 1973, subjective methods continue in many organizations; when challenged, the courts will almost always declare the method in violation of Title VII.[21] In the Crawford case the court said that because the standard used to evaluate was not written, it was subjective. There is little disagreement among the courts that subjective appraisal methods are in violation of Title VII; however, an appraisal method is bound to have some subjectivity and this is recognized by the courts. The courts have approved subjective methods in hiring if

[19] Wade v. Mississippi Cooperative Extension Service, 528 F.2d 508 (5th Cir. 1976).

[20] Parson v. Kaiser Aluminum & Chemical Corp., 575 F. 2d 1374 (5th Cir. 1978).

[21] Crawford v. Western Electric Co., 614 F.2d 1300 (5th Cir. 1980).

they include objective standards. Where the subjective oral interview was given to applicants for an electrician's job but there was a requirement that the applicant meet certain tests or have eight years of journeyman experience, the court said that the subjective oral interview is not discriminatory as long as objective criteria of certain skill tests or experiences are also used.[22]

It would appear from the rationale of this case that if an objective standard for performance were established and subjective reasons were stated why that performance standard was not met, the appraisal method would be valid. Many progressive employers have changed their performance appraisal methods and have adopted the use of management by objectives (MBO) as a basis for their performance systems.[23] Where performance appraisal uses MBO, it must be an ongoing procedure between the supervisor and the subordinate, not just a meeting every six months during which only the most recent data are used or a meeting at times when the rater has decided to promote or otherwise change the status of the employee and uses the performance appraisal as justification. Those who have been successful with an MBO approach have insisted on the classical form of quantitative and measurable objectives rather than the more subjective type used by some companies.[24]

VALIDATION OF PERFORMANCE APPRAISALS

It is apparent from court decisions that if the employer does not validate performance appraisals, the courts will on a case-by-case basis. In Allen v. City of Mobile, 466 F.2d 1245 (5th Cir. 1972) cert denied, 411 U.S. 909 (1973), the court said that the performance rating system was discriminatory and prescribed another performance rating system. There is no assurance that the judicially prescribed method of appraisal has any more validity or would serve a more useful purpose for promotion than the employer's system; however, the method prescribed by the court is the legal, valid method for those employers within the jurisdiction of the 5th Circuit Court of Appeals. Apparently the courts feel that validation of rating a system can be "unscientific" when applied to a given factual situation.

---

[23] Weyerhauser Co., Tacoma, Wash., and University Research Corp., Chevy Chase, Md.

[22] Hamilton v. General Motors Corp., 606 F.2d 576 (5th Cir. 1979).

[24] The author for many years was eligible for an annual bonus based on his company president's appraisal. It was a practice among those receiving the bonuses to perform above "the call of duty" in November, when the bonus was determined. The bonuses were given out in December and it was determined that only the last month's performance would be remembered.

Another court followed the Allen case and ordered a rating system that would ensure that minorities and nonminorities would be equally graded. The federal district court prescribed the performance appraisal as an alternative to the one that it struck down, but it was not a validation method that could be applied to other factual situations.[24]

The problem of performance appraisal systems as related to court decisions was studied by Feild and Holley of Auburn University. These investigators found that the courts rejected appraisal systems as invalid when no specific instructions were given to the raters, appraisals were trait oriented rather than behavior oriented, and job analysis was not used in developing the content of the rating form.[25]

This is the most comprehensive study of performance appraisals and the law that has come to the author's attention. Sixty-six court cases from 1965 to 1980 with performance appraisals at issue in employment discrimination disputes were studied. The results of this study show that defendants who lost the discrimination suits tended to have appraisal systems described as follows: the case was brought against an industrial organization, evaluators of employees were not given specific instructions on how to complete the appraisals,

the appraisal system was trait-oriented rather than behavior-oriented, job analysis was not utilized in developing the content of the appraisal system, and the results of the appraisals were not reviewed by the ratees. Although the courts have not given criteria for validating performance appraisals, as they have in testing validation situations, this does not prevent the employer from doing so.

The EEOC guidelines state that the same method should be used in test validation and selection, which is at least a start, but test validation is much less subjective than performance appraisals, which have been totally subjective for years. There is a great deal of similarity between selection for employment and selection for promotion. The first step in both is to look at the job and decide the minimum qualifications (job analysis). Then one checks the requirements against the qualifications of employees doing the job. If current employees do not meet the requirement and still do the job adequately, the performance standards are too high.

Recent surveys indicate that employers have a difficult road ahead in implementating a legally accepted appraisal program. Company practices have not changed to conform with the case-by-case guidelines set by the courts. One

[24] Harper v. Mayor City Council of Baltimore, 359 F.Supp. 1187 (DC Md. 1973).

[25] Hubert S. Feild and William H. Holley, "The Relationship of Performance Appraisal Systems Characteristics to Verdicts in Selected Employment Discrimination Cases." Research paper (Auburn, AL: Auburn University, 1980).

survey showed that less than one-half of 217 companies studied used job analysis to develop their evaluation system, and over 60 percent used personal traits rather than behavioral traits to measure job performance.[26]

The personnel professional cannot start too early in validating performance appraisals systems. The first thing to do is to determine whether the system uses personality traits; if so, it should be thrown out. The next thing to do is to determine whether there is any relationship between what the appraisal form measures and job performance; if not, it should be thrown out. The next thing to do is to develop a new system that utilizes some of the court decisions in discrimination cases.

Exhibit V-3 attempts to consider court decisions in the design of a valid appraisal system. It contains all the elements that the various courts have stated necessary for a valid procedure. It is not intended to be a scientific or structured method that can be used in all organizations. It is an outline to develop an appraisal form that will pass the test of the courts in discrimination suits and still fit the needs of a particular organization. Whether it would meet EEOC guidelines is questionable; however, if the courts approve it, the EEOC must follow these decisions.

Whether these steps are used or whether some other validation process is used, one thing is certain. It will be more defensible than if no attempt is made to validate the performance appraisal system.

EXHIBIT V-3

Performance Appraisal Validation Procedure

Steps in developing appraisal validation procedure:

1. State the purpose for which the evaluation results will be used (salary review, promotion, training only, etc.).
2. Develop a job analysis to determine factors necessary for successful performance.
3. Determine the level of skill or competence in each job factor that is necessary for organizational success.
4. Structure rater's interview with the ratee to communicate the rating procedure used and job factors to determine performance levels.
5. Develop and require ratee to make self-assessment of strengths and weaknesses. The analysis should be based on the job factors from the job analysis.
6. Develop and train rater to use a standardized procedure in rating subordinates.
7. Compare ratee self-analysis with rater evaluations and constructively discuss the differences.
8. Mutually establish goals for improvements where appropriate.

---

[26] R.I. Lazer and N.S. Wilstrom, *Appraising Management Performance: Current Practices and Future Directions* (Washington D.C.: The Conference Board, 1977).

SENIORITY AND ANTIDISCRIMINATION LAWS

It might be said that the original message conveyed to the employer concerning subjectivity in employment decisions regarded the seniority method. Seniority has been used to eliminate prejudice or subjective decisions for many years not only in labor agreements but also in the judicial system and many other social institutions. In the federal court system the chief judge of a district or appellate court is usually the senior judge. The U.S. Supreme Court relies heavily on seniority in many of its administrative procedures and customs.

Seniority System That Perpetuates Discrimination

Seniority systems that discriminated against minorities and females were common before the antidiscrimination laws. Unions had segregated locals, employers had separate seniority lists for males and females and for blacks and whites, and companies provided segregated facilities. Since discriminatory seniority systems were established many years before antidiscrimination laws, they would accordingly perpetuate discrimination toward minority or female workers. This problem was dealt with by the Supreme Court regarding the Teamsters Union, which had two separate seniority lists; one for city drivers and one for over-the-road drivers. The system had an adverse impact because there were no minorities on the over-the-road seniority list and there was no practical way for minorities to be put on the list. There was no question that this situation would continue for a considerable period. The Supreme Court held that as long as the system was instituted before Title VII and it was neutral on its face, the seniority system did not violate Title VII although it perpetuated discrimination.[27]

The Supreme Court made it clear in a later case that if there were any evidence of intentional discrimination, such a system would be invalid.[28] In 1982 the court carried the Teamsters case one step further and stated that although the system was instituted after Title VII and had an adverse impact that perpetuated discrimination, it was still valid unless intent to discriminate can be shown.[29]

From these cases it can be concluded that unless intent to discriminate can be shown, a seniority system that has an adverse impact and perpetuates discrimination is valid. This concept can be applied to the situation where a permanent status is required to become a part of the seniority

---

[27] International Brotherhood of Teamsters v. United States, 431 U.S. 324 (1977).

[28] Pullman Standard v. Swint, 102 S.Ct. 1781 (1982).

[29] American Tobacco Company v. Patterson, 102 S.Ct. 1534 (1982).

system. In one situation the employer and union agreed that unless workers worked for 45 weeks during the year, they could not acquire permanent status (permanent-status employees were accorded greater benefits than temporary employees).

Although no minority had ever acquired permanent status, the court said since the policy was based on length of service—as would any seniority system—it was a valid system, following the Teamsters case.[30]

COMMUNICATION OF PROMOTIONAL OPPORTUNITIES

The strong position that the courts have taken on the seniority system imposes an obligation on the employer to make a seniority or promotion system with the least possible discriminatory impact. When the employer fails to communicate to employees that a vacancy exists but as an alternative goes on the labor market to hire a new employee, it is often claimed that such action is discriminatory. In one case the employer could not justify passing over members of a protected class when they were not informed of an opening.[31] A showing must be made that notice of the vacancy was given to all employees who may be eligible before the employer can justify overlooking them. When employees are overlooked and the employer alleges that they are not qualified, it is a weak defense. The courts are quick to disregard any evidence that tries to justify an employment decision that was not in evidence before that decision. In one pertinent case

the court ruled that the failure of female employees to apply for promotion does not mean that the employer did not discriminate.[32]

To avoid litigation, notice of all vacancies should be communicated to eligible employees. When an employee shows an interest in a vacant position but is not selected, the reasons should be well-documented. When an employee's work is unsatisfactory, the fact should be documented immediately. It should not delay until the formal performance review. In legal proceedings or hearings, the best exhibits or testimony are documented communications to the employee showing that the employer attempted to correct the employee's performance promptly.

Some companies have taken affirmative steps to avoid pitfalls of discrimination laws in the area of promotion. Exhibit V-4 is a form that would assure communication of promotion opportunities. This formal method of communication

---

[30] California Brewers Assn. v. Bryant, 444 U.S. 598 (1980).

[31] Patterson v. American Tobacco Co., 535 F.2d 257 (4th Cir. 1976).

[32] Mitchell v. Mid-Continental Spring Co., 583 F.2d 275 (6th Cir. 1978).

EXHIBIT V-4

POSITION OPPORTUNITIES ANNOUNCEMENT

DATE OF ANNOUNCEMENT _____ REMOVE DATE _____

JOB TITLE _____ DIVISION/DEPARTMENT _____

SUPERVISOR _____ SALARY CLASSIFICATION _____

REQUIREMENTS

DUTIES

IF YOU WISH TO BE CONSIDERED FOR
THIS POSITION, PLEASE CONTACT

WE ARE AN EQUAL OPPORTUNITY EMPLOYER

aids the employer in the promotion process and is most often used in the blue-collar area, where promotion may be partially controlled by the labor agreement.

In large multiplant organizations some companies have a standard form to communicate job openings between plants. However, a personnel policy is necessary to permit mobility of employees between plants and eliminate the often protective but unconscious position of the local supervisor to keep qualified employees from being transferred.

It is highly important that the job requirements and duties stated on the form are objective requirements taken from up-to-date job analyses or job descriptions. It is wise to check the job and determine present employees' job duties, and whether they meet the requirements that are stated in the position opportunities announcement.

Care should also be taken in this type of announcement that it does not imply that management's prerogative to select the best-qualified candidate is being waived by the announcement. The complete absence in the announcement as to criteria in the selection of the candidate is one method to retain the prerogative of selection.

Lawsuits are common when minorities and females allege that they have been denied promotional opportunities by not being notified of the vacancy. One reason that employers do not notify is that they have a certain person in mind and they do not want to create an adverse situation where they turn down another employee who feels qualified. This policy will expose the employer to litigation under Title VII, especially if it is determined that the rejected employee is better-qualified.

SUMMARY AND CONCLUSIONS

Affirmative action is a concept that imposes a duty on the employer to take affirmative steps to improve work opportunities for minorities, women, handicapped workers, and veterans. Two conditions are necessary before this obligation is enforceable. First, the employer must be a government contractor or subcontractor. Second, there must be some evidence that job opportunities had not been available to protected individuals on an equal basis with the white male, nonhandicapped, and non-

veteran female population. Affirmative action should be instituted by all employers as a defensive measure in the event of a discriminatory charge being filed by an employee or applicant. An affirmative action program can meet the needs of the organization to select qualified persons and still comply with government standards as long as it contains a few basic elements:

1. A statement from top man-

agement that program will be enforced

2. Procedure for disseminating the affirmative action policy

3. Utilization analysis of protected classes by job categories

4. A program to correct employment practices that cause adverse impact on protected individuals

In an effort to correct discrimination, care must be taken not to give preference to one race over another; otherwise a reverse discrimination charge is possible. Affirmative action programs do not demand that marginally qualified persons be selected or promotion. What they do demand is that an employer make a good faith effort to seek qualified persons in the protected groups.

Traditional performance appraisals have relied on subjective ratings of the supervisors and certain personality traits of the employee. Continuing to rely on these practices exposes the employer to costly litigation and results in substandard promotion policies. A rating system must not be subjective or allow the rater to choose the elements to be emphasized or omitted.

As in testing for selection purposes, performance appraisals, when relied on for promotion purposes, must be validated in order to withstand the scrutiny of the antidiscrimination laws. Subjective evaluation of the rater allows room for discriminatory motives and is therefore invalid. There must be an empirical basis for the raters' conclusions.

An analysis of case law reveals that unless the rating method has been developed through job analysis and is job-related, it has little chance of surviving judicial scrutiny. Furthermore, the rater must base conclusions on consistent observation of the employee's performance; the objective criteria of the rating system must be strong enough to override possible biases.

The courts, in holding performance appraisals invalid, have developed some basic elements necessary to validate a performance appraisal. This might be termed a judicial validation.

1. The appraisal method must be job-related and the same for all job classifications.

2. There must be a consistent observation of the ratee's work performance. It is common practice to begin observing performance shortly before the appraisal date. The courts consider a rating with short observance periods invalid.

3. The rater's evaluation cannot be subjective. There must be an empirical basis for the conclusion, not just standardized conditions. To comply with this requirement, there must be some training of the raters.

Like tests, performance appraisals can be useful. However, unless validated, it must be shown that they do not have an adverse impact on promotion, or the performance appraisal will run afoul of EEOC guidelines and court decisions in the same manner as pre-employment testing did.

Performance appraisals have enjoyed extensive application in both public and private employment, but the decisions of the courts have placed the system in a precarious position. Employers must undertake research as to validation of performance appraisals. Developing empirical standards for performance appraisals will be difficult but if the employers do not develop a validation procedure, the courts will do so on a case-by-case basis. This may not appraise performance, but it will provide relief to the plaintiff.

Personnel management has a huge undertaking in the validation of promotion procedures where they have an adverse impact because few methods of validation of performance appraisals exist.

To the surprise of some equal employment opportunity activists, most seniority systems have received judicial acceptance unless is can be shown that they intentionally discriminate.

Care should be taken by the employer that the opportunity to be promoted is communicated to all employees who may be interested. An otherwise valid method of promoting can be overturned simply because it was not communicated to the employees.

CHAPTER VI

EMPLOYMENT DECISION MAKING—AGE, NATIONAL ORIGIN, RELIGION, AND HANDICAP CONSIDERATIONS

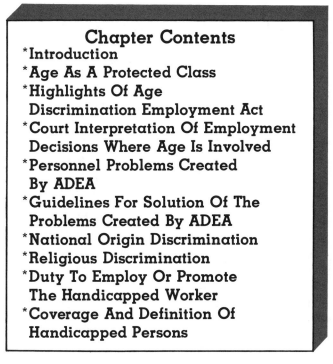

Chapter Contents
*Introduction
*Age As A Protected Class
*Highlights Of Age
  Discrimination Employment Act
*Court Interpretation Of Employment
  Decisions Where Age Is Involved
*Personnel Problems Created
  By ADEA
*Guidelines For Solution Of The
  Problems Created By ADEA
*National Origin Discrimination
*Religious Discrimination
*Duty To Employ Or Promote
  The Handicapped Worker
*Coverage And Definition Of
  Handicapped Persons

INTRODUCTION

As discussed in Chapter I, the law has moved into the office of the personnel practitioner to the extent that any decision must not only consider the employee relations consequences but also the legal implications.

When considering whether there is legal exposure under antidiscrimination laws, the practitioner must look at the personal characteristics of employees involved to determine if they are in a protected class and whether there is exposure to a statute or regulation. A few employee groups are not protected by any statute, but they are becoming more rare as antidiscrimination laws reach maturity through administrative and court rulings and legislative action. In 1983 approximately 25 percent of the work force was not protected by antidiscrimination statutes. The unprotected employee is probably a blue-eyed male, 21 years old without military service, an atheist who works in a job where there are neither females or minorities and who does not believe in suing his employer because he is grateful to his employer for a job.

In most employment decision-making situations it is not a question of whether the employee is covered but under what statute (state or federal) is the employee covered. Although the various protected classes are basically covered under the same statute, compliance is somewhat different, depending on the protected class. Accommodation is necessary for both handicapped and religious activity but not to the same degree. In an area of age discrimination the problems are similar in many respects to sex and race categories; however, the right of jury trial sets this class apart from others. Whether an employee can speak English is a consideration in national origin discrimination cases; other protected classes do not have this problem.

This chapter gives special treatment to each protected class that has different compliance requirements or demand special considerations when making an employment decision.

The legislative history and interpretation of antidiscrimination laws originally involved the race question and accordingly was treated extensively in previous chapters; therefore race will not be considered in this chapter. What has not been covered in previous chapters on racial discrimination is covered in Chapter VIII.

AGE AS A PROTECTED CLASS

The problem of what to do with the older worker has haunted employers for many years. There seemed to be no easy solution to the problem of the marginal worker who has been with the company for 30 years and has substandard performance for 25 of the 30 years. Like many other personnel problems, the solution was an arbitrary one: compulsory retirement at age 65 for all employees, except the board of directors and chief executive officer. This solution was destined to meet with social and political opposition for two reasons. One, many employees were still productive at age 65; physical and mental ability and attitude toward retirement are an individual matter, not one that can be categorized. Second, there is no medical or other authority for age 65 as the time when most employees cease to be productive.[1]

The compulsory retirement at 65 became almost universal in American business as well as in other organizations. In a survey of 400 companies in 1977, 2 of 3 companies had compulsory retirement, typically at age 65. The usual reason given was to create job opportunities for younger persons.[2] When almost all employers have a policy with social and economic implications, political forces will usually step in to correct it. As members of Congress have so often said about employer practices, "You correct it yourself or we will do it for you" (when it becomes politically advisable). As for the older worker, compulsory retirement, demotion, or discharge to make room for a younger person was an easy solution until Congress stopped it in 1978.

---

[1] The basis that a 65-year-old worker was so old as to warrant compulsory retirement came from German Chancellor Otto Von Bismarck in 1887 as the age when German social security system should start. Life expectancy is twice what it was in 1887. Further Bismarck was neither a doctor nor an entrepreneur but an army general.

[2] William W. Mercer, Inc., "Employer Attitudes toward Mandatory Retirement" (New York: June 1977).

HIGHLIGHTS OF AGE DISCRIMINATION EMPLOYMENT ACT

The purpose of the Age Discrimination Employment Act (ADEA)[3] is to promote employment of older persons based on their ability to perform and to prohibit arbitrary age discrimination in employment by requiring employers to solve their problems of the older worker through accommodation rather than by termination or retirement.

The act and its amendments contain the following basic provisions:

1. It forbids employers with 20 or more employees, including public employers, employment agencies, and labor organizations (with 25 or more members), to make employment decisions based on a person's age when that person is between 40 and 70. This is interpreted to mean that preference cannot be shown within the protected group. An employer could not express preference of a 45-to 55-year group as this would discriminate because of age. The Tax Equity and Fiscal Responsibility Act of 1982 amended ADEA to require the same benefits between age 65 and 69 as granted employees below that age group.

2. The act invalidated compulsory retirement in pension plans in the private sector until age 70. It eliminated compulsory retirement at any age in the federal government. If inability to perform the job can be shown, or if an executive in a policy making position, or if the person has a pension above $27,000 (without Social Security), the employee could be retired without consent.

3. Authorizes jury trial of any issue of fact.

4. The act expressly authorizes employers to treat older employees differently in certain circumstances:
   a) If age is a bona fide occupational qualification;
   b) If different treatment of older workers is based on reasonable factors other than age;
   c) If the decision is the result of bona fide seniority system;
   d) If discharge is for just cause, age cannot be used as discriminating reason.

5. The law is enforced by EEOC; however, because of right of jury trial the commission has more legal clout than in other antidiscrimination laws, also the act does not apply to American citizens working abroad for American companies.[4]

---

[3] 29 USC Sect. 613 et seq.

[4] Cleary v. U.S. Lines, 555 F.Supp. 1251 (DC N.J. 1983).

COURT INTERPRETATION OF EMPLOYMENT DECISIONS WHERE AGE IS INVOLVED

The ADEA affects every employment decision where the employee involved is over 40. The courts have interpreted the act to mean that age need not be the only factor but must be the determining or significant employment decision. If there is a finding that there are significant and compelling factors involved in making the decision other than age, the plaintiff will not have established a prima facie case and the action will fail.[5]

Factors other than age may include discharge for just cause. Where a 56-year-old repeatedly ignored specific directions of his supervisors, the court held that discharge was not because of age but for insubordination.[6] By the same reasoning, where discharge of an employee was bad faith and violation by the employer of covenant of fair dealing under the state law, the court awarded the major share of punitive damages for violation of implied covenant and not violation of ADEA.[7]

The inability to perform satisfactorily the particular job or incompetence is a factor other than age that could justify a discharge or transfer; however, performance and incompetency determinations are often subjective. Therefore the burden of proof is greater than in traditional misconduct situations where objective facts are more easily obtainable. It is advisable in incompetency situations to have objective measurements of unsatisfactory performance before a decision involving an older worker's performance. Objective measurements in the case of sales evaluation were considered valid where two older employees failed to meet their sales quota while all others not discharged did.[8] The objective measurement of performance of all workers, not only older workers, is one of the most serious problems for employers in compliance with various employee rights laws, including antidiscrimination laws.

In a decision to hire, promote, or transfer, if the employer can show a reasonable business purpose, such as poor performance with previous employer, a better qualified younger person, an older worker meeting only minimum requirements, or an applicant failing to meet educational requirements, then age will not be considered a factor in the employment decision.[9]

---

[5] Loeb v. Textron, 600 F.2d 1003 (1st Cir. 1979); Spagnuolo v. Whirlpool Corp., 641 F.2d 1109 (4th Cir. 1981).

[6] Havelick v. Julius Wile & Sons, Inc. 445 F.Supp. 919 (S.D. N.Y. 1978).

[7] Cancellier v. Federated Department Stores, dba I. Magnin, 672 F.2d 1312 (9th Cir. 1982).

[8] Marshall v. Roberts Dairy Co., 572 F.2d 1271 (8th Cir. 1978).

[9] Anderson v. Viking Pump Div., 545 F.2d 1127 (8th Cir. 1976).

PERSONNEL PROBLEMS CREATED BY ADEA

The many problems created by ADEA are beginning to show their ugly heads. These problems have been somewhat dormant since the 1978 amendment of the act because of lack of funds in the Labor Department and reluctance of the older workers to exercise their rights under the act. (Until 1979 the Labor Department enforced ADEA; since that time EEOC is charged with enforcement.) In the 1980s the skeleton has come out of the closet and is swinging a big stick. In 1981 EEOC had a whopping increase of 89 percent in litigations under ADEA. This compares with an overall increase of 24 percent for other antidiscrimination statutes that it administers. In a 12-month period (1981) more cases were filed under ADEA than in any other 12-month period since the passage of the act.[10] In 1982, 19,100 charges were filed with EEOC under ADEA.[11] This problem is compounded by the innumerable amount of statistical data, which leaves no doubt that the working population is getting older.[12]

The statute has created several personnel problem areas that are major cost items and difficult personnel problems for any organization unless major steps are taken to eliminate them. Some of these problems are:

1. Promotional opportunities will be greatly reduced by older employees continuing to work.

2. Affirmative action programs will be retarded as new job openings are reduced due to delayed retirements.

3. The marginal employee, over 40 years, will continue to be marginal unless measurement of performance techniques for all employees is objectively developed.

4. Since new employees start at lower salaries, older employees who have received cost of living or longevity increases will cause a company's average salary level to be unnecessarily high.

5. Over 70 percent of ADEA violations involve discharge cases, and employers lose 89 percent of the court cases.[13]

The solution of these problems is found in first recognizing that there is no direct correlation between age and submarginal performance. Second, the employer's

---

[10] Armando M. Rodriguez, "A Look at Equal Employment Opportunity," *Labor Law Journal*, May 1982, pp. 259–264 at 263.

[11] EEOC 17th Annual Report (preliminary May 1983).

[12] From 1981 to 1982 the number in protected classes increased from 74.9 million to 77.9 million, age group being the largest increase. "Employment and Earnings, Washington, D.C. Bureau of Labor Statistics. vol. 29, no. 1, January 1982, vol. 30, no. 1, January 1983.

[13] Robert A. Snyder and Billie Brandon. "Riding the Third Wave—Staying On Top of ADEA Complaints," *Personnel Administrator*, vol. 28, no. 2, February, 1983, p. 42.

desire to make room for the younger worker is no longer a management prerogative that the courts will accept unless there is a reason to replace the older worker other than a management philosophy that younger employees are better for organizational growth (which is a difficult concept for judges to accept when one considers their average age).

Marginal Worker— Measurement Of Performance

When a manager wants to create a vacancy to promote a younger, underutilized worker (or make the president's son president), the usual procedure is to talk to the person blocking the promotion and state that early retirement would be in the best interests of the company. Another common solution to the problem is where the 35-year employee is not motivated to learn new techniques brought about by the computer age or some other modern procedure.

Before ADEA the solution to such problems was early retirement or outright termination. The abolition of a fixed retirement age before age 70 has closed the door to any arbitrary decision by management. ADEA has forced employers to develop standards of performance data and promotability criteria for all age groups. This had not been done by most employers so the task is a momentous one that will not be accomplished for several years. In the meantime, a more immediate solution must be found.

One immediate solution is to make early retirement so attractive to the employee that retirement is voluntary. Another alternative is to assign the employee to a special project or a consulting basis after termination. These alternatives create exposure to benefits other than wages and to other employee relations problems unless the employee voluntarily terminates or a special consulting agreement is drafted. Any special project or "pasture assignment" should have termination provisions or conditions of employment in the form of an employee agreement, or problems result, as illustrated by the following case.

VOLUNTARY RETIREMENT THAT WAS NOT VOLUNTARY—A CASE HISTORY

John Doe, age 64, was for 40 years an administrative manager for a 250-employee manufacturing facility. As most of his work was being computerized, John realized that either he had to learn computer procedures or retire. He went to his supervisor of 20 years and requested special projects for the next year, after which he would retire, at age 65. His supervisor orally agreed. They shook hands and everybody was happy.

During the succeeding year, John trained his replacement to the limit of his ability and performed useful, special project assignments with a high level of competency. In his retirement plans, John had not made sufficient financial planning to allow for inflation. Also, during the year his wife died, and working became much more interesting than a lonely retirement. John saw his supervisor and told him that he had changed his mind and wanted his old job or a similar job, and he was willing to learn the new computer procedures and considered himself more qualified than applicants being considered for a vacancy in another facility. The supervisor called the personnel director and requested advice. The personnel director consulted the legal department. The legal counsel advised that because John had a satisfactory work performance for the past 40 years, it would be difficult to convince a jury in an age discrimination suit that he was not qualified until given an opportunity on the new job and his performance objectively measured.

This case is a classic example of an employer making an employment decision that was considered fair to both parties without anticipating what could happen in the ensuing year. It is possible that the employer could have argued that there was an oral agreement and that the employee had to retire as agreed. However, lengthy litigation, exposure to punitive damages, employee relations consequence of an employee with forty years of employment suing the employer and a jury trial warranted a business decision to make retirement attractive to John so that it would be considered voluntary.

GUIDELINES FOR SOLUTION OF THE PROBLEMS CREATED BY ADEA

Age discrimination will play the same role in the 1980s as race discrimination played in the 1960s and 1970s. The older worker is becoming a powerful force with which the employer must reckon in order to avoid costly litigation and high damage awards. The following are some recommended policies to aid in preventing litigation involving age.

1. First and foremost, management must develop objective standards of performance for employees in all job categories and make decisions based on documented analysis of employee performance and competence. Some practitioners will claim that performances cannot be measured in certain jobs. Any human endeavor can be measured, some more easily than others. Termination policies must specifically state that failure to meet communicated standards of performance is just cause for discharge. In the past, many employers tolerated less than acceptable work performance from older workers who were near retirement age. This situation could always be changed by enforcement of a compulsory retirement plan.

Under ADEA this option is cut off, and the older worker must meet the performance standards like other employees or be transferred to a job that can be performed. The employer under ADEA cannot afford the luxury of a marginal worker with no option to terminate the arrangement until age 70.

2. Mobility among employees must be encouraged. The assistant counsel who will not become general counsel must be encouraged to keep up broad legal training to be ready to join a small law firm when conditions change or the management becomes dissatisfied. Transfers within the organization must be the first consideration.

   The practice of supporting only job-related training programs backfires when early retirement is encouraged. Educational programs must be expanded in order to provide related skills for the second career or a transfer to other jobs in the organization.[14]

3. Preretirement counseling should be designed to fit the individuals' needs and not be structured to what the management thinks that they need, as many contemporary programs are. The employer should not first tell the employees what their problems will be in retirement and then offer a solution. The program should start with each employee stating what problems are anticipated and request aid in solution.

4. Flexible retirement arrangements should be developed with employees as much as possible. Policies should be developed on an individual basis. Phased retirement may fit some individuals (company allows employee to work three days a week and then two or one before retirement). With others, financial security is most important. For others, maintaining prestige is most important. Some employees want to work part-time; others want to be occupied or challenged, if not in their present job, in some other endeavor. Some employees fear domestic problems of being home every day. As one employee put it, "My wife said that she married me for better or worse but not for lunch." Preretirement counseling must be meaningful to the employee, and this can be accomplished only on an individual basis.

It is not too late for the employer to develop positive programs to avoid personnel and legal problems under ADEA. The fed-

---

[14] It is common to give educational financial assistance to employees only for those subjects directly related to their job. If other subjects are desired, the employee does not receive aid for tuition, etc. This should be changed to include broader subjects in the job area.

eral law, as well as state laws,[15] is in its infancy and the potential enforcement is only beginning to be realized. Unless programs are developed soon, ADEA will be the most costly and most disruptive for personnel policies of all antidiscrimination laws.

NATIONAL ORIGIN DISCRIMINATION

Unlawful discrimination occurs when an employment decision is based on the national origin of the person adversely affected by that decision. Although national origin discrimination under Title VII has not been popular compared to other protected classes such as race, religion, and sex, it can be troublesome if totally ignored. National origin bias is unlawful in hiring and promotion, the same as in race, religion, and sex; however, it has one additional feature: where the employee cannot speak English. To require the employee to do so can be violative of Title VII if knowledge of English is not required for successful performance of the job. Where Spanish-Americans were not provided with translated tests for carpentry jobs, there was no violation because English was a requirement for the job.[16] Employers can require a bilingual employee to speak English on the job.[17] Labor unions may also be required to publish collective bargaining agreements in a foreign language in order to ensure adequate representation of their members when a large proportion of the membership speak only a foreign language.

Discrimination because of national origin is unlawful if certain physical requirements such as height tend to exclude certain nationalities unless business necessity can be shown. Prohibition of dress and grooming customs can be a violation of national origin if native appearance or dress does not interfere with the job. National origin under Title VII has nothing to do with citizen status: the employer may refuse to hire noncitizens provided it is applied to noncitizens of all national origins.

Because of the absence of case law and the relatively few national origin cases filed with EEOC further treatment of national origin discrimination would not be the best use of space.

---

[15] All but a few states have laws preventing discrimination because of age.

[16] Frontera v. Sindell, 522 F.2d 1215 (6th Cir. 1975).

[17] Garcia v. Gloor, 609 F.2d 156 (5th Cir. 1980).

RELIGIOUS DISCRIMINATION

Title VII states that it is unlawful to discriminate because of religion. The statute does not require complete religious freedom in an employment situation; in many situations this would interfere with the normal conduct of the business. What it does require of the employer or labor union is to make reasonable efforts to accommodate the religious beliefs of employees or applicants. This duty to accommodate includes religious observance as well as religious beliefs. Teaching a Bible class at night, being a lay preacher, or going to summer Bible camp would be some of the activities that would require an attempt to accommodate.[18]

The extent to which the employer must disrupt the business to accommodate for religious observance was decided by the Supreme Court in the leading case of Hardison v. TWA, 432 U.S. 63 (1977). The court required the employer to show reasonable efforts to accommodate. If rescheduling work assignments or seniority had to be violated, or other changes in normal operations that would cause increased costs in order to accommodate, it would not be religious discrimination to refuse to do so. Under Hardison the Court said that the employer only had to bear de minimus cost to accommodate; otherwise it would be discriminating against other employees for whom no similar expenses are made to allow them time off from work. Subsequent to Hardison, one court held that if accommodation resulted in a compromise of other employees' seniority rights as secured by collective bargaining, this would be undue hardship, and accommodation would not be required. But where the employer failed to show that rescheduling Saturday work was an additional cost and further evidence revealed that other employees volunteered to work, accommodation would not be undue hardship.[19]

One of the most common situations under religious discrimination is where under the labor agreement all employees must pay dues to the labor union, and an employee, because of religious beliefs, refuses to do so. The union demands termination under the terms of the labor agreement; the employer refuses. To date all courts who have considered this question have held that if the employee pays the amount of the dues to charity, this is reasonable

---

[18] Redmond v. GAF Corp., 574 F.2d 897 (7th Cir. 1978).

[19] Brown v. General Motors Corp., 601 F.2d 956 (8th Cir. 1979).

accommodation of employee's religious beliefs by both the union and the employer.[20]

Employees' or applicants' religious observance and beliefs should not be a problem to the employer since the Hardison case. When an applicant is hired and there is some indication that religious beliefs will interfere with the employment situation, the employer should not refuse to hire the applicant, as this would be discrimination because of religion. The applicant, however, should be informed that an attempt will be made to accommodate; if that is not possible, the applicant must decide whether to accept the job or from time to time not be able to observe religious beliefs. It is extremely important for the employer to attempt to accommodate when requested to do so because of religious beliefs. Failure to make a reasonable attempt will invariably result in violation even though it can be shown in retrospect that accommodation was not possible.

DUTY TO EMPLOY OR PROMOTE THE HANDICAPPED WORKER

Contrary to common belief, no federal law covering private employers similar to Title VII makes it unlawful to discriminate in hiring or promotion of handicapped persons. The Rehabilitation Act of 1973 requires federal contractors to take affirmative action to hire qualified or promote handicapped individuals.[21] The affirmative action required of government contractors and employers receiving federal assistance is similar to that required under Executive Order 11246 (discussed in Chapter IV) with one exception; by definition a handicapped worker is not as qualified as a nonhandicapped worker for all job assignments.

Therefore, there is a duty of the employer to accommodate the handicapped worker by making a good faith effort to place the applicant or employee in a job that the person is qualified to perform with the same competency as a nonhandicapped worker.

The Rehabilitation Act of 1973 has several sections dealing with different types of employers. Section 503 requires federal contractors and subcontractors to take affirmative action. Section 504 prohibits discrimination because of a handicap by any private or public institution receiving federal financial assistance.

In the interest of space, this

---

[20] Tooley v. Martin Marietta Corp., 648 F.2d 1239 (9th Cir. 1981). Nottelson v. Smith Steel Workers, 643 F.2d 445 (7th Cir. 1981).

[21] 87 Stat. 355, 29 USC Sect. 701–794.

section does not cover all regulations concerning handicapped persons working for federal state governments and in sheltered workshops. We are concerned only with federal contractors under Section 503 and employers receiving federal financial assistance under Section 504.

COVERAGE AND DEFINITION OF HANDICAPPED PERSONS

The Rehabilitation Act of 1973, Section 503, requires any business that has a contract of $2,500 or more and provides services or personal property to any agency of the federal government to take affirmative action to employ handicapped workers. This requirement also applies to subcontractors. This means that virtually every employer that sells or provides services directly or indirectly to the federal government is covered under the act. If the employer has government contracts that exceed $50,000, a written affirmative action program must be developed.

The statute defines handicapped persons as "any person who has a physical or mental impairment which substantially limits one or more of such person's major life activities and has a record of such an impairment, or is regarded as having such an impairment."[22]

For purposes of Sections 503 and 504 as related to employment, handicapped does not include any individual who is an alcoholic or drug abuser, whose current use of alcohol or drugs prevents such individual from performing the duties of the job in question or whose employment, by reason of such current alcohol or drug abuse would constitute a direct threat to property or the safety of others.[23]

This paragraph was a 1978 amendment to the statute. Before the amendent, Sections 503 and 504 were interpreted by the courts and the Department of Labor to include alcohol and drug abusers.

Many states under their discrimination statutes do consider chemical dependency (alcohol and drug abuse) a handicap. In some states, chemical dependency is a handicap (Wisconsin); in other states it is a sickness (Minnesota). Pennsylvania courts have held that obesity (overweight) is a medical condition and not a handicap.[24] The California court considers high blood pressure a handicap.[25] The Illinois Supreme Court has held

---

[22] Sect. 7 of Rehabilitation of 1973, 29 USC Sect. 706(6).

[23] 29 USC 706 (7) (B).

[24] Phil. Electric Co. v. Commonwealth of Pennsylvania Human Relations Commission, 448 A.2d 701 (Pa. Com. Ct. 1982).

[25] Nat'l Ins v. Fair Employment and Housing Com. 651 P.2d 1151 (Calif 1982). Minnesota in Lewis v. Remmele Engineering, 314 N.W.2d 1 (Minn. 1983) finds an epileptic machine operator to be handicapped because of danger to himself.

that cancer does not qualify as it does not hinder the individual from performing a major life function. The court stated that medical conditions, although permanent, did not comply with the general understanding of the term handicapped.[26]

The regulations say that a qualified handicapped person means, with respect to employment, a handicapped person who with reasonable accommodation can perform the essential functions of the job in question.[27] The Supreme Court, in one of the few handicapped cases that it has decided, interpreted this regulation to mean that the qualified handicapped person is one who is qualified despite a handicap.[28] In this case a deaf person wanted to be admitted to a nursing school. The court said that the school is not required under Section 504 to modify or change the program so that a deaf person could be trained. The Davis case has been strictly interpreted by lower federal courts. A blind law graduate was lawfully denied a position as legal research assistant with EEOC.[29] When a blind teacher wanted to teach sighted students, the school disqualified her from taking the teacher's examination; this was approved by the court.[30]

It appears on the basis of decisions of the circuit courts, that reasonable accommodation does not mean the changing of the qualifications for the job to accommodate the handicapped. In support of this viewpoint is the fact that one court held that accommodation is not required under Section 504 of the Rehabilitation Act if modification of the essential nature or the program of the facility imposes undue burden on the recipient of federal funds.[31] In this case a school bus driver was suspended indefinitely when he was required to wear a hearing aid. His hearing without assistance did not meet department regulations. The use of the hearing aid did bring the driver up to the rating required by the regulations, but the court said that allowing a driver to wear a hearing aid would place an undue burden and a financial hardship on the school district and would necessitate the modification of the program of the district.

---

[26] Lyons v. Heritage House Restaurants, 432 N.E.2d 270 (Ill. 1982).

[27] 45 CFR Sect. 4.32.

[28] Southeastern Community College v. Davis, 99 Sup.Ct. 2361 (1977).

[29] Coleman v. Darden, 595 F.2d 533 (10th Cir. 1979).

[30] Gurmankin v. Costanzo, 556 F.2d 184 (3rd Cir. 1977).

[31] Strathie v. Dept. of Transportation, F.2d (3rd Cir. 1983).

REACTION TO SECONDARY TOBACCO SMOKE AS A HANDICAP

In recent years courts and arbitrators are considering a growing number of situations where employees have an allergy or a hypersensitivity to secondary tobacco smoke generated by fellow employees. The issue in all these cases is whether there is a duty on the employer to accommodate an employee who has an adverse reaction to tobacco smoke.

The federal authority in this area is the Occupational Safety and Health Act of 1970.[32] The OSHA administration has failed to promulgate standard or permissible levels for tobacco smoke, probably because tobacco smoke is not a by-product of the employer's activity. Another source of federal authority could be the Rehabilitation Act of 1973 whereby sensitivity to smoke could be found to be a handicap. Some states have statutes regulating smoking in the work places,[33] where inadequate ventilation causes smoke pollution. These statutes have not been enforced long enough to be of any help to employer's policies on smoking in the work place.

The courts that have considered the problem of the hypersensitive employee have held that there is a duty on the part of the employer to accommodate. The legal origin of this duty is found in two sources; some courts find a common law duty to provide the employee with a safe place to work while others hold that being allergic to smoke is a handicap or a disability.

Two state courts have held that where an employee is allergic to secondary tobacco smoke, the common law right to a safe working environment is being violated. In Shimp v. New Jersey Bell Telephone Co., 368 A.2d 408 (NJ Sup. Ct. 1976) the court restricted smoking to a lounge area after the employee subjected to smoke at the desk had a nose and throat irritation, nosebleeds, headaches, and vomiting. Where the employee developed a sore throat, nausea, dizziness, blackouts and loss of memory, choking sensations, and cold sweat sensations, the court held that the employer owed the employee a duty to use all reason-

---

[32] 29 U.S.C. 651 et. seq.

[33] Col. Rev. Stat. 25-14-103 (4) (1982); Minn. Stat. Ann. Sect. IV 4.413 (1982 Supp.); Mont. Code Ann. Sect. 50-40-104 (1981); Neb. Rev. Sect. 71-577 (1981); Or. Rev. Stat. Sect. 243.350 (1981); Utah Code Ann. Sect. 76-10-106 (1978).

able care to provide a safe place to work and the employee must be removed to a no-smoking area.[34] In both these cases the reaction to smoke was severe[35] and the court did not ban all smoking but required the employer to provide the hypersensitive employee a safe place to work.

Two courts have relied on the handicap concept to find that an employee allergic to tobacco smoke should be accommodated. In Vickers v. Veterans Administration, 549 F.Supp. 85 (D.C. Wash. 1982) the court said that a hypersensitive person was a handicapped person for the purposes of Section 504 of the Rehabilitation Act of 1973. The court found that reasonable accommodation was made when the employer got voluntary agreements from other employees not to smoke, separated the desks, offered a floor-to-ceiling protection around the employee's desk, and offered an outside job.

A circuit court of appeals found that although the employee has no permanent disability, incapacity to work in a smoke-filled environment is a disability. The employer was ordered to remove the employee from the smoke-filled room or the employee would be considered totally "disabled" under the pension plan.[36] In this situation the reaction was severe as the employee developed chest pains and congestion and had trouble breathing and speaking.

The courts in all these situations only required the employer to accommodate and have not totally prohibited smoking at the work site. Also in all cases a severe physical reaction has been shown by the employee.[37] It is doubtful whether the courts would enforce a complete smoking ban. Where a arbitrator ruled that a no-smoking ban was reasonable in an asbestos plant because of the probability of cancer, the court refused to enforce the award, stating that neither OSHA nor the labor agreement permitted the employer to prevent employees from smoking when it had been permitted at the time of hiring.[38]

Generally arbitrators will hold that a no-smoking ban promulgated unilaterally by the employer does not meet the test of reason-

[34] Smith v. Western Electric Co., 643 S.W.2d 10 (Mo. APP 1982).

[35] Where there is only hypersensitivity but no severe physical reaction one court said common duty to accommodate is not a violation of providing safe place to work. Gordon v. Raven Systems Research Inc (D.C. Ct of App. 1983).

[36] Parodi v. Merit Systems Protection Board, 690 F.2d 731 (9th Cir. 1982).

[37] In Gordon v. Raven Systems and Research Corp, A2d (D.C. Ct. App. 1983) it was held not a violation of common law duty to provide a safe place where severe defects are not shown.

[38] Johns-Manville Sales Corp. v. Int'l Assn. of Machinist Local Lodge 1609, 621 F.2d 756 (5th Cir. 1980).

ableness required under the labor agreement.[39] (An employer has a right to promulgate unilaterally a rule that governs the conduct of employees on the job but the union can contest the reasonableness of the rule.)

From the courts' and arbitrators' decisions, it appears that an employer cannot ban smoking entirely. Where a specific employee has severe adverse affects to secondary tobacco smoke, the employer must accommodate either under the common law rule of providing a safe place to work or under the handicap concept.

An employer who is fearful of the nonsmoker-smoker problem could consider hiring only nonsmokers. There is no statute to prevent such a policy.

MEANING OF REASONABLE ACCOMMODATION

It is not certain under present case law what is required of the employer to accommodate the handicapped person in order to comply with affirmative action requirements of Sections 503 and 504 of the rehabilitation act. Most cases under this act come under Section 504, which deals with federal financial assistance programs. Students of handicapped law have concluded that courts will require more effort to accommodate than with religious accommo-dation under the Hardison case.[40] How much more effort is uncertain.[41] In the Southwestern Community College case the Supreme Court said that Section 504 did not require extensive modifications of a program to admit a deaf person to a nurses' training program but left open whether any modification would be required. One certain requirement is that there must be a good faith attempt to accom-modate.[42] The Strathie case has given us a beginning to the insight

---

[39] Union Sanitary District CCH, 82 Ardb. 8593 (Koven).

[40] Jana K. Guy. "The developing law on Equal Employment Opportunity for the Handicapped: An Overview and Analysis of the Major Issues," *University of Baltimore Law Review, 183*, 1983.

[41] In Holland v. Boeing, 583 P.2d 621 (Wash., 1978) the Washington State Supreme Court refused to apply the de minimus test of Hardison because it believed that handicap differs from religious discrimination.

[42] E.E. Black, Ltd. v. Marshall, 497 F.Supp. 1088 (D.C. Hawaii 1980). A person with possible back disability applied for a carpenter's apprentice position and was refused. The court recognized that the employer may disqualify the applicant but failed to look for other jobs within the company.

on the extent of accommodation. If it means substantially changing policies, altering programs or if there is a business purpose for the action, the courts will probably rule in favor of accommodation.

RECOMMENDATIONS FOR ACCOMMODATION POLICY FOR HANDICAPPED PERSONS

The law in the area of handicapped persons is in its infancy. The federal law requires affirmative action only for federal contractors and recipients of federally funded programs. Many states do, however, prohibit discrimination of handicapped persons in all employment decisions; it is predicted that Congress will follow in a few years. There is still time for employers to develop policies and procedures that will be beneficial to the organization and not run afoul of the law. If this is done, the development of law of the handicapped will be what the employer and employees can accept. The first step that an employer should take is to ask the person whether any physical disability will interfere with the job under consideration. If the answer is no and there is in fact no disability, it is then not a question of accommodation but one of qualifications. The regulations are clear that the first step in any handicapped consideration is that the person involved must be regarded as being handicapped.[43] If the person is not considered handicapped, no further steps are necessary except to consider qualifications of a nonhandicapped person.

The next step, if the person is considered handicapped, is to ask what the candidate can do. This may require a physical observance of certain jobs or accurate job description and medical authority. If the individual professes the ability to do a certain job, the supervisor disagrees, and the medical report permits performance, it is advisable to let the person try. This may cause some exposure to worker's compensation losses, but unless the safety of others is involved, it is a poor defense to accept the supervisor's subjective analysis of the ability of a handicapped person to perform a certain job if that person thinks it can be done.

More often than not the handicapped person proves the supervisor wrong, especially if told that there is doubt about the ability to do it and one hopes that the handicapped can prove the supervisor wrong (a motivation technique).

Since supervisors are responsible for the low cost of operations or staying within a budget, they often resist hiring the handicapped. It is advisable to have a written accommodation policy that contains the following provisions:

1. Consultation should be required with the disabled person on what accommodation

---

[43] 29 U.S.C. Sect. 706(7) (b) (i).

is needed to be as qualified as a nonhandicapped person.

2. Accommodation requests should be an individual matter and not what a similar disability may require.

3. Accommodation may create a pattern or practice; it should not be made if consequences result in future accommodations that cannot be economically tolerated. (An example would be to change one architectural barrier.)

4. The cost of accommodation should have an upper limit; hidden costs should be included, if not too subjective.

5. The effect of undue hardship on other employees must be considered. If treatment is substantially different than other employees are treated,

accommodation is probably not required and the Hardison decision would apply.

6. If appropriate, rehabilitation engineers ergonomists, or accommodation experts may be called on for consultation. It is defensible evidence of good faith effort when accommodation is refused based on information from a consultant.

Hiring or promoting the handicapped worker should not be a problem for the employer. In many respects the handicapped worker is as valuable to an organization as a nonhandicapped worker. They must be assigned tasks that they can do as well as any other worker and be treated like any other worker except for the accommodation of the physical disability.

SUMMARY AND CONCLUSIONS

This chapter has dealt with those protected classes where the law is not fully developed. This is one of the most important chapters on discrimination as these are areas where the employer can have an impact in the development of the law by instituting policies and procedures that are defensible. As it has so often been stated by the legal profession, "bad facts make bad law."

Age, religion, national origin, and handicapped regulations, although they have particular problems of compliance, have one common element; compliance is not required if the person is not

qualified for the job. If they are qualified, there is no compliance problem. In the area of age, the employer might say that the problem is to make room for a younger person but why is it necessary if the older person is qualified? It is not good personnel practice to create a job vacancy for morale purposes as it destroys the morale of the older person and the younger promotable person will say, "As he is I will be someday and I do not want to be with a company that will do that to me."

In the areas of religion, only de minimus accommodation is required by the law. This is nothing more than what good employee relations policy would require.

As to the handicapped, a good accommodation policy aids the employer in tapping a human resource that can be beneficial to the goals of the organization. In some instances the handicapped worker can be a better employee than a nonhandicapped worker. For high turnover jobs, jobs that have little supervision, or jobs that are dead-end, the handicapped worker has proved to be the best selection to fill a vacancy. The hiring and promotion of the protected classes discussed in this chapter aid rather than hinder the personnel practitioner's job and organization goals. If a positive approach is taken from the outset, good law will be the result.

CHAPTER VII

MARY HOGAN'S BACK— A CASE HISTORY WITH COMMENTS

Chapter Contents
*Introduction
*Mary Hogan's Back
*Comments
How To Identify The Mary Hogans
*Company Mistakes
*Considerations In Out-of-Court Settlements
*Summary And Conclusions

INTRODUCTION

In Chapter VI back cases were purposely avoided because they deserve special consideration. One of the most rare persons in business is a personnel practitioner who has not experienced the placement or return-to-work problem of an employee with a back disability. These disabilities are sometimes caused by work-related injuries, other times by nonwork-related injuries, all too often by no injury at

121

all. Backs of certain individuals wear out. This can be a person who does physical work, one who does office work, or an executive who because of job requirements can tolerate a bad back and therefore does not become a personnel problem. Although there is little case law on whether a bad back is a handicap,[1] it is predicted that the decision in the Black case will someday be the rule in most courts—that a severe back disability is a handicap because it meets the requirement of "substantially limits one or more major life activities."

For many years employers have been giving preemployment physicals that x-ray backs for certain job applicants. If a back condition is found medically unsuitable for the job under consideration, the employee is not hired. Case law is vague on whether this is considered a handicap and accordingly whether there is a duty to accommodate. It may soon be considered a handicap, and an attempt to accommodate is advisable. The extent that the employer should go to accommodate should be decided by economical considerations and good employee relations policy. The accommodation policy should be the same for employees who have an occupational or nonoccupational back condition as for other applicants applying for a job.

MARY HOGAN'S BACK

Almost every operation, whether small or large, can find a Mary Hogan. Some employees become knowledgeable on how to use the law to their advantage and get paid for not working. Their constant appearance in hearings and courts often make them better lawyers than the company lawyer who spends much time on board of directors' problems.

In reading the Mary Hogan case it should be noted that legal counsel was available at all times to the operating management and, after the charge was filed with the city, legal counsel was involved, except for one action—when Mary was terminated for insubordination.

The Mary Hogan case has an abundance of practical facts that involve many phases of antidiscrimination law, personnel practices, and supervisor techniques. The exhibits were part of the personnel records kept on Mary Hogan, except Exhibit VII-1, which is a summary of the events that shows how a Mary Hogan takes advantage of an employer's mistakes and plans every move in building an effective case. The personnel

---

[1] E.E. Black Ltd. v. Marshall, 497 F.Supp. 1088 (1980) is one of the few cases where the courts have considered a back a disability.

records are available to both parties when the case goes to litigation and are illustrative of the importance of documentation when the dispute is being tried.

MARY HOGAN'S BACK—CASE STUDY

Paul Smith, department superintendent of Acme Bag Company for the past 14 years, notices that the conveyor belt was jammed with paper bags. He told Mary Hogan, a polypropylene (P.E.) inserter on the machine to "get a pallet and remove the bags off the belt."

Mary replied, "I am not able to because my back is bothering me." Paul replied, "Get one that you are able to handle." Mary replied, "I will not do it." Paul said, "I think you can do it." Mary said, "No." Paul said, "You are terminated, clock out, and leave the plant." Mary Hogan did just that.

Acme Bag Company is a facility of 110 employees represented by Teamsters Union. Acme manufactures grocery bags for supermarkets and other grocery and confectionery accounts in Mill City, Minnesota, which has a population of approximately 100,000. Acme Bag Company has been in operation at this location for 15 years, and 3 years ago it became a part of Standard Products Corporation, a conglomerate that operates in all 50 states and Mexico.[2] Standard Products Corporation has an active affirmative action program both at the corporate and local plant levels and the Acme Bag plant had recently passed a compliance review. The Acme plant as well as parent corporation has a good labor relations record and had no previous EEOC charges. Mary Hogan was employed by Acme in October 1974 as an unskilled worker; she worked in various unskilled positions throughout the plant during her employment.

On June 2, 1975, Mary filed a complaint with the Mill City Civil Rights Commission alleging that the Acme Company discriminated because of her sex when she was given a two-day suspension for refusing to mop the floor when males and minorities were not required to do so. (Mary did not file a grievance over the suspension). Section 601A.7 of the city ordinance was alleged to be violated. A similar charge was filed with EEOC under Title VII; EEOC referred it to the Minnesota Civil Rights Commission, a Section 706 referral agency. The charge was investigated by the city in the summer of 1975 and dismissed on November 5, 1975.[3]

---

[2] All names and places are fictitious. Only the facts bear resemblance to an actual case.

[3] Dismissal of the city complaint does not affect the charge filed with EEOC.

Before the investigation by the Minnesota Civil Rights Commission and after the city had dismissed the complaint, Ms. Hogan in May 1976, amended the complaint, alleging that Acme had refused to allow her to return to light duty of 10 pounds or less and that this was a violation of Title VII and state law. However, Acme had not received any medical report of Ms. Hogan's condition from July 1975 to May 1, 1976. This amendment was based on the fact that Ms. Hogan was not given the opportunity to work since August 1975. The state civil rights specialist in June 1976 discovered that Ms. Hogan had not worked since July 31, 1975, and inquired about the absence. She was told by Acme that Ms. Hogan was on a medical leave and Acme would be glad to have her return to work, providing the company doctor approved it. Acme further stated, when questioned, that the reason Ms. Hogan had not returned to work was because she had not contacted Acme stating that she was physically able to return to work and was able to perform the job in the plant that she had previously selected or that she could perform any other job.

On August 29, 1975, Acme had a medical report from the company doctor stating that Ms. Hogan was able to lift only 5 to 20 pounds. Before August 29, 1975, Ms. Hogan had signed a statement that she would perform only the job as bottom feeder and table loader, jobs that required lifting 20 to 35 pounds and 60 to 75 pounds respectively; this caused Acme to give her medical leave.

From August 29, 1975 to June 1976, Ms. Hogan had applied for unemployment insurance, which Acme contested on the grounds that the claimant was on medical leave. It was ruled that Ms. Hogan was available for work, and she received unemployment compensation. The notice to allow unemployment benefits was not received by Acme but was sent to the parent company's office, which failed to forward it to Acme, which would have appealed the decision.

Although the company has forms for a medical leave of absence, no medical leave was applied for by Ms. Hogan under the terms of the labor agreement. However, Ms. Hogan's status was considered a voluntary medical leave during the period of August 29, 1975 to July 12, 1976; premiums for her health insurance were paid by Acme rather than terminating her as required by the labor agreement, which stated that after three months on any leave of absence, an employee is terminated. All during this period Ms. Hogan was not considered by Acme as available for work but was not contacted to determine her status.

When Ms. Hogan was called to return to work after being contacted by the civil rights specialist on June 14, 1976, she stated that she was still under doctor's care and would be until June 26. On June 28 Ms. Hogan inquired when she could see a company doctor; on advice of corporate counsel, the personnel coordinator arranged an appointment. The company doctor on July 2 stated that she could return to light work, but lifting 40 to 50 pounds repetitively would cause back symptoms. Ms. Hogan was notified of her physical condition, which permitted her to return to work on July 8; she agreed to return to her old job of bottom feeder on July 12, 1976 (requiring the lifting of 25 to 40 pounds).

On July 13 she alleged that she hurt her back. A meeting was called to determine what job Ms. Hogan could do. With the union present, she was asked what she wanted to do and she stated table loader and was returned to that job for the remainder of the day (this required the lifting of 40 to 50 pounds). On the following day, July 14, her husband called and stated that she hurt her back on the previous day and wanted an appointment to see another doctor. It was assumed that this other doctor would be somebody other than the company doctor; she was told that she could see any doctor whom she wanted. She requested the company doctor. It was the observance of her supervisor that when she left the plant on July 13, 1976, nothing was wrong with her back. However, an appointment was made with the company doctor for July 14.

Nothing was heard from Ms. Hogan after her physical examination until her husband called on July 19 and wanted to know what the doctor had found, stating that the doctor never told her the results of the July 14 examination. When told that nothing was wrong with her, she stated that she wanted to see another doctor. On July 29 she was ordered to return to work on August 2; however, rather than return to work, she saw another doctor on August 2, who authorized her to return to work on August 3 but "no heavy lifting." She reported to work August 3 and told her supervisor that she could not load tables (a job that she said she could do on July 13, 1976, her last day worked).

As a result of her statement, a meeting was held on the same day with the union and management; Ms. Hogan requested that she be taken off table loader and be assigned to P.E. inserting. It was explained to her that this job requires lifting 50 to 70 pounds. It was a job that she had previously performed and she knew its requirements. It was also stated to Ms. Hogan and the union that she would be used on a temporary basis in other departments. Ms. Hogan performed this job until September 2, 1976, when she was discharged for refusing to get a pallet that weighed 30.1 pounds and required her to only slide the pallet to carry out the order of her supervisor, Paul Smith. The complaint of the civil rights commission was again amended, stating that her discharge was due to retaliation for filing the original complaint. As a result of the discharge, a grievance was filed under the labor agreement and the dispute was arbitrated; the arbitrator found on August 23, 1977 insubordination as the cause for the discharge.[4]

The state civil rights commission, after an investigation, determined in June 1978 (two years after the incident) that there was no reasonable cause as to the sex discrimination charges regarding the suspension for refusing to mop

---

[4] Arbitration decision has no bearing on the pending EEOC charge. In Alexander v. Gardner-Denver, 94 Sup. Ct., 1011 (1974), the Supreme Court held that EEOC can consider arbitrator's decision but it is not controlling.

the floor, but there was reasonable cause to believe that Ms. Hogan was discriminated against for not returning to work during the period of August 29, 1975 to July 12, 1976 and that the discharge on September 2, 1976, was retaliation to filing a complaint. The civil rights commission in its conciliation proposal demanded $9,000 in back pay and reinstatement. The corporate EEO investigator was told by the local manager that he didn't discriminate and any settlement would look like guilt. The parties were requested to attend a conciliation meeting. If this failed, the matter would go before the civil rights commission hearing examiner; an appeal from that decision would be to the district court. What did the Acme Company do wrong to cause the problem?

EXHIBIT VII-1

Sequence of Events in Mary Hogan Case

1. May 2, 1975—Ms. Hogan bid off all jobs except table loader and stacker.

2. May 16, 1975—Ms. Hogan refused to mop floor—laid off for two days.

3. June 2, 1975—Ms. Hogan filed charges with city and state civil rights commission over discipline for refusing to mop the floor.

4. July 29, 1975—Ms. Hogan signed off all jobs but bottom feeder and table loader.

5. July 31, 1975—Last day Ms. Hogan worked until July 12, 1976.

6. August 5, 1975—Ms. Hogan went to Acme's doctor, Dr. Abramson of Golden Springs Hospital for back, released to return to work on August 11, 1975, but no heavy lifting.

7. August 12, 1975—Ms. Hogan went to Dr. Rosenbloom of Golden Springs Hospital for back, released to go to work on August 18, 1975; no heavy lifting.

8. August 12, 1975—Ms. Hogan had x-ray from Dr. Bircher whom Ms. Hogan selected.

9. August 13, 1975—Acme received letter from state industrial commission stating that Ms. Hogan reported an industrial injury to have occurred on April 15, 1975. Stated it was reported to supervisor.

10. August 15, 1975—Firm wrote letter to Ms. Hogan, inquiring about injury.

11. August 21, 1975—Ms. Hogan saw Dr. Gunder, company doctor; released to go to work with lift limitation of 5 to 20 pounds.

12. August 27, 1975—Ms. Hogan saw Dr. Gunder, company doctor; released to go to work with lift limitation of 5 to 20 pounds.

13. August 29, 1975—Ms. Hogan stated supervisor said firm didn't have any work for her with 5- to 10-pound limitation. Acme's last contact with Ms. Hogan until June 1976.

14. November 5, 1975—City dismissed the charge over mop incident.

15. November 14, 1975—Ms. Hogan filed a claim for unemployment insurance.

16. November 24, 1975—Acme protested on basis that Ms. Hogan is on medical leave.

continued

EXHIBIT VII-1

17. December 11, 1975—Minnesota Employment Security Commission rendered decision that she is available for work and allowed benefits. It was not contested.

18. May 12, 1976—Acme amended complaint alleging failure to find work or make reasonable effort in August, 1975.

19. June 6, 1976—Unemployment insurance expired.

20. June 18, 1976—Ms. Hogan talked to Paul Smith, stating she couldn't return until June 26, 1976; called for company doctor appointment.

21. July 2, 1976—Ms. Hogan saw Dr. Gunder; stated that she could return to work and lift 40 to 50 pounds.

22. July 8, 1976—Ms. Hogan called and asked what the doctor said because he hadn't told her.

23. July 9, 1976—Ms. Hogan wrote letter stating that she agreed to return to work on July 12, 1976.

24. July 12, 1976—Ms. Hogan returned to work as bottom feeder.

25. July 12, 1976—Ms. Hogan said she could work as bottom feeder.

26. July 13, 1976—Acme had meeting on what Ms. Hogan could do.

27. July 14, 1976—Husband called and said she hurt her back on July 13.

28. July 14, 1976—Ms. Hogan made appointment to see company doctor.

29. July 18, 1976—Ms. Hogan called, wanted to know if Acme got report from doctor as doctor did not tell her. Acme told her there was nothing wrong according to doctor.

30. July 29, 1976—Ms. Hogan was ordered to return to work on August 2, 1976.

31. August 2, 1976—Ms. Hogan saw another doctor at Dial Clinic; released for work on August 3 with no heavy lifting.

32. August 3, 1976—Ms. Hogan had discussion with supervisor about working as bottom feeder; said that she hurt her back.

33. August 4, 1976—Acme had a meeting with Ms. Hogan about what she could do.

34. August 4, 1976—Ms. Hogan bid off all jobs except P.E. inserter.

35. August 5, 1976—Acme wrote her that she had to report to work by August 10, 1976.

36. August 10, 1976—Ms. Hogan reported to work.

37. August 12, 1976—Ms. Hogan reprimanded for slow production.

38. August 18, 1976—Ms. Hogan reprimanded for not wearing ear protection.

39. August 20, 1976—Ms. Hogan filed grievance for nine paid holidays and one-week vacation for period of September 1975 to July 1976.

40. September 2, 1976—Ms. Hogan discharged for refusing order.

41. September 2, 1976—Ms. Hogan amended charge that she was discharged as retaliation for filing previous charges.

42. September 2, 1976—Ms. Hogan filed grievance over discharge.

43. August 23, 1977—Arbitrator held insubordination a just cause for discharge.

44. June 1978—State civil rights commission found probable cause.

EXHIBIT VII-2

August 29, 1975

Mr. Sam Jones
Plant Manager
Acme Bag Co.
Mill City, Minnesota 55800

Re: Mary Hogan

This 42-year-old female employee had an x-ray at Dr. Bircher's office
on August 19, 1975, and was seen in our office on August 21, 1975,
and August 27, 1975.

Employee states that she hurt her back in April when she had a
sudden pain while twisting vigorously. She states that she kept
at work with varying degrees of pain. She claims to have occasional
leg pains. In July she began to have neck complaints. Recently
she has had pain in the right groin with walking. She states that
any type of activity or lifting aggravates her pain.

X-ray is reported as showing no evidence of old or recent injury
but moderate narrowing of the L-5 and S-1 interspace.

Patient is a slender female weighing approximately 110 pounds. There
is no evidence of muscle atrophy. Reflexes are active, perhaps
greater on the left. There is no demonstrable evidence of limitation
of movement of spine or legs although almost all movement active
or passive is stated to cause pain. Straight leg raising is negative
to 80 degrees. There is no evidence of sensory loss.

Her complaint of rectal bleeding would seem unrelated to factory
work although I did no rectal exam.

There is no doubt in my mind that symptoms exceed objective
findings and that motivation may be a factor. An arthritic process
cannot be ruled out. I see no reason to believe that an episode
in April has produced the problem.

It is quite possible that this female is too small to be doing
relatively heavy factory labor. However, I would think that lifting
of 5 to 20 pound objects could be done routinely unless it required
bending (as opposed to the use of legs by squatting).

While indicating to her a lack of factory connection, I gave her
a prescription for butazolidin alka for a short-term trial.

continued

EXHIBIT VII-2

It is my recommendation that she be encouraged to resume work, but that if she feels unable to do so, she should consult her own physician regarding nonfactory disease. If she insists on the relationship to work, I would recommend consultation with an orthopedic surgeon.

Sincerely,

John E. Gunder, M.D.

EXHIBIT VII-3

July 2, 1976

Acme Bag Co.
Mill City, Minnesota 55800

Re: Mary Hogan

Gentlemen:

Mary Hogan was seen by me on July 2, 1976, and reported that:

1. She had not worked since I saw her last (August 27, 1975);
2. In the last year, she has seen Dr. Bakody, the last time on March 9, 1976, and he had told her that her work at Acme was too heavy;
3. She has continued to have pain in the lower back and legs which is worse after heavy lifting; and
4. She has an appointment with Dr. Bircher on July 26, 1976, arranged by Acme's attorney.

On examination, the patient seems to have full range of motion of back and legs. Straight leg raising is normal. Her reflexes in the lower extremities are equal and active. I find no evidence of atrophy of either leg.

It is my opinion that Ms. Hogan has no significant injury and that she could return to light work without significant physical problem or risk of aggravation. With her light body build, lifting over 40-50 pounds repetitively is likely to produce back symptoms.

Sincerely,

John E. Gunder, M.D.

EXHIBIT VII-4

July 13, 1976

This meeting was called to try to determine problem concerning Mary Hogan whether she is able to work or wants to work. Those present included Sam Jones, plant manager; Mabel Guill, union representative; Paul Smith; and Mary Hogan.

Mary was asked if she wanted union representation and she requested Mabel Guill.

Sam: Mary, I understand there is a problem in that you do not want to load tables.

Mary: My back will not take it. Something in my back is not right.

Sam: I do not understand. We have sent you to the doctor. We have asked if you were ready to come back to work. You said yes. You have been back one day. Do you really want to work? We have a job available if you want to work. If not, we will go another route.

Mary: I will do anything I am able to do.

Sam: We have got the slip where you have disqualified yourself or did not want to do anything except table loading and P.E. liner-inserter.

Mary: I cannot lift that other stuff.

Sam: You are not able to come to work?

Mary: I made out okay yesterday.

Sam: Inserting requires more lifting than table work.

Mary: Not constant lifting is only difference.

Sam: We have a contract with the union and we try to abide by it. One of the requirements is that when we are short, we pull the junior one and table loading and insertion is the only one you are available for by your own choice. According to the doctor, there is no reason you cannot do this work.

Mary: The doctor is not carrying my back around.

Sam: We have to go with the doctor's recommendations. He is more qualified than we are in these things.

Mabel: I want to see a copy of the doctor's report.

Sam: If you want to work, the job is there. We have to put you as a table loader. If you do not want to work, it is another story. The choice is up to you at this point.

Mary: There is no choice but work for me.

Sam: If you want to work, there is a choice and if not—the choice is yours.

Mary: I can do it and suffer the consequences.

Mabel: She has to make a choice. I do not know what the doctors have told her or her lawyers have told her.

Sam: Mabel, we asked Mary if she wanted union representation.

Mabel: Have all doctors released her?

continued

EXHIBIT VII-4

Sam: The company doctor has. I do not know of the rest.

Mary: There is a difference between not wanting and not being able.

Sam: I understand, but the doctor says you are able.

Mary: I have never been lazy here. I toted bags same as men and that is how I got this way.

Sam: We do not discriminate between male and female. What do you want to do?

Mary: I have no choice but to go out and do it if it kills me or not.

August 4, 1976

EXHIBIT VII-5

Had a meeting with Mary Hogan, Mabel Guill, Paul Smith, and myself at 9:00 A.M. this morning.

We discussed the doctors' reports in that two doctors had found nothing wrong with her physical condition at this point she wanted to check into the hospital and have a complete physical. She was told she has had since August of 1975 to do this, and at this time the company did not see any reasons for this request.

The union and Mary requested that she be taken off the bottom feeders and table loading jobs. This only left one job in the plant she wanted to do and that is P.E. liners. I agreed to let her sign to form. I also explained this job required lifting P.E. liners of 50 to 70 pounds. She said she would find a way.

It was also explained to the union we would not put up with continued absenteeism.

It was also explained to the union that if Mary happens to be junior person in the Liner Department and we needed someone in another department, she would be used on a temporary basis in the other department.

Sam Jones

COMMENTS

These comments will be limited to identifying the Mary Hogans in the work force, company mistakes in dealing with employees like Mary Hogan, factors to consider in the decision-making process of whether to settle or contest allegations in court and recommendations on how to deal with chronic physical disabilities such as backs.

HOW TO IDENTIFY THE MARY HOGANS

As the practitioner studies the facts in this case, one conclusion is self-evident: Mary Hogan was knowledgeable (or her attorney was) about her available remedies and how to build a record to allow her to use those remedies. Her various activities were designed to trigger the company into doing something that would enable her to accomplish her objective: being paid for not working. Let's analyze how this was done.

1. Whenever she felt a wrong was committed, she used every available regulatory agency to seek redress, without paying for an attorney. If she filed a charge with the city, federal government, and union, certainly somebody would listen to her and aid her cause.

2. She was an expert at delay. From August 1975 to June 14, 1976, she never contacted the company. When contacted on June 14 to come back to work, by delays she returned to work on July 12. Each step in the delay was just enough not to cause adversity. When returning to work she immediately hurt her back and again a series of delays until ordered to return to work on August 2, 1976.

3. Because she had to report for work, it was time to see another doctor, who released her for work on August 3. It took a letter to force her back to work, but when the letter was written, she complied.

4. When returning to work, she would violate minor rules and continue to exhaust her remedies of getting something for nothing; in this case she filed a grievance with the union.

5. She would continually do something to force the company to take a challengeable action, but not going too far to get a bad record. Refusing to get a pallet, not wearing safety protective equipment, being late for work, etc., are all harassment tactics to trigger company action.

To identify the Mary Hogans one should look for two or more of the following characteristics:

1. Usually a marginal worker.

2. Never commits a major violation of company rules but enough to cause the company to take more severe action than the violation would reasonably demand (Slow production, refusing a minor order, false statements by husband).

3. Is efficient in irritating the supervisor (not wearing protective safety equipment, filing a lot of grievances, etc.).

4. Makes statements that are not logically true, but could be true, so that investigation is required before action can be taken. Investigation also causes exposure of defamation to third parties. (For example, Mary's husband said that the doctor did not inform her that she could return to work.)

5. Solicits sympathy from co-workers (Mary was unsuccessful with this).

6. Forces most supervisors or company statements to be in writing before complying; otherwise denies statement was ever made.

7. Knows what to do when company makes a mistake in handling a situation. Often "plant lawyers" like Mary cannot be identified until a sequence of events similar to Exhibit VII-1 is developed.

COMPANY MISTAKES

The company's major mistake after Mary Hogan was identified as an employee who was a litigator, was to permit her to continue as an employee. In the interest of good employee relations the supervisor or personnel practitioner will often give the employee the benefit of doubt and not apply a strict construction to the rules. This policy will backfire with the Mary Hogans. When the labor agreement said termination after three months, then she should be terminated. If the medical report states that she cannot do a particular job, she should not do it, but a good faith effort should be made to accommodate for other jobs. If none are available, she should not be permitted to return to work.

In Mary Hogan's case, when in August 1975 there were no jobs that she could do, she should have been terminated under the labor agreement and health insurance should not have been paid. On July 13, 1976, when she hurt her back, she should have been taken off the job and not permitted to do other work until medically authorized.

It was not a mistake to permit her to go to several doctors as this is permitted under most state worker's compensation laws. The mistake was made when one doctor said that she could do only certain jobs and she was permitted to do other jobs that doctors said she could not do. When medical advice is conflicting, the company can take action on any one of the conflicting medical statements without being exposed to additional liability. The question of what doctor is right should not be determined before action is taken; this would be impractical. If the company acted on wrong medical advice under most court decisions and statutes there is no additional liability. In worker's compensation cases under most state statutes the extent of the disability as medically determined is what the employer is liable for.

The other mistake was discharging Mary. Sending her home as being physically unfit to work would have been a better solution. The EEOC charge of retaliation is much easier for Mary to sustain than failure to accommodate. Discharge is exactly what Mary wanted. She had successfully irritated her supervisor so that his patience ran out and he discharged her, which set the company up for a retaliation charge.

There is little law on whether there was an obligation on the part of the company to check on Mary's physical condition from August 1975 to June 1976. It appears that if there were other job vacancies that Mary could possibly do, she should have been contacted as a good faith effort to accommodate. Once a good faith effort is made, there is no further obligation unless conditions change. However, as we see when discussing leave of absences in Chapter XIV, a personnel policy for all indefinite leaves of absence is advisable.

Why did the company act the way it did in Mary Hogan's case? First, it thought that if it were lenient, Mary would not have a good reason to complain (this usually backfires with the Mary Hogans). Second, because Mary had been successful in irritating everybody who became involved in her case, the less adverse decisions, the less misery, until the pressure was too great that the only way the supervisor could relieve the emotional pressure was to discharge her. The company's mistakes could have been avoided if it had bit the bullet at the early stages by termination and let Mary exercise whatever remedies available to her.

CONSIDERATIONS IN OUT-OF-COURT SETTLEMENTS

Considerations as to out-of-court settlements should contain legal as well as employee relations consequences. As to legal considerations, the assessment of chances of winning, as discussed in Chapter II, are one consideration. The other consideration is that a settlement would not prevent a retaliation charge if the employee were reinstated. Neither will a court order to reinstate prevent retaliation charges. Therefore, in the settlement negotiations, whether reinstatement is a "must position of the employee" has considerable influence on the decision. EEOC will always propose reinstatement along with full back pay, but that is sometimes a starting point for negotiations.

As to employee relations considerations, the first problem is with the supervisor involved. Any monetary settlement implies discrimination regardless of the settlement agreement. With some managers and supervisors, this stigma is difficult to overcome especially in a sex discrimination case when their wives are active in feminist movements. If any member of management feels that settlement is admission of guilt and the facts show that actually there was no discrimination, settlement for economic reasons is often a mistake, unless management determines that economic considerations override all other considerations.

Usually there is less cost to settling than to litigate the case. When budgeting for litigation, the employer should consider costs for going to district court level. If there is an administrative hearing before the judicial review and if the same commission that made initial determination hears the case and makes the determination, as in Mary Hogan's case, chances of winning at the administrative level are poor. Often attorneys feel that it is economically advisable to waive the administrative-level hearing and go directly into court if permitted by the statute.

Also in consideration of employee relations consequences of a settlement, the effect of lump-sum payment on other employees is important. It has little effect unless the employee is reinstated. If reinstated, the exposure to adverse employee relations is present, but it does not always have adverse effect on employee relations. One way to mitigate an adverse effect on employee relations is to prohibit disclosure of the terms in settlement agreement.

Settling a case where there is little evidence of discrimination is not advisable when consideration is given to the long-range economic and employee relations consequences. In situations where the legal assessment of winning in the courts is better than 50 percent, the long-range economic and employee relations benefits are worth risking a court decision, although the immediate cost may not justify it.

SUMMARY AND CONCLUSIONS

The employer's position in dealing with bad backs similar to Mary Hogan's must be flexible until it is determined whether the physical condition is bona fide or one that enables an able bodied employee to receive compensation without working. When an employee reports a bad back, the first thing to do is look at the employee's record and try to identify if this person is motivated to work or is a professional litigator. If it is determined that this is a legitimate case and the employee will return to work when medically possible, no further strategy is necessary. If it is determined that this is an unmotivated employee and professional litigator, the following steps are advisable. From time to time modification will be necessary according to the situation. These steps will not always work but that does not mean they should not be tried.[5]

1. The first step is to get a medical determination of the employee's condition. This determination should correlate with other facts surrounding the case. If there is reason to believe this is the employee's opinion, but written by the doctor, the employer should require a medical, not a patient's opinion, possibly from another doctor.

2. If the employee believes that a disability exists, every effort to accommodate should be made. Sometimes backs heal rapidly when an employee is put on a substantially lower paying job. This is one of the best ways to heal a back that is medically questionable.

3. If there are continual efforts to return to work and recurrences of injury, the employer should move quickly for a medical leave or termination providing there are no vacancies in the foreseeable future that employee is qualified to fill.

4. During the entire procedure, the employer should avoid adversity whenever possible as not to give the employee a remedy. If the employee is not telling the truth, the employer should take different action.

5. The employer should investigate all doubtful situations of sickness. If the employee is home mowing the lawn or harvesting the hay crop, the employee should immediately be discharged for falsification.

Discharge should be the last resort. When doing so, the firm must have a solid record. Otherwise medical leaves are the best solution until the policy or labor agreement permits termination.

The Mary Hogans will not disappear but the numbers found in each facility will depend on how individual cases are dealt with. The proper attention and action will result in the Mary Hogans appearing less often.

---

[5] The duck hunter's code should be used in this situation: "You don't get a duck unless you shoot at it."

CHAPTER VIII

SEX DISCRIMINATION UNDER TITLE VII

Chapter Contents

*Introduction
*Requirement Of Discrimination
  Based On Gender
*Bona Fide Occupational
  Qualification As A Defense In
  Sex Discrimination
*No-Spouse Rule
*Female Work Assignments
  Under Title VII
*Sexual Harassment: A Legal
  Definition
*Remedies In Sexual Harassment
  Cases
*Recommendations To Minimize
  Exposure To Sexual Harassment
  Litigation
*Summary And Conclusions

137

INTRODUCTION

One of the most difficult provisions of Title VII for some employers to accept is the requirement that persons of equal qualifications be given equal employment opportunities regardless of sex. The social norm that a woman's role is that of a housekeeper and child rearer is often the controlling factor. The norm permits the female to enter the labor market only from economic necessity or when men were not available. During World War II women were encouraged to enter the labor market as a contribution to the war effort. When G.I. Joe returned to the labor market after the war, "Rosey the Riveter" simply did not have the physical strength to do a man's job. This thinking that the woman's place is in the home and not in the work place was accepted in the courts as well as in social institutions. In the often quoted case of Muller v. State of Oregon,[1] Justice Bremer in the Supreme Court at p. 421 stated that "History disclosed the fact that woman has been dependent upon man. He established his control at the outset by superior physical strength and this control in various forms with diminishing intensity has continued to the present."

This stereotyped thinking among males was still in the Congress when Title VII was passed.

Congressman Howard Smith of Virginia, as opposition to the act, reasoned that if sex were included as an amendment to Title VII, it would not pass.[2] Although this maneuver failed, members of Congress expressed their skepticism about women in the work place by stating in Section 703(a)(e)(1) of Title VII that "where sex is a bona fide occupational qualification, reasonably necessary to the normal operation of the business, it would not be unlawful to discriminate on the basis of sex."

The enactment of Title VII did not suddenly change the patterns of sex discrimination that had been around for a hundred years. A start can be made by the law, but the remainder will have to be done by the courts, economics of operating a business or enterprise, and a change in the reluctance on the part of women to bring a lawsuit.

This chapter highlights some of the employment problems under Title VII that are particular to women in the work place and are not as common with the other protected classes. There are different problems for the employer in the administration of equal employment opportunity for a minority or for a Seventh Day Adventist than for a woman being harassed by a male. Sex discrimination in em-

---

[1] 208 U.S. 412 (1908).

[2] Vol. 110, Congressional Record, page 2577–84 (1964).

ployment benefits is treated in Chapter XIV and discrimination in payment of wages is covered in Chapter XIII. This chapter is restricted to sex discrimination in employment opportunities.

REQUIREMENT OF DISCRIMINATION BASED ON GENDER

In some early cases the only issue before the courts was whether women were treated differently than men and, if so, was there a bona fide occupational qualification (BFOQ) that justified a reason for such treatment. When a company refused to hire a woman with preschool children but hired men with preschool children, women were treated differently and the Supreme Court declared such a policy unlawful and remanded the matter to the lower court to determine whether a BFOQ existed.[3] What the court was really saying is that different treatment between males and females based solely on gender raises the issue of BFOQ. Different treatment also raises the question of the Due Process and Equal Protection Clauses of the Fifth and Fourteenth Amendments of the Constitution. Here BFOQ is not a defense for violation of these amendments.

The best example of whether the discrimination is gender-based is found in those cases where pregnancy disabilities payment are excluded from health insurance plans but payments included for men who became ill or disabled. In one situation the Supreme Court said that since men are not given disability for pregnancy, there is no benefit that men are given that women are not.[4] This case was decided under the Equal Protection Clause of the Fourteenth Amendment. The next question was, Would the same reasoning apply to a case under Title VII? Two years later the Court said that it did. The Court reasoned that there is no doubt that Congress did not intend to change the Constitution when Title VII was passed; in order to be in violation of Title VII, it must be gender based.[5]

The requirement that different treatment must be gender-based is still struggling its way through the courts, especially when the requirement seems to have socially undesirable results.

The Pregnancy Disability Act of 1978 was an amendment to Title VII and was passed to change legislatively the ruling in General Electric v. Gilbert, 429 U.S. 125 (1976). The act made it unlawful to

---

[3] Phillips v. Martin Marietta Corp., 400 U.S. 542 (1971).

[4] Geduldig v. Aiello, 417 U.S. 484 (1974).

[5] General Electric v. Gilbert, 429 U.S. 125 (1976).

deny benefits to females on account of pregnancy that males receive for other illnesses.[6] This has been interrupted to mean that a spouse of a male employee can not receive less benefits than a female employee.[7] The Court stated that the Pregnancy Discrimination Act not only overturned the holding in the Gilbert case, but rejected the reasoning of the Court in Gilbert that differential treatment of pregnancy is not gender-based discrimination because only women can become pregnant. The effect of the ruling in the Newport News case on paternity benefits, disability benefits for the spouse of male employees and other benefits granted to female employees due to pregnancy but denied to male employees will have to wait further judicial interpretation.

BONA FIDE OCCUPATIONAL QUALIFICATION AS A DEFENSE IN SEX DISCRIMINATION

Section 703(a)(e)(1) of Title VII specifically states that sex discrimination is lawful if BFOQ[8] can be shown. In race, religion, color, and national groups such an exception is conspicuously absent in the statute. Although the courts have allowed the BFOQ defense in cases concerning these protected classes. When BFOQ is used as a defense, the employer automatically admits sex discrimination under the terms of the statute.

EEOC guidelines construe the exception narrowly, and the courts have followed. Where an airline alleged that females were an essential BFOQ for flight attendants, the court said that "discrimination based on sex is valid only when the essence of the business operation would be undermined by not hiring members of one sex exclusively."[9] The Supreme Court in upholding a BFOQ for an Alabama statue that required minimum height and weight (which excluded 33 percent of the women and only 1 percent of the men) stated that the prison system warranted the exclusion of women. The court was careful to point out that the exception to individual capacity is "extremely narrow."[10]

From the cases decided since Dothard, it appears the BFOQ will be decided on a case-by-case basis and a narrow interpretation will be given. There are few guidelines for BFOQ except that if the employer

---

[6] This is considered in Chapter XIV.

[7] Newport News Shipbuilding & Dry Dock Co. v. EEOC 103 Sup, Ct. 2622 (1983)

[8] Abbreviation for Bona Fide Occupational Qualification. This is often used simultaneously with business necessity.

[9] Diaz v. Pan American World Airways, Inc., 442 F.2d 385 (5th Cir. 1971).

[10] Dothard v. Rawlinson, 433 U.S. 321 (1977). However, usually weight requirements are not considered a BFOQ as in Weeks v. Southern Bell Telephone and Telegraph Co., (5th Cir. 1969).

had reasonable factual basis to believe that substantially all women would be unable to perform safely and efficiently the assigned duties of the job, sex discrimination would be legal.[11] As in other discrimination situations, there is no substitute (if at all feasible) for giving the employee an opportunity to perform before using BFOQ as a defense. Job assignment based on sex cannot be defended except in rare cases such as safety or privacy consideration. Normally customer preference is not considered as BFOQ. When an employer stated that foreign customers are prejudiced against women, the court said that sex discrimination for sales persons is invalid as a matter of law.[12]

NO-SPOUSE RULE

The presence of the historical social norm that the work place is not for women makes it only appropriate that when women get married they should be encouraged to leave the labor market. Airlines for years had a no-marriage rule for stewardesses. The federal postal service in 1913 decided that married women should not hold classified position.[13] The Economy Act of 1932 (Section 213) stated that married women in the federal service would be retained only if they were more efficient than their husbands.[14]

Title VII declares a no-marriage rule unlawful when it does not apply to both sexes equally,[15] but it does allow the application of BFOQ as provided in Section 703(e). What this means to the struggling personnel practitioner is that if two employees get married, a rule could require that one must go but the rule could not state which one unless some basis were used other than sex. The rule also means that if one had a superior-subordinate relationship, BFOQ could be a defense on a showing that the spouse relationship interferred with the efficient operation of the business.

The leading decision pertaining to no-spouse rule was a case where there was a statistical evidence that because of a no-spouse rule, an adverse impact in hiring females resulted (73 female applicants were rejected compared to 3 males).[16] The court found that what most personnel practitioners know: problems between married

---

[11] Weeks v. Southern Bell Telephone Co., 408 F.2d 228 (5th Cir. 1969).

[12] Fernandez v. Wynn Oil Co., 653 F.2d 1275 (9th Cir. 1981).

[13] U.S. Civil Service Commission, *Women in the Federal Service*, 2d ed. (Washington, D.C.: Government Printing Office, 1938).

[14] Cited in Note 13.

[15] 42 U.S.C. Sect. 2000(d) et al.

[16] Yuhas v. Libbey Owen Ford Co., 562 F.2d 496 (7th Cir. 1977) cert denied.

employees lead to grief for employers, and BFOQ permits the rule. The court also said that married couples working together could cause emotional problems that would affect their work performance. If one spouse has a dispute with the employer or co-worker, the other spouse may become involved.

The Yuhas decision has been followed by other courts to the extent that if the no-spouse rule is administered properly, it is not sex discrimination although there may be an adverse impact. This rule applies to transfers as well as termination or refusal to hire. In one situation two teachers were married; without her consent the female was transferred to another school because her husband was made department head. The court said that marriage, not sex, caused the transfer and this was a BFOQ.[17]

The rule also applies when the unmarried employees are living together. The court said that the no-spouse rule was broad enough to apply to unmarried employees and it was immaterial that the state did not recognize common law marriages.[18] The fact that the plaintiff gave birth to a child out of wedlock may have influenced the decision, but based on subsequent decisions, this is doubtful. Some states included marriage as a protected class in their discrimination laws. If this is the case, it is possible that the no-spouse rule would be held to be sex discrimination.[19]

FEMALE WORK ASSIGNMENTS UNDER TITLE VII

It is a well-established principle in antidiscrimination law that one cannot determine categorically that all females are incapable of performing certain tasks. Where a female held a job for 10 years and was bumped by a male, the company argued that it had a policy of giving seniority only to certain job classifications of roustabouts and roughnecks. It was argued that the policy was neutral on its face, that no female was either a roughneck or roustabout; therefore under the policy the plaintiff could not retain her job and bumping by a less senior male was not sex discrimination. The court found that the plaintiff performed the same job as males so she must have been a roughneck or roustabout, and the plaintiff was improperly excluded from the seniority system.[20]

When considering qualifications for promotion under a labor agreement, labor relations practi-

---

[17] Meier v. Evansville Vanderburgh School Corp., 416 F.Supp. 748 (S.D. Ind. 1975).

[18] Espinoza v. Thomas, 580 F.2d 346 (8th Cir. 1978).

[19] This is the case in Minnesota where it was held that no-spouse rule violated the marital provision of the state discrimination law. Kraft Inc. v. State, 284 N.W.2d 386 (Minn. 1979).

[20] Danner v. Phillips Petroleum Co., 447 F.2d 159 (5th Cir. 1971).

tioners discovered early in their careers that unless the applicant is given an opportunity to perform, it is difficult to win in arbitration. In some cases legitimate reason can be shown for not giving the opportunity to perform other than subjective reasons such as safety or exposure to property damage; then the failure to give the opportunity would not be a damaging factor to the case.

In work assignments for females it is advisable to permit performance before rejection unless there is substantial, objective evidence why they cannot do the job or the safety of others would be jeopardized if permitted to perform. Courts that have considered the issue of female work assignments have held that employer cannot determine employment opportunities on the basis of physical capabilities and endur-ance of women as a group. Where it was required to lift heavy objects, the job could not be denied the employee because she was a female.[21]

In another heavy-lifting case the employer rejected a female because it was alleged that she did not have the physical ability to perform the job. The court said that the applicant must be given a reasonable opportunity to demonstrate her ability to perform the duties.[22] In the Long case the court also applied the same rule when a job was refused because of race. The employer who denies work assignments to females because of alleged limitations of females needs to be reminded of the song about Rosey the Riveter of the World War II era, who performed well but would not have been given the chance except for the war.

SEXUAL HARASSMENT: A LEGAL DEFINITION

Harassment at the work place is outlawed by Title VII when a member of the protected class is involved. The act does not have a specific provision prohibiting harassment as such, but the courts and EEOC have so interpreted the statute. Where a white employee resigned because of racial harassment by a black supervisor, it was actually constructive discharge ac-cording to the court. Treatment by the black supervisor amounted to harassment by the creation of intolerable conditions.[23]

A nationality harassment situation involved a supervisor who, in order to communicate a no-smoking rule to a single violator (who was German), posted a no-smoking sign in German. Harassment was admitted but employee

---

[21] Rosefeld v. Southern Pacific Co., 444 F.2d 1219 (9th Cir. 1971).

[22] Long v. Sapp, 502 F.2d 34 (5th Cir. 1974).

[23] Calcote v. Texas Educational Foundation, Inc., 578 F.2d 95 (5th Cir. 1978).

did not subsequently violate the no-smoking rule. (The relief requested was removal of the sign).

Most harassment situations involve sexual harassment. It is difficult to determine what came first in the work place: sexual relations or sexual harassment. Until recently management did not have to contend with the sexual relations between employees either within or outside the working relationship as long as they did not interfere with work performance or it did not occur on company time.[24] If management were aware of sexual advances, it would ignore them as a normal result of the attraction between the sexes and something that would be worked out between the parties involved. If in extreme cases correction were needed, the matter was handled on a confidential and individual basis. The typical manager reasoned (and many still do) that because of the personal nature of sexual harassment, dealing with it openly would sometimes create more problems than it would solve.

Another reason for management's reluctance is that sexual advances are often difficult to define. Acquiescence and encouragement are always possibilities. Female employees are frequently reluctant to bring the matter to the attention of the employer for fear of embarrassment or because

of uncertainty about what action, if any, management will take.

Types Of Sexual Harassment

In recent years several surveys have been made to determine whether sexual harassment in the work place is common. In general these surveys found that unwanted sexual harassment existed for more than 40 percent of the employees reporting; 1 to 2 percent reported being coerced into sexual relations, which is the most extreme form of sexual harassment. The 1 or 2 percent may not seem large but if the figures are accurate, based on the number of women employed, about 400,000 working women a year have unwanted sexual relations, which could be called employment rape.[25]

Based on these data the total absence of sexual harassment in any organization is a rarity. These surveys may not be entirely reliable because when they were taken there was no legal definition of sexual harassment. The courts have considered whether harassment existed on a case-by-case basis rather than applying a legal precedent to a factual situation.

A study of all the court decisions on sexual harassment does, however, permit categorization of certain factual situations to give some prognosis of what the courts will do. One of the early types of

---

[24] No-sexual-relations rules are almost unenforceable even when it takes place on company time as it is difficult to witness.

[25] "Sexual Harassment and Labor Relations: A BNA Special Report" *Labor Relations Reporter* 107, no. 23, July 20, 1981, p. 23 (Washington DC: Bureau of National Affairs).

sexual harassment is sexual favors being exchanged for employment opportunities. In order for this type of activity to be harassment under Title VII, it must be shown that job opportunities would be denied if sexual favors were refused.

At the outset the employee is made to understand by a superior than when sexual favors stop, so do job opportunities. Denial of employment opportunities short of discharge may be denial of promotions for which the employee is qualified; granting others leaves of absence but denying leaves for the person refusing sexual favors; less pleasant job assignments; lenient enforcement of rules in exchange for sexual favors, etc.[26]

The second type of sexual harassment has been referred to by the courts as environmental sexual harassment. This is where no job opportunities are involved, just unwanted attraction of one sex to another. The comments or innuendos of a sexual nature, physical contact, or other overt acts that convey a message that going further would be desirable but this is neither the time or the place: these fall in this category.

The acts about which the employees most commonly complain are comments, innuendos, and jokes of a sexual nature. This type of harassment is considered a violation by some courts because the employees contend that it interferes with work performance. This claim may appear ironic since in most other situations, the employer is the one who is most concerned with interference with work performance. Some courts ignore the issue of work performance completely and simply say that the employee deserves a better work environment.[27]

The work environment type of harassment can be caused by a co-worker or by a supervisor who cannot affect the job status of the victim or otherwise influence conditions of employment but could affect work performance. For example, the refusal of sexual favors or being the subject to unwelcome comments or jokes by co-workers would make some employees extremely nervous and thereby affect work performance. This should be distinguished from mere flirtation which is not harassment according to some court decisions.[28]

Sexual Harassment Under Case Law

The law in the area of sexual harassment is too new to guide the employer with any degree of certainty in every situation. The

---

[26] One of the common indications of sexual favors is the supervisor protecting the subordinate's unsatisfactory work performance or approving pay for time not worked.

[27] The interference with job performance has been extended to be an interference with any employment relationship, Kryriazi v. Western Electric Co., 461 F.Supp. 894 (D.N.J. 1978). Job performance interference that is required in other antidiscrimination situations must be more objective than in sexual harassment cases.

[28] Heelan v. Johns Mansville Corp., 451 F.Supp. 1382 (D. Colo. 1978).

Supreme Court has not defined the term, and the EEOC guidelines have not received judicial approval in all respects. Court decisions, however, have given the necessary elements to establish sexual harassment as a violation of Title VII. Two key characteristics are necessary:

1. The alleged conduct must be of a sexual nature where the accused favors one sex over the other.

2. The sexual conduct must be unwelcome; if tolerated, it is not considered harassment.

The existence of sexual harassment is often difficult to determine because consent is not known until after the act is committed. Any element of consent or acquiescence would cause the conduct to be considered a normal consequence of one sex being attracted to the other. Asking for sexual favors is not harassment or any other offense under the law; only at the time of refusal does harassment start.

Case law looks for two other elements besides acquiescence and favoring of one sex: Did the employer know or should the employer have known about the alleged conduct and did the conduct affect employment opportunities? In the leading case in the area of em-ployer knowledge, a worker subjected a female co-worker to verbal sexual advances, made sexually derogatory remarks and on one occasion physically grabbed her between the legs while she was bending over. The female complained to her supervisors, who did nothing to stop the unwelcome advances. In holding the company liable under the Minnesota Discrimination Law the court paid particular attention to the fact that the employee complained and the company took no action.[29]

Another element that the courts look for is a link between sexual favors or advances and employment opportunities. In this situation an offer of employment may be made in exchange for sexual favors. Obviously the superior-subordinate relationship is involved. Some courts require proof that direct employment consequences flow from refusal of sexual favors.[30]

Other courts like the D.C. Circuit Court of Appeals find that the sexual activity need not be linked to employment opportunities if notice is given to the employer. In this respect the federal court agrees with the Minnesota Supreme Court in the Continental Can case.[31]

From these cases cited, where there is no notice to the employer and no employment opportunities

---

[29] Continental Can Co. v. State of Minnesota, 297 N.W. 241 (Minn. Sup. Ct. 1980).

[30] Tomkins v. Public Service Electric & Gas Co., 568 F.2d 1044 (3rd Cir. 1977); Barnes v. Costle, 561 F.2d 983 (D.C. Cir. 1977); Garber v. Saxon Business Prod., Inc., 552 F.2d 1032 (4th Cir. 1977).

[31] Bundy v. Jackson, 641 F.2d 934 (D.C. Cir. 1981).

are involved, no sexual harassment exists. All courts that have considered the issue agree with this statement. This conclusion is reinforced by one situation where a supervisor kept an apartment for a female bank teller. The teller testified that she and the supervisor had sexual intercourse 40 or 50 times in a two-year period, often during working hours in the bank vault. Later the teller fell in love with another person and refused further contacts; no further advances were made by the supervisor. The teller subsequently resigned and filed a sexual harassment charge. The court held that no violation of Title VII had occurred since the employer did not have notice of any unwelcome advances and no employment opportunities were involved. It was merely a broken love affair.[32] This decision should not be interpreted to mean that such activity is proper during working hours. It may be a personnel problem but not a legal problem under Title VII.

EEOC Guidelines On Sexual Harassment

The EEOC guidelines on sexual harassment[33] differ from most EEOC guidelines in that they were issued long after the courts held that sexual harassment is a violation of Title VII. Several court decisions on sexual harassment were issued in 1977, and the EEOC guidelines were not issued until 1980. By this time the courts had already determined that where there was no notice, there was no violation, and where refusal effected employment opportunities, there was a violation even when there was no notice.

The guidelines state that the reason sexual harassment is unlawful is because Title VII prevents one sex from being favored over another; where a male favors a female and not other males, there is a violation. By the same principle a male could be sexually harassed by a female and the courts have so held. A male sexually harassing a male is unlawful because females are not given the same attention;[34] however, a bisexual can not be guilty of harassment because favors are shown to both sexes.

Using the same reasoning, a transsexual would not be protected by Title VII since it is yet to be determined medically which sex is being favored.[35] Where a transsexual was denied use of female restroom facilities, claiming to be a female at the time of applying for a job and the employer discharged for misrepresentation since the plaintiff was a male in employer's

---

[32] Vinson v. Taylor, 23 FEP cases 37 (D.C. D.C. 1980).

[33] 29 CFR Sect. 1604.11 (1980).

[34] Wright v. Methodist Youth Service, Inc., 511 F.Supp. 307 (N.D. Ill. 1981).

[35] A transsexual is described as an individual who is mentally of one sex but physically of another, 63 ALR3d 1199 (1975).

opinion, the court said discharge was not a violation of Title VII as the act not intended to cover transsexualism.[36]

The EEOC guidelines ignored the court decisions and imputed knowledge to the employer whenever the supervisor is involved. The commission applies the legal doctrine of respondeat superior (let the principle be held responsible). The EEOC defends its guidelines by reference to the decision in a case where the supervisor violated the management policy and the court imputed knowledge. This argument overlooks the fact that an important second element was involved, namely, that the supervisor could influence the employment status of the female employee and case law does not require management knowledge when employment opportunities are involved.[37]

The guidelines do follow court decisions where co-workers are involved. Both EEOC and the courts state that the employer must know or be in a position to have known of the harassment before liability exists. The guidelines further state that the employer can be held for actions of nonemployees in sexual harassment situations. No legal precedent for this position has been found, and the EEOC does not explain how this would be applied. By inference one can conclude that the employer's actions must have a relationship to the nonemployee's action. This was the situation where the employer discharged a receptionist, who after two days refused to wear a short, revealing, and sexually provocative uniform. The woman complained that the uniform caused unwelcomed sexual comments and gestures from passersby. The court said that the defendant caused the plaintiff to be subjected to sexual harassment by the public.[38]

The EEOC guidelines also deal with what might be called sexual harassment in reverse. In this type of case an employee climbs the corporate ladder, at the expense of other qualified persons, by giving sexual favors to the supervisor. The qualified employees passed over have a claim for sexual discrimination. One court that has considered this situation (Toscano v. Nimmo, 570 F. Supp. 1197 D.C. Del. 1983) has upheld EEOC guidelines stating that when a less qualified employee is promoted because of sexual favors, the more qualified employee not promoted was sexually harrassed when refused the promotion.

In general the EEOC guidelines seem to support a case-by-case approach. The agency has stated that it will look at the totality of the circumstances to determine violation. It might be safe to interpret this to mean that when a charge is made, the agency will consider what affirmative action the em-

---

[36] Sommers v. Budget Marketing, Inc., 667 F.2d 748 (8th Cir. 1982).

[37] Miller v. Bank of America, 600 F.2d 211 (9th Cir. 1979). In author's opinion the fact that supervisor referred to plaintiff as a "black chick" also influenced the court. Bad facts always made bad law.

[38] EEOC v. Sage Realty Corp., 507 F.Supp. 599 (S.D.N.Y. 1981).

ployer has taken to prevent or control harassment.

Situations Where Legal Issues Are Undecided

When neither notice nor employment opportunities are involved, what conduct constitutes sexual harassment? The law is unsettled. All the courts will say is that each case must be decided on the basis of all the facts and circumstances related to the alleged conduct.

As a hypothetical case, suppose a consental relationship exists between supervisor and subordinate and the relationship dissolves and the supervisor discharges the subordinate for poor performance or some other subjective reason. Few courts have considered this situation. The court might say that the employee has a duty to disclose at the first sign of adverse employment opportunities or threats; after the relationship ceases on the other hand it could be argued that refusal at any time is harassment provided denial of employment opportunities occurred.

In one case it was established that the supervisor and the subordinate were in love with each other. The sexual affair was broken off by the female because the supervisor would not marry her after she obtained a divorce. The New York Supreme Court ruled that this was a love affair, which sex discrimination laws were not intended to prohibit.[39]

Another common problem concerns substandard performance on the part of a sexually willing employee that is overlooked by the supervisor for 10 or 15 years in return for sexual favors. When further sexual activity is refused or the supervisor retires and the poor performance continues, the new supervisor terminates the employee for poor performance.

Neither the courts nor the EEOC have considered this problem. It could be argued that the existence of a sexual affair does not obligate the employer to permit poor performance. However, after 10 years of acquiescence to poor performance, proof is difficult. Substandard performance is a strong reason for termination and usually overrides all other reasons even when those reasons standing alone would be considered an unlawful termination. A court might hold that the employee must be given an opportunity to perform when sexual favors are not involved before termination for poor performance.

Normally a third party does not have a cause of action. In Blaw-Knox Foundry and Mill v. NLRB, 646 F. 2d. 113 (4th Cir., 1981) the Court stated that employee action in protecting a female cousin from a supervisor was not a protected activity. However, where a supervisor supported the employee's protest of sexual harassment and was discharged, the court held a protected activity, NLRB v. Downslopes Industries 676 F. 2d 1114 (6th Cir. 1981).

---

[39] Fletcher v. Greiner, 106 N.Y. Misc. 564 (1982).

REMEDIES IN SEXUAL HARASSMENT CASES

Where an employee voluntarily terminates because of sexual harassment[40] or is discharged after refusal of sexual favors, it would be logical to conclude that the remedy would be the same as other violations under Title VII. The remedy would be to make the employee whole by reinstatement and back pay plus attorney's fees. Attorney's fees sometimes exceed the amount of damages awarded to the plaintiff.[41]

Because sexual harassment often involves unwanted contact, a sexual assault charge could be brought under a state tort law or under the common law.[42] Tort actions allow consequential or punitive damages for sexual harassment, which may be the reason that harassment cases under tort law are increasing. The main exposure to damages in a sexual harassment lawsuit brought under the tort theory is that jury trial is available, which increases exposure to large awards. In one case the employee's action for sexual harassment under Title VII was dismissed, but under a state law in a claim of sexual assault the jury awarded $50,000, which was largely punitive damages.[43]

In the Clark case the court held off-color remarks, offensive touching, and rebuffed sexual advances not a violation because no employment retaliation was involved, but the jury held sexual assault as a tort was committed, for which damages could be awarded. Where there is environmental harassment and neither constructive discharge is involved nor any employment opportunities are denied, it is difficult under Title VII to provide a remedy except to cease and desist; thus plaintiff looks to other laws for a remedy. In one situation the court issued a restraining order to cease management-tolerated remarks of "did you get any over the week-end?"[44]

The actual extent of liability whether under Title VII or sexual assault will depend less on EEOC guidelines and previous court decisions and more on employer competency in dealing with sexual harassment problems. Courts conceivably would accept the defense of an affirmative action program to eliminate employer liability for sexual harassment. Affirmative action appears to be the best defense against claims by employees.

---

[40] This would be constructive discharge, which is discussed in Chapter XVI.

[41] In the Sage case, discussed on page 148 (Note 38), the plaintiff's back pay amounted to $33,000 and attorney's fees, $90,000.

[42] A tort is a violation of general duty that one person owes to another and is imposed by law. *Black's Dictionary of Law*, 5th ed. 1979.

[43] Clark v. World Airways, Inc., 24 FEP Cases 354 (BNA) (D.C.D.C. 1980).

[44] Morgan v. Hertz Corp., 27 FEP Cases 990 (BNA) (W.D. Tenn. 1981).

RECOMMENDATIONS TO MINIMIZE EXPOSURE TO SEXUAL HARASSMENT LITIGATION

In court decisions, when the employer has notice of sexual harassment and does nothing to correct the situation, the employer will be held liable. The courts will always ask, "What has the employer done to prevent or correct the wrongful employment practice?"[45] Where the employer develops procedures to prevent sexual harassment, at least two courts have found no liability even though it was determined that the conduct existed. In one case the employer was spared liability because the conduct was quickly investigated and management fairly adjudicated the complaint.[46] In the other situation female students alleged sexual harassment by male faculty members. The court of appeals was impressed by the university's procedure for dealing with the complaints, which was established between the time the case was filed in lower court and was argued before the circuit court. The case was dismissed even though the conduct was acknowledged to exist and plaintiff had a cause of action before the program was instituted.[47]

Sexual harassment suits need not result in liability if the employer is willing to admit the probability that such conduct will take place at the work site and is willing to institute a policy prohibiting it. Some employers have been reluctant to establish a policy because they feel that it will trigger a feeling among employees that they have been unjustly accused. If the employer determines that this is the case, it should be made clear to the employees that their private lives and their activities outside the work place are none of the company's business, as long as they do not interfere with work performance of the consenting employees or co-workers.[48] A harassment policy should contain the following elements:

1. The employer establishes and communicates to all levels of employees the policy against sexual harassment or any type of harassment.

2. One person with rapport with all levels of employees actively encourages complaints and assures employees that complaints will be kept in strict confidence.

---

[45] In Katz v. Dole 709 F.2d 251 (4th Cir. 1983) the Court held the federal agency liable for failure to do something about environmental harassment after employee complaints.

[46] Neidhardt v. D.H. Holmes Co., 624 F.2d 1097 (5th Cir. 1980).

[47] Alexander v. Yale University, 631 F.2d 178 (2nd Cir. 1980).

[48] Some employers may want to include the parking lot as the work place because sexual relations during lunch and work breaks can sometimes occur in the parking lot.

3. The employer investigates complaints quickly and takes appropriate action where harassment is found.

4. The employer exposes supervisors to sexual harassment case law and EEOC guidelines as well as clearly explains company enforcement procedures.

5. Rarely should corrective action be taken at the first incident as the person involved has no way of knowing that it is unwelcomed until told so.

Rather than having a formal policy, some organizations may want to post a notice such as Exhibit VIII-1, on the bulletin board.

EXHIBIT VIII-1

Date _____

HARASSMENT NOTICE

For many years the management of this Company has by policy and to the public, stated that it is an equal opportunity employer. All management employees have, without exception, been instructed to adhere strictly to this policy. There are, however, rare instances of harassment of minorities, nationalities, and females that distinguishes them as a class from other employees. Any type of discriminatory action or harassment of one employee against another because of race, age, religion, sex, or national origin that interferes with good working conditions is a violation of Company policy and employees responsible will be subject to disciplinary action. Our commitment as an equal opportunity employer applies to all employees and we intend to enforce it by investigating all known incidents or complaints of employees and that necessary disciplinary action where found to be in violation of Company policy. Employees who are subjected to harassment of any type are encouraged to report to management any violations of the above policy.

The notice refers to all types of harassment, not just sexual harassment. Unwelcome Polish or Swedish ethnic stories could be called environmental harassment in the same manner as sex jokes. EEOC guidelines for national origin prohibit harassment because of nationality.[49]

SUMMARY AND CONCLUSIONS

More certain law will emerge through the maze of court allegations and defenses now present in sex discrimination cases. The stereotyped thinking of male decision makers will be changed on a

---

[49] 29 CFR 1606.8

case-by-case basis. Interpretations of the law on sex discrimination in employment will be instrumental in redefining sexual roles in the work place. How well the employer accepts the role of women in the work place will be directly correlated with how soon it will happen and how livable the law will be.

In sexual harassment the contours of how the courts will treat such conduct have been established. In the period ahead there will be some smoothing of the rough edges but the problem is defined to the extent that the employer can solve it. Where no knowledge and no job opportunities are involved, there is no liability. Knowledge on the part of the employer is fatal when nothing is done about sexual harassment in the work place. What else is necessary for employer preventive procedures?

The employer's definition of sexual harassment in a policy statement should be the same as in the courts. If it is unwanted, it is harassment; if the employee does not complain to management, it is legally acceptable, sexual attraction that may even help rather than hinder work environment. Sexual harassment conduct is not any different from any other undesirable conduct with which the employer must cope in the work place. Enforcement of house rules is always a problem; prohibition of sexual harassment is just another rule that must be enforced.

Because sexual harassment is before the employers as a problem to be solved, an effective program of prevention is a must if liability is to be avoided. Employers that think that the problem will go away or will not become one of major consequences will realize their mistake only after they have paid large monetary sums in damages or have adverse public and employee reaction because of their failure to respond to employee harassment complaints.

CHAPTER IX

DEFENSIVE PROCEDURES TO PREVENT LITIGATION AND LIABILITY UNDER ANTIDISCRIMINATION LAWS

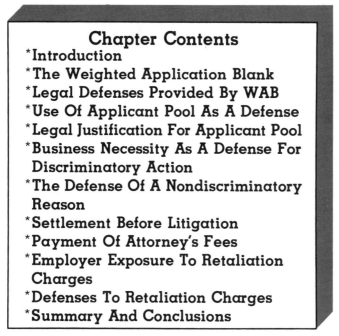

Chapter Contents
*Introduction
*The Weighted Application Blank
*Legal Defenses Provided By WAB
*Use Of Applicant Pool As A Defense
*Legal Justification For Applicant Pool
*Business Necessity As A Defense For Discriminatory Action
*The Defense Of A Nondiscriminatory Reason
*Settlement Before Litigation
*Payment Of Attorney's Fees
*Employer Exposure To Retaliation Charges
*Defenses To Retaliation Charges
*Summary And Conclusions

INTRODUCTION

The preceding chapters discussed the major personnel problems created by antidiscrimination laws in a somewhat negative fashion. After reading these chapters the reader could get the impression that antidiscrimination laws not only are costly but seriously interfere with the operation of an enterprise. This impression is contrary to congressional history of the antidiscrimination laws and their subsequent interpretations. The selection and promotion of the best-qualified persons is completely protected by Supreme Court interpretations of all antidiscrimination laws. The right to terminate an employee because of lack of qualifications or violation of rules has never been questioned by the courts. What the courts do say is that the reason for an employment decision should not be influenced by the fact that an employee is a member of a particular social class that is protected by the antidiscrimination statutes. This position is not any different from what good personnel practices have been advocating for three or more decades. Qualifications and ability to perform the job are the determining factors in any employment decision. The only change that the law has made is that qualifications must be objectively determined; often personnel professionals have practiced subjective methods.

The courts have further stated that any nondiscriminatory reason for making a decision is not in violation of antidiscrimination statutes. These basic principles of antidiscrimination laws are sometimes challenged by regulatory agencies and individuals who would like a more favorable interpretation of the law.

Under the legal system, a person cannot be stopped from challenging the law by filing a lawsuit. What the employer can do, however, is establish such policies and procedures that challenges through the legal process are discouraged. If the issue does go to court in spite of the discouraging efforts, the record should be in such shape as to allow a minimum amount of exposure to liability.

The personnel practitioner should be aware of those policies and procedures and defensive techniques available that, if adopted by the employer, will either prevent litigation or keep exposure to liability at a minimum if the dispute is tried in the courts. Preventive policies and procedures should be designed as to not interfere with the primary purpose of an enterprise of hiring and promoting the best-qualified persons available, as well as transferring or eliminating those employees who cannot meet all of the employer's legitimate job performance standards.

THE WEIGHTED APPLICATION BLANK

The federal, state, and city requirements of affirmative action regulations and antidiscrimination laws make it imperative that an organization adopt nondiscriminatory recruitment, selection, and promotion procedures that result in the best-qualified applicant filling the vacancy. By doing so the organization will avoid exposure to litigation. Although previous chapters discussed some defensive measures that must be taken to prevent litigation and liability, adoption of positive programs is necessary. The weighted application blank (WAB) is one of those programs. This is a technique that for many years was used to control turnover by the selection of job applicants according to defined personal history factors. WAB is more accurately defined as structured method for determining which characteristics and other variables found in a job applicant are important for success on certain specified jobs.[1]

The concept on which this method was developed is that certain quantitative and objective information is found in each applicant that will determine behavior for a particular job category. For many years employment managers and supervisors have subjectively determined that a certain type of person will or will not succeed in a certain job (for example, a supervisor who believed that all persons from Wisconsin were lazy). This was usually based on limited experience that employees who lived far away, had high wages on previous jobs, did not have a car, were divorced, either quit or were discharged from the previous job, were all job hoppers or were turnover employees. The WAB seeks to establish a profile by the use of statistical techniques and analysis that with some degree of accuracy predicts whether certain factors have any influence on job tenure.[2]

Exhibit IX-1 shows some of these factors. The data are taken from a sample of employees on the payroll for a period of three months or less and from another group of employees with one or more years of service. The purpose of this study using WAB was to control

---

[1] "Development and Use of Weighted Application Blanks," rev. ed, no. 55 (Minneapolis: University of Minnesota, Industrial Relations Center, 1971).

[2] Although there is not an absolute correlation between tenure and success on the job, for the purpose of WAB analysis, tenure of one or more years on the job is predictive of some degree of success based on the assumption that if an employee lasts one year or longer, performance has been rated as acceptable.

turnover in the unskilled and semiskilled job categories.[3]

The original list of factors was based on the opinions of the employment manager and over 30 supervisors on what characteristics determine the ideal employee. Of 16 original factors, only 9 were found to differentiate between active groups and terminee groups. This is illustrative of what regulatory agencies are referring to when they insist that a question on the application blank have a business purpose rather than reflecting subjective thinking of the employer. Exhibit IX-1 shows the ideal employee for the paper stock division. In Exhibit IX-2 the same factors were used for the container division employees, but the ideal employee has different distinguishing characteristics. Exhibit IX-2 shows why it is necessary to make WAB studies for each employee group.

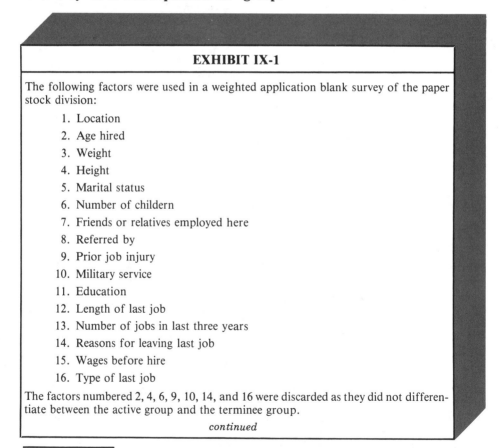

EXHIBIT IX-1

The following factors were used in a weighted application blank survey of the paper stock division:

1. Location
2. Age hired
3. Weight
4. Height
5. Marital status
6. Number of childern
7. Friends or relatives employed here
8. Referred by
9. Prior job injury
10. Military service
11. Education
12. Length of last job
13. Number of jobs in last three years
14. Reasons for leaving last job
15. Wages before hire
16. Type of last job

The factors numbered 2, 4, 6, 9, 10, 14, and 16 were discarded as they did not differentiate between the active group and the terminee group.

continued

[3] The WAB technique assumes that there is an opportunity to select from the labor market. In a tight labor market, as in some areas during the Korean War, the employer moved the employment office upstairs; if applicants could walk up the stairs, they were hired.

EXHIBIT IX-1

The ideal employee in the paper stock division had the following characteristics at the time of hire:

1. Is from local or labor market area of approximately 20 miles of plant site
2. Weighs between 151 and 170 pounds
3. Is married
4. Has friends or relatives who work here
5. Was a walk-in
6. Has education of 8 yrs or less or is a high school graduate
7. Last job was 12 to 23 months in duration
8. Had 1 to 2 jobs in the last 3 years
9. Wages before hire were less than or equal to employer's starting rate

A cutoff score of 11 or better was arrived at by using the greatest differentiation between the active group and the terminee group. This would mean that 72 percent of the actives would have been hired and 4 percent of the terminees would have been hired.

Source: **All exhibits relating to the WAB method are from personnel files of Hoerner Waldorf Corporation, St. Paul, Minnesota, 1969–1970.**

Exhibit IX-2 also shows the importance of cross-validation. The 48 percent hiring figure for terminees is only a little better than guessing; however, the 68 percent cross-validation figure for activees makes the study worthwhile for the control of turnover when the original data showed 80 percent accuracy in hiring; 78 percent (32 percent hired) of the terminees would have been eliminated if a cutting score of 7 were used in hiring.

EXHIBIT IX-2

The following factors were used in a weighted application blank survey of the container division:

1. Location
2. Age hired
3. Weight
4. Height
5. Marital status
6. Number of childern

continued

EXHIBIT IX-2

   7. Friends or relatives employed here

   8. Referred by

   9. Prior job injury

  10. Military service

  11. Education

  12. Length of last job

  13. Number of jobs in last 3 years

  14. Reasons for leaving last job

  15. Wages before hire

  16. Type of last job

The factors numbered 1, 3, 6, 9, and 13 were discarded as they did not differentiate between the active group and the terminee group.

The ideal employee in the container division had the following characteristics at the time of hire:

   1. Is 31 to 40 years old

   2. Height is 6'2" or more

   3. Is married

   4. Has friends or relatives who work here

   5. Was referred by a friend, relative, state agency, or came in on his own

   6. Has served in the military

   7. Has an education of 11 years or less

   8. Last job was for longer than 24 months

   9. Was laid off from his last job

  10. Wages were higher on the last job

  11. Was a semiskilled worker

A cutoff score of 7 or better was arrived at by using the greatest differentiation between the active group and the terminee group. This would mean that 80 percent of the actives would have been hired and 32 percent of the terminees would have been hired.

Using another group of 50 employees to cross-validate the results, the same cutoff score of 7 or better was arrived at by using the greatest differentation between the active group and the terminee group. In this group 68 percent of the actives would have been hired and 48 percent of the terminees would have been hired.

Exhibit IX-3 shows the work sheet to establish a hiring profile for the paper stock division. This calculation is the correlation of the personal histories with the tenure on the job. It is a mathematical formula that provides relative weighing of each significant independent characteristic. The characteristics are given a point value, and a cutting score is developed by drawing a line between the number that shows where the most terminees would be eliminated and the most actives would have hired.

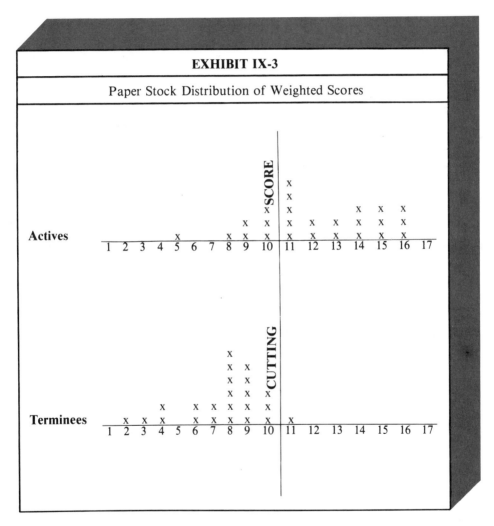

EXHIBIT IX-3

Paper Stock Distribution of Weighted Scores

Exhibit IX-4 shows in graphic form that for the paper stock division a cutting of 11 would be effective in eliminating hires who will be terminated within a year. In this study of actives and terminations, no data were compiled as to the reason for termination except that an applicant with certain (point value) characteristics of less than 11 would be more likely to be terminated than an applicant above 11.

The WAB is most effective in the factory and office semiskilled jobs. There is little or no use for the higher skilled jobs or managerial jobs because factors other than personal characteristics such as job assignment, supervision, training, and work experience would outweigh the personal characteristics used in WAB. Most personnel practitioners can develop the WAB to fit their needs with some research and a little training. More sophisticated WABs can be found in the literature, and study of this literature is advisable.[4]

The system described in this chapter is a simplified one that works; if a method works, it should be used without becoming too academic.[5]

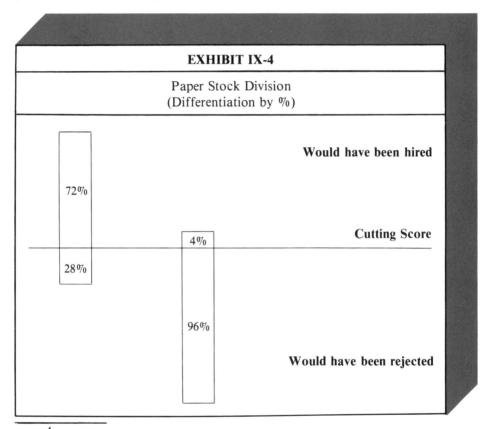

EXHIBIT IX-4

Paper Stock Division
(Differentiation by %)

72%

Would have been hired

4%

Cutting Score

28%

96%

Would have been rejected

[4] Daniel G. Lawrance, Barbara L. Salsbury, John G. Dawson, and Zachary D. Fasman, "Design and Use of Weighted Application Blank," *Personnel Administrator* 27, no. 3 (1982), 47: "Study in Predicting Voluntary Labor Turnover with Weighted Application Blank," *Marquette Business Review* 21, no. 1 (Spring 1977): 1. Study cited in Note 1.

[5] Sometimes your company's president goes to lunch with another company president who has a more sophisticated program and then on request you must get academic with a sophisticated program.

LEGAL DEFENSES PROVIDED BY WAB

The WAB replaces the possible subjective interviewer's biases which are often artificial barriers in the selection and promotion of the protected classes. It is certainly more defensible in showing nondiscriminatory reasons than the less objective measures used by many interviewers. Like any other selection device, it should first be determined whether the WAB has any adverse impact in the selection of protected classes; if so, then the method used to develop it should be tuned up to be sufficient for validation purposes. The experience of those who use WAB has been that there is no adverse impact provided that the characteristics used and sample comes from all classes of employees. If the present work force used as a sample has a statistical imbalance, then WAB would probably be challenged on perpetuating discrimination. The WAB also serves to establish reason for asking certain questions in the interview that have found to be predictive of tenure and success on the job. Affirmative action compliance officers and EEOC have consistently stated that there must be a legitimate purpose for asking questions in the interview. Questions to determine characteristics used to score the WAB would have a legitimate nondiscriminatory purpose.

The WAB should be used in the initial screening interview; if the applicant fails at this level, further interviews would not be necessary. This would eliminate the opportunity for supervisor and manager bias at the second level of the hiring process.

USE OF APPLICANT POOL AS A DEFENSE

After the use of WAB is established, the next step is to make sure that the qualifications for the job are determined by job analysis from current job descriptions. What has caused these techniques to be subject to judicial suspicion is that many times they are developed for ad hoc purposes, as a method to justify the wage and salary or promotion decisions. An audit of the job analysis and job descriptions often discloses that any resemblance between what the employee is doing and what the job analysis or job description says is purely coincidental. Often job descriptions are valuable for exhibits in EEOC hearings or disputes under the Fair Labor Standards Act; however, they can be damaging when they are not kept up to date or are developed to get an employee a raise or to upgrade the job content on paper. Actual observance of job content for purposes of job analysis and job descriptions is necessary if they are to be used as a basis for employment decisions. When the job analysis and job descriptions are developed by objective methods, the employer is then in a position to establish an applicant pool of qualified candidates.[6]

The applicant pool is a technique by which the employment manager has made an attempt to have available qualified candidates to fill future vacancies. It is developed by predicting job vacancies in the next six-month period (or whatever period is appropriate) in certain job categories. After determining the need or size of the pool, the employment manager immediately recruits and selects the best-qualified applicants for that job category. When all candidates are selected for the anticipated vacancies, recruiting and selection would stop until job offers were made to those placed in the applicant pool.

In selecting candidates for the applicant pool, those selected would be told that when a vacancy occurs they will be hired; if they are not available when a vacancy occurs, other candidates in the pool will be selected according to the order in which they were accepted in the pool.[7]

Elimination Of Pitfalls In The Selection By Applicant Pool

Often the employment manager or supervisor establishes certain criteria for selection. When applicants do not meet those standards and the employment manager can feel the heat on the telephone from the anxious supervisor who placed the urgent requisition, the most expeditious thing to do is to drop or modify the hiring standards in order to fill the vacancy. A less-qualified white male is hired; however, the applicant rejected three weeks before happens to be a neighbor of the less-qualified applicant accepted. Since she was pregnant, black female who had a wooden leg from Vietnam War, a discrimination charge is filed. Such a charge is difficult to defend, if better qualifications can be shown by the first applicant. A case history may illustrate this point.

---

[6] Job analysis and job descriptions should be developed by persons who are not supervisors or members of the personnel staff. In the author's experience, industrial engineers or outside consultants are persons most likely to develop unbiased job analyses and job descriptions.

[7] The practice of telling applicants that their application blank will be kept on file and if a vacancy occurs they will be called for an interview, is troublesome as all too often they are not called and a less-qualified person is hired through normal recruiting sources.

THE CASE OF THE BLUE-EYED BLOND

The department head requested a secretary. The labor market for secretaries is extremely tight. A month goes by and the department head by this time has completely discredited the personnel department to the chief executive officer for failure to fill the vacancy. The CEO calls in the personnel director, who relieves the pressure by agreeing to recruit a secretary personally as the employment manager was unable to do so and if anybody is to be accountable it should be the personnel director. Another two weeks pass, and top management continued to apply the pressure. A beautiful blue-eyed blond, physically well proportioned applies for the job. The personnel director interviews her and gives her a typing test. She can neither type nor spell the position for which she is applying. The department head immediately accepts her. The personnel director, from professional pride, tells the department head that she can neither type nor take shorthand and has about a eighth-grade spelling level. The department head answers, "She can learn, she can learn." This kind of crisis selection can be avoided by an applicant pool.

LEGAL JUSTIFICATION FOR APPLICANT POOL

One of the common criticisms of affirmative action programs by compliance agencies is that a good faith effort is not made to correct underutilized job categories. In order to comply with these demands many marginal applicants must be hired; when they do not perform, the justification for termination is also challenged. This pitfall can be avoided by the applicant pool. The courts often require quotas to correct discriminatory practices. An offer of a job that is refused is the same as a hire to satisfy quota requirements.[8] This concept is reinforced by the Supreme Court, where it held that a job offer after discriminatory refusal to hire stops liability even

---

[8] A remedy for a statistical imbalance caused by discriminatory practices is to require the employer to hire a certain percentage of the protected class discriminated against. The employer therefore must take the best-qualified within those classes to comply with court order. Contractor's Association of Eastern Pa. v. Secy. of Labor, 442 F.2d 159 (3rd Cir. 1971).

though retroactive seniority of six years was not included in the job offer.[9] In view of the rule in the courts that a job offer is the same as a hire, one criticism of the applicant pool is eliminated, i.e., that once placed in the pool the best-qualified will not be available when the vacancy occurs and the underutilized category is not filled. Whether the vacancy is filled or not, as long as the offer is made, the good faith effort has been made to correct the underutilization under the court rule.

The applicant pool gives almost zero exposure to affirmative action problems and still allows the employer to hire the best-qualified applicant. The applicant pool must be properly structured to include qualified persons of all classes. Where the employer established an applicant pool that had a height requirement that excluded more women than men, the court held that although some women were not discriminated against, others were by the requirement.[10]

Where an employer had a labor pool that had a majority of whites and of 234 clerical staff hires only 7 whites were hired, the court held discrimination against whites.[11] The establishment of an applicant pool of whites does not protect the employer unless selection is made from that pool. In the Craig case the applicant pool was properly structured with whites but there was an adverse impact in selecting only blacks from the pool.

The Supreme Court in Regents of University of California v. Bakke alluded to the acceptance of the pool concept.[12] Justice Powell's appendix to his opinion described the Harvard University concept of admissions pools. At Harvard applications for admission exceed the openings available in the freshman class. A qualified group is selected for the pool and from that group admissions are based on a number of criteria, none of which is not solely dependent on race but could be associated with it. No quotas are used; however, attention is paid to distribution among many types and categories of students. The Harvard concept described by the court seems to give a indirect approval to the applicant pool. Those employers interested in establishing an applicant pool are advised to study the appendix opinion of J. Powell in Regents of University of California v. Bakke.

---

[9] Ford Motor Co. v. EEOC, 102 Sup.Ct. 3057 (1982).

[10] Costa v. Markey, 677 F.2d 1582 (1st Cir. 1982).

[11] Craig v. Alabama State University, 451 F.Supp. 1207 (Ala., 1978).

[12] 438 U.S. 265 at 321 (1978).

BUSINESS NECESSITY AS A DEFENSE FOR DISCRIMINATORY ACTION

Business necessity is a term that originated with the Supreme Court.[13] In the Griggs case the Court stated that business necessity is justification for a policy that discriminates against a member of a protected class. Although originated under Title VII the term has also been applied to age discrimination statutes[14] as well as other antidiscrimination statutes. Business necessity has been defined as "that which is reasonably necessary to the safe and efficient operation of the business."[15] Business necessity has not been as useful as a defense to the employers as it might appear because of the narrow interpretation by the courts of what is efficient (or normal) and safe operation of the business.

The courts have held that business necessity cannot be used as a defense unless there is a showing of no other acceptable alternative that will serve the employer equally well and has a lesser impact on members of protected groups.[16] With a defense of business necessity, the employer admits discrimination, but argues that there is a reason for it.

Similarity Between Business Necessity And Bona Fide Occupational Qualification

Bona fide occupational qualification differs from business necessity in that it is defined by 703(e) of Title VII and originally referred only to sex. Section 703(e) states that sex discrimination is valid in certain circumstances where sex is "a bona fide occupational qualification reasonably necessary to meet the normal operation of that particular business or enterprise."

The application of Section 703 (e), discussed in Chapter VII, is mentioned here only to show the similarity with business necessity. In sex discrimination cases business necessity is often used where there is a disparate impact on a

---

[13] Griggs v. Duke Power, 401 U.S. 424 (1971).

[14] Hodgson v. Greyhound Lines, Inc., 499 F.2d 859 (7th Cir. 1974) cert denied, 419 U.S. 1122 (1975).

[15] This was first defined in Robinson v. Lorillard Corp., 444 F.2d 791, at 798 (4th Cir. 1971), cert denied, 404 U.S. 950. However, in the Hodgson case the court substituted "normal" for efficient.

[16] Robinson v. Lorillard Corp. (cited in Note 15). Also Wallace v. Debron Corp., 494 F.2d 674 (8th Cir. 1974).

group of employees; BFOQ is used where there is a disparate treatment on an individual.[17] As a practical matter there is very little difference between the two and often they are interchanged when used as a defense for discrimination in an employment decision.

BUSINESS NECESSITY AS A DEFENSE FOR DISCRIMINATORY ACTION

The courts usually reject the employer's perception of business necessity when it is not supported by objective data that show a particular job requirement necessary for the efficient operation of the business. The courts demand evidence that the traditional qualifications used by an employer are necessary to the safe and efficient performance of the job.[18]

When asserting business necessity as a defense, the employer has the burden to show that the discriminatory action was necessary for the safe and efficient operation of the business. In the deLaurier case the school board was able to show that teachers in the ninth month of pregnancy were not physically able to carry out teaching duties or administrative requirements of the job.

The employer often fails to sustain this burden because of subjective beliefs of what is necessary for the safe and efficient operation of the business. Where there was no evidence except the employer's statement that black employees could not safely and efficiently perform work in other job categories, a bar of a transfer to those jobs could not be justified as a business necessity.[19]

In the Chesapeake case, if the employer's statement had been supported by acceptable evidence that the employees were tried on the job and their performance was not unsatisfactory or was unsafe for "the following reasons," the result would have been different.

Where others' safety is involved, the courts have readily applied the business necessity defense. Greyhound Lines had a policy of limiting driver applications to persons under age 35, as statistics showed that its safest drivers were between the ages of 50 and 55 and had 16 to 20 years' experience. This policy "on its face" discriminated because of age but was held to be necessary for the safety of others.[20]

Where a county civil service commission assigned a black to

---

[17] This distinction was stated by the court in Dothard v. Rawlinson, 433 U.S. 321 (1977).

[18] deLaurier v. San Diego Unified School District, 588 F.2d 674 (9th Cir. 1978).

[19] United States v. Chesapeake & Ohio Ry. Co., 471 F.2d 582 (4th Cir. 1972).

[20] Hodgson v. Greyhound Lines, Inc., Note 14. The same result in Usery v. Tamiami Trail Tours, Inc., 531 F.2d 224 (5th Cir. 1976), where hiring age of 40 was upheld.

minority recruiting because the commission thought that it would develop rapport with members of minority groups whom the commission was trying to recruit, the court held that Title VII does not authorize race to be used as a business necessity.[21]

Business necessity is applied on a case-by-case basis. Whether a particular discriminatory action can be justified depends on how well the employer objectively justifies that the action was necessary for the safe and efficient operation of the business.

THE DEFENSE OF A NONDISCRIMINATORY REASON

In Chapter III, page 50, when describing a prima facie case it was stated that under court decisions a statistical imbalance will establish a prima facie case. If a facility or job category within that facility has no minorities or females employed, a statistical imbalance exists; the employer then has to show a nondiscriminatory reason for not employing or promoting members of the protected groups. For example, plant A has no minorities; on investigation it was found that recruiting was broadly based, but few minorities applied for job vacancies and there were few minorities unemployed in the labor market area. With these facts the absence of minorities could be justified.

In many situations the facts do not justify a statistically imbalanced work force and the employers must seek other defenses to justify their hiring policies. The question of what defenses are acceptable has been

before the Supreme Court several times. In the first case, the employer had to defend what appeared to be a discriminatory action of refusing to hire three black bricklayers who were fully qualified. The employer justified the action on the basis that the firm hired only bricklayers known to be experienced and competent or recommended by others as skilled workers (this was temporary work force). Evidence showed that the firm did hire black bricklayers by this method; 13 percent of the jobs in question were performed by blacks and the remainder by whites. The Supreme Court held that the employer had only to give a legitimate reason for not hiring the blacks, which was the selection method used for all applicants; further, there is no obligation that the hiring procedure maximize the hiring of minorities.[22]

The second case involved a female college professor who had been denied promotion while

---

[21] Knight v. Nassau County Civil Service Commission 649 F.2d 157 (2nd Cir. 1981).

[22] Furnco Construction Corp. v. Waters, 438 U.S. 567 (1978).

similarly qualified males were promoted. She produced statistics to show that a higher proportion of males were promoted than females. The court said the employer must give only a legitimate non-discriminatory reason for its action; there is no requirement that the employer must prove an absence of discriminatory motive to rebut a prima facie case.[23]

In 1981 the Supreme Court provided the employer with a stronger defense for alleged discriminatory action where statistics indicated that discrimination had been practiced. In this situation a female alleged that she was discharged on the basis of her sex and replaced by a male. The issue before the Court was the kind of proof necessary to show that such action was not discriminatory. The lower court held that the employer must prove by objective evidence that males hired were better qualified than the female discharged. The Supreme Court outlined three stages of proof for discriminatory action: (1) the prima facie case that the plaintiff must establish; (2) the employer's articulation of the non-discriminatory reason for its action; and (3) the employee's rebuttal that the reason was only a pretext for the employer's discriminatory action. It then becomes a factual question that the trial court must decide. The court said that only a non-discriminatory reason had to be given and there is no burden of persuasion on the employer that its action was not discriminatory. The important point in this decision is that the court said that the employer is not required to prove that a person hired or promoted is more qualified than the plaintiff, as long as legitimate reasons for the decision are stated; then it is question of fact whether those reasons are discriminatory.[24]

The courts have subsequently enlarged on this concept. In Perry v. Johnson Products, 698 F.2d 1138 (1st Cir. 1983) the Court stated that rebuttal of prima facie case may be "exceedingly light" and the plaintiff must show by direct evidence discrimination.

The employer has sufficient defenses other than business necessity to show that discrimination was not involved in the employment decision. Other factors such as hiring methods or other personnel procedures may rebut the employee's claim of discrimination.

SETTLEMENT BEFORE LITIGATION

When an employer is faced with a lawsuit over alleged discriminatory practices, settlement is always a consideration. If the EEOC, state, or city regulatory agency is involved, settlement will

---

[23] Board of Trustees of Kenne State College v. Sweeney, 439 U.S. 25 (1978).

[24] Texas Department of Community Affairs v. Burdine, 101 Sup.Ct. 1089 (1981).

be encouraged, often before the preliminary investigation is made. Sometimes the first proposed settlement terms by the agency or charging party is reinstatement with back pay. This is capitulation rather than compromise. This is usually a base from which the parties negotiate. How much negotiation room exists depends on what the charging party will take or what the regulatory agency will accept. In rare cases the agency will not accept terms, even though the charging party will.

Before agreeing to settlement, the employer must consider the economic consequences of pursuing the case in the courts as well as employee relations consequences. The considerations discussed in Chapter VII (Mary Hogan case) would apply to any other settlement situation. However, it is appropriate at this point to discuss provisions of settlement agreements.

Essential Elements Of Settlement Agreements

When the employer is presented with a settlement agreement, the provisions should be reviewed to determine whether it contains necessary protective clauses to effectuate a settlement. The essential parts of a settlement agreement are:

1. The charging party must waive the right to sue as an individual and further waive the right to participate in any

class action involving the same charge.

2. If a regulatory agency is involved, that agency should waive the right to sue.

3. That the relief granted to the charging party settles all claims should be clearly spelled out with a provision that the terms are to be kept confidential by the charging party.

4. Specific statements should be made in the agreement that there is no admission of a violation nor has any determination been made that a party's violation exists.

5. Payment of charging party's attorneys should be specifically denied or otherwise disposed of. A settlement agreement does not prevent the charging party from collecting attorney fees.[25]

In return for these provisions, the regulatory agency will ask for certain provisions and the employer should determine whether these provisions will prevent the economical and efficient operation of the enterprise. Some of the provisions to be carefully considered are:

1. If affirmative action to correct practices is requested, does compliance substantially change hiring or promotions standards?

---

[25] Miller v. Staats 706 F.2d 336 (DC Cir. 1983).

2. Does the agreement require the employer to go beyond what the law requires (regulatory agencies will sometimes require the employer to accept provisions of their guidelines or interpretations that have not been judicially approved)?

3. Although prohibition of retaliation for bringing the charge is an acceptable clause, as that is required by law, the language should not prevent the employer from treating the charging party any differently than other employees.

Progress-reporting requirements for compliance with the agreement should not be administratively burdensome. One or two progress reports over a short period is usually all that is necessary. Unreasonable provisions can be prevented by hard negotiations; usually the agency and plaintiff will agree rather than not settle when there is disagreement over these provisions. It is the remedy such as reinstatement that often prevents settlement.

PAYMENT OF ATTORNEY'S FEES

One of the economic considerations in the decision on whether to settle or litigate is the payment of attorney's fees. In discrimination suits attorney's fees are usually awarded to the plaintiff if the prevailing party. The prevailing defendant is only awarded attorney's fees if plaintiff's action is frivolous, unreasonable or without merit. The Supreme Court has held that in order to award the defendant attorney's fees the defendant must show that no reasonable belief existed by plaintiff that discrimination occurred.[26]

The reasoning of the courts in requiring a different standard for payment of attorney's fees to plaintiff than to the defendant is that where plaintiff prevails, the law has been violated, but where defendant prevails, it is only bad faith by the plaintiff in filing the lawsuit.

Often attorney's fees exceed the amount of liability in making the employee whole; therefore, it is an important cost consideration when determining whether to settle. On the other hand filing a counterclaim for attorney's fees could have a chilling effect on the plaintiff's position to pursue the case as exposure to paying the defendant's attorney's fees is far greater for an individual than for an employer. For this reason it is advisable to give serious consideration to filing a counterclaim for at-

---

[26] Christiansburg Garment v. EEOC, 434 U.S. 412 (1978).

torney's fees in these situations where there is an apparent unreasonable or meritless complaint. A claim for attorney's fees can also be filed against the EEOC, which would have a sobering affect on some of the overly zealous district or regional officers who believe that all employers are guilty of discrimination and their mission in life is to save the poor struggling employee from this discriminating employer. The court in a Michigan case stated:

> Here the charging party cries discrimination and the EEOC, despite an utter lack of evidence, sympathetically files suit, hoping that defendant will surrender rather than go to trial. When, as here, defendant refuses to knuckle under, EEOC goes to a lengthy trial, tries the case poorly, loses, and hopes a lesson has been taught. A better case for an award of attorneys' fees could not be made.[27]

EMPLOYER EXPOSURE TO RETALIATION CHARGES

In every statute that grants certain rights to employees, a provision prohibits the employer to retaliate against any employee who attempts to aid in the enforcement of the statute. The legislative purpose of such a provision is that Congress recognizes that unless the employee is encouraged to report the violation of these statutes, enforcement is difficult; therefore, the employee should be protected.

Because most retaliation charges are brought under Title VII, we will consider case law under that statute. The same principle would apply for a violation of retaliation provisions in the Fair Labor Standards Act, National Labor Relations Act, Age Discrimination in Employment, or Occupational Safety and Health Act.

Situations Where Retaliation Is Alleged

Retaliation is defined as an unlawful employment practice of an employer whereby the employer discriminated against the employee for participating in the enforcement of a statute. These cases usually arise in discipline and discharge cases. They are also common in sexual harassment situations where the employee complains of sexual harassment to management and the supervisor retaliates by denial of job opportunities. In retaliation charges the employee has only to have a belief of being discriminated against to bring a retaliation charge.[28] Under the same reasoning some courts hold that a retaliation charge can be maintained even though the

---

[27] EEOC v. Union Camp Corp., 536 F.Supp. 64, at 66 (W.D. Mich. 1982).

[28] Payne v. McLemores Wholesale and Retail Stores, 654 F.2d 1130 (5th Cir. 1981).

original charges on which the retaliation was based were false and malicious.[29]

When a settlement is made for a large sum of money and the employee is reinstated, any reprimand, disciplinary action, or adverse employment situation may bring a retaliation charge. Such a charge is usually vigorously pursued by regulatory agencies and attorneys because of an alleged unethical conduct involved of discriminating against a person who exercises a right under the law. For this reason the burden of proof for the employer is greater than in other discrimination charges. When defending retaliation charges before an agency or court, the author often had the feeling that the employer was thought to be partially guilty by the fact that a retaliation charge was filed.

DEFENSES TO RETALIATION CHARGES

Not every employer's action against an employee can be considered retaliation for the enforcement of a statute. Where a female doctor engaged in cancer research filed a salary discrimination charge with the state commission alleging that she was paid less than a male scientist, the employer settled for $20,000. She continued after the settlement to investigate other discriminatory practices of the employer on behalf of other employees; the employee was discharged because of a disruptive influence and liability threats toward the institution. The court held no retaliation as the employer is entitled to loyalty and cooperativeness from its employees.[30]

The retaliation on the part of employer must be intentional, showing that the employer treated the plaintiff differently than the firm would have treated other employees under similar circumstances.[31] The most important elements in the defense of retaliation cases is that the discipline or employment decision is applied to all employees when the situation is the same. The mistake that employers often make is either to treat a person who has filed a charge more leniently (the Mary Hogan situation, which backfired) or more strictly; then retaliation charges are filed. Either policy is troublesome in retaliation charges. The more lenient policy reaches the point of no return; when enforcement takes place, retaliation is alleged. The overly strict policy will cause almost indefensible retaliation charges.

The establishment of proper

---

[29] Pettway v. American Case Iron Pipe Co., 411 F.2d 998 (5th Cir. 1969).

[30] Hochstadt v. Worcester Foundation for Experimental Biology, 545 F.2d 222 (1st Cir. 1976).

[31] Monteiro v. Poole Silver Co., 615 F.2d 4 (1st Cir. 1980).

procedures for discharge as discussed under wrongful discharges in Chapter XVI and the employee complaint procedure as discussed in Chapter X are the best defenses to retaliation charges. All that is necessary for a defense under the Supreme Court decisions of Furnco[32] and Burdine[33] is to be able to establish a nondiscriminatory reason. The employer does not have to prove the absence of retaliatory motive. If the employer's discipline, grievance, and discharge procedures are uniformly applied, no violation of statutory retaliation provision will be found.[34]

SUMMARY AND CONCLUSIONS

The antidiscrimination laws and their interpretation do not restrain the employer from running the enterprise in what is believed the most economical and proper method. Those employers who permit antidiscrimination regulations to disrupt their operations by playing dead and comply with whims or desires of employees or regulatory agency have not taken advantage of the defenses granted to them by the courts.

To insulate the operation from costly litigation and interruption of the operation by antidiscrimination laws, it is necessary to adopt some preventive policies and procedures. These policies and procedures are not contrary to but supplement good personnel practices and in some cases change those personnel practices that have not been effective.

If the successful personnel practitioner treats employees as individuals, antidiscrimination laws will not interfere. It is not what females, minorities, or older persons as groups cannot do, but what are the qualifications of the individual worker or applicant involved in the employment decision. Antidiscrimination laws do not interfere with employment of a qualified person; they do eliminate subjective employment decisions and force employers to justify their decisions on criteria that reflect job requirements. This mandate from antidiscrimination laws enhances business growth and profits. Those employers who have experienced otherwise have refused to challenge regulatory agencies or employees when an attempt is made to force decisions on them that are not in the best interests of the business or they refuse to make legitimate business changes in policy or procedures to eliminate exposure to litigation.

---

[32] Furnco cited in Note 22.

[33] Burdine cited in Note 24.

[34] See EECO *Compliance Manual*, Sect. 1.89, Part III.

CHAPTER X

RIGHTS OF NONUNION EMPLOYEES UNDER THE NATIONAL LABOR RELATIONS ACT

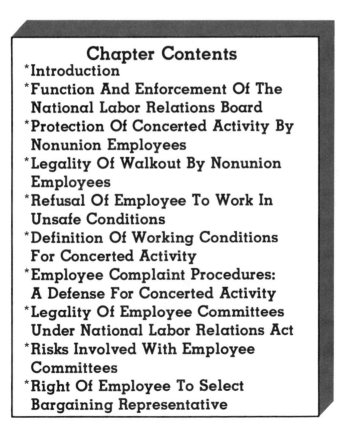

Chapter Contents

> **Chapter Contents (continued)**
> *Procedures In Selection Of A
> Bargaining Representative
> *Supervisor Conduct In Support Of
> Union Activity
> *Summary And Conclusions

INTRODUCTION

This book discusses employee rights granted to them by the various statutes. Previous chapters covered those obligations under antidiscrimination statutes. Restriction on the payment of wages is another employee right, covered in subsequent chapters. Some employers are unaware that nonunion employees have the same rights as union employees under the National Labor Relations Act.[1] This lack of knowledge of the rights of a nonunion employee sometimes extends to attorneys who only rarely deal in labor law. The law is clear that the employee does not have to be a member of a union, a certified union does not have to be involved, nor does there have to be an organizing drive in existence for the employee to have protection under the National Labor Relations Act.[2] Section 7 of the act guarantees all employees the right "to engage in concerted activities for the purpose of collective bargaining or for other mutual aid or protection." Section 7 refers "to all employees." If the employee chooses to act through a bargaining representative (com-

monly called a union), the right to do so is also protected by the act, or employees can represent their own interests by collective action.

Section 8(a)(1) of the act prevents the employer from interfering with these protected rights by making it an unfair labor practice to "interfere with, restrain or coerce employees in the exercise of the rights guaranteed in Section 7." If the employer violates the act, the National Labor Relations Board (NLRB) can take remedial action to make the employees affected whole or can order the employer to cease and desist from the unfair labor practice.

This chapter reviews the case law that grants nonunion employees certain rights under the act and will state what the employer can do to recognize nonunion employees' rights the same as they would in a union setting. Because the nonunion employee has the right to union representation, the complex subject of employer interference in employee's right to organize is also discussed.

---

[1] 29 USC Sect. 151 et seq.

[2] When the act is referred to in this book, it includes its major amendments, which are sometimes known as the Taft-Hartley Act of 1947 and Landrum-Griffin Act of 1959.

FUNCTION AND ENFORCEMENT OF THE NATIONAL LABOR RELATIONS BOARD

The NLRB is the administering agency of the National Labor Relations Act. It has two main functions: the determination of appropriate collective bargaining representatives for employees and the deciding of unfair labor practice charges and, if found, providing a remedy.

If an employee or its representative feels that an unfair labor practice has been committed, a charge may be filed with the board. The charge is then investigated. If substance to the unfair labor practice charge is found, an informal settlement is attempted. If settlement fails, a formal complaint is filed as in any other legal proceeding. A hearing is then held before an administrative law judge, who gives a finding of facts, conclusions of law, and a recommendation order to the board. Either party can contest this recommendation and ask the board for discretionary review of the judges recommendations. The board may grant the review or follow the recommendation of the administrative law judge. The board has no enforcement power of its orders as its function is only to interpret the law.

If either party does not agree with the order, they do nothing and the board then must go to the circuit court of appeals for enforcement of the order. The board order is argued as to whether it is proper under the law. The court either enforces or denies enforcement of the order. Appeal from the circuit court decision goes to the U.S. Supreme Court, which decides like any other appeal whether to hear it or let the decision stand and become law of the circuit. The board does not publish guidelines or interpretative opinions like other agencies. Board law is decided on a case-by-case basis. (It does, however, issue procedural rules and regulations for the conduct of hearings.)

This chapter and the next cite several cases that will be board orders with which the employer complied without appeal. This will be cited as *Volume number NLRB No. ____.* (In board cases only one party is involved.) Where the employer refuses to comply with board orders and the board is forced to seek enforcement in the circuit court of appeals, it will be cited as any other circuit court case.

PROTECTION OF CONCERTED ACTIVITY BY NONUNION EMPLOYEE

Board statistics show that there is a continual increase of cases where nonunion employees are contesting the employer's denial of their right of concerted activity. This concerted activity is common in wage demands, safety matters, working conditions, and employee walkouts over failure to settle employee dissatisfactions. The nonunion employer that does not recognize employee's rights to engage in concerted activity exposes the organization to violating the law and the obligation to compensate the affected employees for whatever statutory wrong was committed.[3]

The board does not define concerted activity, but case law indicates that two conditions must exist before concerted activity is protected by the act. One, the activity must be for mutual aid or protection for a group of employees. Two, employee activity must involve wages, hours, or other conditions of employment defined in the act.

The leading case for concerted activity is where a group of nonunion employees left their jobs over the cold working conditions in the plant. The walkout took place after repeated complaints about the lack of heat at the work site. The employees were discharged for walking out and stopping production. The board held that their discharge violated Section 8(a)(1) of the act and ordered reinstatement with back pay because the employees were engaged in a protected activity to improve working conditions. On appeal the Supreme Court held that the board's action was proper because the employer interfered with concerted activity as guaranteed by Section 7 of the act and the employees' request was neither unlawful nor indefensible.[4]

Usually concerted activity involves two or more employees; however, it is possible that only one employee can be engaged in concerted activity. Where an employee complained of numerous safety hazards and little was done about it, the employee filed a complaint with the California Occupational Safety and Health Administration. The employer discharged the employee;[5] the board held that although the employee acted alone, it was for the benefit of all employees and therefore was concerted activity and ordered reinstatement.[6]

In a previous situation a single employee who attempted to enforce the terms of a collective bargaining agreement was protected under the concerted activity rule.[7] The board in the Alleluia case (nonunion) used the Interboro case (union) as authority for its decision, thus reaffirming its policy that no distinction is to be made between rights of union or nonunion employees under Section

---

[3] For rights of nonunion employees in a disciplinary interview, see the section on the Weingarten doctrine, p. 210.

[4] NLRB v. Washington Aluminum Co., 370 U.S. 9 (1962).

[5] As has been so often said by a manager, "We must git rid of those troublemakers."

[6] Alleluia Cushion Company, 221 NLRB 999 (1975).

[7] NLRB v. Interboro Contractors, Inc., 388 F.2d 495 (2nd Cir. 1967). The court's theory was the same as in the Alleluia case; benefits that accrue to others from individual activity is a protected concerted activity.

7. In the single-employee cases the board has gone further than the courts in holding concerted activity.

Where an employee asked for a wage increase for himself, independent from other employees, the board stated that this implied concerted complaint because other employees would be affected by employer's uniform pay system.[8] This would probably not be enforced by the circuit courts in view of the refusal to enforce a board order where an employee was discharged for filing a safety complaint with the Montana Department of Health and Environment Science (the facts were similar to Alleluia). The court said that concerted activity must be established by direct evidence and it cannot be assumed in this case that other employees would be affected.[9]

It appears from a review of the board and court cases that the courts consider an activity to be concerted only if a group action is in some way involved or several employees are directly affected by a single action. The board requires only that the complaint be of common concern to all the employees. Because the board requires less evidence of group activity than the courts in defining concerted activity, it is advisable for the employer to follow the board rule unless the issue warrants going to the circuit courts, where enforcement would be determined according to court decisions. The court may give some direction on what is considered concerted activity when it rules on the City Disposal Systems case, cited in note 17 of this chapter.

LEGALITY OF WALKOUT BY NONUNION EMPLOYEES

When nonunion employees leave their jobs over working conditions, the first question is whether this is insubordination of an employer's work order (usually the work order is to return to work or be discharged). The law is quite clear that when a group of employees leave their jobs over working conditions, this is protected activity in the same manner as a work

stoppage if a union were involved.[10] In the Vic Tanny case the court refused to listen to the employer's argument that the discharges were because of employee insubordination in the refusal to carry out a work order.

This concept can be carried into a situation where 15 nonunion employees walked off their jobs in protest over a discharge of an em-

---

[8] Hansen Chevrolet, 237 NLRB 584 (1978). The employer complied with the order; therefore an enforcement proceeding for the board's order was not necessary.

[9] NLRB v. Bighorn Beverage, 614 F.2d 1238 (9th Cir. 1980).

[10] Vic Tanny International v. NLRB, 662 F.2d 237 (6th Cir. 1980). In East Chicago Rehabilitation Center v. NLRB, 710 F.2d 397 (6th Cir. 1983) the Court held that employees did not have to file a ten-day strike notice because they were not a union.

ployee who had another employee sign out for her. Both employees were discharged. The employer then discharged the 15 employees for walking off their jobs.

The board ordered reinstatement, as this was concerted activity protected by the act. The court enforced the order, noting that irrespective of the employer's right to discharge the two employees for time-card infraction, their co-workers had a right to protest the discharges by concerted activity.[11]

REFUSAL OF EMPLOYEE TO WORK IN UNSAFE CONDITIONS

The right of an employee to refuse to work in unsafe conditions is protected by two different statutes: Sections 7 and 502[12] of the Labor Management Relations Act of 1947 (LMRA) and Section 11(c)(1) of the Occupational Safety and Health Act.[13]

The refusal to work is usually expressed by walking off the job. Under the LRMA the question arises whether this is an illegal strike or one protected by Sections 7 and 502 of the act. Under OSHA the issue would be whether the employee could be discharged for refusal to work and if the discharge would be a violation of the discrimination clause in the statute.

In the interpretation of Section 502 of the LRMA the courts

have stated that a refusal to work is protected by the act if there is a good faith belief that the working conditions are abnormally dangerous and that workers are competent to testify as to the physical conditions. Where a fan was blowing dust and other abrasives into the workers' faces, the employer inspected the ventilation system and stated that it was operating properly. The employees were told that they would be discharged if they walked out. Despite the warning, they walked off the job, and the court held that this was a protected activity.[14]

In a nonunion facility, employees walked off the job alleging that it was too cold to work as there was no heat in the area (out-

---

[11] United Merchants & Manufacturers Inc. v. NLRB, 554 F.2d 1276 (4th Cir. 1977).

[12] LMRA Sect. 502 states: . . . nor shall the quitting of labor by an employee or employees in good faith because of abnormally dangerous conditions for work at the place of employment of such employee or employees be deemed a strike under this Act.
Section 7 of the act gives the employees the right to strike.

[13] OSHA Sect. 660(c)(1) states: (c)(1) No person shall discharge or in any manner discriminate against any employee because such employee has filed any complaint or instituted or caused to be instituted any proceeding under or related to this Act or has testified or is about to testify in any such proceeding or because of the exercise by such employee on behalf of himself or others of any right afforded by this Act.

[14] NLRB v. Knight Marley Corp., 251 F.2d 753 (6th Cir. 1958). This would be protected even though it was a violation of company and OSHA rules according to NLRB v. Tamara Foods, 692 F.2d 1171 (8th Cir. 1982).

side temperature was about 20 degrees). The employees were discharged for violation of a rule of leaving the plant without permission. The U.S. Supreme Court held that this was a protected activity under the statute.[15]

Subsequent to these decisions, the courts seem to adhere to the doctrine that good faith belief must be accompanied by the existence of objective physical evidence or at least ascertainable evidence that an abnormally dangerous condition exists.[16] If an abnormally dangerous condition is found not to exist, then the employees can be discharged; the act does not afford them the protection for walking off the job. The protection under Sections 7 and 502 of LRMA is exclusive. A no-strike clause in the labor agreement or an arbitration clause does not affect the employees' rights, although the arbitration is permitted if the labor representatives want to seek that remedy under the labor agreement.

As in other situations under the LMRA, in order to receive the protection under the LMRA the protest over the unsafe conditions must be such that the employee is acting in behalf of others or there are several employees affected or involved. The concerted activity test under the act must be met by the facts in the case. Where the employee acted unilaterally over refusing to drive a truck that he contended was unsafe, the court held that this was a unilateral action and not concerted action with the object of inducing or preparing for group action. The issue is now before the Supreme Court.[17]

The right under OSHA of the employee to refuse to work under unsafe conditions is found in the Secretary of Labor's interpretation of what constitutes discrimination under Section 11(c)(1) of OSHA. The secretary's directive interpreting this section stated that if (a) the employee's fear were objectively reasonable, (b) the employee attempted to get employer to correct, and (c) resorting to normal enforcement procedures under the OSHA were inadequate, the employee then could refuse to work.

Whether this interpretation of Section 11(c)(1) is correct came before the Supreme Court in Whirlpool Corp. v. Marshall, 445 U.S. 1 (1980). In the Whirlpool situation the employees had previously complained about the condition of a screen. An employee had fallen to his death and the company subsequently made some alterations to make the screen more safe when it became necessary to remove objects from the screen. Also the firm established a safety procedure when working on the screen. The employees who had complained about the unsafe condition of the screen were ordered to perform their usual maintenance tasks on the screen and they refused. They were ordered to go home, were not paid for the remainder of the shift, and given a written reprimand. The

---

[15] Cited in Note 4.

[16] Gateway Coal Co. v. United Mine Workers of America, 414 U.S. 368 (1974, NLRB).

[17] City Disposal Systems v. NLRB, 683 F.2d 1005 (6th Cir. 1982). Cert. Granted 103 Sup. Ct. 1496. (NLRB v. City Disposal Systems).

Supreme Court held that in order to have a violation of 11(c)(1) of OSHA two conditions must exist: (1) reasonable belief that the employees will be placed in jeopardy of injury or death and (2) reasonable belief that there was no other alternative but to disobey the employer's order (no opportunity to go to a OSHA office or seek redress from another level of management).

The court further held that this may be termed a strike and although the employees would be protected, they would not receive pay for not working. The court also reaffirmed the rule established under Section 502 of LRMA that if a hazardous condition were found not to exist or employees were acting in bad faith, they could be discharged for insubordination.

If an OSHA regulation is violated and employees walk off the job, because in spite of OSHA regulations it is unsafe, it is questionable whether they are protected under Section 502. One court said it was protected activity under 502 in spite of OSHA (NLRB v. Tamara Foods, 692 F.2d 1171 (8th, 1982). The Supreme Court will have to decide the issue sometime in the future.

DEFINITION OF WORKING CONDITIONS FOR CONCERTED ACTIVITY

As in the United Merchants case (See Note 11) where the court held that protest over a justifiable discharge is concerted activity, the question is raised as to the scope of work issues and the extension beyond the direct control of the employer. This question was answered by the Supreme Court regarding employees who were distributing a union newsletter in nonwork areas during nonwork time. Two of the four sections of the newsletter dealt with union matters and the remainder urged the employees to oppose state right-to-work legislation. It criticized a presidential veto of an increase in the federal minimum wage. The court, in upholding the Fifth Circuit's enforcement of the board's order, stated that although the issues in the dispute had only an indirect impact on relations between the employer and employees, they bore a direct relationship to all employees' interests in general.[18] The court rejected the employer's argument that Section 7 does not extend to situations where the employer has no power to change.

In an expansion of the scope of the employee's rights of concerted activity, the courts have extended the right of employees to make disparaging remarks against the employer. A non-union employee complained over television about working conditions and later quit. One year later the former employee was refused employment although qualified for the position.

---

[18] Eastex Inc. v. NLRB, 437 U.S. 556 (1978).

The court held that the reason for the employer, a hospital in this case, refused to hire the person was because of the televised remarks the year before. The hospital argued that the remarks constituted disloyal conduct.[19]

From these cases one could conclude that almost any activity concerning working conditions is protected under the act unless they involve individual problems. The best example of an individual problem is where an employee consistently harassed the employer to obtain a merit wage increase without support or the involvement of other workers. The board held that discharge was lawful[20] because the employee's action did not directly further the interests of other employees. Where a non-union employee requested to have a witness present when signing a performance appraisal required for continued employment, the court held this was not a protected activity as the employee was not acting for others.[21] The same result where there is a violation of dress code, or job transfers are involved. If disloyalty or insubordination can be shown, it will also lose protection of the act.

The "Bible case" for employee disloyalty involved employees of a television station who were distributing handbills criticizing the station's quality of programs. The Supreme Court, in holding that the employer had just cause for discharging the employees said, "There is no more elemental cause for discharge of an employee than disloyalty to his employer."[22] (The handbills being distributed made no reference to a labor dispute or improvement of working conditions.)

The rights of nonunion employees to engage in concerted activity without retaliation is a well-established law. The employer, when faced with the problem, need only act reasonably: listen to the problem, investigate, and take a position as to its correction rather than try to eliminate the problem by retaliation against the employee who called it to management's attention.

EMPLOYEE COMPLAINT PROCEDURES: A DEFENSE FOR CONCERTED ACTIVITY

One of the most common causes of employee's concerted activity over working conditions is the failure of the employer to have an effective complaint procedure. There must be a place to go to let the steam off. After attempts to do so fail with the employee's super-

---

[19] NLRB v. Mount Desert Island Hospital, 695 F.2d 634 (1st Cir. 1982).

[20] It was once said that "anybody can discharge an employee, but it takes a good personnel practitioner to discharge a troublemaker and make it stick."

[21] E.I. duPont deNemours & Co. v. NLRB, 707 F.2d 1076 (9th Cir. 1983).

[22] NLRB v. Local Union 1229, IBEW (Jefferson Standard Broadcasting Co.), 346 U.S. 464 at 472 (1953).

visor (who often is the source of the problem), concerted activity results. Such activity usually would not be protected if a complaint procedure were available. For example, if a complaint procedure were available when co-workers protested discharge of a fellow employee, as in the United Merchants case,[23] a work stoppage would probably not be justified because other means would be available to adjudicate the dissatisfaction.[24]

Nothing in the act prevents any employer from establishing an informal or formal complaint procedure. There are two reasons why complaint procedures avoid concerted activity. One, if the employee is offered a forum for the solution of the problem, concerted action is less likely. Second, the employer is forced to take a position that is documented, and this often satisfies the employee. Sometimes a forum to discuss the dissatisfaction is all that is needed to satisfy the employee.[25]

Elements Of An Effective Complaint Procedure

There are many types of complaint procedures in union and nonunion organizations. What is effective for one organization may be ineffective for another. However, all procedures should be designed to contain the following elements:

1. The procedure should be designed so that it encourages the employee to use it. If the employee at the first instance is required to discuss the complaint with the immediate supervisor, who probably caused the problem, the use of the procedure is discouraged.

2. The personnel practitioner should be indirectly involved in the solution of the problem; leaving it up solely to operating management causes inconsistency.

3. The final appeals procedure should permit employees and management representatives to make the decision.

4. The objective of settling complaints should be what's right, not who's right.

5. All complaints are real to the employee and should never be considered ridiculous, although they may be to management.

6. Management must be able to discontinue the procedure if it does not work.

Recommended Complaint Procedure

Exhibit X-1 is a complaint procedure that contains these elements. It is an effective procedure

---

[23] Cited in Note 11.

[24] The author purposely has avoided the use of the term *grievance*. A grievance is defined as an employer action in violation of a labor agreement. A dissatisfaction or complaint is any employee concern over wages and working conditions.

[25] Many dissatisfactions or grievances are settled by permitting the employee (union or nonunion) to talk while the employer just listens. Often employees talk themselves out of the dissatisfaction.

to avoid protective concerted activity as well as to promote good employee relations.

This procedure is often difficult to sell to management because it gives up a management right to make final decisions. However, if the employee's rights were represented by a union, this management's right is given up in over 90 percent of all labor agreements by arbitration clauses. Another objection that top management often gives in opposition to the procedure outlined in Exhibit X-1 is that where employees are represented on the committee, they will always rule for the employee. However, the most strict constructionist of a rule violation is usually another employee.

The complaint procedure is one area with which personnel law does not concern itself except to avoid retaliation liability and protect concerted activity. However, complaint procedures are an important part of effective personnel administration and an effective method to prevent litigation. The personnel practitioner should spend considerable time and effort in developing a procedure that will work for the particular operation.[26]

EXHIBIT X-1

Complaint Procedure for Nonsupervisory and Hourly Employees Not Represented by a Union

When an employee becomes dissatisfied with the working relationship or some other problem for which a solution is desired, the employee may discuss this dissatisfaction with the immediate supervisor or with the supervisor's supervisor. If a satisfactory solution is not received at these levels, the dissatisfaction or problem shall be put in writing and submitted to the employee relation's representative.

The employee relations representative shall investigate the matter and make a recommendation in writing to the manager of the department. The manager shall, after due consideration and consultation, make a determination and so inform the employee in a person-to-person meeting, by presenting a copy of the decision to the employee and sending a copy to the employee relations representative and employee's immediate supervisor.

If the employee is dissatisfied with the manager's decision, the employee may refer it to a employee-management committee consisting of two management representatives and three employee representatives, whose majority decision shall be final and binding on both the company and the employee. This procedure shall be communicated to all employees affected; employees must be made to feel, beyond any reasonable doubt, that they will not be in any way penalized for using this procedure.

The employee-management committee shall be discontinued on 30 days' notice of either party to discontinue. Such discontinuance date shall not be effective until all pending employee's problems or dissatisfactions have been resolved.

---

[26] For further discussion of complaint procedures see K.L. Sovereign and Mario Bognanno, "Positive Contract Administration," Chapter 7.6, and Willy L. Beavers "Employee Relations without a Union," Chapter 7.3 in *ASPA Handbook of Personnel and Industrial Relations* (Washington, D.C.: Bureau of National Affairs, 1979).

LEGALITY OF EMPLOYEE COMMITTEES UNDER NATIONAL LABOR RELATIONS ACT

Employee discontent is often based on the lack of communications. As many labor relations experts think, the cause of employees joining a union can be traced to a lack of communications. Some employers believe that the solution to these problems is the formation of an employee committee. Although the employee committees may provide a two-way management-employee communication system and is often an effective substitute for employee representation by a union, if not properly constituted it can run afoul of the National Labor Relations Act. Section 15.2(5) which states:

The term 'labor organization' means any organization of any kind, or any agency or employee representation committee or plan, in which employees participate and which exists for the purpose, in whole or in part, of dealing with employers concerning grievances, labor disputes, wages, rates of pay, hours of employment, or conditions of work.

Section 158(a)(2) provides:

It shall be an unfair labor practice for an employer to dominate or interfere with the formation or administration of any labor organization or contribute financial or other support to it: *Provided*, that subject to rules and regulations made and published by the Board pursuant to section 6, an employer shall not be prohibited from permitting employees to confer with him during working hours without loss of time or pay.

It is evident from the language of these two sections of the act that interpretation is needed to determine whether in a given case an employee committee is in violation of the act.

In the leading case on employee committees, the evidence showed that the committee had bylaws that were prepared by the company. The employee representatives on the committee established a procedure for handling grievances in nonunion plants. They also made proposals to management as to seniority, job classifications, job bidding, holiday and vacation pay, etc., in the same manner as a union negotiating committee. The Supreme Court held that this was clearly a labor organization under the act and was company-dominated.[27]

The Court had the most concern over the fact that the committee handled employee complaints. Although Section 9(a) of the act permits nonunion employees to present their own complaints to the employer, they cannot do so on behalf of other employees (unless through concerted activity) as this would be a representation situation and come within the definition of a labor organization.

Courts hold that it is not necessary to bargain with employees to come within the definition of a labor organization. If the committee makes demands as to working conditions on the employer and the employer does not recognize its

---

[27] NLRB v. Cabot Carbon Co., 360 U.S. 203 (1959).

power to make such request, the committee would not be considered a labor union.[28]

Facts That Determine Whether A Committee Is A Union

Review of court decisions indicates that one must look to each factual situation and determine whether the committee is acting as a union and whether it is employer-dominated.

Did the company choose the committee members or force a change of members? If so, it would be held to be a company-dominated union.[29] If there were continuous rotation of members for the purpose of communicating to all employees about working conditions, one court held that this was management communicating to its employees, which does not establish a union.[30] Generally, an ad hoc committee is not considered in violation, such as where a committee is formed to discuss inadequate supervision, quality control circles, or similar groups organized to improve quality and quantity of production.

Recommendations To Keep An Employee Committee Legal

Because an employee committee affords exposure to a violation of the act (the remedy for which is to cease and desist, in other words, discontinue the committee), does this mean that it should not be used? If properly structured, employee committees can be a useful tool in an employee communication program and be instrumental in keeping the employees nonunion.[31] An employee committee should be structured to contain the following provisions:

1. The declared purpose of the committee should be for communicatons both to management and from management.

2. Individual problems should not be discussed, but a separate complaint system should be instituted.

3. The broad problems should be in the form of communicating dissatisfaction and the employer explaining its position on employee problems.

4. Changes in working conditions such as lunch hour or wage and salary program should be in the form of two-way communication of employees asking why, and management explaining its position.

5. If employees express a general dissatisfaction, management should consider it and correct it or give a rational reason for not doing it.

---

[28] NLRB v. Jas H. Mathews & Co., 156 F.2d 706 (3rd Cir. 1946).

[29] Irving Air Chute Co. v. NLRB, 350 F.2d 176 (2nd Cir. 1965).

[30] NLRB v. Scott Fetzer, 691 F.2d 288 (6th Cir. 1982).

[31] Pitney-Bowes of Stamford, Connecticut, believes that its communication program is instrumental in preventing unionization of their employees. See Fred T. Allen. "Profile of a Winner" *Industry Week* (Cleveland, Ohio: Penton, IPC) October 29, 1979, p. 53.

If such dissatisfaction is in the form of a threat or forceful demand, it should not be considered as consideration of a demand is permitting the committee to be similar to a union.

Exhibit X-2 contains the recommendations listed. It also illustrates that the committee should not have elaborate bylaws and procedures. Formal written guidelines should only be what is necessary to permit the committee to function under broad informal procedures.

The committee structured in Exhibit X-2 of four management representatives and five employee representatives is designed to

---

EXHIBIT X-2

Employee-Management Communications Committee

The general purpose of this committee, consisting of employee and management representatives, is to promote better communications between the company and its employees.

The purpose of employee representatives shall be to communicate to management the acceptability of management policies and practices, to make suggestions for improving management-employee relationships, and to communicate generally their problems and dissatisfactions.

The purpose of management representatives shall be to communicate business conditions, customer relations, employee benefits, wage and salary policies, community and governmental problems, management policies and practices, and new developments and to represent management's position concerning general employee problems and dissatisfactions.

Selection of Committee

The committee shall consist of management representatives from production, administration, and management, except that the plant manager or employee relations representative shall not sit on the committee. Employee representatives shall be selected by the employees whom they represent; representation from different departments is desirable but not essential. There shall be a maximum of five employee representatives and a maximum of four management representatives. Each member of the committee shall serve for one year and shall not be eligible for reappointment. Vacancies shall be filled in the same manner as they were appointed.

Committee Organization

The committee shall meet once each month until discontinued on request of either party. They shall elect a chair and a secretary. The chair shall be alternated from year to year between an employee and management representative. Minutes of the meeting shall be kept and distributed to all employees. The committee shall adopt such other rules and procedures as necessary to carry out its function.

make the committee a more effective communications device. Usually management representatives have easily communicated subjects as the information comes from one or two sources. The employee representatives have a less homogeneous group to represent; therefore, their communication problem is more difficult. There is more of a tendency to discuss wages and working conditions, which may result in the board declaring it a company-dominated union if there are only a few employee representatives.

With an unbalanced committee, the thought should be conveyed that this is not a voting situation where the majority vote will make a decision; management being underrepresented clearly communicates this to the employees.

RISKS INVOLVED WITH EMPLOYEE COMMITTEES

An employer who intends to use the employee committee should also be aware of the risks involved apart from the legal exposure of committing an unfair labor practice. If there is irresponsible leadership on the committee, a whole host of employee relations problems could be created that would cause a "bushey haired" personnel practitioner to become bald.[32]

If a large number of differences between management and the committee remain unresolved or are settled on the basis of an arbitrary management answer, a tailor-made organization is handed to a union on a silver platter. For these reasons a committee should be carefully formed before a threat of union organization.

Management can avoid these pitfalls by continual audit of the effectiveness of the committee. If there is not a harmonious relationship, it can diplomatically discontinue the committee. The advantages of an employee committee outweigh the disadvantages. Positive personnel administration should seriously consider employee communication committees in spite of the solvable problems that they create.

RIGHT OF EMPLOYEE TO SELECT BARGAINING REPRESENTATIVES

The basic authority for the right employees to select bargaining representatives is Section 7 of the National Labor Relations Act. This section provides that employees "shall have the right to self-organization to form, join, or assist labor organizations to bargain col-

---

[32] The author is bald.

lectively through representatives of their own choosing and to engage in other concerted activities for the purpose of collective bargaining or other mutual aids or protection."

Section 7 was amended by the Taft-Hartley Act to state specifically that an individual shall have the right to refrain from any or all union activities. This was a loophole in the original act. The interpretation of Section 7 by the board and the courts has become complex and voluminous. It is only possible here to give a brief overview of the procedures. Important decisions concerning union-employer posture and remedies for violations are covered only briefly.

When an employer is faced with a union organizational drive, a general knowledge of the law prevents mistakes in the initial stage of organization drive. Professional advice and counsel by a person thoroughly versed in this area is advisable immediately after knowledge of an organizational attempt exists.

PROCEDURES IN SELECTION OF A BARGAINING REPRESENTATIVE

If a company becomes aware of an organizational effort at its inception, it will probably be through supervisors, by loyal or ambitious employees ("apple polishers"), or by observation of an organizer passing out handbills. Sometimes, however, organizational efforts are kept secret, and the employer is not aware of the effort until a letter or telegram demanding recognition is received from the union. If this happens, the initial stages of the organizational campaign have passed.

Authorization To Represent Employees

The initial organizational objective by a union is to obtain sufficient number of authorization cards or authority (some unions use a list similar to a petition) for the union to represent the signatory employee for collective bargaining purpose. There is no specified form as long as the document or card states that the employee wants to be a member of the union or requests on the card that the union be certified as the bargaining representative.[33] Various meetings, coffee parties, beer sessions, calls at the employee's home, and hard sell from other employees are all part of the procedure to get employees to sign authorization for representation. When the union gets 30 percent or more of the eligible employees in the job categories that they claim is an appropriate bargaining unit to sign authorizations, they may, under board procedural rules, petition for an election. As a practical matter, to ensure winning an election, most unions will not petition the board for an election unless

---

[33] NLRB v. Valley Broadcasting Co., 189 F.2d 582 (6th Cir. 1951).

they have 60 percent or more authorizations from those eligible to vote.

Request To Bargain Without An Election

Before the union petitions the board for an election, it sometimes requests orally or in writing that the employer bargain without an election. The union states that the union represents the majority of the employees and would like to be recognized as a bargaining representative and suggests a date for the first meeting.

Sometimes the union presents the authorization forms to prove its claim of majority status. The employer should not look at those cards or in any other way gain knowledge of who signed the cards unless it has been decided to recognize the union without an election. The courts have enforced the board's position that if the employer has knowledge of who signed the authorization form, the employer cannot later demand an election or question the majority status of the union.[34] The employer should always demand an election unless there are rare circumstances that dictate otherwise[35]

Signed authorizations are not always predictive of how the employee will vote. Sometimes an employee signs cards for reasons other than union representation. A person may have signed a card to get rid of the union organizer and changed his mind after hearing all the issues. The beer party may have lasted too long and the employee did not reflect true feelings.[36] Once an employee signs a card, the board will not accept any testimony on why the person signed the card.[37] However, persuasion to withdraw authorization is not in itself illegal.[38]

If the employer denies recognition and requests the board to hold an election, the board must do so in the absence of an unfair labor practice.[39] When the board orders the election, the time and place are determined as well as the eligible list of voters. If the employer or union agree with all the conditions, a consent election petition is signed. If they do not agree, a hearing is held and the board makes a determination of the issues and then orders the election. This order is

---

[34] Retail Clerks Union v. NLRB (John L. Serpa, Inc.), 376 F.2d 186 (9th Cir. 1967).

[35] The author as state agency representative once held an election where all voters were dues-paying members of the union but they all voted not to have the union represent them.

[36] Cards signed after drinking 26 bottles of beer were held to be valid. American Art, 170 NLRB No. 70 (1968).

[37] Midstate Beverages, 153 NLRB No. 14 (1965).

[38] NLRB v. Monroe Tube Co., 545 F.2d 1320 (2nd Cir. 1976).

[39] Linden Lumber Division & Summer Co. v. NLRB, 419 U.S. 301 (1974). One technique to chill union organizational efforts is to argue over a list of eligible voters, especially in the area of confidential employees; such employees must be directly exposed to labor relations policy to be confidential. This was defined in NLRB v. Hendricks County Rural Electric Membership Corp., 450 U.S. 964 (1981).

appealable to the circuit court. After the election is ordered, the campaign to influence the employees on how to vote starts.

Union-Employer Conduct In Representation Election

Section 8(a)(1) of the act states that is is a violation to interfere with, restrain, or coerce employees in exercising their rights under Section 7 to join or not to join a labor organization. Violation by the employer usually takes the form of threatening the loss of jobs or benefits, questioning employees about their union activities or membership, spying on union gatherings, or granting wage increases deliberately timed to discourage employees from joining or voting for the union.

The important thing to remember about conduct in representation campaigns is that coercion, promises, or seeking information on whether employees are members of the union and how they individually feel about union representation is usually held to be an unfair labor practice. One of the most common violations is where the employer solicits dissatisfaction or grievances in order to determine why employees joined the union and then corrects the conditions before the election. This is always held to be an unfair labor practice.

Soliciting complaints is permissible, but promises to remedy them is unlawful.[40] Other employer conduct held to be unlawful is a statement that a plant shutdown was a possibility because the union would make it impossible to survive.[41] The company granted an unusual number of employee loans a week before the election.[42] Some permissible conduct is making a misstatement in a letter or document unless such a document is forged or deceitful.[43] (If letters are to be used, they should be carefully drafted; it is sometimes better not to use letters, especially if it is the first one that the employee has ever received from management.)

Other permissible conduct is granting benefits and wage increases—a past practice[44]—withholding from paychecks and paying separately, sums equivalent to union dues.[45] Holding a raffle for $84 worth of groceries stating that this was the amount of union dues for one year.[46]

Unions are also held to the same standard of conduct as employers under the law. However, it is often difficult to get evidence of union conduct because of the reluctance of employees to testify against each other. Where a union waived initiation fees to those who signed authorization cards before the election, the Supreme Court held this to be unfair labor prac-

---

[40] Montgomery Ward & Co., 225 NLRB No. 15 (1976).

[41] W.A. Kruger Co., 224 NLRB No. 148 (1976).

[42] Bradley Lumber Co. v. NLRB, 128 F.2d 768 (8th Cir. 1942).

[43] Midland National Life Insurance Co., 263 NLRB No. 24 (1982).

[44] NLRB v. Otis Hospital, 545 F.2d 252 (1st Cir. 1976).

[45] Geyer Mfg. Co., 120 NLRB No. 33 (1958).

[46] Buzza Cardozo, 177 NLRB No. 38 (1969).

tice.[47] However, the union was within its right to give a free turkey to all employees attending a union meeting.[48] There has also been developed a large body of law on what the union and employers can say and what they cannot say, which also involves the constitutional right of the freedom of speech.

One problem that often comes up when a union is attempting to organize is what degree of solicitation by pro-union employees must be permitted by the employer. The general rule is that the employer must permit employees to engage in union activity during nonwork time. The Supreme Court held that prohibition of union activity during nonwork time would interfere with employee's right to organize unless the rule is necessary to maintain discipline or production.[49]

A rule that requires permission from management for any kind of solicitation is usually held to be too broad as it could include nonwork time.[50] Another rule was struck down where all talking during work time was prohibited. The court said that such a rule was unreasonable.[51]

The Supreme Court put some restriction on solicitation during nonwork time in hospitals and health care institutions, where such activity would interfere with visitors and patient care, such as in patients' rooms and corridors. However, the court stated that solicitation in a cafeteria would not interfere with patient care or visitors.[52]

The situation that most often confronts employers is where, as a matter of good employee relations, the employer has permitted conversation or solicitation of the other subjects during work time. Then, when a union campaign takes place, the employer prevents conversation or activity for union organization as well as other subjects.

The board and courts usually hold this as discrimination except where the United Fund was permitted.[53] If selling Girl Scout cookies or tickets for the Shrine circus or charity ball were permitted during work time, the employer would have exposure to an unfair labor practice charge if union solicitation were prohibited during work time after a petition for election has been filed. If the union activity were far more excessive than what had been permitted, tuning it down to what was permitted in other areas would probably be legal.

The employer who had a past practice of permitting conversation and civic projects during work

---

[47] NLRB v. Savair Mfg. Co., 414 U.S. 270 (1973).

[48] Jacqueline Cochran, Inc., 177 NLRB No. 39 (1969).

[49] Republic Aviation Corp. v. NLRB, 324 U.S. 793, 16 LRRM 620 (1945).

[50] Birmingham Ornamental Co. v. NLRB 615 F.2d 661 (5th Cir. 1980).

[51] NLRB v. Chem Fab Corp., 691 F.2d 1252 (8th Cir. 1982).

[52] Beth Israel Hospital v. NLRB, 437 U.S. 483 (1978); also NLRB v. Baptist Hospital, 442 U.S. 773 (1979).

[53] PACECO Co., Div. of Fruehauf Corp. v. NLRB, 601 F.2d 180 (5th Cir. 1979).

time should be cautious when establishing a rule to prevent union activity during work time.

As in other situations concerning employer conduct in representation elections, the employer should receive professional advice before too much is said, however, to state that one does not want a union is always safe.

Remedy For Misconduct In Representation Campaign

When the board finds that the union or employer has committed an unfair labor practice, it will order a new election; if the offense is severe enough, it will order certification without an election. In order to certify a union without an election, there must be substantial proof that the company committed a serious unfair labor practice.[54] The court said in Gissel that the employer's action must have a marked impact on employee sentiment that is expressed on the authorization forms and the election results. The employer's action under the Gissel doctrine must undermine the majority status of the union.[55]

SUPERVISOR CONDUCT IN SUPPORT OF UNION ACTIVITY

In combating union organization efforts, the single-most important management representative is the front-line supervisor. These supervisors' rapport with the employees gives them the greatest exposure to unfair labor practices in management's attempt to oppose the union. For this reason they must be briefed on their legal rights in representing management. Most managements assume that the supervisor will support their position but what happens with the supervisor who supports union activity? Is there any restriction on discharging a supervisor who supports union activity? Supervisor support of union activity is not uncommon because dissatisfied supervisors will often reason that if a union represents the employees and their wages or benefits are increased, theirs will also be increased.

Sections 2(3), 2(11), and 14(a) of the Taft-Hartley amendments to the act specifically exempt supervisors from the protection under the act. The question arises that if a supervisor is discharged for supporting union activity, is this in any way interfering with the employee's right to join a union? The

---

[54] NLRB v. Gissel Packaging Co., 395 U.S. 575 (1969).

[55] Since the Gissel decision, some courts say that 30 percent of authorization cards is sufficient for the doctrine to apply while others say that there must be an actual majority: United Dairy Farmers v. NLRB, 633 F.2d 1054 (3rd Cir. 1980). In United Supermarkets, 261 NLRB No. 179 (1982), board took the position that no majority is needed if outrageous conduct is shown.

courts have declared that discharge of a supervisor for engaging in union activities in not unlawful; however, in certain situations the board and the courts have reversed the discharge of a supervisor who supports the union, which is contrary to management orders. Discharge of a pro-union supervisor for pro-union activity can interfere with, restrain, or coerce rank-and-file employees in their rights to join a union; therefore, it is violation of Section 8(a)(1) of the act. Where the employer discharged a supervisor for refusal to commit an unfair labor practice, it was held unlawful discharge.[56]

The basic rule of the board and courts in supervisor's cases, is the discharge of supervisors for pro-union activity is not unlawful where they participate in union concerted activity because supervisors have no protection under the act. It is only unlawful under the to discharge a supervisor (1) for refusing to commit an unfair labor practice, (2) for giving adverse testimony at a board or grievance proceeding, and (3) for failing to prevent union organization. The supervisor's activity must directly interfere with employees' right to organize.[57]

SUMMARY AND CONCLUSIONS

It can be readily determined that a nonunion employee has as much protection under the National Labor Relations Act as a union employee. It is also apparent that the employer can institute certain programs that will substitute for third-party employee representation and aid in the prevention of union organization. The most important of these programs is the complaint procedure, which has little or no legal restraint as to its function. The employee committee is also an effective tool but does have its legal restrictions. That does not mean that it should not be used but it does mean that it should be designed to be immune from the board declaring it a company-dominated union and ordering it to be discontinued. The employee committee also has exposure to the very thing that it was designed to prevent: employee representation through a union. The risk of employee representation is far greater than the board's cease-and-desist order; for this reason a continual audit of the committee effectiveness is necessary to prevent its deterioration into a ready-made union. Employees' committees are worthwhile because the risks can be kept to a minimum by management audit.

The act exempts supervisors from protection for union activity; however, the employer does not have complete authority to discharge for support of union activity. The rule in the Automobile

---

[56] NLRB v. Talladega Cotton Factory, 213 F.2d 204 (5th Cir. 1954).

[57] Automobile Salesmen's Union Local 1095 v. NLRB, 711 F.2d 383 (DC Cir. 1983).

Salesmen's Local 1095 case gives the employer the authority to discharge a supervisor for pro-union activity as long as that supervisor is not prevented from giving testimony, blamed for union organization, or forced to commit an unfair labor practice. A pro-union supervisor should be discharged if there is refusal to obey legitimate instructions and those instructions do not directly interfere with employees' right to organize and the Automobile Salesmen case gives that authority.

CHAPTER XI

RIGHTS OF UNION STATUS EMPLOYEES UNDER THE NATIONAL LABOR RELATIONS ACT

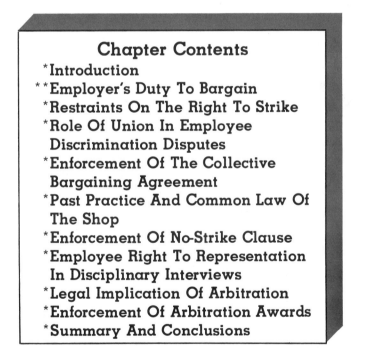

Chapter Contents
*Introduction
**Employer's Duty To Bargain
*Restraints On The Right To Strike
*Role Of Union In Employee
 Discrimination Disputes
*Enforcement Of The Collective
 Bargaining Agreement
*Past Practice And Common Law Of
 The Shop
*Enforcement Of No-Strike Clause
*Employee Right To Representation
 In Disciplinary Interviews
*Legal Implication Of Arbitration
*Enforcement Of Arbitration Awards
*Summary And Conclusions

INTRODUCTION

When the personnel practitioner looks at the title of this chapter, the thought may occur that since one does not have a union or expect to have one in the foreseeable future, this would be one chapter to skip. This would be a mistake. One of the best defenses to employee organization is for the employer always to consider whether one could make the same employment decision if a union were representing the employees.

For example, a nonunion employer in an effort to get workers to work the graveyard shift decided to pay all workers an extra four hours' pay per shift. When economic conditions changed and jobs became less plentiful, it was decided to change this expensive policy and pay only for time worked. How can one change the policy to have the least impact on worker's attitude? It must be done very carefully. If workers were organized, it could not be done without union acceptance, which would be unlikely. Without a union the policy change must be well-communicated to the employees or the employer will have a union.

Nonunion employers should know the rights of union employees and what restrictions labor agreements contain in order to make decisions that will have the least impact on employee relations. The union should not be given the opportunity to say, "If you were represented by a union, the employer could not do this."

Chapter X stated that a nonunion employee has the same rights under the National Labor Relations Act (NLRA) as an employee who is a member of a union. What difference does it make whether an employee be-longs to a union? Why is there such effort by employers to

keep out unions? The major difference is in the procedures. Employees represented by a union cannot individually discuss with the employer the wages and working conditions but must do so through elected representative, which is the union. The second difference is that in a union situation a labor agreement exists that may restrict the employer in making employment decisions.

To select a representative for the purpose of discussing wages or other conditions of employment is a right granted to the employee by Section 7 of the act. When the National Labor Relations Board holds an election and the majority of those voting select a union or some other organization to represent them for bargaining purposes, the employees can no longer individually represent themselves. Under the law, if the majority chooses a bargaining representative, that representative must act for all the employees and all employees must go through the union with their problems.

From the employer's point of view, a third party has come between the employee and the employer. The employer no longer can grant wage increases or change working conditions without agreement by the employee representative.

When the union is certified as the bargaining agent for the employees, the employer is obligated under the law to make a good faith effort to reach written agreement as to the terms and conditions of employment. Once an agreement is reached, both the union and employer must follow it and the employee may force the union and employer to do so through the National Labor Relations Board. Whatever rights are granted in the labor agreement are additional rights that a nonunion employee may not have.

This chapter describes the procedures under the law that forces the employer to deal with the union as opposed to dealing with employee individually as in Chapter X. It also reviews the additional rights that an employee has through the enforcement of the labor agreement to which the employer agreed.

EMPLOYER'S DUTY TO BARGAIN

After a union wins an election and is certified by the NLRB as the bargaining representative of the employees, the first real contact that the employer has with the union is the request made by the union to meet for the purpose of bargaining over wages and working conditions. The usual procedure is for the union to make several proposals to be put into a written agreement between the union and the company.[1] Under the act the company must meet with the union for the purpose of collective bargaining but they do not have to agree to anything; however, Section 8(d) of the act requires that both parties bargain in good faith.

If there is evidence that the employer has no intention to reach any agreement, the union can file an unfair labor practice charge; if it is found that the employer was

bargaining in bad faith, the board can issue a cease-and-desist order to require the parties to bargain in good faith. Bad faith bargaining is most likely to occur when the initial contract is being negotiated. Often the employer who is still trying to recover from the shock of the loss of the representation election will be reluctant to change conditions. The employer's objective at the bargaining table is to give as little as possible, with the hope that next year the employees will see how little the union had done for them and will vote the union out or at least stop paying dues.[2]

It takes a skillful negotiator to give nothing or little and not be charged with bad faith bargaining (this is sometimes called surface bargaining). Often there is a fine line between bad faith bargaining and saying no. There is no legal

---

[1] At these initial bargaining sessions most union proposals are the promises that the union made during the campaign of what it would force the employer to do if the employees voted for it.

[2] Under board rules, an election to decertify the union cannot be held until one year after the first election.

definition of bad faith bargaining, as the board relies on a case-by-case basis for its decisions. What the board looks at is the total conduct of the parties at the bargaining table. This requires a subjective evaluation by the board or the courts of the parties' attitude toward intent to reach an agreement. For example, if the employer took the position that in promotions the supervisor would have the sole discretion on who would be promoted, this would indicate that the employer did not want to reach an agreement because the employer is well aware that seniority is the life blood of a union and it could never accept such a proposal.

In a similar situation the employer, after one year of bargaining, presented 13 new proposals calling for major changes in the prior agreement, such as elimination of the union security clause, changing the work week from 35 to 40 hours, etc. The board said that if the union would accept these proposals, it would be stripped of its capacity to represent employees.[3]

Where the union bargained for an interest arbitration clause (this requires the parties to submit disputes over wages and other contract provisions to final and binding arbitration) and the company refused, the union then proposed that the bargaining issues be submitted to arbitration. The company filed with the board a refusal to bargain charge. The court held that interest arbitration is not a mandatory subject of bargaining and because the union insisted on the clause, this could be interpreted only as evidence of never intending to reach an agreement.[4]

Unilateral Action As Bad Faith Bargaining

Where a union is certified by the board, the employer is bound to deal exclusively with that union as a bargaining agent for the employees. Sometimes an employer would like to give a superior employee an extra bonus or wages above the contract rate. If this is done without the union's consent, it is bad faith bargaining. The rule in plain language is "no side deals" with union employees.[5]

Other conduct that may support a strong inference of bad faith bargaining is failing to give management representatives sufficient authority to bind the employer, refusal to sign an agreement already reached, withdrawal of concessions previously granted, or delaying tactics (this is tough to stop or prove). One of the problems of the board in bad faith bargaining cases is that the only remedy for the unfair labor practice is a cease-and-desist order; there is not much liability if found guilty of bad faith bargaining. The board tried to remedy this in a situation where the employer engaged in flagrant bad faith bargaining and one of the

---

[3] Yearbook House, a subsidiary of Shaw-Barton, 223 NLRB No. 214 (1976).

[4] NLRB v. Greensboro News, 549 F.2d 308 (4th Cir. 1977).

[5] NLRB v. American National Insurance, 343 U.S. 395 (1952).

union's demands was a union shop.[6] The board in an attempt to remedy the violation ordered the company to include a union shop provision in the agreement. The Supreme Court said that such action was going beyond the intent and scope of the act. Congress never intended to give the board such powers to compel a union or the employer to agree on any contract provision.[7]

Bad faith or surface bargaining complaints usually come before the board when the employees do not want to strike but the company will not concede to their demands; the union hopes that they will be in a better position after the company is found guilty of an unfair labor practice.[8] The union reasons that the employees might be willing to strike or the employer will concede to a few more demands after being found guilty.[9]

Regulation Of The Bargaining Process

One of the most common situations that causes refusal-to-bargain charges is the unwill-ingness of either party (usually the employer) to bargain over certain subjects. This issue is important to the union because if the employer does not have to bargain over certain conditions, the employer can always make the decision and the union does not have the right to strike over a nonbargainable issue. The employer or the union must bargain over hours of work, working conditions, and wages because this is stated in the act. Where these subjects are involved, the court does not consider the attitude of the parties at the bargaining table for those subjects are specifically required by the act.[10] These are called mandatory bargaining topics and refusal to bargain over them is per se violation of the bargaining duty.[11]

Other bargaining topics are not so clear-cut under Section 8(d); the courts must decide whether a particular subject at issue is a working condition or whether it is a management right to operate the business. The guideline used in these questionable areas is if the action taken by the company results in an economic impact on

---

[6] Union shop is a contract provision that requires all new employees to become members of the union within a certain period after hiring, usually 30 days. It also requires all present employees to become and remain members of the union.

[7] H.K. Porter Co. v. NLRB, 397 U.S. 99 (1970).

[8] When the employer is found guilty of an unfair labor practice, the board requires that a notice be put on the bulletin board that the employer has been guilty and reassures the employees that in the future the firm will follow the law.

[9] This situation reaffirms what the employer should have told the employees before the election; the union can make all the promises that it wants, but the employer has to agree before any benefits are granted.

[10] Section 8(d).

[11] Per se as used in legal context means; taken by itself; it constitutes a violation. (Black's Dictionary of Law, 5th ed. 1979).

the employees, it is a bargainable subject. This comes up regularly in a situation where the company wants to contract work out to a third party rather than have the employees do it and labor agreement is silent on this right.

Where a company contracted maintenance work out to another company and laid off employees in the maintenance department, the court held that contracting out was a subject that the firm had to discuss with the union.[12] However, if the contracting out did not result in the layoff of employees, the results would have been different.

The economic impact rule is not always followed where certain subjects are traditionally management concerns. Where a company for economic reasons closed part of its operation, the court held that the employer was required to bargain about the effect of the decision on the employees but not the decision itself because the plant closing was purely for economic reasons. The court reasoned that the economic burden placed on the employer in continuing the operation outweighed a benefit gained over labor management relations by the bargaining process.[13]

On the other hand where a company subsidized in-plant food services by an independent caterer, the court held that the company must bargain over the prices. The court affirmed the board's position that food services are "other terms and conditions of employment" under Section 8(d) of the act.[14] If the employer had not subsidized the food services, it would probably not have to bargain over such services because a subsidy is a benefit to the employees and price affects the amount of the subsidy; therefore, it is a working condition.

Another frequent issue is in the benefit area, such as Christmas bonuses or turkeys at Christmas time. This situation arises where the company has a profitable year; it gives a Christmas present to the employees (turkey, ham, fruit). Next year profits are down so the firm decides not to do it. Sometimes when profits are down, some employers continue it. The general rule in this case is that if the bonuses are intermittently given with some consistency as to their basis, they are considered gifts; where they are unilaterally skipped after consistently being given, regardless of conditions, the courts reason that they are compensation that must be bargained over.[15]

Where the employer unilaterally polled the employees and instituted a trial program of shift rotation, this was held to be refusal to bargain because shifts are conditions of employment.[16] Whether a particular subject is bargainable or

---

[12] Fibreboard Paper Products Corp. v. NLRB, 379 U.S. 203 (1964).

[13] First National Maintenance Corp. v. NLRB, 101 Sup.Ct. 2573 (1981).

[14] Ford Motor Co. v. NLRB, 441 U.S. 488 (1979).

[15] NLRB v. Wonder State Mfg. Co., 344 F.2d 210 (8th Cir. 1965).

[16] NLRB v. Southwestern Pipe, Inc., 444 F.2d 340 (5th Cir. 1971).

not is important to the parties; for this reason the board and the courts hear a reasonable number of these cases.

Because a subject is bargainable does not mean that the company must agree, but it does mean that the union has a right to strike, if it does not agree. Once the employer consistently grants a benefit like a Christmas bonus, it may not be able to stop the benefit. Although this additional compensation was not bargained for by the union, the union can bargain over taking it away.

Duty To Disclose Information

Another area where the law regulates the relationship between the union and the employer is the disclosure of information to be used for bargaining purposes. This subject is covered in Chapter XIV, where the entire subject of disclosure of employee information to third parties is detailed.

For the purpose of this chapter, it is sufficient to state that the employer has a duty to furnish the information necessary to represent the bargaining function and the administration of the labor agreement adequately. What is necessary is often a point of disagreement between the union and employer; the board must step in and determine whether the information in question is necessary.

The provision requiring information be furnished to the union by the employer has been interpreted broadly by the board. This broad interpretation has been supported by the courts as long as the union gives a reason why the information is needed.

Regulation Of The Bargaining Process

Other than the good faith bargaining requirement and the furnishing of information, there are few regulations controlling the bargaining process. Most collective bargaining sessions are unstructured and the parties establish their own ground rules. Conduct such as bluffing, misstatements, wrong figures, and arguments over certain facts are part of the bargaining process with which the law does not interfere.

Once an agreement is reached, the board can order the employer to sign the contract that contains all the agreed terms. To agree on terms and not sign is bad faith bargaining according to the Supreme Court.[17]

RESTRAINTS ON THE RIGHT TO STRIKE

If an impasse is reached in bargaining, the parties are not required to continue. The Supreme Court has held that neither party is required to continue fruitless, marathon discussions.[18]

[17] H.J. Heinz Co. v. NLRB, 311 U.S. 514 (1941).

[18] NLRB v. Am. Nat'l Insurance Co., 343 U.S. 395 (1952).

Under the Taft-Hartley Amendments of the act the initiating party (which is almost always the union) must give a 60-day notice to the Federal Mediation and Conciliation Service of intent to modify or terminate the contract. The party must also notify the state mediation agencies of intent to modify or terminate within 30 days after the 60-day notice to the federal agency.

Although all that is required is the intent to modify or terminate the contract, in practice the union or employer will notify the Federal Mediation and Conciliation Service or state agency that an impasse in bargaining has been reached; the mediation service will enter the case and attempt to get the parties to reach an agreement. Where an agreement is not reached, a strike is the usual action by the union.

Restrictions On Conduct During Strike

Most legal restrictions on conduct during a strike are under state and municipal laws. These governmental bodies under their authority to maintain the peace and to promote the public welfare have invoked a wide variety of restrictions on strike activity. The only time the National Labor Relations Board gets into the strike situation is when the employer decides to operate during a strike and hires economic replacements or when the conduct of the parties is inconsistent with good faith bargaining.

The leading case on employee rights during a strike is NLRB v. Mackay Radio & Telegraph Co., decided in 1938.[19] In that case the court held that when employees go on strike, they continue to be employees; to hold otherwise would deny them their right to strike, which is granted under the act. Although they remain employees, the employer has the right to hire permanent replacements, if it is done before the striking employees apply for reinstatement. If the striking employees request reinstatement after the job is abolished, they cease to be employees. If the jobs are not abolished, the striking employees are entitled to an offer of reinstatement whenever a vacancy occurs. The court in the Fleetwood case stated that to hold otherwise would discourage union activity.[20]

The only exception to the rule of reinstatement is those rare instances where the strike is an unfair labor practice (usually the board will act before an unfair labor practice strike takes place). In that case the courts hold that the strike is for a lawful purpose; thus the employers have an absolute right of reinstatement and the employer must terminate the

---

[19] 304 U.S. 333 (1938).

[20] NLRB v. Fleetwood Trailers Co., 389 U.S. 375 (1967).

replacements and reinstate the strikers when the strike is over.[21]

Since striking employees do not cease being employees,[22] the duty to bargain does not change because they are on strike. However, neither party is under obligation to take the initiative in getting the bargaining sessions started after the strike takes place.[23]

The collective bargaining process is not a legal process. The less use that the parties depend upon the law the sooner their differences will be settled and good employee relations reestablished.

ROLE OF UNION IN EMPLOYEE DISCRIMINATION DISPUTES

For more than 30 years the National Labor Relations Act was the only legislation concerned with labor management relationships except for some occasional disputes under the Fair Labor Standards Act.

In 1972, when Title VII was amended, a third party entered the relationship. EEOC could sue both the union and employer for discrimination. The problem immediately arises who has jurisdiction, the board or EEOC, especially when procedures are different. If the union discriminates, does the board still hold a representation election under the act? What happens to the employee's right to strike over discriminatory practices of both the company and the union?

For the purpose of this chapter it is important only to review a few basic principles concerning the role of the union in discrimination cases.

1. The Supreme Court, long before Title VII, held that where the union entered into a collective bargaining agreement with the employer that discriminated against blacks, this is a violation of the duty of fair representation because under the act all classes of employees must be represented.[24] Based on this decision the courts refuse to enforce an unfair labor practice against a union where it discriminates.[25]

2. Since the employees have elected the union to be their bargaining representative, they cannot discuss discrimination matters directly with

---

[21] NLRB v. Thayer Co., 213 F.2d 748 (1st Cir. 1954).

[22] This does not mean that they retain all benefits as employees while on strike. This will be discussed in more detail in Chapter XIV.

[23] Exposition Cotton Mills Co., 76 NLRB No. 183 (1948).

[24] Steele v. Louisville & Nashville Co., 323 U.S. 192 (1944).

[25] NLRB v. Mansion House Center Management, 473 F.2d 471 (8th Cir. 1973).

the employer but must go through the union. Where there is evidence that the union approves of employer discriminatory practices, the employees must still go to the union. Where the employees went out on strike over discriminatory practices without going through the grievance procedure, it is not a protected activity, therefore, discharging the employees is not an unfair labor practice.[26] (Discharge because of strike activity is otherwise unlawful.) The court said that although employees have a right to be free from discrimination under Title VII, the right cannot be pursued at the expense of orderly collective bargaining.

ENFORCEMENT OF THE COLLECTIVE BARGAINING AGREEMENT

One right that a union employee has that a nonunion employee does not is enforcement of the collective bargaining agreement. The Supreme Court has interpreted Section 301 of the act to mean that the individual rights of an employee under a collective bargaining agreement can be enforced in the courts. Suits can be brought by the union on behalf of the employees, by individual employees against the union and employer, and by the employer against the union.[27] This decision opened an area for employees to sue their union when the union does not enforce the contract against the employer. These are called fair representation cases. The most famous is a situation where several over-the-road drivers were discharged for falsifying their expense account; when their grievance was denied before a joint Labor-Management Arbitration Committee, the employees as individuals sued the union and the employer. The basis of their suit was that the charges of dishonesty were false and that the union made no effort to investigate to determine whether others were involved. The court held that this was a breach of union duty to represent adequately the employees under

---

[26] Emporium Capwell Co. & Western Addition Community Organization v. NLRB, 420 U.S. 50 (1975).

[27] In W.R. Grace v. Rubber Works Local 759 *103,* Sup. C. 2177 (1983) the Court held the contract could be enforced through arbitration even though management and EEOC had made a settlement to the contrary. The issue was over seniority.

the collective bargaining agreement.[28] The extent of liability of the union is what it contributed to the damages. In Bowen v. Postal Service, 103 Sup. C. 588 (1983) the Court said that the union's failure to process the grievance caused employees to lose wages and union was liable to the extent of this loss.

Because the union is subject to fair representation charges by the employee, the union will often arbitrate weak cases rather than take the exposure to fair representation charges. This has greatly increased the use of arbitration in disputes over interpretation of the labor agreement.

PAST PRACTICE AND COMMON LAW OF THE SHOP

Another area in the enforcement of the labor agreement is where the employer believes that it has the sole discretion in making a decision except where restricted by the labor agreement. The employer's belief is based on the theory that the firm retain everything that it did not specifically give away in the bargaining process. If the agreement is silent about a particular subject or practice, under this theory, management had the right to act without interference from the union.

In 1960 three cases called the Steelworkers Trilogy went to the Supreme Court.[29] In all three cases

the issue was whether the company had to arbitrate an issue not covered in the labor agreement. The Supreme Court said yes, a labor agreement cannot cover every situation and the employee has certain rights not specifically stated in the labor agreement by virtue of the employer/employee relationship. This became known as the common-law-of-the-shop theory, which was expanded into the past practice rule of labor agreements. This rule usually applies in arbitration cases where a clause is ambiguous or the agreement is silent on a particular practice. The rule as

---

[28] Hines v. Anchor Motor Freight, Inc., 424 U.S. 554 (1976). The author had a related experience. He found 25 maintenance employees drinking in the local bar. He recommended discharging five of the least productive workers. The union objected as there were others in the bar. The author told the union that if they would disclose the names, he would discharge them too. This was the end of the grievance as the union did not want to investigate further. In this situation the Hines case would apply for the five workers discharged.

[29] United Steelworkers of America v. Warrior and Gulf Navigation Co., 363 U.S. 574; United Steelworkers of America v. Enterprise Wheel and Car Corp., 363 U.S. 593; United Steelworkers v. American Mfg. Co, 363 U.S. 564 (1960).

followed by most arbitrators is that a past practice is a part of the contract unless the contract clearly states otherwise.[30]

The courts have continued to follow the Steelworkers Trilogy cases and have said that a past practice is an integral part of the contract.[31] The past practice concept has been followed into nonunion situations; in discrimination cases the court or agency looks to past practice to determine whether employees are treated differently than the past practice because of race, sex, etc.

How To Change
A Past Practice

If a union employer were to change a past practice, it would be a bargainable issue if the practice is clearly contrary to the labor agreement. For a nonunion employer it is advisable to give sufficient notice before a practice is changed. The mistake that nonunion employers usually make is that they are confronted with a glaring immediate problem where the previous practice, if followed, would result in a real economic or employee relations problems. To change it for that particular situation without notice is risky if the employee involved is a member of a protected class. It is also an exposure to union organization. The employer is well-advised to apply the past practice to the situation at hand and bite the bullet but give notice effective on a certain date that the practice will no longer be followed.

ENFORCEMENT OF NO-STRIKE CLAUSE

The law permits the employee to enforce the labor agreement against the union and the employer. It also permits the union to sue employer or the employer to enforce the labor agreement against the union. The employer enforcement of the agreement against the union usually appears in a situation where the union authorizes a strike in violation of no-strike clause in the agreement. Under Norris-La Guardia Act of 1932, the courts are prohibited from granting injunctions for strike activity. But where there is a no-strike clause, the question is whether it can be enforced in view of the Norris-La Guardia Act. Until 1970 no-strike clauses could not be enforced as the Supreme Court held

---

[30] For discussion of past practice in arbitration see Frank Elkouri and Edna Elkouri, *How Arbitration Works,* 3d ed. (Washington, DC: Bureau of National Affairs, 1973), Chapt. 12.

[31] Norfolk Ship Building Corp. v. Local 684, 671 F.2d 797 (4th Cir. 1982).

that Norris-La Guardia Act superseded the contractual no-strike clause.[32]

However, in certain situations the Court partially reversed itself; in 1970 it held that a no-strike clause can be enforced provided the labor agreement contains a mandatory grievance adjustment or arbitration clause. The Court reasoned that a no-strike clause is a trade-off for an arbitration clause; therefore, the union must arbitrate rather than go on strike.[33] In subsequent cases the court has made it clear that an arbitration clause is a prerequisite to issuing an injunction to enforce a no-strike clause. Where employees went on strike in sympathy of other employees from another company, the court held that such a strike could not be enjoined because the strike was not over a dispute of the employer in the labor agreement but in support of others not subject to arbitration.[34] This case reaffirms the court's position in the Boys Market case that the decision is narrow; the Norris-La Guardia Act is by no means dead.

EMPLOYEE RIGHT TO REPRESENTATION IN DISCIPLINARY INTERVIEWS

This chapter has emphasized that the big difference between union and nonunion status is that in a union facility the employee is represented by an agent. The question sometimes arises of whether the employee can demand that the union be present when the employer talks to the employee about discipline or other matters.

One such situation is where an employee is interviewed to determine whether discipline should be given for an alleged infraction of a rule. The Supreme Court in what is known as the Weingarten doctrine[35] held that under Section 7 of the act an employee has a right of representation if two conditions exist. First, the employee requests the representation; second, this is limited to situations where the employee reasonably believes that the investigation will result in disciplinary action. The doctrine as applied by the courts in subsequent cases does not prevent the employer from canceling the interview after the request. The interviewer can

---

[32] Sinclair Refining Co. v. Atkinson, 370 U.S. 238 (1962).

[33] Boys Market v. Retail Clerks Union, 398 U.S. 235 (1970).

[34] Buffalo Forge Co. v. United Steelworkers of America, 428 U.S. 397 (1976). This was a 5 to 4 decision. Political science students are taught that 9 reasonable persons sit on the Supreme Court, but often lawyers in 5 to 4 decisions say that 4 persons were unreasonable.

[35] NLRB v. Weingarten Inc., 420 U.S. 251 (1975).

decide whether to invoke discipline based on the established facts without further investigation. The doctrine states that the union cannot take an active part in the discussion as it is not a grievance meeting but a only meeting to investigate the facts to determine whether disciplinary action should be taken. Under the doctrine the representative (whether union representative or a co-worker) does have a right to meet on company premises and on company time with the employee before the interview according to a board ruling that was enforced by the courts.[36]

The doctrine does not apply where the employer has already decided to invoke discipline without further investigation and does not seek other facts to make a determination.[37] The courts have also stated that the request for representation must be made according to an established practice (no duty to inform employee that there is a right of representation). Where an employee stormed out of a supervisor's office stating, "I am going to get my steward," and left the office despite the supervisor's order to the contrary, the court held this was insubordination, not a Weingarten request; discharge was lawful.[38]

Where an employer violates the Weingarten doctrine and the employee is disciplined, the remedy is to make the employee whole by canceling the discipline and granting back pay. [See the Chromally Alloy case, 263 NLRB No. 20 (1982).] However, if no discipline if given, then a cease-and-desist order is the remedy.[39]

Although the doctrine may be violated if the rule violation was severe such as stealing, or for some other strong cause, the courts will not reinstate the employee, reasoning that the discharge was for just cause.[40]

Weingarten Doctrine Applied To Nonunion Employees

The question arises whether the same right exists when a nonunion employee requests representation. The board has ruled that a nonunion employee can request a coworker to be present during an investigatory interview under the Weingarten doctrine.[41] This has been reaffirmed by the appellate court in the E.I. duPont deNemours

---

[36] Pacific Telephone and Telegraph Co., v. NLRB, 711 F.2d 134 (9th Cir. 1983).

[37] NLRB v. Certified Grocers of California, 587 F.2d 449 (9th Cir. 1978).

[38] Spartan Stores v. NLRB, 628 F.2d 953 (6th Cir. 1980).

[39] ITT Corp, 261 NLRB No. 24 (1982).

[40] NLRB v. Southern Bell, 676 F.2d 499 (11 Cir. 1982). Also in Montgomery Ward and Co. v. NLRB 664 F.2d 1095 (8th Cir. 1981), and in Pacific Telephone and Telegraph Co. v. NLRB, 711 F.2d 134 (9th Cir. 1983).

[41] In Materials Research Corp., 262 NLRB No. 122 (1982) the board said there is a relative imbalance between unrepresented employees and employers and forcing an employee to attend a disciplinary interview alone does not correct the imbalance.

v. NLRB cited in Note 21 on page 185. However, the non-union employee can not be acting in his or her own behalf, but the action must affect other employees. This board ruling is consistent with the doctrine that a nonunion employee has the same rights under Section 7 as a union employee. To prevent liability under the Weingarten doctrine supervisors must be informed of the board decision and a company policy to comply.

LEGAL IMPLICATION OF ARBITRATION

Since arbitration is not a legal process,[42] this section considers only those situations where the law affects arbitration, such as under the Collyer doctrine of the National Labor Relations Board and enforcement of arbitration awards.

Under Section 10(a) of the act the board may defer to arbitration rather than process an unfair labor practice. This is commonly called a Collyer situation.[43] The board takes the position that where arbitration is provided in the labor agreement, arbitration is the forum to settle that dispute.[44] The exception to the rule that the board will not defer to arbitration is if there is a discharge for union activity or where either party is not willing to arbitrate.

When an unfair labor practice charge by the union comes under the Collyer doctrine and the employer asserts the Collyer doctrine, the matter is usually dropped and arbitration seldom takes place. One can only guess that arbitration was considered by the union before filing the unfair labor practice charges; if the board will not hear the matter, it is better to drop the case than to arbitrate it. Wherever possible, the employer should assert the Collyer doctrine when unfair labor practice charges are filed.

Relationship Of Arbitration Process To The Law

Lawyers and labor relations practitioners often disagree on what power and authority arbitrators should have. Should the arbitrator in certain areas (like discharge) be able to consider whether the law has been violated or be limited to the four corners of the labor agreement?

The Supreme Court in the Gardner Denver decision answered these question when it held that an

---

[42] In Virgin Islands' Nursing Assn. v. Schneider, 668 F.2d 221 (3rd Cir. 1982), the court held that an arbitrator does not have to give a reason for a decision to have the award enforced. This is something that a judge could not get away with.

[43] Collyer Insulated Wire, 192 NLRB No. 150 (1971).

[44] Approximately 95 percent of all labor agreements contain arbitration clauses.

arbitration award has no bearing on EEOC case.[45] In making the distinction the court said:

Arbitral procedures, while well suited to the resolution of contractual disputes, make arbitration a comparatively inappropriate forum for the final resolution of rights created by Title VII. This conclusion rests on the special role of the arbitrator, whose task is to effectuate the intent of the parties rather than the requirements of enacted legislation ... But other facts may still render arbitral processes comparatively inferior to judicial processes in the protection of Title VII rights. Among these is the fact that the specialized competence of arbitrators pertains primarily to the law of the shop, not the law of the land.

In the Gardner Denver case the discharge of the employee was upheld by the arbitrator, who never considered the discrimination charge filed with the EEOC. When the employee took the discrimination charge to court, the lower court said that he was bound by the arbitration award. The Supreme Court reversed and said that the award is only a part of the evidence to be weighed, eliminating all hope that arbitrators would be able to receive the increased caseload before the courts in discrimination cases.

ENFORCEMENT OF ARBITRATION AWARDS

Arbitration is not a judicial process: there are no standard rules of evidence or pretrial discovery procedure[46] and one arbitrator is not bound by another's decision. (Most arbitration decisions ignore decisions of other arbitrators except to justify their position.)

Facts and contract language are seldom the same. Reliance on prior decisions may be interpreted as a sign of weakness by the parties involved and could reflect on the arbitrator's professional ability to decide the facts on the merits of the case.

The law interferes with the arbitration process only when an award is challenged in the courts.[47] The challenge is either on the grounds that the arbitrator went beyond the scope of the agreement, or there was arbitrary or other misconduct on the part of the arbitrator. Normally courts are reluctant to reverse rewards as arbitration is

---

[45] Alexander v. Gardner Denver, 94 Sup. Ct. 1101 (1974).

[46] This practice may change if other courts follow C&P Telephone v. NLRB, 687 2d. 633 (2nd Cir. 1982) where information relating to the grievance had to be given to the union after the demand for arbitration, amounting requiring discovery in the arbitration process.

[47] For further information on the arbitration process see Robert Coulson, *Labor Arbitration—What You Need to Know* (New York: American Arbitration Association, 1978); Edwin Moberly Teple, *Arbitration and Conflict Resolution* (Washington, DC: BNA, 1979); Edward Paul Peters, *Arbitration and Collective Bargaining* (New York: McGraw-Hill Book Co., 1970).

a nationally recognized way to settle labor disputes. In one situation the arbitrator awarded back pay where the labor agreement did not authorize it and the court held that it is not necessary for the labor agreement to authorize back pay as long as the arbitrator does not act contrary to the agreement.[48] This decision is indicative of the wide discretion that the courts afford arbitrators. However, when they do go outside the scope of the agreement, the courts are quick to reverse the award.

Where an employee was discharged for stealing and the labor agreement was clear that the employer had a right to discharge for stealing, the court held that reinstatement of the employee by the arbitrator violated the clear language of the contract and refused to enforce it.[49]

The courts will also refuse to enforce an award if it is vague, ambiguous, or contrary to the general good of the public. It is a subjective decision by the particular court whether the award is too vague, ambiguous, or against public policy.[50]

One question that sometimes arises in the arbitration process is the enforcement of a previous award. Where one party seeks to enforce a previous award without rearbitrating the issue, it must be shown that the disputed conduct as well as the facts falls within the prior award. When the plaintiff shows that the conduct does fall within the previous award, the defendant must show that there is an exception to the previous award. Otherwise the courts will enforce a previous award, because the conduct is the same and no exception to the previous award can be shown.[51]

Beyond the enforcement of awards, the law considers arbitration a nonlegal method of settling disputes over the interpretation of a labor agreement.

The limited treatment of arbitration in this chapter should not give the impression that arbitration is necessarily a simple process and seldom-used method of settling disputes. If the subject of this book were contract administration, the nonlegal aspects of the arbitration process would cover several chapters but arbitration demands much less consideration in a book on personnel law.

---

[48] Resilient Floor & Decorative Covering Workers v. Welco Mfg. Co., 542 F.2d 1029 (8th Cir. 1976).

[49] Mistletow Express Service v. Motor Expressman Union, 566 F.2d 692 (10th Cir. 1977). Also in NLRB v. Fixture Mfg., Co., 669 F.2d 547 (8th Cir. 1982) the Court refused to reinstate an employee under an arbitration award when a contract gave the employer a clear right to discharge.

[50] In Meat Cutters Local v. Great Western Food Co., 712 F.2d 122 (5th Cir. 1983) the court refused to enforce a reinstatement award as contrary to public policy when an employee was discharged for drinking when driving a truck.

[51] NLRB v. Owners Maintenance Corp., 581 F. 2d 44 (2nd Cir. 1978); Oil, Chemical Workers Int'l Union v. Ethyl Corp., 644 F.2d 1044 (5th Cir. 1981).

SUMMARY AND CONCLUSIONS

The existence of union representation places an additional burden on the employer to bargain over wages and other working conditions. In the bargaining process management rights are exchanged for an agreement from the union that the employees will not strike. Management agrees to inform employees of all vacancies and promote according to qualifications and seniority; it agrees to certain wages and benefits; it often gives up a right to change hours of work without notice, etc., in return the employees agree not to strike, a right that they had under Section 7 of the act. The law imposes a duty on the employer to discuss with the union certain conditions of employment, but it does not require either party to agree to anything. However, once it is agreed, the courts will enforce the agreement. The employee can sue the union and the employer. Each party to a labor agreement can sue to enforce terms of a labor agreement. However, it is rare for an employer to sue the employee; instead the union, as the employee's representative is subject to the lawsuit.

Arbitration is a recognized nonlegal method to settle labor disputes. Neither the board nor the courts will interfere with the process unless the award goes beyond the labor agreement or rights of the employees granted to them under Section 7 of the act are interfered with. The arbitration process usually does not affect the employees' rights under the law. When an employee is discharged and alleges a violation of the labor agreement and also an antidiscrimination statute, the employee has "two bites on the apple"; if not reinstated, through one process, maybe the other process will do so.

The rights of the employee through representation are not increased by the law. The law does enforce the agreement that has been voluntarily entered into between the employer and employee representative. Through that agreement the rights of employees are increased to the extent that employer grants them.

CHAPTER XII

PAYMENT OF WAGES UNDER THE FAIR LABOR STANDARDS ACT

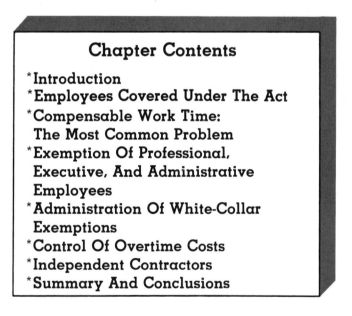

Chapter Contents

*Introduction
*Employees Covered Under The Act
*Compensable Work Time:
  The Most Common Problem
*Exemption Of Professional,
  Executive, And Administrative
  Employees
*Administration Of White-Collar
  Exemptions
*Control Of Overtime Costs
*Independent Contractors
*Summary And Conclusions

INTRODUCTION

The problem of the proper worth of a job is as old as the employment of one person by another. Judging the worth of a job raises questions involving philosophy, economics and sociology. From a practical standpoint the important issue is what the employer is willing to pay and what the employees are willing to accept.

Until the enactment of the Fair Labor Standards Act of 1938[1] (the act) the employer and employee decided between themselves what compensation should be paid for services rendered. The employer developed compensation systems that attempted to reward the worker for output and for contribution to the organizational objectives, taking into consideration the supply and demand for a particular skill in the marketplace.

The act interfered with the employer-employee relationship in determining the amount of compensation to be paid an employee by requiring the payment of a minimum wage to employees and prohibited the employer to employ a person for more than specified number of hours per week without paying time and one-half of the regular rate. After the Fair Labor Standards Act, Congress passed several other statutes to control wages: Walsh-Healey Public Contracts Act,[2] Davis-Bacon Act,[3] Service Contract Act,[4] and Equal Pay Act.[5]

Because the principles established by the Fair Labor Standards Act are followed by the administrator of the Wage and Hour Division of the Department of Labor in determining hours of work and related subjects under Walsh-Healey, Davis-Bacon, and Service Contract Act, these statutes are not considered here. This chapter is concerned with the situations that frequently arise under the Fair Labor Standards Act and the problems involved in compliance. Minimum wage requirements under the act involve a relatively small percentage of the gainfully employed and have less compliance problems than other sections of the act. Therefore it is not discussed in this chapter.

EMPLOYEES COVERED UNDER THE ACT

The act covers employees of any enterprise engaged in interstate or foreign commerce if such an enterprise has two or more employees who produce goods exceeding $275,000 per year. This definition excludes several enterprises: however, most states have enacted little fair labor standards acts that cover employees not in-

[1] 29 USC Sect. 201 et seq.

[2] 41 USC Sect. 35–45.

[3] 40 USC Sect. 276.

[4] 41 USC Sect. 351–58.

[5] 29 USC Sect. 206 et seq.

cluded in the federal act. For this reason whenever an employer-employee relationship exists, it is rare that employees are not covered unless the enterprise or employees are specifically exempted by the federal or state act. Section 203 exempts enterprises such as mom-and-pop businesses where only the family is employed, and owners of nonprofit organizations not having a business purpose. Seasonal recreational establishments are also exempted under the act. State and local governments are exempt under the Supreme Court decision of the National League of Cities v. Usery, 426 U.S. 833 (1976). Several types of employees are also exempted, such as professional, executive, and administrative. The determination of when an employee comes under these exemptions is discussed later.

Penalties For Violation

The act is enforced by the Wage and Hour Division of the Department of Labor and carries with it a criminal penalty for willful violations. Penalty for willful violations include fines up to $10,000 and imprisonment up to six months. A willful violation must be deliberate, voluntary, or intentional as distinguished from accidental, negligent, or inadvertent.[6]

Where no violation is found, the penalty is restitutionary back pay; under certain conditions liquidated damages equaling the amount of the back pay can be awarded. That amount of back pay and liquidated damages awarded is discretionary with the court. Often in determining the damages for failure to pay overtime, the amount of overtime worked is difficult to determine. The courts have stated that in the absence of employer records, the employee's recollections of the hours worked is sufficient if reasonable.[7]

In all situations under the act the defendant has a right of jury trial; the successful plaintiff may obtain attorney's fees and costs from the defendant.

Many questions concerning enforcement and interpretation of the act by the Department of Labor can be found in its interpretive bulletins. Such bulletins as "What Are Hours Worked," #785; "Overtime Compensation,"#778; "General Coverage of the Act," #776; and "White Collar Workers," #541 are useful in understanding the division's position on the interpretation of the act. For the most part these interpretations have judicial acceptance but cannot be entirely relied on as law.

---

[6] Nabob Oil Co. v. United States, 190 F.2d 478 (10th Cir. 1951).

[7] Mumbower v. Callicott, 526 F.2d 1183, 1186 (8th Cir. 1975).

COMPENSABLE WORK TIME: THE MOST COMMON PROBLEM

The act does not limit the hours that an employee can work but requires that the employee be compensated for all the time worked. It also provides that the employee must be compensated at time and one-half for all hours over 40 in one workweek. The act contains no definition of *work* and only a partial definition of *hours worked*. A study of the countless court cases on the subject of time worked discloses that if the employee is serving the interests of the employer, it is considered time worked under the act.

It is immaterial whether the work were requested by the employer or authorized as long as it was performed and the employer had reason to believe that the work is being performed.[8] Where work is being performed, it is difficult for the employer to plead no knowledge because the results of the work performance or existence of it is something the employer knows about or should know with reasonable diligence. Where the employee works and the employer fails to pay for the work, overtime problems arise.

Payment Of Meal Periods

The act does not require the payment for meal periods when employees are serving their own interests. However, in many work situations they are not. A shipping clerk is not required but chooses to remain at the desk during meal periods eating a brown bag lunch and directing the unloading of a truck while chewing on a sandwich. A secretary knits at her desk, the supervisor asks for a file. A maintenance mechanic is called to repair a machine during lunch hour. In all these situations the employer often does not pay for meal periods, because the employee is serving the interest of the employer while eating lunch, the courts have held in these situations that the employee is not really relieved of duty and whether inactive or active all meal periods must be paid for. If the shipping clerk is active only occasionally, all meal periods are considered time worked unless special arrangements are made the work week is 42.5 hours rather than the 40 hours that the employer intended when granting half-hour meal periods.[9]

These examples are common situations where the employer unknowingly has considerable exposure. The employer falsely reasons that since the employee is not required to work or remain at the

---

[8] Handler v. Thrasher, 191 F.2d 120 (10th Cir. 1951). The author once discharged an employee on Christmas day. The author knew that the employee was working overtime without recording it to keep up but could never catch him. The employee never suspected somebody would be around on Christmas day to find him working.

[9] Mumblower v. Callicott, cited in Note 7. A special arrangement could be made to allow a 45-minute lunch period, deducting 30 minutes per day for the meal period.

work site and does so as a matter of convenience, it is not work time. Rest or snack periods are usually paid for as a policy matter. Under the Department Regulations,[10] 29 CFR Sect. 785.18, if less than 20 minutes they are compensable.

However, some courts state that because employees are serving their own interests, they are not compensable[11] and do not support the Wage and Hour Division's position as stated in Section 785.18. Other courts enforce the regulation on the presumption that rest periods promote efficiency, which is in the employer's interest. A safer approach, if the employer does not want to pay for rest periods or snack periods, would be, if possible, to offset rest periods against other working time such as compensable waiting time or on-call time so total hours worked do not exceed 40. This offset has been approved by at least two courts.[12] However, this is not always possible, and employee relations problems could become prevalent.

Off-Duty And On-Call Time

The general rule is that if an employee is completely relieved from duty and such time is long enough to enable the employee to use the time for one's own purpose, it is not considered time worked. This often comes up where waiting time is involved. If the waiting time is part of the job, it is compensable; if the employee is free to use the time for one's own purpose, it is not considered waiting time.[13] Another problem often arises when the employee is required to be on call. The usual rule is if the employee is not required to remain on the premises but is required to leave word with the company officials or at home where to be reached, it is not considered work time while on call.[14]

The 10-Minute Meal Period

In one situation the employees made a deal with the manager that if they took a 10-minute lunch period they would be able to quit 20 minutes early and still work 8 hours per day. (They also had two rest periods.) After a 3-year period one employee evidently got indigestion or a nervous stomach and complained to the Wage and Hour Division.

The division took the position that under its regulations, CFR Sect. 785.18, this must be a paid period because it was less than 20 minutes. Investigation revealed that employees left their machines and went to the lunchroom for 10 minutes (one even stated that he

---

[10] "What Are the Hours Worked?" Interpretative Bulletin No. 785 (29 CFR, Sect. 785.18).

[11] Blain v. General Electric, 371 F.Supp. 857 (D.C. Ky. 1971).

[12] Mitchell v. Greinetz, 235 F.2d 621 (10th Cir. 1956); Ballard v. Consolidated Steel Corp., 61 F.Supp. 996 (S.D. Cal. 1945).

[13] Skidmore v. Swift & Co., 323 U.S. 134 (1944).

[14] Armour & Co. v. Wantock, 323 U.S. 126 (1944).

went home for lunch). When the bell rang then all returned to their machines. The Wage and Hour Division demanded two year's back pay because employees worked 40 hours and 50 minutes per week under their interpretation. This amounted to over $12,000 for about 60 employees. The employer took the position that because employees were serving their own interest for the 10-minute meal period, it was not work time, therefore not compensable, and refused to pay the back pay. After a period of threatening litigation, the Wage and Hour Division dropped the matter. Since employees for the 10-minute period were serving their own purposes, the 10-minute period was not work time.

Compensable Waiting Time

Another common exposure of an employer is where an employee comes to work well before the regular starting time. This happens when a spouse drops an employee off or with car pools, which causes the employee to get to the work site early, being a good employee the person performs duties before being clocked in. This is compensable work time about which employer does not consider. It is neither stopped nor approved but tolerated. Preshift work is almost always held compensable. Where a butcher sharpened his knives outside shift hours, the Supreme Court held it compensable.[15] The same result occurred where preshift paperwork was performed.[16]

In these situations where employees arrive at the worksite from 15 to 20 minutes early and the employer has no knowledge of whether they are working or not, the rule of thumb used by some courts is that if they arrive 15 or more minutes early, they are presumed to be working unless the employer can prove otherwise.[17]

Compensatory Travel Time

The Portal to Portal Act[18] eliminates from working time certain travel and walking time or other similar activities before or following the workday unless considered compensable by custom or practice. If travel time is integrated with work, it is compensable, as those traveling on employer business or field repair crews often do.

If a nonexempted employee regularly works in Chicago and is sent to Minneapolis, travel time would be compensable[19] (deducting time between home and airport). If as a routine assignment the employee goes to Minneapolis, under certain conditions the courts

---

[15] Mitchell v. King Packing Co., 350 U.S. 260 (1956).

[16] Dunlop v. City Electric, 527 F.2d 394 (5th Cir. 1976).

[17] Ibid.

[18] 29 USC Sec. 251–262

[19] Marshall v. R & M Erectors, Inc. 429 F.Supp. 771 (D. Del. 1977).

may conclude that travel to Minneapolis comes under the Portal to Portal Act and travel to Minneapolis is merely a change of work site. Travel time also must be considered on a weekly basis; the employer can avoid excessive overtime due to travel by giving compensatory time off in the same workweek in which the overtime was earned.

Often travel time is spent for meetings and training programs.

Such time, whether travel time or time spent in training sessions or meetings, is not compensable under division rules if all these four conditions are present: (1) the event is held outside working hours; (2) attendance is voluntary; (3) training or meeting is not directly related to the employee's job; and (4) the employee does not perform any productive work while attending the meeting or training sessions.

EXEMPTION OF PROFESSIONAL, EXECUTIVE, AND ADMINISTRATIVE EMPLOYEES

The most common problem under exemptions is whether the duties of an employee are such that they are exempted under the act. The act specifically exempts professional, executive, and administrative employees.[20] In determining whether an employee is exempt, Interpretative Bulletin 541[21] is helpful. The Wage and Hour Division uses a salary test to determine whether an employee is included under one of the exemptions. If an employee is paid over a certain salary (this is regularly increased by the department), an employee can spend 20 percent of work time in nonexempt work and still be considered exempt. Whether an employee is exempt often depends on the nature of the business and the

job content. Job titles may indicate job content, but the title is not controlling. When a job title listed in Bulletin #541 as exempt, it is seldom audited.

Most employees tend to stress the importance of their jobs. Often when interviewed by a compliance officer they rate their jobs at a level higher than reality, which makes them exempt but in fact they are nonexempt (unless they are complainants who feel that they are denied overtime pay). From an employee relations standpoint the personnel practitioner tends to classify an employee as exempt in questionable cases. Another reason why the employees are often classified as exempt is where they can control their own

---

[20] Sec. 13(a) (1). Besides exemptions for white-collar employees, the act has several other exemptions such as motor carriers, air carriers, agriculture workers.

[21] CFR Sect. 29, Part 541.

overtime. One way to eliminate the problem is for the employer to make them exempt and hope that it can be defended in a wage-and-hour audit. Because there are many gray areas where exempt and nonexempt classifications are being interpreted for reasons other than payment of overtime, the employer is continually exposed to violations. A policy is necessary on whether to take the exposure for employee relations considerations or strictly to construe the act in order to avoid the penalties of back pay.[22]

Another exempt classification is outside sales persons. Under Section 213(a) (1) of the act they are exempted if they sell regularly or obtain orders for goods or services while off the employer's premises. Comparatively speaking this classification is less troublesome than administrative, professional, or executive classifications as the activities can objectively be defined.

ADMINISTRATION OF WHITE-COLLAR EXEMPTIONS

The first step in an exemption policy is to assign one person the responsibility for handling exemptions. This person should be given the final authority in each case to determine whether an employee is exempt or nonexempt. Every supervisor or manager has a special interest in making an employee exempt or nonexempt; often it has nothing to do with job content.

Certain guidelines should be established and communicated to all supervisors as to exempt or nonexempt classifications in those gray areas where the risk of violation is the greatest. Job description should be developed for wage and hour compliance; they should include the distinctions in Bulletin #541. As a defensive measure, one should require employees to write their own job description. The job descriptions should be reviewed by the supervisor or personnel department to ensure that all the activities are included. In compliance reviews when the investigator interviews the employee; it is difficult for the employee to change a position during the interview when the employee wrote it originally (There is often an incentive to change job content if the employee becomes aware of the amount of back pay.) Also when the job de-

---

[22] Often the practitioner has a difficult time with an executive secretary who wants to be part of management and not record her time although job content makes her nonexempt. She goes to her boss; he calls personnel; she is exempt.

scription is in writing, made out by the employee, the compliance officer is more likely to accept the job description.

Most job descriptions for wage and hour compliance are either too vague or merely follow the wording of the regulations and are therefore meaningless to determine exempt or nonexempt status. The best job descriptions for wage and hour compliance are those that list specific duties and their frequency of performance. The job description should pinpoint those activities that answer whether the exempt or nonexempt requirements are met. The job description for wage and hour compliance is for the purpose of documenting management position on the exempt or nonexempt classifications and may not be applicable for other purposes for which job descriptions are used, such as hiring, promotion, compensation, etc.

When determining exempt or nonexempt classifications there is no exposure to violations if an employee is wrongly classified as nonexempt and paid overtime. It is only when an employee is wrongly classified as exempt that the employer has liability for overtime pay. An employee can be misclassified as exempt for a considerable time and nothing happens until the employee complains and the Wage and Hour Division investigates and

takes a position. For this reason in those gray areas it is advisable to keep a record of hours worked by exempt employees, although it is not necessary under division rules.

Since the issue of nonexempt disputes usually involves a small number of employees in any one company, few disputes ever go to litigation; economically it isn't feasible for either party. Where a large number of employees is involved, the Wage and Hour Division takes the issue to court to get some guidelines. Where a fast-food chain had all their assistant managers classified as exempt supervisors and the Wage and Hour Division claimed that they were nonexempt employees, the court gave the following rules to determine whether assistant managers were supervisors:[23]

1. They must recommend hiring and firing.

2. They must direct the work of two or more persons.

3. They have management duties.

4. They regularly and customarily exercise descretion .

Two of the four requirements are subjective; the gray areas were not eliminated. In any given situation subjective determination must be made whether management duties existed and discretion is customarily and regularly exercised.

---

[23] Donovan v. Burger King, 672 F.2d 221 (1st Cir. 1982).

CONTROL OF OVERTIME COSTS

One of the difficult problems for the employer in the control of overtime costs is that many times the employee's desire to earn overtime pay is stronger than any action that the employer can take. A waste control clerk or sales service expediter can always find a reason to work overtime when money is needed to buy a new boat.[24] The first step in the control of overtime is to remove from the employee as much as possible the decision of when overtime should be worked. This can be done by requiring authorization before overtime can be worked. The enforcement of the rule of requiring authorization must be by discipline; if the employee works the overtime, it must be paid for. The Wage and Hour Division takes the position that unauthorized overtime still must be paid if known or tolerated;[25] the courts are likely to sustain this position.

Compensatory Time-Off As Control Of Overtime

Because the law requires that overtime be paid only after 40 hours in one workweek, compensatory time-off can be given any time during the workweek in order to avoid overtime payment.[26] Overtime hours worked in one week cannot be offset by a subsequent workweek or by providing compensatory time-off at a later date.[27]

Where the employer pays premium pay for time worked such as for working on a holiday or double the regular rate for working on Sundays, the premium pay may be excluded from the employee's regular rate and credited toward overtime pay where employee works more than 40 hours in week that premium pay was granted. Under this rule an employee could work 42 hours in the week where double-time was granted and not be paid overtime for work over 40 hours. However, this policy may cause some employee relations problems.

Belo Contract As Control Of Overtime

The Belo contract is a guaranteed wage contract made with the nonexempt employee who receives constant weekly wage and hours varying widely from week to week. This plan is an effective

---

[24] The author once made a study of overtime for nonexempt group leaders and found that their overtime increased before they went on vacation and before Christmas.

[25] 29 CFR Sect. 778.316 and 785.11 and 13.

[26] Walsh-Healey Act and Davis-Bacon require in most areas overtime after 8 hours per day. Employers that are government contractors as defined by these statutes could not avoid overtime payment by compensatory time-off.

[27] *Opinion Letter* No. 971 (Washington, DC: Department of Labor, Wage and Hour Division), March 26, 1974.

method to control overtime where the employee can control hours of work. It is widely used for field repair service, customer service jobs, and other situations where the job requires work off the premises by nonexempt employees.

The conditions necessary to quality for a Belo contract were stated by the Supreme Court in Walling v. Belo Corp., 317 U.S. 706 (1941). The court listed five requirements:

1. The duties of the job covered by the contract must require irregular number of hours per week. This is the key requirement. The fluctuation must not be caused by economic conditions or employer control but by job duties of the employee.

2. Hours must fluctuate below as well as above 40 hours per week.

3. The contract must pay the employee a regular hourly rate above the statutory minimum wage requirements.

4. The weekly guarantees must pay at least one and one-half times the regular rate for all hours over 40.

5. The contract cannot cover more than 60 hours a week.

Exhibit XII-1 is a Belo contract that complies with these requirements, except #2 which is obtained from payroll records.

EXHIBIT XII-1

BELO CONTRACT

_____ (Company Name) _____ , hereby agrees to employ _____ (Name of Employee) _____ as _____ at a regular hourly rate of pay of $ _____ per hour for the first forty (40) hours in any work week and at the rate of at least time and one-half or $ _____ per hour for all hours in excess of forty (40) in any work week, with the guarantee that _____ (Name of Employee) _____ will receive in any work week in which he or she performs any work for the company, the sum of $ _____ as total compensation for all hours performed up to and including (insert the total hours agreed upon, however hours agreed upon cannot exceed 60 hours per week) hours.

COMPANY NAME

By _____

Accepted:

_____
(Employee's Signature)

The average hours inserted in the last line must bear a "reasonable relationship to the hours an employee actually works." This is usually determined in the first contract by past overtime records. However, the actual hours worked before a Belo contract is usually greater than what is worked after the employee is paid for a set number of hours per week under the new arrangement. When the incentive is removed to earn more overtime pay, the overtime hours usually decrease with no effect on job performance. To anticipate a decrease in hours by entering less than the previous average would not be in violation of the Belo requirements but may result in poor employee relations. A better plan would be to review the contract in six months or a year and base the average hours on the experience under the Belo.

In the second contract year the hours could be reduced if the average shows it but should not be reduced to the average. Otherwise the employee is not being rewarded for efforts in doing the work in less hours.

INDEPENDENT CONTRACTORS

Sometimes an employee who wants to earn extra money will offer to clean the office or do yard work during off hours at a predetermined fee. The employer, to avoid paying overtime and promote good employee relations, will sever the employee-employer relationship for this job assignment and create an independent contractor relationship, for which no overtime need be paid. In determining independent contractor status the courts look to the totality of the circumstances.

To determine whether an independent contractor relationship exists, the following questions should be asked. A favorable answer to one does not make the person an independent contractor; several affirmative answers are necessary, especially to 1, 2, 3, and 4.

1. Who supervises and employs the workers, who pays Social Security, worker's compensation taxes, etc.?
2. Who controls the progress of the work except for completion and final inspection?
3. Does the nature of the work imply independence?
4. Who controls how the work should be done as distinguished from what should be done?
5. Does the person perform similar work for other employers?
6. Is the work to be performed for a fixed price and for a fixed amount of services?

The Supreme Court has said that not only should an independent contractor have independence in the performance of the assigned job but initiative and decision making authority should be associated with the independent contractor. Otherwise an employer/employee relationship exists.[28]

The major factor in the determination of independent contractor status is the degree of control. The more control, the more likely the worker will be found to be an employee. A person who is required to comply with instructions about when, where, and how to work is ordinarily an employee. Some employees who are experienced or proficient in their work need little instruction; however, this does not put them in an independent contractor status as the control element is present if the employer retains the right to instruct. For the purpose of determining employer/-employee relationship under the National Labor Relations Act, the board applies only the right of control test. If the person for whom services are performed retains the right of control of the end result and also the manner and reasoning to be used in reaching that result, an employer/employee relationship exists.[29]

It is difficult not to retain the right to instruct for a person who works for the employer 8 hours a day in one job and cleans the office at night or mows the lawn on Saturday. If an employer/employee relationship exists overtime compensation is due for all hours worked over 40 unless the flat fee paid for cleaning the office exceeds what the employee would have received on a time and one-half basis under the Fair Labor Standards Act.

If an employer assumes that an independent contractor relationship exists and in fact it does not exist, the exposure in other areas is far greater than the payment of overtime. There is no insurance coverage of worker's compensation for the independent contractor; if a person is hurt and an employer/employee relationship in fact existed, the employer is liable even though there is no worker's compensation insurance coverage. Income tax withholding, unemployment compensation, and Social Security withholding and payments by the employer are required for an employee but not for an independent contractor. If the employer is wrong as to the relationship, the employer is liable for all payments including the employee's withholding and Social Security payments. Because of this exposure the employer should be cautious when treating the relationship as independent contractor status.

Situations Where An Employee Relationship Exists Rather Than Independent Contractor

To prevent exposure to liability where an employer assumes an independent contractor relationship

---

[28] NLRB v. United Insurance Co., 390 U.S. 254 (1968).

[29] National Freight, Inc., 146 NLRB No. 144 (1964).

exists but an employer/employee relationship legally exists, some examples may be helpful.

Where a gasoline distributor leased stations to operators, the court found that not only was the lessee an employee, but those persons whom the lessee hired were also employees of the distributor. The evidence showed that the distributor controlled the hours of operation, prices of major items, and daily management of money and took the risk of profits and loss. The court reasoned that the employees of the lessee were an integral part of the operation; therefore, they were also employees of the distributors and the lessee.[30] Other cases where the court found an employee/employer relationship are where an agent operated a retail cleaning outlet under a contract was held to be an employee of the owner[31] and where crew leaders for a builder registered under a state law as labor contractors but were in practice employees.[32] In the Fifth Circuit a contract laborer who was a mechanic and supervisor was held to be an employee; however where the contract laborer was a concrete subcontractor of this employee, he was held to be an independent contractor.[33]

SUMMARY AND CONCLUSIONS

Violations under the Fair Labor Standards Act can exist for a long time before anything happens. Often the employee is content with the violation either because it is not known to be a violation or it is more convenient (such as coming to work early and working) to ignore the requirements of the act.[34] When the honeymoon is over, the employers are caught with egg on their face.

An investigation by the Wage and Hour Division of the Department of Labor for compliance can be caused by complaints from the employee, unions, or competitors or by routine industry check by the agency. Most investigations occur through employee or union complaints. Seldom does the agency make spotchecks unless it finds a flagrant violation in one company and wants to determine if it is a practice in the industry, such as in the fast-food industry after the Burger King case. Compliance with the certain provisions of the act is not difficult while in other situations it can be an employee relations problem. Often the employer, when a violation is questionable, is

---

[30] Marshall v. Truman Arnold Distributing Co., 640 F.2d 906 (8th Cir. 1981).

[31] Donovan v. Sureway Cleaners, 656 F.2d 1368 (9th Cir. 1981).

[32] Marshall v. Presidio Valley Farms, Inc., 512 F.Supp. 1195 (W.D. Tex. 1981).

[33] Donovan v. Techo, Inc., 642 F.2d 141 (5th Cir. 1981).

[34] The basic statutory limitations for liability is two years; three years for willful violations. As one manager told the author, "I have been doing unintentionally for five years. I am already three years ahead if found wrong."

willing to take the risk of being determined in violation, such as in exempt and nonexempt classifications in order to avoid employee relations problems.

In payment for hours worked, if it is remembered that where the employee cannot serve one's own interest, it is considered compensable hours. Some employees like to eat at their desk and answer the phone; the employer lets them and does not consider it time worked. In this situation to avoid compensation the employee must leave the work site or be granted a longer meal period.

In determining whether a job is exempt, from the employee relations point of view the firm should make it exempt if the job content makes it doubtful. This may cause problems later, but some employers feel that it is worth the exposure rather than to disrupt employee morale. Unless the employee complains the problem seldom emerges.

Travel time is a difficult problem to control. However, the employer can consider compensatory time-off or interpret the Portal to Portal Act to exempt payment of travel time where travel to work site is on a regular basis.

For the employer to control overtime, two strong positions must be taken. One, enforcement of a strong overtime policy that as much as possible removes the control of hours from the employee.

Second, where control of overtime hours cannot be removed from the employee and exempt status can not be justified, the Belo contract or some other pay plan should be considered. If a pay plan other than Belo is considered, it should be reviewed by the Wage and Hour Division to determine what position the division will take in the event of a compliance review. (Sometimes asking for opinion can instigate a review; maybe it is better to put the plan in and wait for the review. This is a decision that the employer must make.)

Creating an independent contractor status is one way to control overtime. Extreme care should be taken to make certain that although an independent contractor status was intended, an actual employee/employer relationship does not exist. Liability for uninsured worker's compensation and payment of unemployment, Social Security and withholding taxes often offset the advantages of establishing a questionable independent contractor status. In any independent contractor status a written contract should be executed and contain the requirement of independent contractors outlined in this chapter. Professional advice should also be considered when establishing an independent contractor relationship that may be questionable.

CHAPTER XIII

COMPLIANCE PROBLEMS WITH EQUAL PAY ACT AND ITS CHILD, THE COMPARABLE WORTH THEORY

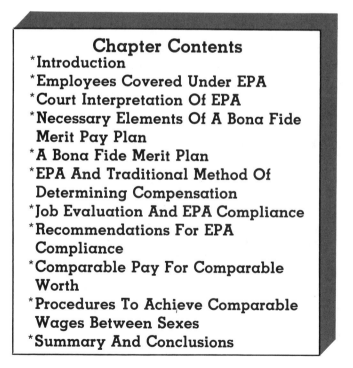

Chapter Contents
*Introduction
*Employees Covered Under EPA
*Court Interpretation Of EPA
*Necessary Elements Of A Bona Fide Merit Pay Plan
*A Bona Fide Merit Plan
*EPA And Traditional Method Of Determining Compensation
*Job Evaluation And EPA Compliance
*Recommendations For EPA Compliance
*Comparable Pay For Comparable Worth
*Procedures To Achieve Comparable Wages Between Sexes
*Summary And Conclusions

INTRODUCTION

As stated in Chapter XII, the first interference by the federal government in the payment of wages was in 1938, when the Fair Labor Standards Act was passed and employers were told that they had to pay minimum wage and overtime premium to their employees. For the next 25 years there was no further interference with the employer's right to determine wages of their employees. By 1962 the percentage of women in the workforce increased from 25 percent to about 35 percent; earnings of women average 60 percent to 70 percent that of men for year-round, full-time work.[1]

Congress considered this a social problem in the same manner as minimum wage legislation. In 1963 it amended Section 6 of the Fair Labor Standards Act, and called the amendment the Equal Pay Act (EPA).[2] EPA simply states that no employer shall discriminate in the payment of wages within a facility on the basis of sex for equal work on jobs that require equal skill, equal effort, and equal responsibility and are performed under similar working conditions, unless the differential is based on seniority, a merit system, an incentive pay system, or any factor other than sex.

The EPA statute is easily defined but can cause problems in wage and salary systems. Many employers have depended on loopholes and other defensive provisions for the survival of their wage and salary systems. Since 1979 vigorous enforcement by EEOC has jeopardized such a policy.

EMPLOYEES COVERED UNDER EPA

Because EPA was an amendment to the Fair Labor Standards Act, it basically covers the same employees as FLSA. However, coverage was extended by amendments to certain employees exempt under the FLSA. EPA was amended in 1966 to include workers in schools, hospitals, laundries, drycleaning establishments, nursing homes, retail, and on large farms. In 1972 professional, administrative, and executive employees were included. Finally in 1974 EPA was extended to all levels of state, local, and federal government employees. Equal pay standards are limited to each facility of a company and are

---

[1] U.S. Department of Labor, Women's Bureau, Pamphlet #9 "Economic Indicators Relating to Equal Pay" (Washington, D.C.: Government Printing Office, 1962).

[2] 29 USC 206 et seq.

not to be applied between various facilities of the employer. Before the EPA amendment was passed, about 20 states had already passed equal pay laws; 45 states, the District of Columbia, and Puerto Rico presently have equal pay laws that include employees not covered under the federal law.

EPA provisions are enforced in the same manner as other provisions of FLSA with one distinction. Since 1979, EEOC enforces EPA, while FLSA is still enforced by the Wage and Hour Division of the Department of Labor. This distinction is important.

COURT INTERPRETATION OF EPA

While EPA can be simply defined, it is not as simple to interpret. The first problem is how different must a job be in terms of skills, effort, responsibilities, and what are the similar working conditions under which the job must be performed. The first opportunity that the courts had to answer these questions was in Schultz v. Wheaton Glass Co. where male selector packers were receiving $.21 per hour more than female selector packers.[3] They performed substantially the same work, which was inspection work, except that approximately 18 percent of the time the male selectors did materials handling tasks.[4] Females were not permitted to perform these tasks because they were restricted from lifting anything over 35 pounds. Material handling was also performed by male snap-up boys who made $.20 more than

male selectors. The court, in a landmark opinion on the interpretation of EPA, established a legal principle in finding a violation of EPA; it has been followed by other courts in many decisions. In view of the refusal of the Supreme Court to review the decision, these principles can be considered as controlling. These principles are sometimes called the "equal work standard."

1. The equal work standard requires only that the jobs be substantially equal and not identical. Small differences will not make them unequal.

2. When a wage differential exists between men and women doing substantially equal work, the burden is on the employer to show that the differential was for some reason other than sex.

---

[3] Schultz v. Wheaton Glass Co., 421 F.2d 259 (3rd Cir. 1970); cert denied, 398 U.S. 905 (1970).

[4] Right after the enactment of EPA, the first loophole that employers conceived in EPA was to change the job content to include tasks that women did not normally perform. The author in 1965 spent a lot of time writing "compliance job descriptions."

3. Where some but not all members of one sex performed extra duties in their jobs, these extra duties do not justify giving all members of that sex extra pay.

4. That men can perform extra duties does justify extra pay unless women are also offered opportunity to perform these jobs.[5]

5. Job titles and job descriptions are not material in showing that work is unequal unless they accurately reflect actual job content.[6]

This decision was followed four years later in a case where male orderlies were assigned extra duties that nurse aides were not required to perform. These duties were primarily turning over patients and helping them when physical support was required. The court held that the difference was not substantial to justify the wage differential.[7]

What is a substantially different job is decided on a case-by-case basis. Where there is a substantial difference in effort, skill or responsibility, the courts permit a pay differential between the sexes.[8] The

principle that job content, not job titles or job descriptions, is what determines whether jobs are equal was also followed in the Eighth Circuit.[9]

Definition Of Similar Working Conditions

Another justification for a wage differential between men and women on which the employer relied was shift work. Where all men worked the night shift and women the day shift, it was argued by employers that the differential was justified because they were not similar working conditions. In the only EPA case to reach the Supreme Court, it was held that working conditions as used in EPA do not refer to the time of day when work was performed and different shifts do not justify a pay differential.[10]

This case also established the rule that equal pay violations could be remedied only by raising the women's wages, not reducing the men's but left open the question of whether changes in job content could remedy the violation. Often employers attempted to justify pay differentials between men and women by arguing that working

---

[5] To offer the extra duties to women would often destroy the purpose of the extra performance to justify the differential.

[6] In the author's experience, they may be accurate for a short time in reflecting job content but if a women could do the job, the supervisor would let her do it and the job description would become obsolete; the jobs would become equal, but the pay would be unequal.

[7] Brennan v. Prince William Hospital Corp., 503 F.2d 282 (4th Cir. 1974).

[8] Usery v. Columbia University, 568 F.2d 953 (2nd Cir. 1977).

[9] Katz v. School Dist. of Clayton Missouri, 557 F.2d 153 (8th Cir. 1977).

[10] Corning Glass Works v. Brennan, 417 U.S. 188 (1974).

conditions were not similar, that the jobs, performed by males were more hazardous tasks than ones performed by females. There are situations where this might be a defense. However, such a defense should be used with extreme caution. Statistics show that 70 percent to 85 percent of all industrial accidents are not caused by physical conditions but by unsafe acts of the employee. Under these statistics hazardous working conditions would not justify the differential if accidents are caused by the employee and not the hazardous conditions.

Equal Skills As A Defense

For the purpose of the Equal Pay Act, skills have been defined as those skills that the employee must possess to meet the performance requirements of the job. These skills are usually measured by experience, education, training, and ability to perform the job. A common "equal skill" situation that courts have struck down is where the employer trains men for promotional purposes but does not offer to train women who for some reason are not considered in the promotion plans; when the jobs are compared, the trained men have more skills than women.[11]

Where male tellers were paid more than female tellers, the employer argued that the males were being trained in all aspects of banking to replace senior officers;

because they were in a bona fide training program, the differential was justified. The court said that mere recognition by management of the ability to be promoted does not constitute a bona fide job-training program. Subjective evaluation of potential for promotion standing alone cannot justify pay differentials under EPA.[12] In order to justify pay differentials under EPA through a bona fide training program (1) it must be open to both sexes, (2) employees must be notified of the training opportunities (3) there must be a defined beginning and ending of the training program, and (4) a definite course of study and advancement opportunities upon completion are essential. It is also advisable to put the program in writing.

Equal Responsibility As A Defense For Unequal Pay

The defense of a difference in responsibility to justify unequal pay occurs mostly in administrative, professional, and executive jobs, where before the 1972 amendment these employees were excluded from coverage under EPA.

One of the first cases under the responsibility defense was where the employer claimed that men had to make decisions that women did not have to make. The court found that although men did make decisions that women did not, such decisions were subject to review by supervisors. Therefore,

---

[11] Schultz v. First Victoria Bank, 420 F.2d 648 (5th Cir. 1969).

[12] Marshall v. Security Bank & Trust Co., 572 F.2d 276 (10 Cir. 1978).

the differential was not justified under the responsibility defense.[13]

Often the employer justifies a pay differential between sexes in the same job categories in that one type of work is more difficult than another. Where the employer claimed that management of soft-line departments such as clothing, usually managed by women, had less responsibility than hard-line departments as sporting goods, usually managed by men, the courts have held that there is no substantial difference.[14] The same result occurred where a female softball coach was paid less than a male baseball coach in a high school.[15]

NECESSARY ELEMENTS OF A BONA FIDE MERIT PAY PLAN

One of the factors that will justify differentials is where a properly communicated bona fide merit system is applied without regard to sex. All too often the term *merit pay* is used to include cost-of-living increases, longevity increases, and other, general, across-the-board increases that have no relationship to meritorious performance.[16] Merit increases that will survive judicial review under EPA are individual increases in pay related to job performance of that individual. A bona fide merit policy is a pat on the back with dollar bills in the palm of the hand.

Where the merit system determined earnings above the base pay by quality and quantity of production, the court held that there was no violation of EPA when males were paid higher than females.[17] On the other hand the merit system must do what it is designed to do, i.e., pay extra for better performance.

Where a merit system included seniority as well as quality of work and pay was based only on seniority, the courts said that lower

---

[13] Hodgson v. Fairmont Supply Co., 454 F.2d 490 (4th Cir. 1972).

[14] Brennan v. T.M. Fields, Inc., 488 F.2d 443 (5th Cir. 1973).

[15] Brennan v. Woodbridge School District, 74 Labor Cases CCH 33,121 (D.C. DC, 1974).

[16] This usually happens when the employer does not want to set a precedent of granting cost-of-living increases or longevity increases; thus it is called merit. The misuse of the term becomes evident in EEO cases where a merit increase is given one month and employee is discharged the next month for poor performance.

[17] Cupples v. Transport Insurance Co., 371 F.Supp. 146 (N.D. TX, 1974).

female rates were not justified because seniority factors were not applied uniformly to males and females.[18] This situation is an example of the employer who gave performance as a pretext for additional earnings and then determined the wages on some other subjective factor to justify the wage level. Determining a wage level on some factor other than performance is the major fault with merit pay plans and why they do not stand judicial scrutiny. In an inflationary period the employer wants to keep earnings in line with the labor market conditions, yet does not want to set a precedent by implying that pay increases are automatic or based on labor market conditions. Rationalization sets in and any believable reason is given.

Where the employer uses a reason for an increase in compensation that is not related to performance, it is not a bona fide merit plan. The following study is an example of how the term is misused in business. In 1983, 248 "large companies"were surveyed to determine what merit increases they would give in 1984; they reported 6.3 percent for exempt and 6.1 for nonexempt. If these companies had a bona fide merit plan, how would they know in 1983 what level of meritorious performance would be achieved in 1984 and further what have exempt and nonexempt classifications to do with performance?[19]

A merit pay plan should not be related to inflation or labor market conditions. That should be taken care of by an increase in base pay. The problem is that most companies call it a merit plan; to the courts this denotes an award for performance. A merit pay plan based on performance is compensation paid above the base pay; if the employer wants to reflect inflation in merit pay, the firm can do so by the merit pay being determined by a percentage of the base pay.

In order for a compensation plan to be based truly on merit, it should be given at a time when some significant performance has been completed. For administrative purposes, that could be done by periods, providing that the waiting period is not too long as to chill motivation. In production incentive plans for factory workers, merit pay for the previous three-month period should be the maximum waiting period and paid within two weeks after the end of the merit pay period.

---

[18] Hodgson v. Washington Hospital, 19 Wage and Hour Cases 1101 (BNA) (D.C. PA, 1971).

[19] Survey by Towers, Perrin, Foster and Crosby as reported in *Ideals and Trends* a Commerce Clearing House editorial staff publication, #43, July 15, 1983 (Chicago: Commerce Clearing House, Inc.).

A BONA FIDE MERIT PLAN

In order for a merit pay plan to be bona fide under the various statutes, it should be in writing and contain all or most of the following elements.[20]

1. The employee must believe that good performance will result in additional compensation.[21]

2. There should be a direct correlation between the amount of pay and the exceptional performance, without any upper limits. Upper limits tend to dampen the motivation of certain workers.

3. The employee should understand the merit plan before it is adopted so that there are no surprises at evaluation time. (The author can recall working with the most motivated incentive worker he has ever known. She was asked at 10:30 A.M. how much incentive pay she had earned so far that day and she knew. This employee understood the incentive plan.)

4. The performance should be accurately measured either by objective performance appraisals or standards of performance with which employee agrees. If agreement cannot be accomplished, the employer should be sure that it is right and adopt it. Sometimes employees have to work with the plan before they are convinced they can earn additional money.

5. The base pay should not be reduced because an employee is on a merit system. Merit pay should be given when performance is above the average worker's base pay.

6. The merit system must be updated periodically. Job content affects the performance; if not current, either the company or employee is unfairly affected.

7. Managers must believe in the system and be trained to properly administer it.

8. The plan must be monitored. It will not run by itself. This may require full-time standards engineers where large number of jobs are involved, but the increased production justifies the added costs.

9. Follow-up procedures are necessary to prevent bias and leniency. Nothing can defeat

---

[20] In EEOC v. Aetna Insurance Co., 616 F.2d 719 (4th Cir. 1980) and Brennan v. Victoria Bank & Trust Co., 493 F.2d 896 (5th Cir. 1974). The Courts allowed discrimination when a merit plan contained these elements.

[21] A prominent industrial engineer once told the author that an incentive plan is 10 percent technical knowledge and 90 percent selling it to the employees involved.

a merit plan faster than leniency or bias.[22]

Pay Based On Factors Other Than Sex

Wage and salary plans based on seniority are not in violation of EPA if there is a direct correlation between seniority and pay levels and it is otherwise a bona fide seniority plan. Most seniority plans fail under EPA because they are not applied to males and females in a like manner. Departmental seniority that excludes females is a good example.

Another factor, other than sex, that employers tested in the courts is the area of employee fringe benefits. This is further discussed in Chapter XIV; however, it is sufficient to say here that a difference in employee benefits does not justify a differential in pay. The employer's argument that requiring a greater pension contribution for females than for males because women live longer was not justified under EPA. The Supreme Court adopted the lower court's position that actuarial distinctions based entirely on sex could not qualify as an exception based on any factor other than sex.[23] In a situation where a deferred compensation plan with optional contributions and optional method of receiving benefits one of which was an insured annuity plan that women would receive less benefits for same contribution than men because of use of sex segregated actuarial tables the court said that this was not a factor other than sex i.e. longevity of life, that would justify a differential under the Equal Pay Act.[24]

An example of valid factors other than sex according to the Labor Department's opinion (not yet reversed by EEOC since it obtained jurisdiction in 1979) is temporary assignments made to a lower rated job with the employee retaining the rate of the old job (sometimes called a red circle rate), which is greater than for the female doing the same work. Another example would be a male permanently transferred to another job and is "red circled" to his old job rate which is greater than the female rate. A bona fide training program as discussed in this chapter could be a factor other than sex.

One factor other than sex that has not been judicially reviewed is part-time work. Such review is unlikely unless EEOC brings it to court. The Department of Labor has taken the position that part-time employment (under 20 hours per week) is a factor other than sex to justify a pay differential.

---

[22] For further discussion on effective merit pay plan, see Nathan B. Winstanley, "Are Merit Increases Really Effective," *Personnel Administrator*, April 1982, p. 37.

[23] City of Los Angeles v. Manhart, 553 F.2d 581 (9th Cir. 1976), 435 U.S. 702 (U.S. S.Ct. 1978).

[24] Arizona Governing Committee For Tax Deferred Annuity and Deferred Compensation Plans, Etc., et. al. v. Nathalie Norris Etc. 103 Sup Ct. 3492 (1983).

EPA AND TRADITIONAL METHOD OF DETERMINING COMPENSATION

Until the Equal Pay Amendment, the employer and employee were left to decide what should be paid males and females for services rendered. The employer developed compensation systems that attempted to reward the worker for output and for contribution to organizational objectives, taking into consideration the supply and demand for a particular skill in the marketplace.

As the empoyer later hired large numbers of persons, some evaluation system had to be designed to compare one job with another. Faced with this problem, employers developed or purchased various programs to prevent inequities in the wage structure. Employee contributions were rated by subjective measurements that would justify wage levels that the supervisor had already decided were appropriate. The systems, whether developed or purchased, tended to lack ingenuity and general applicability. At best they offered an easy solution to a troublesome problem Sometimes it would have been better to use a simple description of wage-and-salary administration, give the employee a periodic increase or tell why not—and be sure the plan is right on the why not.

The traditional methods of determining what to pay new em-ployees did not start in a scientific or formal way. Typically the employer looked at the marketplace and offered the minimum rate that would attract applicants. If too few would work at this rate, the employer would increase it. When more employees were needed, the employer would see what was being paid elsewhere and offer the new hires slightly less if possible. If this rate did not attract qualified applicants, it would be increased or the difference would be justified by job content if comparison had to be made with employees already working in the same job. In short the labor market conditions and the profitability needs of the employer would determine the starting wages to be paid.

Frequently, while the starting rate was set by the wage and salary administrator or the employment manager, the supervisor would subjectively determine any increases. The wage policy always had enough flexibility to permit justification of an increase. A new job description, a new job title, or a reevaluation might be necessary, but the supervisor's position was usually justifiable within the policy. This method was bound to create inequities. The method of determining wages developed so many problems that something had to be done. The best solution initially seemed to be a job evaluation system that would set a value for each job. These systems were quickly accepted by personnel practitioners as the way to lay to rest once and for all the troublesome—and somewhat boring—wage-and-salary problem.

Job evaluation was easy to sell to top management and to supervisors who still had their loopholes.

It was often complicated and too difficult for employees to understand. Some dissatisfied employee would quit rather than try to buck the system; others would join the union. The personnel director appointed a wage-and-salary person to administer the program and the title of wage-and-salary administrator was created.

JOB EVALUATION AND EPA COMPLIANCE

The EPA was destined from the beginning to run head on into job evaluation systems and compensation policies such as those discussed. The most common job evaluation systems were based on job descriptions that measured the same areas of the job with which EPA was concerned, such as knowledge or skill, responsibility or accountability, effort and working conditions. Job evaluation differed from EPA in that the numerical scores in job evaluation were measured against market conditions and internal compensation structures that EPA did not recognize. Neither did it recognize the methods used by supervisors in giving increases. To the extent that the job evaluation became subjective, it violated EPA.

Court interpretations of EPA have made it clear that only those jobs within the same category

must be compared. If there are no males and females in the same job categories, EPA does not apply.[25] This eliminated effective coverage of large groups of employees because most women are concentrated in relatively few job categories, traditional female jobs could not be compared with traditional male jobs.

Failure Of EPA To Correct Differences Between Sexes

From the outset EPA did not correct wage differences that existed before the act. The employer took the position that existing wage and salary systems did give equal pay for equal work; thus there was no need to change the policy of determining wages by job evaluation, market conditions, profitability, or competitive practices. The determination of wages

---

[25] Orr v. Frank R. MacNeil and Son, Inc., 511 F.2d 166 (5th Cir. 1975).

by market conditions and job evaluation were found by researchers to have built-in sex bias.[26]

Starting salaries in job categories that are predominantly female are traditionally lower and will stay that way, as long as the supply of labor is adequate. In 1955 women workers received 64 percent of the rate of male workers'; in 1975, 12 years after EPA, they received 59 percent.[27]

If starting salaries for the same work are different between the sexes, the differential continues as salary increases are granted. The justification usually given by employers is that the jobs are not the same. Frequently the differences in job content are no more than might be observed between two workers of the same sex receiving the same pay. The law permits pay discrimination as long as the employers give legally acceptable reasons. If these reasons are not challenged by the employee or by the enforcement agency, it is never determined whether they are legally acceptable. Where violations are found under EPA, the correction is made only within the specific job categories. The basic wage and salary procedures are not considered by the courts nor will the courts require the employers to change them. Often within a short time due to changes in job assignments, the violations recur and remain that way unless another complaint is filed.

This section has shown why present wage and salary procedures have failed to eliminate wage differentials between the sexes. It would be presumptuous to assume that the factors that determined wages and salaries in the past will be abandoned by employers. Such considerations as employee qualifications, job content, union membership, labor market conditions, employee work behavior and contribution, local practices, profitability, and competition will continue to determine the compensation level unless the courts or Congress intervenes. As long as these factors determine compensation compliance with EPA, it will continue to be a problem.

The lower starting rates traditional for females in the labor market are carried over in transfers and promotions or job integration.[28] This carryover effect is well illustrated in the case of the female plaintiff who held the position of

---

[26] "Women, work, and wages; equal pay for jobs of equal value," National Academy of Sciences Committee on Occupational Classification and Analysis, Washington, DC, 1981.

[27] U.S. Department of Labor, Bureau of Labor Statistics, "U.S. Working Women: A Databook," 1977, p. 35.

[28] Some courts have held that labor conditions justify differential hiring rates for the same job. Where females received lower starting rates than males, the courts have this justified under the EPA. See Kouba v. All State Insurance Co., 691 F.2d 873 (9th Cir. 1982). Also Horner v. Mary Institute, 613 F.2d 706 (8th Cir. 1980).

assistant to a male advertising director. When the director was transferred, the plaintiff assumed the duties but not the title of director. She was not compensated at the same level as the former director. The court said that she was entitled to the same compensation under EPA.[29]

RECOMMENDATIONS FOR EPA COMPLIANCE

Although the failure of employers to abandon traditional methods of determining pay levels and pressures of the labor market conditions make compliance with EPA difficult, that does not mean that the statute should be ignored. Programs and procedures that show good faith efforts to eliminate differences between sexes will minimize exposure to litigation. They are also an effective defense in the event a lawsuit is started.

An effective EPA compliance program should:

1. Pay careful attention to job structure, document jobs with concise, content-oriented descriptions, and be wary of slight modifications of jobs to fit a specific individual or of "fudging" in a job description to classify (and pay) one employee at a higher level than other employees doing substantially equal work.

2. Examine pay relationships between a new hire and employees hired earlier, in the same or higher level jobs and correct inequities promptly. Differences should be based on defensible criteria, such as relevant education or experience, bona fide training or merit pay programs.

3. Examine pay differentials among all jobs involving equal skills, effort, responsibility, and working conditions. If the firm finds an instance where a pay differential may be based on sex, it should eliminate the inequity by bringing the pay of the lower paid employee to the level of the higher paid or substantially changing the job content of one of the jobs.

4. Be consistent in the application of hiring, promotion, and pay increase practices and criteria used to determine wage levels.

5. Document reasons for pay actions that may later be questioned and be reasonably sure that the position is legally defensible.

---

[29] Fitzgerald v. Sirloin Stockage, Inc., 624 F.2d 945 (10th Cir. 1980).

COMPARABLE PAY FOR COMPARABLE WORTH

The language of EPA and its legislative history make it clear that only jobs that are substantially equal in all respects are to be compared. The concept of evaluation of comparable jobs was expressly rejected by Congress.[30] Every court that has considered the question has agreed the EPA requires equal work not comparable work. As the 3rd Circuit said:

In sum, we conclude that Gottlieb's testimony established no more than that the positions at issue were "comparable." We hold that such a showing of comparability of positions was not sufficient to give rise to an inference that those positions were "equal," as that term is used in the Equal Pay Act.[31]

In the House of Representatives debate on Title VII, sex was added to race, color, religion, and national origin shortly before the bill was voted on. This addition introduced a possible conflict with EPA.[32] To clear up the conflict, the Senate added the Bennett Amendment to Title VII [Sect. 703(h)]. This amendment provides that in determining compensation, an employer may differentiate on the basis of sex if such differentiation is authorized by EPA.

In 1979 the EEOC took the position that the Bennett Amendment-EPA defenses of equal skill, effort, and responsibility under similar working conditions were not applicable under Title VII but that other provisions of Title VII still applied, thus allowing a comparison between job categories.

The application of the comparable worth theory to Title VII by EEOC gave rebirth to the World War II National War Labor Board's policy of requiring equal pay for comparable work. However, wages then were controlled by law. The board used job evaluation to determine whether inequities existed between dissimilar jobs and would order equalization whether the jobs were performed by men or women under its emergency power to control wages.[33]

The courts have rejected the EEOC position.[34] In Gilbert v. General Electric the Supreme Court said that Congress did not intend to put the courts into the business of evaluating jobs. Another court, in considering the question under EPA, would not allow the comparison of nurses with tree trimmers but would look only at the comparison of females and males in the nursing category.[35] In still another situation a court required that the EPA defenses apply to Title VII cases and refused comparison between physical plant

---

[30] *Congressional Record* 9209, 88th Congress, 1st session (1963).

[31] Angelo v. Bacharach Instrument Company, 555 F.2d 1164 (3rd Cir. 1977).

[32] House of Representatives Report No. 414, 88th Cong., 1st session (1963).

[33] General Order 16, November 1942.

[34] General Electric v. Gilbert, 429 U.S. 125 (1976).

[35] Lemons v. City and County of Denver, 620 F.2d 228 (10th Cir. 1980).

employees and clerks, secretaries, library assistants, and computer operators.[36]

Some proponents of the comparable wage theory argue that one court decision opened the door.[37] The court in this case said that if an action is brought under EPA, one cannot compare between job categories, but that this exclusion does not prevent an action for sex discrimination from being started under Title VII. The basic reasoning of the court is that Congress did not intend the Bennett Amendment to insulate discriminatory practices from judicial redress under Title VII. This narrow 5-to-4 decision decided a procedural issue only and specifically ignored the comparable worth issue. Post-Gunther decisions have followed the Supreme Court in allowing an action to be brought under Title VII, but courts have construed Gunther narrowly, stating it is not up to the courts to value the worth of jobs.[38] When a male supervisor brought action under Title VII on the basis that female clerks were paid an attendance bonus and male supervisors were not, the court said that there is good reason for the bonus because clerks are often absent and supervisors are not.[39] In Kouba v. All State Insurance, 691 F.2d 873 (9th Cir., 1982) the use of past salaries as one hiring criterion was permitted although females' rates were lower than males.

It may be concluded that under present court decisions the comparable worth theory has no judicial acceptance but neither has it been completely rejected by the courts under Title VII. The only thing that appears reasonably certain is that litigation will be encouraged under the Gunther decision because fear that comparable worth theory will be blocked by EPA has been eliminated when action is brought under Title VII.

Under the present wage system, if an employer attempted to adopt a procedure that would comply with the comparable worth theory, it would be economic disaster, as well as fatal to the personnel practitioner attempting it. The methods used by the War Labor Board to equate dissimilar jobs is not applicable where wages are not controlled by law and there is no scarcity of labor as during World War II. Although some unions are advocating the theory (especially the International Union of Electrical Workers),[40] collective bargaining would be in turmoil. Who would negotiate first in a hospital: the janitors or the nurses? Would the liquor store clerks or the librarians negotiate for city employees? Certainly the good

---

[36] Christensen v. University of Iowa, 563 F.2d 353 (8th Cir. 1977).

[37] County of Washington v. Gunther, 101 Sup.Ct. 2242 (1981).

[38] Plemer v. Parson's Gilbane 713 F.2d 1127 (5th Cir. 1983).

[39] In Bartelt. Berlitz School of Language, 698 F.2d 1003 (9th Cir. 1983), the court permitted evidence to support Title VII even though it would not be permitted under the EPA.

[40] IUE v. Westinghouse Electric Corp., 631 F.2d 1094 (3rd Cir. 1980).

faith bargaining provisions under the National Labor Relations Act would have to be changed if hospitals refused to bargain with nurses until the janitors' contract was settled.

One cannot relate wages to job values when the wages of the tree trimmer were not set by job values but by various other factors discussed in this chapter. Comparison of job values in setting wages could work only if all jobs would start at zero compensation and the level of wages determined by a job analysis procedure. This approach would require a criterion set by law that would be isolated from market conditions, supervisor's subjective judgments, and pressures by labor unions. (Certainly there never could be agreement on what criteria to use unless Congress passed a law dictating the criteria.)

This is not to say that employers should ignore the social and political pressures of the comparable worth theory any more than they should ignore compliance problems with EPA and Title VII. Seventeen states have passed laws that contain comparable worth or similar language for employees in the public sector. The jury is still out on the impact of such legislation on wage and salary procedures.

One thing seems certain. The problem of governmental regulations over wages is in its infancy and is almost certain to increase during the 1980s. The law in this field is new enough to enable the employer to seek a solution before unwanted legislation is passed.

PROCEDURES TO ACHIEVE COMPARABLE WAGES BETWEEN SEXES

Some suggested ways to lessen the impact on wage and salary structure by the comparable worth argument is as follows:

1. The firm should strive for more objective methods of determining wage levels through job evaluation. This method must consider labor market conditions and leave fewer loopholes for subjective judgments by supervisors, such as present job evaluations that do not explain differences between male and female rates or rates deter-mined by conditions and internal considerations other than job values.

2. Administration of wage and salary policies must have as an objective the determination of wages by criteria that are applied in all situations. If applied equally to males and females, any criterion would be acceptable to the courts as being in compliance with EPA and Title VII.

3. Male job categories must be integrated with female as the best solution to the com-

parable worth problem. As long as a large percentage of female workers are concentrated in very few job categories, pressures will increase to raise female wages rates artificially by attempting to establish the comparative value with other wages that were artificially determined. Integration will be difficult since factors other than wages attract females and males to certain job categories, but it is not too soon to try.

SUMMARY AND CONCLUSIONS

The Equal Pay Act states that no employer shall discriminate in payment of wages within any facility on the basis of sex for equal work on jobs whose performance requires equal skill, effort, and responsibility under similar working conditions unless such differential is based on a seniority system, merit system, or any other factor than sex.

Under the court interpretation of this act, the jobs need not be identical in all respects but must be substantially equal. Most employers mistakenly believe that minor difference in the job content justifies the differential between sexes; therefore, most violations occur in this area.

In order for the seniority system, merit plan, or factor other than sex to justify a pay difference it must be a bona fide system that actually grants additional pay for seniority or for additional performance under a merit system. A merit system to be bona fide must objectively measure performance and reasonably compensate for additional performance.

Traditional compensation systems have a built-in headwind for compliance with EPA and Title VII. Job evaluation systems that use a point count and then are not followed in every case because of market conditions or supervisor considerations are especially dangerous. The comparable worth theory, if implemented, will not only result in the redistribution of wage benefits but force out traditional methods of setting wages and cause even greater inequities between jobs. Even if values could be set for each job, this development would not eliminate employer exposure to equal pay litigation. The court in Gerlach v. Michigan Bell Telephone stated that comparable worth undervaluations alone will not establish cause of action for sex-based discrimination.[41]

Other courts have followed the Gerlach case and found that unequal pay for comparable work did not violate Title VII.[42] The

---

[41] Gerlach v. Michigan Bell Telephone Co., 501 F.Supp. 1300 (E.D. MI, 1980).

[42] Walter v. KFGO Radio, 518 F.Supp. 1309 (D.N.D. 1981); also see Plemer v. Parsons Gilbane, cited in Note 38.

solution to the problem of pay differentials is to become more objective and forceful in job evaluation procedures. A second step is to recognize that market conditions influence wage levels, as the court did in Kouba v. All State Insurance. The employer must control, as much as possible, the supervisor's emotional or subjective reasons for setting wages and must also integrate job categories and recognize that the comparable worth theory is neither a solution to equal pay problems nor a concept that can be implemented. Comparable worth is an academic concept that tells the employer that existing differences between male and female compensation is a social problem that must be corrected.

CHAPTER XIV

REGULATION OF EMPLOYEE BENEFITS PLANS AND EFFECTIVE USE OF EMPLOYEE AGREEMENTS

Chapter Contents

*Introduction
*Regulations Of Pregnancy Disability Benefits
*Case Law On Pregnancy Disability
*The Effect Of The Law On Upaid-Leave-Of-Absence Policy
*Personnel Policy Restrictions Of Military Selective Service Act
*Vacations—Compensation Or Time-Off
*Overview Of Employment Retirement Income Security Act Of 1974
*Requirement Of Alternative Health Insurance Plan
*Sex Discrimination In Benefit Plans
*Impact Of Mandatory Retirement On Benefit Plans
*Effective Use Of Employment

INTRODUCTION

An employee benefit is something of a monetary value that is not related to work performed and either paid for in whole or in part by the employer. Health insurance, life insurance and pensions are employee benefits when the employer is the purchaser of the plans for the benefit of the employee. Normally this type of benefit is granted by a policy decision of the employer, is not taxable and ceases when employment terminates.

Another type of benefit discussed here is payment for time not worked, such as holiday pay, vacation pay, disability leave, and in some cases leaves of absence for reasons other than medical. Usually these benefits are defined in a benefit policy statement and vested in all employees when hired or shortly thereafter. In certain circumstances the employer does not want to treat all employees alike when it comes to terms and conditions of employment; in separating these employees from others an employment agreement is necessary. Chapters XII and XIII described how the payment of wages are regulated by statute. This chapter describes how statutes have regulated employee benefits even though they were granted voluntarily by the employer. No statute requires the employer to grant any employee benefits or to pay for time not worked. It must be emphasized that if the employer decides to grant employee benefits, it then becomes regulated except in those instances where regulations can be mitigated by an employment agreement.

REGULATIONS OF PREGNANCY DISABILITY BENEFITS

The EEOC guidelines issued in 1972 stated that pregnancy-related disabilities must be covered in health benefit plans like all other temporary disabilities. These guidelines were challenged by

General Electric Company, whose health plan excluded pregnancy-related disabilities. The Supreme Court rejected the EEOC guidelines and stated that there was no disparity between men and women since the disability plan was not worth more to men than to women.[1] In a related situation where the employer denied women seniority standing upon return from pregnancy, the Court said that this differs from denial of benefits as the women are being denied employment opportunities that men were not denied when returning from an illness; this is a violation of Title VII.[2]

Provisions Of The Pregnancy Disability Amendment

The Civil Rights movement took the issue back to Congress, asserting that the decision would have serious economic consequences for millions of working women who were either the sole wage earners or married to husbands earning less than $7,000 per year (at that time considered poverty level).[3] Two years after the General Electric case, Congress amended Section 701 of Title VII of the Civil Rights Act of 1964. The amendment required the employers to include disability for pregnancy in their existing temporary disability sick leave or health insurance benefits programs. The only exception is in the case of abortion which could be excluded unless the life of the mother is endangered if the fetus were carried to term.

Where medical complications result from an abortion, it is considered an illness and must be covered. The amendment, however, does not prevent abortion coverage on voluntary basis.

The amendment expands the definition of sex discrimination in employment to include all employment practices where there is discriminatory treatment due to pregnancy. The refusal to hire, promote, or transfer because of pregnancy is discriminatory and is considered a violation of the act.

The congressional intent of the amendment is clear. In all employment practices, pregnancy must be treated like any other illness. The disability period begins when the employee can no longer perform her duties satisfactorily and ends when she is able to do so. The amendment does not require the employer to grant any more benefits for pregnancy than for any other type of disability, but they must be the same.[4]

---

[1] General Electric Co. v. Gilbert, 429 U.S. 125 (1976). This case also established a legal principle used in all discrimination cases that in order for an employer's action to be sexually discriminatory it must be gender-based.

[2] Nashville Gas Co. v. Satty, 434 U.S. 136 (1977).

[3] Testimony before a congressional committee stated that twenty million women were in this category. A report "Prohibition of Sex Discrimination Based on Pregnancy," to the committee on Education and Labor, 95th Congress 2nd session, Report no. 95-948 March 13, 1978.

[4] Zichy v. City of Philadelphia, 590 F.2d 503 (3rd Cir. 1979).

Problem Areas Of The Pregnancy Amendment

The problem of treating pregnancy like any other illness is that pregnancy is not any other illness. The employee has notice of the forthcoming situation. After the birth there is a natural tendency of the mother to want to be with the baby after she is physically able to return to work. In some cases it could be argued that she may not be mentally able to return if forced to leave the baby too soon after birth. Another problem occurs when the mother is physically able to return to work, but chooses to stay home to nurse the baby. Another difference is that after any other illness the employee usually returns to work; this is less likely in the case of pregnancy leave. Because these differences inherently exist, the courts have had difficulty in interpreting the law according to the congressional intent of the act.

CASE LAW ON PREGNANCY DISABILITY

The first problem for the courts was the period of illness. It was obvious from the language of the statute that the period of disability cannot be arbitrary as was the practice before the act.[5] The case law is quite clear that an arbitrary determination of the leave of absence period due to pregnancy would violate the act. Where leave was mandatory upon learning of the pregnancy and must wait 60 days after delivery to return to work, the court said that employer failed to show that such a policy was BFOQ under the sex discrimination exception of Title VII although safety of the public was involved.[6]

The court in another situation stated that a forced-leave pregnancy policy violated the act if leave were required when first learning of the pregnancy, but did not violate the act when it applied to flight attendants in their second and third trimesters of pregnancy. The court reasoned that in the later stages of pregnancy BFOQ is a defense. The court said that evidence showed that in the second stage of trimester (13 to 28 weeks) it is a medical question and after 28 weeks (third stage) there is a substantial growth of passenger safety risks to warrant the policy.[7]

Many practitioners have difficulty in treating pregnancy like

---

[5] Common practice was to force unpaid leave of absence after five months of pregnancy and require return to work within three months after birth of child.

[6] Harriss v. Pan American Airways, 649 F.2d 670 (9th Cir. 1980).

[7] Burwell v. Eastern Airlines, 633 F.2d 361 (4th Cir. 1980). Also in National City Airlines 700 F.2d 695 (11 Cir. 1983).

any other illness in keeping the job open until the employee returns. There is a tendency to make the policy different for pregnancy because of the large number of female employees do not return to work after delivery; the employer has no knowledge of this unless the employee advises before the leave that she will not return to work.[8] Under the statute the employer must hold the job open to the same extent as for the male employee who broke a leg skiing.[9]

Another problem with the pregnancy disability amendment is where different benefits are allowed for female employees than for spouses of male employees. The EEOC argues that a policy is not gender-based, and male and female employees must be treated alike.

Where the employer provided full costs of hospital room and 100 percent of all other medical expenses for the first $750 and 80 percent thereafter, the plan made no distinction between male and female employees, but imposed a $500 deductible on the spouse of male employees for maternity benefits in the absence of complications. The male employees complained to EEOC that they were being discriminated against because their spouses were not covered in the same manner as female employees.[10] The Supreme Court agreed, reasoning that the statute makes it discriminatory to give married male employees a benefit package for their dependents that is less than provided to married female employees.[11] The full impact of this decision and its extension to other situations will be determined by future litigation.

State Laws Concerning Pregnancy Disability

Most states have passed laws specially prohibiting discrimination based on pregnancy or interpret their fair employment practice laws, state constitutions, or other laws to prohibit treating pregnancy differently than illness.

Because Title VII only covers employers in interstate commerce with 15 or more employees, there is no conflict with the federal law for this group of employers. Where there is dual coverage and the state

---

[8] This would be a mistake on the part of the employee as it would amount to termination and the employee could be denied all disability benefits, as well as other benefits. A personnel practitioner who wants rapport with the employees should not accept notice without explaining the consequences.

[9] Southwestern Bell Telephone Co. v. Maternity Benefit Litigation, 602 F.2d 845 (8th Cir. 1979).

[10] According to the U.S. Bureau of Census (1982), 20.1 percent of the employed population has dependent spouses.

[11] Newport News Shipbuilding and Dry Dock Company v. EEOC 103 Sup Ct. 2622 1983.

law conflicts with the federal law, the same rule applies as in all other Title VII provisions, i.e., the state statute can be more restrictive but not conflict with federal law or the constitution. This sometimes comes up in the abortion section of the pregnancy disability amendment where state laws are different and can run afoul of the constitutional right to terminate a pregnancy.[12] The practitioner should be familiar with state law before drafting a policy on pregnancy disability.

THE EFFECT OF THE LAW ON UNPAID-LEAVE-OF-ABSENCE POLICY

In granting unpaid leaves of absence, most enterprises determined cases individually, depending on the reason for the leave and whether an employee was needed or could be replaced during leave of absence period. In many cases it depended on the whims of the supervisor. Often one department within a facility would have a different rule than another. Most labor agreements provide for granting an unpaid leave for specific reasons such as medical or extended leave for union business; Beyond these specific reasons there is broad language in the labor agreement, which usually leaves it up to the employer when to grant an unpaid leave of absence, subject to challenge by the union.

With the present requirements of antidiscrimination statutes and courts that all employees should be treated alike, the unilateral right to grant unpaid leaves of absence is rapidly diminishing. For example, where an employee wants a leave to see his dying mother in Sweden, a leave of absence is granted by extending the vacation period. Another employee wants to see her dying mother in California; another employee has a 22nd cousin who is dying in Florida (the only relative whom he knows of); another wants to go to a religious summer camp for four months; another wants to work for passage of the Equal Rights Amendment for one year or the right-to-work law for six months. If the employer does not have a written detailed policy that is uniformly applied to all these situations, there is exposure to discrimination and retaliation charges.

The court will not question the conditions under which a leave is granted but will question the subjective determination of who should be allowed a leave. Retaliation charges can develop over a refusal to grant an employee an unpaid leave of absence who sued the employer under Title VII or some other statute if there is a loose policy. Sexual harassment and religious discrimination are among the

---

[12] Roe v. Wade, 410 U.S. 113 (1973).

retaliation charges that often has to be defended in granting an unpaid leave of absence to one individual and not another. The employer, in view of exposure to discrimination charges, should review the leave of absence policy and if needed set a few broad guidelines.

PERSONNEL POLICY RESTRICTIONS OF MILITARY SELECTION SERVICE ACT

One of the first restrictions on personnel policies was the Military Selective Service Act of 1967 and its predecessor amendments that protect reemployment rights of veterans. These statutes restrict promotion, probationary periods, payment of wages, leaves of absence, and vacation policies.

Promotion Policy Restrictions

An employee enters the military service for four years. During that time 15 promotions occur within the organization. The veteran returns. The personnel practitioner offers the returning veteran the old job. The veteran asks to review the 15 promotions. Does the returning veteran have a right to those promotions? The Supreme Court said yes, the veteran is not only entitled to the precise seniority status but also to improvements that one would have received without military leave.[13]

This decision has been extended by one circuit court to mean that you must allow selection if it requires "bumping" a nonveteran.[14]

However, there are some conditions on this right. It has to be reasonably certain that the veteran would have received the promotion if not for the military leave.[15] The Supreme Court left open the question of whether the employer had to inform the veteran of all the vacancies during the absence. The Eighth Circuit says that one does, but other circuits have not ruled on this.[16] Only in the Eighth Circuit does one have to inform the returning veteran. This veteran's right can be disruptive to the seniority and training system, and the law should be carefully administered as to not deny the veteran of rights but still not disrupt manpower planning and employee training programs.

---

[13] Fishgold v. Sullivan Drydock and Repair Corp., 328 U.S. 275 (1946).

[14] Goggins v. Lincoln of St. Louis, 702 F2d 698 (8th Cir. 1983). In a related situation, another court held that a veteran could turn down a lesser job without losing any rights, Stevens v. Tennessee Valley Authority, 699 F2d 314 (6th Cir. 1983).

[15] Tiltan v. Missouri Pacific Railroad Co., 376 U.S. 169 (1964).

[16] Alber v. Norfolk and Western R.R. Co., 654 F.2d 1271 (8th Cir. 1981).

Probationary Period For Returning Veteran

Under the Military Selective Service Act temporary employment is excluded. The question is whether a probationary period is temporary employment.

Where an employee begins work with either a 30-, 60-, or 90-day probationary period, has worked two weeks, and then joins the military and leaves for service, is the veteran returning four years later on probation or not?

Two circuits have considered this question and have held that the probationary employee is not a temporary employee; when the veteran returns, the probationary period by reason of seniority has been served.[17] If the purpose of probationary period is to observe the employee's work performance for a period, then these decisions would be contrary to the employer's interests. However, the argument fails unless the employer is willing to admit that after the probationary period work performance is rated differently.[18]

Except in the Fourth and Fifth Circuits, probationary periods for returning veterans have not been considered; employers in other jurisdictions could exercise legally untested discretion in the treatment of the returning veteran's probationary period.

Rights Of Vacation Benefits While In The Service

Suppose that an employee exercises all vacation benefits before going into the service. On the day of return the veteran asks for entitled to vacation benefits under the seniority accumulated while in the service.[19] The act does entitle the veteran to retroactive vacation benefits while in the service; however, it does require that the time spent in the service be used to determine vacation eligibility.

Because in this example the employee had a vacation before leaving for the service, would the veteran be entitled to another vacation four years later? The Supreme Court in considering this question in Foster v. Dravo reasoned that inasmuch as the veteran accumulates seniority during military service, the veteran would be en-

---

[17] Collins v. Weirton Steel Co., 398 F.2d 305 (4th Cir. 1968); Montgomery v. Southern Electric Steel Co., 410 F.2d 611 (5th Cir. 1969).

[18] Probationary period is a misleading term except where specified in the labor agreement that after the probationary period just cause for discharge must be shown. All workers are on probation at all times. If they do not perform, they can be terminated after two months or two years of employment. Why should the employees be misled to feel if they last the probationary period, they are permanent employees and have more rights than before the probationary period? Employers would be well-advised if they eliminated the term probationary period, as it denotes permanence after the period ends.

[19] This usually happens when the returning veteran does not want permanent employment with the old employer but wants vacation time before notifying the employer of quitting.

titled to another vacation upon returning, unless there were a work requirement before vacation benefits could be granted.[20] Some employers require that an employee work a certain length of time before qualifying for a vacation benefit (this eliminates those who have been ill for a year). If the returning veteran in the example had not worked the required time, the veteran would not be entitled to vacation on returning, under the Foster case. One circuit has held that where sick benefits are based on a work requirement, the veteran is not entitled to such benefits until the work requirement is met.[21]

Entitlement To Pay Increases While In Military Service

Returning veterans are entitled to certain types of pay increases granted while in the military service. These increases must be of a general type, such as group increases, cost-of-living, or longevity increases. Individual merit increases are excluded.[22] A loose compensation policy that does not define the real reason for an increase can be troublesome if the employer denies the increase to the veteran because it was a merit increase and in fact it was a cost-of-living increase. As mentioned in Chapter XIII all too often the

reason given for a wage increase is merit but everybody is granted one, without any reference to meritorious performance. Such an increase would not come under the exclusion in the Hatton case.

Legality Of Veteran's Preference In Hiring Laws

Many states, as well as the federal government, give a lifetime employment preference to veterans. A female employee challenged the Massachusetts law on the basis that it had an exclusionary impact on the employment rights of women. The Supreme Court in following the reasoning of the General Electric Gilbert case[23] stated that veteran's preference was not pretext for sex discrimination nor was it gender-based because the women who served in the armed forces received the same preferences.[24]

Leaves Of Absence For Military Service

The statute requires that veterans must be given a leave of absence when going into military service. This also applies when the reservist is called into active service, the annual two- or four-week training period, or active duty for an emergency. All such leaves of absence are unpaid unless the employer's policy states otherwise.

---

[20] Foster v. Dravo, 420 U.S. 92 (1975).

[21] LiPani V. Bohack Corp., 546 F.2d 487 (2nd Cir. 1976).

[22] Hatton v. The Tabard Press Corp., 406 F. 2d 592 (2nd Cir. 1969).

[23] Cited in Note 1.

[24] Personnel Administrator of Massachusetts v. Feeney, 442 U.S. 256 (1979).

But time-off for reserve duty weekly training is treated a little differently. The employer must accommodate but not to the extent of changing the work schedule.[25] The unsettled question is where the employee in the reserves voluntarily enlists for officers training school for a six-month period. There is no case law on this, probably because where the employer says no, the employee does not want to gamble; the issue does not arise until returning from unauthorized leave and the reservist wants the job back.

VACATIONS—COMPENSATION OR TIME-OFF

From the beginning when the employer granted vacation benefits, it was considered time-off with pay. The purpose of granting vacations was to grant a period of relaxation from day-to-day activities; on returning to work the employee would be a better employee.[26] As vacations became longer, employers began to make vacation payments in lieu of time-off for several reasons. One, a replacement for a long period of time was difficult and costly in quality and quantity of work performed. Second, some employees could not afford a four-week vacation trip but could afford two weeks. The employer would give four weeks' vacation pay, and the employee would take a two-week trip and work the other two weeks; everybody was happy. The granting of vacation pay in lieu of time-off was extended to where an employee terminated and was paid unused vacation time if certain conditions were met at the time of termination. This caused the thinking that vacation benefits were not necessarily time-off but wages for nonworking time.

Many states have statutes that permit a state agency to be used for collection of wages from an employer. Some of the states have held that because payment is made in lieu of time-off, vacation benefits are wages and therefore take jurisdiction over payment of vacation benefits.

In one situation, an employee was terminated due to loss of

---

[25] Monroe v. The Standard Oil Co., 101 Sup.Ct. 2510 (1981).

[26] This was the stated purpose; however, some employers would reason that the purpose of long vacations is to find out whom they can do without and some employees never want to take a vacation as they were afraid the employer would find that out. Probably a better reason could be to provide a training period for vacation replacements if one did not want to believe the relaxation purpose.

customers. She demanded her vacation pay and sued her former employer for it. One year later the employer paid the vacation pay, but not her accumulated attorney's fees. The court ruled that vacation pay is wages and attorney's fees are due under the Nonwage Payment Statute even though the statute makes no mention of the vacation pay.[27]

Where employees went on strike, the NLRB held that they were entitled to vacation pay accrued before the strike since the employer paid one employee vacation pay in lieu of vacation time-off.[28]

New Mexico is another of the states that considers vacation benefits wages. (Iowa, Montana, Connecticut, and Kansas as well as others concur.) An employee in a New Mexico bank in April told the employer that she would take her vacation in September. She quit in July and requested vacation pay in lieu of her scheduled vacation. The New Mexico State Labor Commission agreed with her. The court disagreed; the employer's vacation policy said that vacations must be actually taken and also stated that no compensation could be paid in lieu of vacation.[29] If the Deming Bank had a history of paying compensation in lieu of vacation time-off and not had an expressed policy prohibiting it, the result would have been different. The practice of granting vacation pay in lieu of time-off is an employee relations decision, but the employer should be aware that it can be considered wages. Unless the policy is properly written, some courts call it wages; if wages, the employer loses discretion in how it is paid.[30]

One technique not to have vacation pay interpreted as wages is to make a distinction between the last day worked and termination date if vacation pay is granted upon termination. The period between the last day worked and termination date is vacation time-off. If the California Supreme Court's position is adopted by other jurisdictions, this technique would not be necessary, nor would the foregoing discussion be necessary. This court takes the position that an employee has a "vested right to vacation pay which accrues at the

---

[27] Becnel v. Answer Inc., *et. al,* 428 SO2d 539 (La. app. 1983).

[28] Thorwin Mfg. Co., 243 NLRB No. 118 (1979).

[29] New Mexico State Labor and Industrial Commission v. Deming National Bank, 634 F.2d 695 (N.M. 1981).

[30] It is costly practice because vacation for many job categories is not a cost item. The employee works to get caught up before leaving on vacation and works twice as hard when returning as no replacement is made. If pay is given, it is straight-cost item.

time of hire."[31] The company had the usual requirement of earning vacation time during the previous year, however the employee had to work one full year before vacation time was due. The employee was terminated after six months into the vacation period. The court in a unanimous decision held the rule invalid and granted a prorated vacation plus 30 paid working days if denial of vacation pay was found to be willful.

OVERVIEW OF EMPLOYEE RETIREMENT INCOME SECURITY ACT OF 1974

The Employee Retirement Income Security Act of 1974 (ERISA) is a difficult statute to understand, and even more difficult to stay in compliance. If the employer wants assurance that benefit plans are in compliance with ERISA, it is necessary either to seek outside professional advice or to employ a full-time specialist. Anything less results in unnecessary risks. The personnel practitioner should have a general knowledge of the law and its regulations, but time can be better spent in other problems than to attempt to become an expert in ERISA. For these reasons this section only gives an overview of the law and leaves the details to ERISA specialists.

Purposes Of ERISA

ERISA was passed by Congress to solve the social problems created by private pension plans and other benefit plans such as the following.

1. When a company goes out of business, often it had inadequate funding of past service credits, which allowed only a small percentage of pension benefits anticipated.

2. Inadequate vesting provisions would often result in the employee who frequently changed jobs having no pension plan at the time of retirement.

3. The law lacked adequate control of administration of pension funds.

4. Communications to the employees of the provisions of the pension plan were often inadequte to enable the employee to understand what benefits one would receive at retirement age.

Congress, through ERISA, attempted to correct these problems by the following provisions:

1. Requiring a minimum level of funding for past service credits to better protect benefits

---

[31] Suastez v. Plastic Press-up Co., 647 P.2d 122 (Cal. Sup.Ct. 1982). In California Hospital Ass'n. v. Henning 569 F. Suppl. 1544 (C.D. Calif. 1983). The court stated that statutes concerning benefits were preempted by ERISA. This would make the Suastez decision unenforceable. The California Hospital case has been appealed to the 9th Circuit Court. It is a decision that should be followed as its final decision could stop a trend.

if the company went out of business.

2. Requiring termination insurance so that if a company went out of business, the pension credits already earned would be protected until retirement.

3. Requiring a minimum vesting provision after 10 years service; vesting must begin at age 25.

4. Permitting ready access to the federal courts when it appeared that there were improper investment and administration of pension funds.

5. Employee communication programs must meet certain standards by simplification of terms and more frequent explanation to provisions of the plans to enable the employee to have a better knowledge of the plan in order to know what one will receive at retirement.

Problem Areas Under ERISA

ERISA regulates not only pension plans but also all other types of benefit plans.[32] The regulation of benefit plans raises the question of whether state benefit plans are pre-empted by ERISA.[33]

The Supreme Court on two different occasions has considered the issue. It has held that if state law prohibits reduction of pension benefits while workers compensation is being paid that such a law is invalid.[34] In another situation a state law required the employer to pay disability benefits to all employees. This was contested by employers who argued that the law was unenforceable because ERISA pre-empted the state law. The Court held that ERISA pre-empts state laws if they prohibit practices that are lawful under ERISA.[35] The disability plan in question was not prohibited by ERISA and therefore was enforceable.

Another problem area is where an employee is discharged and is denied certain benefits under the terms of the plan as the result of termination. If it can be shown that the discharge were solely to avoid vesting of the pension plan or otherwise deny health or pension benefits, it would be in violation of the act.[36] When an employer is considering the discharge of an employee with nine years and 11 months of employment and that employee would be vested in pension rights in one month, a good and valid reason should be established before the

---

[32] Severance pay plan is not considered a pension plan if the total amount paid does not exceed twice the amount of annual salary and is paid within two years after termination; 29 CFR 2510.3-2.

[33] Section 514(a) of ERISA states that ERISA shall supersede "any and all state laws insofar as they may now or hereafter relate to any employee benefit plan." The purpose of this section was to ensure employers that they would not face conflicting or inconsistent state and local regulation of employee benefit plans.

[34] Buczynski v. General Motors Corp., 101 Sup. Ct. 1895 (1981).

[35] Shaw v. Delta Air Lines, Inc. 103 Sup. Ct. 2890 (1983).

[36] Moore v. Home Insurance Co., 601 F.2d 1072 (9th Cir. 1979).

termination action is taken or a pretext to avoid vesting could be alleged. The enforcement would be by the Department of Labor if the employee files a complaint.

The compliance to ERISA is through the Internal Revenue Service (IRS). All plans must be qualified plans in order to receive tax credits when contributions are made to the trust funds or payment of premiums if an insured plan. If the plan does not meet the requirements of ERISA, it is not a qualified plan and does not receive the tax deductions. Not many other enforcement procedures are necessary.

REQUIREMENT OF ALTERNATIVE HEALTH INSURANCE PLAN

The Health Maintenance Organization Act of 1976, as amended, requires employers to include in any health plan offered to its employee the option of membership in qualified health maintenance organization (HMO).[37] It covers all employers who have 25 employees or more and is subject to the Fair Labor Standards Act. Once the employer is contacted by a qualified HMO, the employer must offer the option either to the union that can speak for the employees or to individual employees. The HMO option can not increase the employer's cost unless the employee is willing to make up the difference.

The HMO has given the personnel practitioner little or no problems except occasionally in the communication area. Often when the employer attempts to communicate, there is a tendency to favor either the employer's plan or the HMO. For this reason it is advisable to let the HMO organization communicate its own plan and the employer-sponsored plan be communicated by the insurance carrier or, if self-insured, by someone other than the one responsible for administration of the plan. Many states have their own HMO laws; the state regulations laws must be reviewed when an HMO problem occurs to determine whether state or federal law applies.

SEX DISCRIMINATION IN BENEFIT PLANS

A preceding section considered sex discrimination in pregnancy disability plans, but in other benefit plans sex differences may also occur. For example, sex differences appear in pension plans

---

[37] 42 USC 300(e).

because of greater life expectancy of women, benefits are greater for females for the same cost, or the cost of the plans are more than for males if the same benefit level is to be maintained for females. Where the employer required women to make greater contributions than men to the pension fund in order to receive an equal benefit on retirement because they live longer, the Supreme Court held that this policy violated Title VII.[38] The Court stated that the basic policy of Title VII is "fairness to individuals rather than fairness to classes." Although women as a class may live longer than men, some do not; for those individuals it would be discriminatory according to the Court.

In a related situation, where the employer's plan allowed equal contributions but provided lesser benefits (based on greater life expectancy) the Court reached the same result as in City of Los Angeles Case.[39] In subsequent discrimination cases the Supreme Court has been consistent in considering the effect on individuals rather than a class or group of employees.[40] The position of the Court was reaffirmed when they had to decide whether an annuity plan that was voluntary, amount of contributions optional with the employee. The plan had three options (lumpsum, periodic payments for a fixed period or an insured annuity plan) was in violation of Title VII.[41] The women received less annuity payments than the men for the same amount of contributions, however if the other two options were selected the pay-out would be the same. The reason why the annuity option had a smaller payment for women than men is because of the use of sex segregated actuarial tables by the insurance industry. The Court held that this was no different than Manhart case and less annuity payments for women violated Title VII. The dissent distinguished this case from Manhart in that the participation was voluntary, for each employee could contribute as much as he/she wanted to and Manhart was an employer operated fund whereas in Norris case the State of Arizona was merely making a deferred compensation plan benefit available to its employees for tax purposes and the annuity plan was one of three options. The majority says this makes no difference. The effect of the decision seems to be that the use of sex segregated actuarial tables is illegal regardless of the type of plan.

---

[38] City of Los Angeles v. Manhart, 435 U.S. 702 (1978).

[39] EEOC v. Colby College, 589 F.2d 1139 (1st Cir. 1978).

[40] In Connecticut v. Teal, 102 Sup.Ct. 2525 (1982), they said that discrimination is an individual matter and that the fact that other employees were not discriminated against is irrevelant if the plaintiff is discriminated against.

[41] Arizona Governing Committee For Tax Deferred Annuity and Deferred Compensation Plans, Etc., Et Al., v. Nathalie Norris Etc. 103 Sup. Ct. 3492 1983.

IMPACT OF MANDATORY RETIREMENT ON BENEFIT PLANS

The Age Discrimination in Employment Act gives little indication of what Congress intended as to the affect on employee benefits except that pension plans need not yield added benefits for those employees working after 65. However, the 1982 Tax Equity and Fiscal Responsibility Act amended ADEA and requires that the employer provide the same benefits between age 65 and 69 as for other employees.

The combination of employee relations consequences, federal and state legislation, and a practical analysis[42] all indicate that there will be little distinction in benefit plan coverage based on age. The employer who gradually eliminates such a distinction, if it exists, should do so in a painless and economical way.

EFFECTIVE USE OF EMPLOYMENT AGREEMENTS

An employment agreement is any agreement whether written or oral between an employer and employee concerning the conditions of employment. This chapter considers only the written agreement; the oral agreement has legal problems of proof that would be inappropriate to consider here. The written employment agreement sets out specific conditions of employment, but these conditions should not be interpreted as eliminating all other conditions normally granted to employees who do not have an agreement.

Employers often fail to consider the employment agreement as a useful tool in administering a personnel policy. Many practitioners have the misconception that employment agreements are suited only to determine the duration of employment or job duties and is therefore difficult to enforce. In reality employment agreements are practical for any situation where the employer wants to set out certain conditions for one or more employees apart from other employees.

Suppose that the employer wants to hire a qualified manager and one of the demands of the applicant (often it is more a demand of his family) is that the four-week vacation granted by the former employer be continued. Since the employer's vacation policy is that four weeks' vacation is not granted until after 12 years of service, the policy must be

---

[42] Since in most organizations the executives of an advanced age are the decision makers it is unlikely that the older worker will be treated differently on benefits.

violated or the applicant not hired. An employment agreement would solve the problem and grant the four weeks as an exception to the vacation program. Other benefits would come under the regular benefit plan. (Sometimes applicants don't want to lose higher life insurance benefits when changing jobs and an exception can be made by purchasing an insurance policy different than what other employees have.) Some practitioners feel that agreements of this type may set a precedent that makes it difficult to deny others the same benefit. This has not been the author's experience, nor can the author find any court case law that supports this feeling.

When To Use Employment Agreements

An employment agreement should not be used unless it changes the working conditions for the employee from what other employees have without an agreement. Here are some situations where employment agreements make good sense:

1. Where it is necessary, to define specially the rights, responsibilities, terms of employment, including duration of those special conditions.

2. To deter acts of unfair competition while employed or after being terminated.

3. Where job content exposes the employee to trade secrets or to patentable inventions.

4. To define duration of employment because of the nature of the job (athletic coaches and players, executives hired away from competitor, etc.).

5. Where employees are on commission and salary draws or have selling expenses as part of their commission.

6. To simplify proof on the part of both parties in a dispute over the conditions of employment or oral statements made at the time of employment.

7. To deal with routine matters that are often overlooked at the time of termination, such as travel advances, return of keys, records, and other company property.

PROVISIONS IN AN EMPLOYMENT AGREEMENT

Some of the usual clauses in an employment agreement are terms of employment, duties of the employee, compensation including benefits, confidentiality of information, and protection from disclosure to competitors.

Terms Of Employment

This clause states the beginning and end of the employment agreement. It does not necessarily mean that the employee is terminated at the end of the period; it means that the terms and conditions specified under the agreement are terminated. Some agreements have an evergreen clause; after the end of the period, the contract continues on a month-to-month relationship until either party gives notice to terminate.

Duties Of The Employee

Normally this is a general outline of the duties; it is advisable not to be too specific. Specific duties are not appropriate as that limits job assignments and negates a common law principle, which states that when a person undertakes a task, it is the person's duty to do any and all tasks that are necessary to perform the assignment related to the task undertaken without the cooperation of other persons.

Compensation, Including Benefits

This section should be carefully written so items that may be considered compensation are not left to later interpretation. This is especially true with several types of compensation, such as bonuses, commissions, vacations, stock options, etc. The trend in judicial decisions is to call any form of employee benefit compensation. A benefit was often considered something received only if one used it, such as vacation or sick leave pay; seldom was pay granted in lieu of the benefit, as to imply that it was compensation. A properly written employment agreement clears up this confusion as to benefits.

Confidentiality Of Trade Secrets

Although the employee owes a certain loyalty to the employer not to perform any acts that will adversely affect the business, it is essential that where the job content causes unusual exposure to trade secrets, the employee is contractually bound not to expose the trade secrets. Enforcement of this provision is usually against the employee and the person or corporation to whom this trade secret is revealed.

Some employment agreements have covenants not to compete with the employer for a certain period after termination. These covenants are generally enforceable. However, it is a defense to show unless there is no legitimate business interest of the employer to be protected from the employee's breach of confidentiality and the employee is not completely deprived of a livelihood by its enforcement.

Some employee agreements have special provisions that do not exist in a normal employee-employer relationship. These special provisions would not be enforceable in the absence of a formal contract or a policy that is communicated to all employees and consistently applied. One example of a special provision is a conflict-of-interest clause. This type of clause prevents the employee from engaging in any activity that would interfere with decision making or in making a judgment in performing the duties, on behalf of the employer.

Employers are often concerned about an employee who has two

jobs, which interfere with job duties and performance. This is commonly called "moonlighting." Unless there is an overall corporate policy against moonlighting that applies to all employees, it is necessary to put the restriction on moonlighting in an employment agreement if it is to be enforceable against certain individuals.

Enforcement Of Employment Agreements

Employment agreements are generally enforceable in the courts if they meet the three basic requirements of a contract: (1) offer, (2) acceptance, and (3) consideration. The offer is the conditons of employment set out by the employer. Acceptance is the employee agreeing to those conditions. Continued employment has been stated by the courts to be an adequate consideration.[43] The offer and acceptance requirement of a legally binding contract is self-serving when the applicant starts work or continues to work after an agreement is executed.[44]

Most employees will accept the obligations of the agreement if clearly defined and if the agreement is entered under amiable conditions. Accordingly enforcement during the term of employment agreement is seldom a problem.

Although the terms and conditions of the employment agreement can be readily enforced, many employers choose not to do so. Any employee who is working under the threat of a breach of contract is seldom a motivated employee who will contribute to the attainment of the goals of the organization. The enforcement problem becomes more common when the employee voluntarily terminates or is discharged. Damages for breach of the employment agreement are often difficult to prove except in rare instances. Accounting techniques have not been sophisticated enough to determine the loss of profits due to the single employee breach of contract.

Case Law On Breach-Of-Employment Agreements

The courts generally require employment agreements to be specific. In the interpretation of the agreement, the interests of the employer are weighed against the employee's right to earn a livelihood.

Where an employee agreed not to disclose to anyone the names of customers or any other information acquired during employment and not to compete with employer for two years after termination, the court refused to enforce the agreement because the information that

---

[43] Some jurisdictions hold that where a no compete agreement is signed after employment, continued employment is not a consideration and other independent considerations are necessary before the contract is valid. Modern Controls, Inc. v. Andreadakis, 578 F.2d 1263 (8th Cir. 1978).

[44] Under this principle a written contract is not necessary to find a contract of employment. The problem arises in unwritten contracts or oral agreements before employment of what parties understood to be the agreement.

the employee disclosed was public information, and the noncompete clause was too broad when it covered the entire United States.[45]

In another situation an employee began to form his own company while working for the employer as a plant manager. He copied all the records, purchased same machines, took customer lists, and quit eight months after he had started his company. At the time of his hire the employee had signed an employment agreement with a confidentiality clause and noncompete clause.[46] The employer sued for using trade secrets and confidential information and violating the noncompete agreement. The court had no problem in finding a breach of contract by the manager, the new company was also held liable for inducing the breach of contract.[47] Some jurisdictions are reluctant to enforce covenants of noncompete, but the agreement not to disclose trade secrets is almost always enforceable; therefore, both clauses should be in an employment agreement.[48]

Some employers do not like to use employment agreements because they feel that this limits their right to discharge for poor perform-ance or some other legitimate reason. An employment agreement does not protect a poor performance or violation of company policies but usually describes what is expected of the employee. Where a sales person worked harder than anyone else but did not sell anything, the court said that working hard is not enough and discharge for ineffective performance was held not to be a breach of the employment agreement.[49]

Arbitration Of Employment Agreements

Some employment agreements provide for final and binding arbitration when there is a dispute over its terms. If arbitration is not specifically provided for in an agreement, the parties may still arbitrate the dispute by entering a mutual agreement to do so when the dispute occurs. The alternative to arbitration is litigation. In this situation the parties must decide whether arbitration is most desirable or whether judicial review of the dispute should be pursued. If the dispute is arbitrated, it does not have the legal exposure as in a judicial review; arbitration awards are seldom appealable.

---

[45] Columbia Ribbon & Carbon Mfg. Co., Inc. v. A.I.A. Corp. et al., 42 N.Y. 2d 496 (1977).

[46] In the author's experience this is one of the most effective uses of employment agreements. The starting of a new plant by a manager on the employer's time and with records and equipment is not uncommon. Without an employment agreement the employer has few remedies to stop it.

[47] Lear Siegler Inc. v. Ark-Ell Springs, Inc., et al., 569 F.2d 286 (5th Cir. 1978).

[48] When an employee violates a noncomplete agreement with Company A, the new employer, Company B, is also liable. To avoid having to imply knowledge of Company B, that employee has breached the contract. Company A will notify Company B that the employee has signed a noncomplete agreement and Company B will be held liable if the employee is permitted to violate it.

[49] Freeman v. Danal Jewelry Co., 397 A.2d 1323 (R.I. Sup. Ct. 1980).

One consideration when determining whether a disputed employment agreement should be arbitrated or litigated is that some courts have awarded punitive damages, which are rarely awarded in arbitration awards.

Arbitration serves a purpose in disputes involving small amounts of monetary damages. When large sums are involved, it is better to have the matter decided under legal procedures. The best arbitration clause is one that limits arbitration to small claims such as $25,000, with court determination thereafter.

AGREEMENTS WITH EMPLOYMENT AGENCIES

When the personnel manager needs to fill a vacancy in the skilled or managerial job category, the use of an employment agency is one way to find a qualified applicant. Relationships with an employment agency can result in legal consequences that often the personnel practitioner is not aware of. Problems and misunderstandings concerning fees, pro rata refunds when the employee is discharged or resigns, and the right to deal with applicant privately without being "feeable" are all exposures to lawsuits when using an employment agency.

Most of these problems can be avoided by an initial agreement between the employer and the agency that anticipates these problems and provides for their solution. A contract between the applicant and the agency often does not affect relationships between the employer and agency. There is no federal law regulates employment agencies; only a few states have laws that regulate through licensing the relationship with the applicant. Usually the employer is left out.

A REFERRAL THAT WASN'T—CASE HISTORY

The agency called the sales manager to inquire whether there was a vacancy for a sales person. The manager stated that he was always looking for good sales persons but there was no specific vacancy at that time. On persuasion by the agency he agreed to interview an applicant. The agency stated that its fee was 10 percent of annual compensation if the applicant were hired. The applicant was not hired because his qualifications were not exceptional enough to hire him when there was no vacancy.

Four months later the applicant stopped to see the sales manager. There happened to be a vacancy and he was hired. The employment agency alleged that the hire was feeable since the initial interview was through its referral, the fee was explained, and the employee hired. A fee of $4,500 was payable. The legal basis for the suit was an implied contract because the employer interviewed the applicant four months before the second interview, after which he was hired. The case was settled out of court for the cost of litigation.[50] An agreement containing time limits on referrals would have prevented this lawsuit.

Essential Clauses In An Employment Agency Agreement

Where an employment agency is requested to find applicants at the high salary level jobs, an agreement should be executed. The agreement should contain the following clauses:

1. Fees, the amount of payment, payment dates. If a year-end bonus is paid, is that included in the annual salary for fee purposes?

2. Refunds if the employee does not work out. This is often detailed in the applicant's contract with the agency. Usually the employer that agrees to pay the fee has no contractual relationship with the agency as to refunds except through applicant's contract.

3. Services that the agency performs for its fees; only to find an applicant or to check references? Is the agency liable for discriminatory practice or other acts that may violate the law or acting as agent of the employer?

4. Time limits on referrals. The time between referral and hiring should be agreed. Once the applicant is interviewed and not hired and reapplies later, should it be feeable? If so, how long?

5. If the same resume is received from other sources, who gets the fee? As so often happens, the employer places the vacancy with an agency, a referral is made by the agency of an applicant whose resume the firm already has received but not interviewed. Would this be feeable? Another common situation is that a firm places a vacancy with two agencies; a referral comes within an hour from both agencies for the same applicant. Which one is the fee payable to?

6. Where the applicant is hired for a different job. The referral applicant is not qualified for the job vacancy placed with the agency but is hired for another job later. In the absence of an agreement, some courts say that it is feeable. A contract prevents litigation in this area.

7. Miscellaneous clauses such as a clause that compliance with EEOC laws is required. Confidentiality clauses may be desirable. If an out-of-state agency, what state law is controlling? (This should always be the state of the employer, not the agency; litigation costs are high for the employer if out-of-state).

If an agreement contains all or most of these clauses, costly litigation can be avoided.

---

[50] As happens so often, the only persons to win were the two attorneys, who received the $4,500 in fees.

SUMMARY AND CONCLUSIONS

Leaves of absence due to pregnancy or military service are controlled by statutes, but other reasons for leaves of absence are also indirectly controlled. This occurs when the reason for refusal may be interpreted as being discriminatory or in retaliation for exercising a right under a statute. Because leaves of absence are either directly or indirectly affected by the law, decisions to grant leaves of absence should not be left to the whims of the supervisor but should be uniformly applied as much as possible throughout the organization.

Vacation policies that give vacation pay in lieu of time-off are in effect admitting that vacation pay is wages. The right of the employee to recover wages is often defined by a state statute that removes from the employer the right to determine under what conditions vacation benefits will be paid. To avoid vacation time being considered as wages, the employer should consider making a distinction between last day worked and termination date if vacation pay is paid in lieu of time off at time of termination (this has some problems such as continuation of health insurance, etc.).

Pensions and health plans are regulated by statute. Compliance with these statutes is complicated and usually requires professional assistance. No statute requires the employer to grant employee benefits but, once granted, they give the employee additional enforcement rights that were not present before the benefits were granted.

The employment agreement is a useful tool to set aside the employee from policy requirements that do not fit the situation. It is also effective in preventing employees from competing with the employer after termination or starting a competitor company while working for the employer and using all the employer's facilities and records to start the company.

The personnel practitioner should also consider executing an agreement with employment agencies. It need not be formal, but many disputes over referral fees can be avoided if a written agreement has been executed.

CHAPTER XV

REFERENCE CHECKS AND OTHER DISCLOSURES OF EMPLOYEE INFORMATION

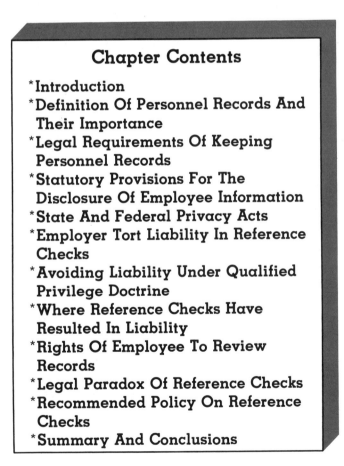

Chapter Contents

*Introduction
*Definition Of Personnel Records And Their Importance
*Legal Requirements Of Keeping Personnel Records
*Statutory Provisions For The Disclosure Of Employee Information
*State And Federal Privacy Acts
*Employer Tort Liability In Reference Checks
*Avoiding Liability Under Qualified Privilege Doctrine
*Where Reference Checks Have Resulted In Liability
*Rights Of Employee To Review Records
*Legal Paradox Of Reference Checks
*Recommended Policy On Reference Checks
*Summary And Conclusions

INTRODUCTION

Professional literature and personnel textbooks neglect almost entirely the subject of disclosure of information about employees that is under the control of the employer. It would be logical to assume that, first, such information is confidential, and second, the employer has an obligation not to disclose it to third persons. Both assumptions are wrong.

Under present legal doctrine, personnel records (defined as all information about employees kept by an employer) are not confidential but are the property of the employer to be used at its discretion. The employee can do little to stop disclosure.[1]

Releasing information about employees is largely a consideration by the employer of who wants the information and for what purpose. The discretionary control of personnel records by the employer has often been considered by civil rights advocates, academics, and the general public as an unjust infringement on employee privacy.[2]

With the advent of the discrimination laws in the late 1960s and 1970s, certain restrictions were made on the employer in the disclosure of information to or about employees. This upsurge in the interest of employee privacy along with a recognition of the judicial system of individual rights has caused the employer to become aware of the employee privacy problem in the use of personnel records. The employee privacy problem has two distinct facets. On one side is the need of the employer for data on the employee for benefit packages, job placement, promotion, and compliance with government information requests. On the other hand employees have an interest in preventing unwarranted intrusions into their private lives as well as adverse consequences should certain information be released.

How has recent privacy interest affected the employer-employee relationship? What has it done to the ability of the employer to attract qualified persons? What has it done to the supervisor's willingness to record and disclose adverse information? What has happened to the doctrine that disclosure of information about individuals is for the public good? What adjustments must personnel policies make to comply with legal developments in the confidentiality of information concerning the employee? The personnel practitioner

[1] In Cort v. Bristol-Myers, 431 N.E. 2nd 908 (Mass., 1982) the court held that there is no cause of action for failure to furnish personal information.

[2] David W. Ewing, "What Business Thinks About Employee Rights." From Allan F. Westin and Stephen Salisbury's *Individual Rights in the Corporation—A Reader on Employee Rights* (New York: Pantheon Books 1980).

must answer some of these questions by becoming familiar with court decisions regarding disclosure of employee information. When will the employer incur liability by revealing employee information? What are the terms and conditions under which the employer can disclose without exposure to litigation by the employee? The use of a subpoena to obtain employee records is excluded from this discussion, as it can be used only in legal proceedings after a complaint is filed with a court and therefore is not normally discretionary with the personnel practitioner.

DEFINITION OF PERSONNEL RECORDS AND THEIR IMPORTANCE

It is common practice for employers to keep individual records on each employee. These records are commonly called employee records or individual personnel files. An employee record is defined as records that contain initial application forms, results of physical examinations, interviewer's notations, test scores, periodic appraisals, transfers and promotions, disciplinary actions, releases and rehirings, wages, salaries, taxes paid, contributions, and similar items.[3] It is highly important that everything about the employee go into the employee's individual file.

All too often important arbitration, EEOC cases, or court decisions are lost because the employer fails to produce the proper evidence to substantiate a fact. Some practitioners believe that separate personnel files according to subject matter should be kept for each employee. They suggest a general file, job performance file, medical file, and closed file where all letters of references, records of investigation, or other matters that employees should not see are filed. The justification often given for the separation of files is that sensitive information would not be given to outsiders, and further the person reviewing the file would not be able to consider irrelevant material that may be damaging in litigation or in other employee relations problems. The reason given by proponents for keeping everything in one file is that, when segregated, relevant information is often missed; further, an employee problem is seldom categorized according to the way the data are filed and data in one file may not offer a solution to a particular problem unless all the files are reviewed. The author's experience favors the one-file concept as the most reliable method to keep employee records.

[3] Dale Yoder, *Personnel Management in Industrial Relations*, 6th ed. (Englewood Cliffs NJ: Prentice-Hall Company, 1970).

LEGAL REQUIREMENTS OF KEEPING PERSONNEL RECORDS

There are few statutory requirements stating that an employer must keep records on an individual employee. The discrimination laws, OSHA, and Fair Labor Standards Act require that relevant information be available for investigation purposes and ensure the proper administration of the laws. Beyond this, the employer has legally few record-keeping requirements.[4] Proper personnel practice in the areas of discipline, performance appraisals, skills inventories, etc., demands the personnel manager to go beyond what the law requires in the area of personnel record keeping.

The question of how long does one have to retain personnel records was discussed in Chapter III? What records the employer should maintain is a policy as well as a legal question. The employer should have records to show that company policy and procedures are complying with the law. On the other hand, too many records can be damaging in the event of a lawsuit. If the employer does not have certain information, it cannot be disclosed and a decision by the regulatory agency must be made only on the information available, which at times can be advantageous to the employer. For this reason, the employer should audit personnel records at least every three years and destroy irrelevant, immaterial or damaging records if not required to keep them. It is also advisable to separate certain records that you are required to keep and note a destroy date. This policy will give stature to the records you retain and at the same time not subject damaging records to the subpoena process in the event of a lawsuit.

STATUTORY PROVISIONS FOR THE DISCLOSURE OF EMPLOYEE INFORMATION

Although records are the property of the employer, certain statutes require the employer to disclose specific information for certain reasons. These reasons are usually to enable a government regulatory agency to carry out its function of enforcing the law.

---

[4] Payroll records for the Walsh-Healey Act, unemployment compensation, and Social Security are usually not considered as personnel records and are kept in the accounting or payroll department. This is a usual industry practice.

Union Demands
For Information

Often a labor organization that is the certified bargaining representative of the employees will request information on an employee or group of employees. The information requested must be relevant to the collective bargaining agreement or needed for the union to represent the employee properly concerning wages and working conditions and protect the collective bargaining relationship. The National Labor Relations Board has given a liberal interpretation to this general principle, except for medical information on the employee, which the board will sometimes require disclosure, if relevant, although such information is highly sensitive. Where disabilities were discovered during physical examination, the board said:

In view of the generally recognized confidential nature of a physician's report, employer (sic) acted reasonably in taking the position that such records should not be publicized without permission of the employee involved, unless and until that individual's physical capabilities became relevant to some particular problem.[5]

By this language the board is saying that it does not matter whether the employee agrees that the union representative should see the file; as long as the information is relevant to the labor union's function, the employer must surrender it. This seems somewhat contrary to what the Supreme Court ruled, that because of the sensitive nature of test scores, such scores need not be given to the union without employee permission. Where test scores were involved, the Court said that the right of privacy was greater than the need of the union for the information.[6]

Where wage data are requested to be withheld by a nonunion employee because it is confidential, one court considered this matter related to union business and required disclosure when a union requested wage data on the nonunion employees. The information requested was wage data on supervisors who occasionally did bargaining unit work (work where a union represents the employees). The court reasoned that the information was relevant to the administration of the contract, and the request of nonunion employees to withhold it does not make it confidential.[7] This must be distinguished from situations where information requested dealt with employees outside the union's jurisdiction. The court said that the employer could lawfully refuse such information.[8]

---

[5] United Aircraft Co., 192 NLRB No. 62 (1971).

[6] Detroit Edison v. NLRB, 440 U.S. 301 (1979).

[7] NLRB v. Jaggars-Chile Stovall, 639 F.2d 1344 (5th Cir. 1981).

[8] Western Electric, Inc. v. NLRB, 559 F.2d 1131 (8th Cir. 1977).

In a related situation a union requested information on employees who were trained in nonbargaining unit work as well as bargaining unit work. The union received the information on nonunion employees, called them scabs, and then requested additional information, which the employer denied. The court agreed with the employer and stated that improper use of similar information furnished to the union earlier showed that the information was not needed for bargaining purposes.[9]

Release Of Employee Information Under Occupational Safety And Health Act

Another statutory requirement to release limited employee information comes from a regulation promulgated under the authority of OSHA, which states that an employer must give access of the records to employees or their representives and to other employees who are exposed to toxic and hazardous substances if requested.[10] The person requesting the records must show a need and have professional qualifications to interpret the information requested. The regulation requires that the medical records on exposure to toxic substances be kept for 30 years and the employee must be in-

formed at the time of hiring and each year thereafter that such records are available.

This regulation has been reviewed by two courts, and it appears it will be judicially accepted.[11] In both cases the court required that the National Institute for Occupational Safety and Health (NIOSH) be given the information. However, the court said that the employee's privacy is a factor to be considered in the use of that information by the governmental agency.

Disclosure Under Discrimination Laws

As in other areas under antidiscrimination laws (Title VII of the Civil Rights Act of 1964 as amended, Age Discrimination Act of 1967, and Rehabilitation Act of 1973) if reference-checking information has an adverse impact on the categories of individuals being protected, it is unlawful to use such information for making an employment decision unless a business necessity can be shown. This does not mean that background investigations are prohibited, but it does mean there must be a nondiscriminatory use and purpose for such information.

In one situation a union requested information on an affirmative action plan and also

---

[9] NLRB v. A.S. Abell Co., 590 F.2d 554 (4th Cir. 1979).

[10] 29 CFR Part 1910.20 and 29 CFR Part 1913.10.

[11] United States v. Westinghouse, 638 F.2d 570 (3rd Cir. 1980) and E.I. duPont de Nemours and Co. v. Finklea, 442 F.Supp. 821 (S.D. W.Va. 1977).

classification data. The court determined that the classification data may be related to union business but not the affirmative action plan.[12] However, complaints filed by union members under discrimination statutes have been held a concern of the union and must be disclosed.[13] The courts also required that relevant information be given when a charge is being investigated or in the case of a compliance review.

The employer in an EEO investigation can challenge the request for information from the personnel file, and, like the NLRB cases, the courts give broad interpretation on relevancy, especially where the allegations in the charge are general as to race and national origin. In one case an original charge was racial discrimination. On investigation EEOC found no grounds to substantiate the racial discrimination charge, but from the information voluntarily given found a sex violation. The court held that it was relevant where the employer produced the information voluntarily.[14] This case illustrates the importance of disclosing only relevant information.

An employer that discloses information not legally required because it lacks relevancy risks a lawsuit as a result of the information voluntarily disclosed. The expenditure of funds and time resulting from litigation could be avoided by insisting on the test of relevancy from the outset.

When a charge is broad and includes several allegations, information must be furnished for all of the allegations. In this kind of charge the agency has considerable latitude in seeking information if the charge is properly worded. In this type of charge the employer has less opportunity to refuse information, and the defense of relevancy must be used with discretion. Where a charge stated in general terms that blacks were discriminated against in promotion, were harassed by supervisors, had segregated locker facilities, and were hired only for certain jobs, the courts permitted almost unlimited access to the employee records.[15]

The restrictions on the enforcement agency to receive only employee information that is relevant restates the common law principle that employee information is the property of the employer, and only under certain conditions as defined by statute or court interpretation may the property of the employer be used by a governmental agency.

---

[12] NLRB v. Westinghouse Electric 610 F2d 956 (D.C. 1979).

[13] International Union Electric Radio and Machine Workers v. NLRB, 650 F.2d 334 (D.C. Cir. 1980).

[14] EEOC v. General Electric, 532 F.2d 359 (4th Cir. 1976).

[15] Graniteville Co. Sibley Div. v. EEOC, 438 F.2d 32 (4th Cir. 1971).

STATE AND FEDERAL PRIVACY ACTS

There is no comprehensive federal regulation for the private sector to require employers to disclose employee information to anyone. Federal employees are protected by the Privacy Act of 1974.[16] The act requires federal agencies to permit employees to examine, copy, correct, or amend employee information. If there is a dispute on the accuracy of the information or what is to be included, an appeal procedure is provided. The act prohibits, with certain exceptions, the disclosure of information to outsiders without written consent of the employee to whom the information pertains. The agency has no obligation to inform the employee that the information exists except to publish it annually in the *Federal Register*.

Several states have enacted comprehensive privacy acts for the public sector.[17] Other state legislatures have not gone quite as far as a comprehensive plan but have imposed certain restrictions on employee information practices in the public sector.[18]

Other states have enacted legislation that requires employers

in the private sector to permit employees to examine their own personnel files.[19] The Michigan statute is the most detailed in that it gives employees the right to examine and copy their own records.[20] The act requires that reference letters, comparative evaluations, medical reports, and grievance files be kept separately. It provides that if an employee disputes the accuracy of the information, dissenting statements made by the employee become part of the file. The statute also restricts the types of information that can be collected about an employee and imposes limitations on disclosure to third parties. Other states permit only disclosure and copying but do not permit the method by which employee can dissent. Most states that require disclosure permit the employer to classify certain information as confidential and withhold it from employees.

Although the Federal Fair Credit Reporting Act[21] regulates the activities of consumer reporting agencies, it does affect the disclosure of information by the employer where the employer en-

---

[16] 5 U.S.C. Sect. 552 (a).

[17] Arkansas, Connecticut, Indiana, Massachusetts, Minnesota, Ohio, Utah, and Virginia are some of the states that have privacy acts.

[18] New York and Colorado are examples.

[19] California, Connecticut, Maine, Michigan, North Carolina, Oregon, Pennsylvania, Utah, and Wisconsin are some of the states that have privacy acts in the private sector.

[20] Michigan Comp. Laws Ann. 423.501.

[21] 15 USC Sect. 1681 et. seq.

gaged a consumer agency to make an investigation. The employer, when using a consumer agency, must inform the employee that an investigation is being made as to character, general reputation, personal characteristics, and mode of hiring. If the employee so requests, the employer must provide a complete disclosure of the nature and scope of the investigation.

The Freedom of Information Act (FOIA) states that where a federal agency maintains a system of records, on request any individual or representative may gain access to that record if the proper authorization is shown by the representative.[22] The FOIA further provides that an individual or representative may request amendment to the record; if refused, adversary proceedings to determine the facts are triggered. Such proceedings are subject to judicial review.

FOIA's stated purpose is to require the information to be released and to inform the public; it is not for the purpose of benefiting the litigants in a lawsuit.[23] The rules and regulations in compliance with this purpose are promulgated with emphasis on disclosing information to the public and not to allow litigants to use the information for their own purposes.

There are exceptions under the act that an individual may examine personnel records. The federal agency may promulgate challengeable rules where revealing such information will obstruct the agency's enforcement function. If the right of disclosure is doubtful, the courts normally rule in favor of disclosure. Medical records are exempted under FOIA, but under certain conditions they can be revealed under Section 552A of the act.

EMPLOYER TORT LIABILITY IN REFERENCE CHECKS

The employer has no obligation to grant requests for disclosure of personnel records unless required by statute. At the same time almost nothing can prevent voluntary disclosure by the employer. If the employer wants to cooperate with the local law enforcement agencies or with the Federal Bureau of Investigation (FBI), it may do so. If the employer chooses

not to do so, the law enforcement agency must decide on the facts that it has and whether to start court action and obtain the information by subpoena.

Where the employer decides to reveal information in the personnel file that is detrimental to the employee, the employee may sue for damages under certain conditions. This usually occurs when such facts

---

[22] 5 USC Sect. 552A (FOIA).

[23] Cuneo v. Rumsfeld, 553 F.2d 1360 (DC Cir. 1977).

that invade privacy under the common law are revealed to the public. The public is interpreted by the courts to mean a small group of people. If it is revealed to only one person regardless of the seriousness of the injury, the employee has no tort action.[24] Under the common law of privacy public disclosure of embarrassing private facts about a person is an invasion of the individual's interest in acquiring, retaining, and enjoying a good reputation. The violation of this interest is called libel or defamation.[25] (This is sometimes referred to as slander.)

Liability for this tort usually arises when an employer communicates to a prospective employer or a credit agency information that is injurious to the reputation of an employee or former employee. Since nothing prevents an individual from filing a lawsuit, one might say that every time an employer discloses adverse information about an employee to a prospective employer, this could result in a lawsuit. This would be true if not for the qualified privilege doctrine that the employer enjoys when revealing information about former or present employees. Privilege is defined as:

... the modern term applied to those considerations which avoid liability where it might otherwise follow ... in its more common usage, it signified that the defendant has acted to further an interest of such social importance that it is entitled to protection, even at the expense of damage to the plaintiff. He is allowed freedom of action because his own interests or those of the public require it, and social policy will best be served by permitting it.[26]

This definition of privilege has been applied to employee records. The courts have taken the position that the public good is best served by a free exchange of information between the prospective employer and former employer as to the work habits and performance while employed. Where an employee falsified production records and the employer told other employers about it, the court said that the employer was justified in that it would discourage other employees from committing the same act.[27] However, this immunity from liability when disclosing adverse injurious information is not without limitations; an employer must take certain precautions if liability is to be avoided.[28]

---

[24] Biderman's of Springfield, Inc. v Wright, 322 S.W.2d 892 Mo (1959).

[25] William L. Prosser, *Handbook of the Law of Torts*, 4th ed. (St. Paul, MN: West Publishing Co., 1971) Section 111, p. 737.

[26] Ibid., p. 98.

[27] Ponticelli v. Mine Safety Appliance Co., 247 A.2d 303 (R.I. 1968).

[28] For additional information on this privilege, see Jack Turner and Terry Esser. "Reference and Background Checks: Myth and Fact," *Human Resources Management Ideas and Trends,* no. 36 (Chicago, IL, Commerce Clearing House, April, 1983).

AVOIDING LIABILITY UNDER QUALIFIED PRIVILEGE DOCTRINE

Many employers are adopting a policy that information disclosed about former employees should be limited to verification of employment and the length of employment. This policy may be considered the safest in the avoidance of lawsuits. But from an employee relations point of view it could result in the hiring of many undesirable applicants and create ill will among former employees who are refused favorable references. An employer can reduce the risk of litigation to near zero and still maintain good recruiting practices as well as good employee relations by taking advantage of the qualified privilege doctrine. However, this doctrine is not applicable unless certain conditions exist. These conditions are that:

1. The information must be given in good faith. Where a supervisor accused an employee of starting a competitive company and repeated other office rumors which he failed to investigate, the court awarded $19,000 in punitive damages.[29] (Punitive damages are damages that compensate above actual loss are punishment for evil behavior.)

2. The information given must be limited to the inquiry. Asking about work habits does not require facts on personal life or information on union activities.[30]

3. The statement must be given under the proper occasion and in the proper manner. If given at a cocktail party or while playing bridge, an otherwise proper statement could be construed an invasion of privacy or libelous.

4. The information must be communicated to the proper parties and not the general public. In one case an inquiry was made by an aunt, uncle, and spouse as to an employee's whereabouts and the reason given for the inquiry was that he was accused of misappropriating company funds. The court said that it was not privileged because relatives had no job-related interest in receiving the information.[31]

---

[29] Calero v. Del Chemical Corp., 228 N.W.2d 737 (Wisc. 1975).

[30] Sindorf v. Jacron Sales, 341 A.2d 856 (Md. 1975).

[31] Stewart v. Nation-Wide Check Corp., 182 S.E.2d 410 (N.C. 1971).

5. Information requested must be related to the requirements of the job.

6. Information revealed must be true or a reasonable effort must be made to seek the truth.

Where a routine reference check with a former employer of a black minority applicant revealed a poor attendance record and the applicant was turned down for the job, the applicant alleged that whites had similar absentee records with the former employer. The court said that refusal of employment based on a reference check was a "legitimate job related non-discriminatory justification for refusal to hire" and that an employer may lawfully make employment decisions on the basis of reference reports from prior employers of job applicants.[32]

The result may have been different if the employer that was considering the applicant had employees on the payroll with similar absentee records as the applicant had with her former employer. If this were so, a discriminatory reason for the refusal could be implied.

Reference checks run afoul of anti-discrimination laws only where it can be shown that the reference check was for a discriminatory purpose or information received was used in a discriminatory manner. If conclusions drawn from reference reports are biased, the result will be considered discriminatory or malicious. A minority applicant may receive a poor reference report because of poor performance on the job for a former employer. This does not necessarily mean that the applicant is unqualified for a different position and different employer. The reasons for poor performance must be considered; poor performance cannot always be used as a pretext for not hiring a member of the protected class. Often the prospective employer will ask if the former employee is eligible for rehire; if the answer is negative, the person will not be hired. Relying solely on this answer may indicate a discriminatory motive in refusal to hire, if the applicant is a member of a protected class.

WHERE REFERENCE CHECKS HAVE RESULTED IN LIABILITY

One of the best sources for information about an employee is the performance appraisal found in the employee's file.[33] However, where there is no causal connection between information provided in the performance appraisal and job performance, reliance on a subjective performance appraisal can result in exposure to liability when such

---

[32] Reeves v. Southern Bell Telephone and Telegraph Company (BNA), 17 FEP Cases 1133 (DC SC 1978).

[33] Validity of performance appraisals is discussed in Chapter V.

information is challenged by the applicant.

This is especially true if the information is damaging to the applicant's chance of being hired. Damaging information must be true according to the belief and to the best of knowledge of the person disclosing it. The best-of-knowledge principle requires that a reasonable effort be made to seek the true facts and not rely on rumors or hearsay reports.

It is advisable not to repeat any suspicion or subjective opinions about an employee in reference checks. Often opinions or suspicions can be interpreted as malicious and libelous as shown by the following case.

August Bobenhausen joined Charles Boucher's Casat Avenue Mobile Homes, Inc. as a sales manager in October 1974. Seven months later Bobenhausen was terminated. Boucher claimed that he had fired him. Bobenhausen for his part claimed that he had quit because the company was cheating him on his commission.

Bobenhausen sought work with numerous other mobile home dealers. One of them, Gil Sausa, offered him a job at $18,000 a year plus $9,000 to $12,000 in commissions. Everything seemed agreeable until Sausa contacted Boucher for a reference and was told that Bobenhausen was a "thief and a crook" who "stole us blind." Sausa withdrew the job offer. Bobenhausen never heard from several other prospective employers after they asked him to identify his previous employer. Bobenhausen eventually purchased his own mobile home company, obtaining financing through a bank and a finance company. A few months later he needed additional credit, but the bank refused any further extension of credit without a character reference. He then went to a finance company, which also refused, saying that it had received a credit report stating that Bobenhausen had been suspected of stealing.

At this point Bobenhausen sued Boucher for slander, charging that he has ruined his reputation. A Florida jury awarded Bobenhausen $30,000 in compensatory damages and $50,000 in punitive damages.

The court said that because Boucher knew the charges were false and repeated them, Bobenhausen was entitled to punitive damages for malice.[34]

An employer that discharges for dishonesty can repeat the information as long as it can be shown to be true; such information is privileged under the public policy doctrine. However, those disclosing must be aware that they might be required to satisfy the jury that the statement was true to the best of their knowledge and belief and was given without malice. This was the situation in a case where the Minnesota Supreme Court stated that the information must

---

[34] Bobenhausen v. Cassat Avenue Mobile Homes, Inc., et al., 344 S.2d 279 (Fla. 1978).

be given in good faith and be accurate.[35] A Wisconsin court put it another way when it said that information must be believed to be true or reasonable steps taken to verify the information if there is any doubt.[36]

Another situation where an employer's action can result in liability is where the reference report shows unlawful retaliation for exercising a right under a statute, such as making worker's compensation claim or filing a charge under EEO. This information is usually not relevant to job performance or job placement. In one situation it was shown that the employer disclosed that the applicant filed an EEO claim while working with the former employer but it had nothing to do with refusal. However, the court still held unlawful retaliation since disclosing the information was not relevant to job performance.[37]

RIGHTS OF EMPLOYEE TO REVIEW RECORDS

The well-established principle of common law that information obtained by the employer about an employee relating to the employment relationship is that the property of the employer also applies to the request of the employees to see their own records.

In the public sector employees have the right to see their own personnel records. The Privacy Act of 1974 (5 U.S.C. Sect. 5229) permits employees of the federal government to inspect their own records, make corrections, and copy the record. The agency cannot disclose the information to anyone without the employee's consent.

Most states have passed legislation similar to the Federal Privacy Act. Some states such as California, Connecticut, Maine, Michigan, North Carolina, Oregon, Pennsylvania, Utah, and Wisconsin have laws requiring the employer to give employees access to their own records. Those states that require it in the private sector usually permit the employer to remove certain information before disclosing the file to the employee. These statutes should not be confused with the Freedom of Information Act (5 U.S.C. Sect. 552), which requires federal agencies to disclose information about agency activities to the general public.

Several employers, particularly large ones such as IBM, AT&T, General Electric, and Sentry Insurance Co., have adopted policies allowing an employee access to one's records. They argue that denying an employee access to such records is not good employee relations. Many advocates of the

---

[35] Stuempges v. Parke Davis & Co., 297 N.W.2d 252 (Minn. 1980).

[36] Cited in Note 29.

[37] Rutherford v. American Bank of Commerce, 565 F.2d 1162 (10th Cir. 1977).

employee privacy doctrine state that if the employers continue to deny employees access to their own records, Congress will do something about it; it is better to establish their internal policies rather than have Congress do it.

Those companies allowing employees to see information from their own files have a policy that usually states that the employer can remove certain information that it chooses not to disclose. Normally the policy does not define the information that may be removed. Determinations are made on a case-by-case basis. Information that probably would be withheld from the employee might include consideration for promotion, the fact that an employee is suspected of violating a rule and must be watched, and the scheduled elimination of the job or that of the supervisor.

LEGAL PARADOX OF REFERENCE CHECKS

It is a legal paradox that the courts are granting immunity from prosecution and ruling that it is in the public interest to exchange information about employees to discourage hiring of undesirable applicants; at the same time many employers are unwilling to disclose because of the danger of being sued.

It has been a common practice among employment managers to check the references of an applicant by calling the applicant's former employer and requesting specific information for preemployment purposes. Large court awards and expensive litigation, where limitations on the qualified privilege have been disregarded, have alerted some employers to the exposure to litigation to the point where they refuse to give reference information except for dates of employment and job title. If this trend continues, reference checks as a source of preemployment information will be as obsolete as the corner blacksmith shop.

Whether exposure to litigation will have a damaging effect on the hiring of qualified applicants depends on how valid reference information has been. It has probably been as valid as other subjective selection procedures that have been common in the past. Some personnel administrators feel that the abolition of reference checks would have no effect on hiring persons qualified to perform because reference checks are not a valid method of determining an applicant's acceptability. Reference checks are somewhat unreliable unless a personal confidential relationship exists between the person requesting the information and the person disclosing the information, in which case legal implications are not usually present,[38] however, the

---

[38] This is one advantage in being active in local personnel associations and professional and civic organizations.

disclosure of trait characteristics is more objective than the ability to perform the job and accordingly no personal relationship is needed.

The only absolute protection against being sued is not to give any reference information to anybody, but an employer that is interested in objective selecting of qualified and stable applicants must obtain background information from some source in order to succeed. If no reference information is provided by employers concerning an applicant's qualifications and trait characteristics, then the selection process is at least in part a subjective one. A subjective selection process is almost certain to run afoul of the anti-discrimination laws. The employer will avoid privacy laws, but a new exposure will be created.

In some jurisdictions the employer can be sued for "negligent maintenance of employment records" as when an employer gives inaccurate information that has adverse consequences on the employee.[39] Following this theory it appears that the employer has some responsibility to other employees to hire desirable persons, and accordingly there would be some duty to investigate before hiring. Failure to investigate might be considered negligence if an employee is adversely affected by the hiring of an undesirable applicant.

For example, a rental car company hired a car washer. Because this is normally a high turnover job, the firm did not do any investigation of the applicant. The person hired had a known record as a rapist. He victimized a secretary in the employer's office after starting to work. The secretary sued and was awarded $750,000 in damages. The court said that there is a duty to other employees to investigate applicants selected.[40]

Another court followed the same reasoning. In Stephanie Ponticas et al. v K.M.S. Investments, 331 N.W. 2nd 907 (Minn. 1983), the employer hired a caretaker for an apartment building. The employee had been convicted of armed robbery, burglary, and auto theft. Using his passkey to enter an apartment, he raped one of the tenants. The court held that an employer has a duty to exercise reasonable care in hiring individuals who because of the nature of their employment may pose a threat to members of the public. The court in Keck v. American Employment Agency, 632 S.W.2d 2 (Ark. 1983) held that an employment agency was liable when an applicant was raped. The person interviewing him said the agency had a duty to its clients.

These three cases point out the fact that if the practice by employers of supplying only name,

---

[39] Quinones v. United States, 492 F.2d 1269 (3rd Cir. 1974). This was also followed with Bulkin v. Western Kraft East, Inc., 422 F.Supp. 437 (E.D. Pa. 1976).

[40] Jones v. Avis Rent-a-Car (Ind. D.C. 1981).

rank and serial number becomes universal, the policy may ultimately be as problematic to employers as disclosing information about employees.

An employer's policy of refusing reference information may eliminate litigation in one area and promote it in two other areas: antidiscrimination laws and liability involving other employees.

RECOMMENDED POLICY ON REFERENCE CHECKS

In any policy on disclosure of employee information, consideration must be given to the employee's right to enjoy a good reputation as well as the employer's concern to employ qualified and desirable people. The employer must also be concerned with the welfare of other employees. The failure to discover that the person hired is a kleptomaniac or has a history of sex crimes is not in the best interest of the employer or employees. A policy, therefore, must not discourage reference information but must be drafted in a way that it reflects a real concern for the employee's privacy and the employer's protection from litigation.

The following provisions are designed to accomplish this goal:

1. Only certain designated and trained persons should be permitted to release information. These persons should be trained in the legal requirements of disclosing employee information. The practice of allowing the supervisor to disclose reference information over the telephone should be eliminated. This practice probably was started because many application forms ask the applicant, "Who was your immediate supervisor on your former job?" If the application form asks, "Who was the immediate supervisor?" the question should be eliminated.

2. Except for dates of employment, all requests for information should be in writing. Since information should be given only to persons who have a reason to receive it, this cannot be ascertained over the telephone. Sometimes former employees seek information under disguise of a prospective employer; requiring the request in writing will eliminate this problem.

3. The firm should give out only information that is requested and is job-related.

When the inquirer asks the time of day, don't tell how to build a watch. If there is any doubt as to its accuracy, one should do not release the information.

4. The employee should be required to consent to the release of the information requested. Although the courts state that this is not needed, it is convenient to have this consent when the employer is being sued by an employee who consented to its release. In one situation where the employee was a member of an association, the court said that he consented to the written cause of his dismissal through his membership.[41] The Restatement of Torts puts it this way: "Moreover, one who agrees to submit his conduct to investigation knowing that its results will be published, consents to the publication of the honest findings of the investigators."[42]

It is also good employee relations to get the employee's consent; the employee feels the right to determine whether certain information should be released. For example, the employee may not want disclosure of an address to a mother-in-law but may want full disclosure of all information to the promoter of an exclusive country club.

5. Information should be put in the employee's file only if it is accurate and there is a job-related or business need for it. Particular attention should be paid to records kept by persons outside the personnel office (for example, front-line supervisors or group leaders) because many problems are found in these records. Collecting irrelevant or inaccurate information adversely affects the quality of the relevant information as well as causing legal problems.

6. Information should be collected from reliable sources. Hearsay and subjective evaluations should be avoided, especially as to work performance, trait characteristics, arrest records, and results of interviews that have no other purpose except to prove somebody right.

7. Employee personnel files should be released within the company to only those who have a job-related purpose to know it. Only that

---

[41] Joftes v. Kaufman, 324 F.Supp. 660 (D.C.D.C. 1972).

[42] Restatement of Torts, Sect. 583.

information in the file that pertains to the stated purpose of the inquiry should be released.

8. Employee access to the file should be permitted but the file should be sanitized if necessary. Such information as comparative evaluations, mental problems, investigative interviews, and physical conditions could do more harm to employee relations than good.

9. When an employee disagrees with the information in the file, the disputed statement should be put in the file without comment in the event it becomes material.

10. The policy should detail what, to whom, by whom, and under what limitations the information should be disclosed.

If a policy contains most of these provisions, the employer not only will be exchanging information for the public good, but will also be able to select qualified and desirable applicants objectively while enjoying good employee relations.

SUMMARY AND CONCLUSIONS

This chapter has reviewed the legal implications of disclosing employee information. The exchange of information between employers is privileged. An employee whose reputation is impaired because of the release of such information (if done properly) cannot sue for damages.

This privilege has some limitations in that the person receiving it must have a legitimate business purpose to receive it, there must be a business relationship between the person saying it and the person receiving it, and the release of the information cannot be malicious or given in bad faith but must be accurate and restricted to the inquiry.

Reference checks properly administered do not expose the employer to liability. A policy of not releasing employee information to other employers is not only contrary to public policy but could lead to more exposure to litigation than it prevents if the practice is universal. Employers who have a total restriction on reference information should reconsider their policy in light of the law presented in this chapter.

Since the law does not restrict disclosure of employee information, an employer policy that respects the privacy of the employee but gives prospective employers certain accurate and nonmalicious facts will prevent unwanted litigation as well as legislation that neither the employer nor the employee will like.

CHAPTER XVI

EMPLOYERS' RIGHT
TO DISCHARGE

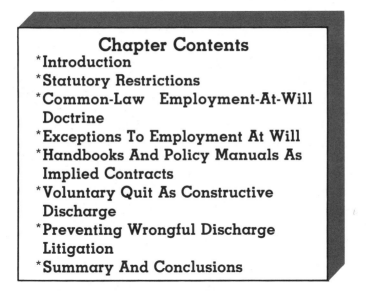

Chapter Contents
*Introduction
*Statutory Restrictions
*Common-Law Employment-At-Will Doctrine
*Exceptions To Employment At Will
*Handbooks And Policy Manuals As Implied Contracts
*Voluntary Quit As Constructive Discharge
*Preventing Wrongful Discharge Litigation
*Summary And Conclusions

INTRODUCTION

When an employer in the private sector hires an employee to work for an indefinite period, in the absence of a formal contract or union agreement, the employee can be terminated at any time without legal liability for good cause, bad cause, no cause at all unless there is an express statutory prohibition. This general rule of the common law is stated in the American Law Reports (A.L.R.) as follows:

Despite its sometimes harsh operation and the obvious opportunities for abuse it affords an unscrupulous employer, few legal principles would seem to be better settled than the broad generality that an employment for an indefinite term is regarded as an employment at will which may be terminated at any time by either party for any reason or for no reason at all.[1]

The early 1980s was a period of the beginning for the erosion of the common law doctrine of employment at will. As one court stated, "It represents an area of the law undergoing dynamic development."[2] Aiding the erosion of the employment-at-will doctrine is the fact that the courts have awarded substantial punitive damages in cases where the doctrine is opposed. As a result, employees and lawyers are more willing to pursue discharge cases that they consider wrongful than in the past. For these and other reasons, discharges are receiving considerable attention in employee relations law literature. Another important fact is that the reporting of court settlements by the news media has resulted in more exposure by the employer to litigation related to discharges than at any other time.

There has been considerable discussion in the labor law journals as well as personnel periodicals where the commentators have taken the position that the doctrine should be abandoned because of its harshness. In the *Harvard Law Review* an article entitled "Protecting at Will Employees against Wrongful Discharge; The Duty to Terminate Only in Good Faith," the author proposed a comprehensive economic rationale for judicial revision of common law rule to provide at-will employees with an expanded private remedy for wrongful discharge.[3] *Business Week* #2682 at page 95, "The Growing Costs of Firing Non-Union Workers" (April 6, 1981) pointed out the alarming awards of wrongful discharge settlements as the reason for increased litigation by employees.[4]

The proponents of eliminating the at-will doctrine are quick to point out that the United States is the only industrialized country that does not provide employees with some form of comprehensive protection against wrongful discharge. The just-cause provisions of labor agreements cover some employees, but union membership has failed to keep pace with the

---

[1] 62 A.L.R. 3d 271 (1975).

[2] Savodnik v. Korvettes, Inc., 488 F.Supp. 822, at 824 (E.D. N.Y. 1980).

[3] 93 *Harv. L. Rev.* 1816, 1817 (1980). See also "Limiting the Abusive Exercise of Employer's Power," 67 *Columbia Law Review* 1404 (1967). The pressure to change the common law rule is continuing. See "Protecting Unorganized Employees Against Unjust Discharge," a publication by the Michigan State University School of Labor Relations, College of Social Science, East Lansing, MI, no. 488, p. 24 (1983).

[4] For other references on employment at will see: Gary E. Murg and Clifford Scharman "Employment at will: do exceptions overwhelm the Rule?" *Boston College Law Review,* vol. 23, 329-84. (1982) Randy A. Weiss "State by State Chipping away at Employment at Will" *National Law Journal,* January 18, 1982, 26-28 (New York: Law Publishing Co.). Edward L. Harrison "Legal Restrictions on the Employers Authority to Discipline" vol. 61, February, 1982 (Costa Mesa CA: Personnel Journal Inc.).

growing work force; a continually smaller percentage of workers are covered. More than 75 percent of the work force is not covered by labor agreements and have no external appeal procedure when discharged.

The employer should not be deceived into believing that the at-will doctrine has been suddenly abolished by the courts and that they must show just cause in all cases of discharge. But they must become aware of the rapid changes in this area of employee relations law.

This chapter examines those factual situations where the doctrine has been successfully challenged in the courts, the legal position that employers may take in defense of their actions, and what personnel policies and procedures are helpful in the prevention of expensive litigation.

STATUTORY RESTRICTIONS

The common law rule allowing discharge at will may be modified by state and federal laws. The laws usually state that an employer cannot discharge an employee for a certain reason similar to what is stated in the federal antidiscrimination laws. Some states prevent discharge for garnishment of wages, refusing to take a polygraph test, or running for a political office. The statute that is most often used in wrongful discharge cases is the Age Discrimination in Employment Act of 1967 as amended in 1978 [29 U.S.C. 631(a)].

Over 70 percent of the complaints under ADEA deal with termination, either direct discharge or involuntary retirement.[5] Because the statute grants the right of jury trial, age discrimination cases are especially troublesome in wrongful discharge cases. A further complication under ADEA is the failure of employers to accurately measure performance.

Another statute that is often resorted to in wrongful discharges is Title VII, when sex discrimination by sexual harassment is alleged. It is a stronger complaint to file for a violation of Title VII than to attempt to establish that wrongful discharge for refusal to sexual favors than to allege the exception to at-will doctrine because it is contrary to public policy.

Various state antidiscrimination statutes specify that discharge for certain reasons is a violation. For example, in Minnesota alcoholism is considered a disability under certain conditions and discrimination due to a disability is prohibited.[6] Many states such as

---

[5] R. Snyder and R. Brandon, "Riding the Third Wave; Staying on Top of ADEA Complaints," *Personnel Administrator* (Berea, Ohio: American Society for Personnel Administration.) February, 1983, p. 42.

[6] Minnesota statutes annotated. 363.03.

California and Michigan have statutes that make it illegal to discharge because of a physical handicap unless a good faith attempt is made to accommodate the disability in other available jobs.

Mixed Reasons For Discharge

An employee may be a union activist, filing discrimination charges, representing employees in his or her group for wages, or otherwise exercising a right under a statute, but in an unrelated activity is guilty of violating a rule that results in his or her being discharged. The National Labor Relations Board (NLRB) formulated a rule that stated the burden of proof is on the employer to show that the employee would have been discharged even if he or she had not been involved in an activity protected by the law. This rule was enforced by the 1st Circuit Court of Appeals.[7] Not all courts agreed and the split of authority continued until the Supreme Court settled the issue.

In NLRB v. Transportation Management Corp. 103 Sup. Ct. 2469 (1983) a bus driver was discharged for "leaving his keys in the bus and taking unauthorized breaks." The employee previous to his discharge had talked to the Teamsters Union about representation and was attempting to convince his fellow workers to join the union. His supervisor stated to other workers that he had heard of the driver's organizing activities and "would get even with the employee."

Testimony showed that it was not unusual for a driver to leave his keys in the bus and the employee was never admonished for taking unauthorized breaks. The NLRB contended that the reason for the discharge was for union activity and that the employee would not have been otherwise discharged for leaving the keys in the bus and taking unauthorized breaks. The Court held that the NLRB was correct in placing the burden on the employer to show by a preponderance of evidence that the employer would have discharged even if he had not been involved in the protected of activity of trying to organize a union. The court held that the board's allocation of the burden is reasonable and it was justified in finding that the discharge would not have occurred had the employer not considered the employee's protected activities.

Statutory Protection Of Supervisors From Discharge

The supervisor has little statutory protection from discharge, except what might be offered in the exceptions to the employment at will doctrine. Section 7 of the National Labor Relations Act does afford the supervisor some protection where the employer discharges the supervisor for:

1. refusal to commit an unfair labor practice,

2. refusal to testify on behalf of management in a board hearing involving union activity,

---

[7] NLRB v. Wright Lines, 662 F.2d 899 (1st Cir. 1981).

3. giving adverse testimony in a board hearing, and
4. failure to prevent a union from organizing employees.

Although Section 2(II) of the act states that supervisors are not employees, the board and the courts have held that it is a violation of employee Section 7 rights if a supervisor is discharged for such reasons.[8] The court in Talladega was quick to point out that it is not extending the act to nonemployees but merely giving protection to nonemployees where their action adversely affects employees as defined by the act.

The failure to prevent a union must be distinguished from the situation where a supervisor does not do enough to prevent a union or where the supervisor sympathizes with the union. In Automobile Salesmen's Union v. NLRB 711 F.2d 383 (D.C. Cir. 1983) the supervisors attended a union meeting and generally sympathized with the employees' organizational activities. The board refused to extend protection of the act to the supervisors upon discharge, stating that it was within the prerogative of management to discipline its supervisors for sympathizing with the employees' desire to join a union, the court affirmed the board's position stating that in order to receive protection under Section 7, the supervisor's activity must directly interfere with employee rights to organize.

The act does not prevent the supervisor from taking a vigorous role in the management campaign to prevent a union. It is where the supervisor refuses to commit an unfair labor practice or to do something such as surveillance of union activities and is discharged that is protected by the act. The discharge for the refusal is the crux of the protection.[9] If the supervisor commits an unfair labor practice, this is not protected because the action would be prohibited by the act. An employer would be enforcing the law by the discharge. When the employer discharges a supervisor for activity that has a direct impact on the employee's rights under the NLRA and it is considered an unfair labor practice, the discharge would be protected.[10]

COMMON-LAW EMPLOYMENT-AT-WILL DOCTRINE

Few legal doctrines have been more firmly established than the at-will doctrine. Under this doctrine the employer could do no wrong. Where an employee was discharged for trading in a certain store that the railroad decided to put out of business, the court said

---

[8] NLRB v. Talladega Cotton Factory, Inc., 213 F.2d 209 (5th Cir. 1954).

[9] NLRB v. Miami Coca Cola Bottling Co., 341 F.2d 524 (5th Cir. 1965).

[10] Howard Johnson Co. v. NLRB, 702 F.2d 1 (1st Cir., 1983).

that the employer had a right to discharge even if it is morally wrong and "'the law cannot compel them (employers) to employ workers, nor to keep them employed."[11]

The employer's discretion to terminate or not to hire was so secure that the Supreme Court held that a statute forbidding yellow dog contracts (contracts that require an applicant to sign an anti-union pledge) was unconstitutional.[12] As late as 1949 a court took the same position that an employer could discharge for no reason at all.[13]

With legislation concerning employees' rights, such as the Labor Management Relations Act as amended,[14] Title VII of the Civil Rights Act of 1964 as amended,[15] Age Discrimination in Employment Act of 1967 as amended,[16] and Occupational Safety and Health Act of 1970,[17] the courts started to take a look at this unblemished common law doctrine by listening to numerous theories

asserted by discharged workers that the doctrine should have certain exceptions. Some argued that their employment was for a fixed period either expressed or implied while other discharged workers argued that the employer had an obligation to evaluate job performance in good faith and therefore could terminate only on just cause. Others would rely more on the traditional reasons such as due process, contrary to fair and good faith dealing, or malicious action by the employer to justify their claims for relief.

The courts in a climate of employee rights created by Congress in other areas began to favorably receive the wrongfully discharged employee's arguments and seek an exception to the common law doctrine. Because almost all of these cases involve either a breach of contract or tort action, they are tried in state courts and accordingly there is a variation of law among the states.

EXCEPTIONS TO EMPLOYMENT AT WILL

Public Policy

This exception, which is the most widely adopted by the courts, states that the employer should

not be permitted to discipline or discharge an employee for reasons that are violative of public policy. Public policy is a broad term used by the courts as a reason for an ex-

---

[11] Payne v. Western and Atlantic R. R. Co., 81 Tenn. 507 (1884).

[12] Copperage v. Kansas, 236 U.S. 1 (1915).

[13] Lewis v. Minnesota Mutual Life Insurance Co., 37 N.W. 2d 316 (Iowa 1949).

[14] 29 U.S.C. Sect. 158 et seq.

[15] 42 U.S.C. Sect. 2000 et seq.

[16] 29 U.S.C. Sect. 621 et seq.

[17] 29 U.S.C. Sect. 660 et seq.

ception to an otherwise well-accepted principle of law. Some law journals define it as a private dealing that is restricted by law for the good of the community.[18] Another definition is "whatever contravenes good morals or established interests of society."[19] Public policy is decided on a case-by-case basis and is not defined by the court until violated. For example, the courts have said that a gambling contract, although it complies with all necessary elements of a contract, will not be enforced because it is not for the benefit or for the convenience of the public to do so. Other exceptions to principles of law are not as widely accepted as the enforcement of gambling contracts; exception to employment at will is one of them.

Where a discharge has been held to be a violation of a public policy, the reason for the discharge is probably against a good employee relations policy. Four distinctly different reasons for discharge have been held to be contrary to public policy: first, exercising a right under a statute; second, refusing to disobey a law when requested to do so by employer; third, disclosing the employer to authorities when the law is being violated, commonly called the whistle-blower cases; and fourth, employer's actions amounting to malice, bad faith or breach of public trust.

In all these situations the employee alleges that a public policy exists. When the employer refused to acknowledge the policy, the employee was discharged in retaliation for following the policy.

Where Employee Exercises a Right under a Statute

A violation of an explicit provision in a statute is not considered an exception to employment at will but simply a violation of the statute for which a remedy is provided in the statute. This straightforward situation does not warrant further consideration in this chapter. For this reason, discharged in violation of statutory provisions in Title VII of the Civil Rights Act as amended, Labor Management Relations Act as amended, Age Discrimination in Employment Act of 1967 as amended, Fair Labor Standard Act as amended, and Occupational Safety and Health Act of 1970 are not discussed in detail. The chapter does discuss where the statute gives the employee a remedy and the employee is discharged for using it.

One of the employment-related rights that employers sometimes object to is the employee's right to file for and receive worker's compensation benefits. The Central Indiana Gas Company discharged an employee without a reason after she obtained a settlement on a worker's compensation claim.[20] In this landmark case the court explains the reasoning behind other situations when an employee exer-

---

[18] 72 C.J.S. policy, p. 212.

[19] Billingsley v. Clelland 23 S.E., 812 @815 (W. Va. 1895).

[20] Frampton v. Central Indiana Gas Co., 297 N.E. 2d 425 (Ind. 1973).

cises a right under the statute when it said:

> If employers are permitted to penalize employees for filing workmen's compensation claims, a most important public policy will be undermined. The fear of being discharged would have a deleterious effect on the exercise of a statutory right. Employees will not file claims for justly deserved compensation—opting, instead, to continue their employment without incident. The end result, of course, is that the employer is effectively relieved of his obligation.[21]

Discharge is an employer's most common retaliation for employees' filing worker's compensation claims or exercising other rights based on various statutes.[22] In one situation a discharge was held wrongful because an employee's wife obtained an attorney to investigate violations of a state minimum wage law.[23] In a rather strange decision, an Idaho court held wrongful discharge for an employee who was appropriating his employer's funds for a Christmas party; the employee successfully alleged that his discharge was to avoid his vesting in the company's pension fund.[24]

Employee Refusal to Disobey the Law

The theory behind this exception is that it is contrary to public policy to force an employee to choose between violating the law and keeping a job. The most-cited case in this area is where the employee refused to testify falsely in a legislative hearing and the employer discharged him.[25] A similar result was reached where an employee refused to falsify pollution reports submitted to the state; however, because the employee failed to plead that this was the reason for the discharge, the employee lost the case.[26]

Sometimes an employee can be wrongfully discharged for telling the truth, as where a police chief was demoted and later discharged because he testified truthfully in criminal prosecution of the former mayor.[27]

Discharge for Jury Duty Participation

Another public policy exception to the at-will doctrine is where the employee is discharged for jury duty or participation in a legal proceeding contrary to employer instructions. Some jurisdictions will hold that discharge for this reason is contrary to public policy. In one case an employee went to the court clerk with a letter from employer to be excused but told the clerk that she did not want to be excused. She

---

[21] Quoted from p. 427 of 297 N.E. 2d, cited in Note 20.

[22] For more complete discussion on retaliation for employees workers' compensation claims, see Theodore A. Olsen, "Wrongful Discharge Claims Raised by at will Employees: A New Legal Concern for Employers." *Labor Law Journal,* vol. 32, no. 5, May 1981 (Chicago: Commerce Clearing House).

[23] Montalvo v. Zamora, 86 Cal. Rptr. 401 (1970).

[24] Jackson v. Minidoka Irrigation Dist., 563 P.2d 54 (Idaho 1977).

[25] Petermann v. International Brotherhood of Teamsters, 344 P.2d 25 (Cal. 1959).

[26] Trombetta v. Detroit, Toledo & Ironton R.R. Company, 265 N.W.2d 385 (Mich. 1978).

[27] Hoopes v. City of Chester, 473 F.Supp. 1214 (E.D. Pa. 1979).

did not tell the employer what she told the clerk. She was discharged after serving on the jury. The court held that discharge was contrary to public policy.[28]

In another situation the employee informed the employer that he was called for jury duty. The employer said that he could get out of it by telling the court in each case that he has a "formed opinion" and therefore would be ineligible to serve. The employee refused to do this or ask to be excused. The employer discharged him on return from jury duty. The court held this to be contrary to public policy.[29]

Only one other jurisdiction has considered the issue of whether discharge for refusal to be excused from jury duty is contrary to public policy. This court held that the employee did not have a cause of action for discharge; the employment at-will doctrine prevailed.[30] Other jurisdictions have considered a related issue, where the employee testifies in a legal proceeding truthfully but adversely to the employer's interest. The courts that have considered this issue have held that no cause of action exists for discharge of an employee for giving adverse testimony and reinstated the employment at-will doctrine.[31]

In another situation the employee refused to drop a personal injury against the employer on behalf of minor daughter. The court held that no cause of action existed for the discharge of the employee.[32]

When Employee Blows the Whistle on Employer

One of the most common public policy exceptions involves the employee who refused to accept assigned duties that furthered the employer's business but were deemed improper or unlawful by the employee. A protest is made to the employer. The protest falls on deaf ears and the employee airs the complaint to public officials, hoping that somebody will do something. These cases are sometimes called whistle blower cases in employee relations law literature.[33]

Many employers believe that if an employee cannot be loyal to the employer, the person should be either demoted or terminated. When this occurs, there is a possibility that the employer could become involved in a whistleblower public policy exception to the employment-at-will doctrine. Loyalty, according to court rationale, is openly expressed where the employee tries to persuade the employer to comply with the law

---

[28] Nees v. Hocks, 536 P.2d 512 (Ore. 1955).

[29] Reuther v. Fowler and Williams, Inc., 386 A.2d 119 (PA. 1978).

[30] Bender Ship Repair Inc. v. Stevens, 379 SO 2d. 594 (Ala., 1980).

[31] Phillips v. Goodyear Tire & Rubber Co., 651 F.2d 1051 (5th Cir. 1981); Ivy v. Army Times Publishing Co., 428 A.2d 831 (D.C. 1981).

[32] DeMarco v. Publix Supermarkets, Inc., 360 So.2d. 134 (Fla. 1978).

[33] See "Protecting the Private Sector At-Will Employee Who 'Blows the Whistle': A Cause of Action Based upon Determinants of Public Policy," *Wisconsin Law Review*, 1977; also Donald D. Cook, "Whistle Blowers, Friend of Foe," *Industry Week*, October 5, 1981, vol. 211, no. 1, pp. 51-56.

and the employer refuses. The frustrated employee then discloses incriminating information to outside investigators; the employer's response is to discharge (such as where the employee-reported overcharges to customers were not rebated).[34]

This situation is more extreme than where the employee refuses to become involved in a scheme to fix gasoline prices because employee under antitrust laws can be individually liable as well as the employer. The California court easily found a wrongful discharge in that situation.[35]

The devious employer that is aware of the consequences of discharging where the employee refuses to take part in an illegal endeavor may attempt to create some other reason for discharge. When an employee refused to take part in special pricing arrangements to some accounts and not others, the employer created a false personnel file to support the discharge. The court was not impressed and held it to be a wrongful discharge.[36]

Whistle-blower cases are receiving a good deal of attention in the media and by state legislatures. Michigan passed the Whistle Blower's Protection Act of 1981; it makes it illegal for an employer "to

discharge, threaten or discriminate against an employee who reports or is about to report a suspected violation of federal, state or local law to a public body."[37] Although there is no federal legislation pending, several members of Congress are investigating the advisability of introducing whistle-blower protection in the private sector. Federal employees are presently protected for blowing the whistle.[38]

Malice And Bad Faith

The malice and bad faith exception is closely related to the public policy exception. Some courts do not bother to make the distinction between the two while others stated it as another public policy exception because emotional harm and suffering are inflicted by the employer by an abusive discharge. An abusive discharge is best illustrated by the case where a restaurant owner lined up all the waitresses in alphabetical order and discharged them one by one when they would not provide information about who was pilfering food.[39]

Few employers would be this abusive and they would not be exposed to this exception to the at-will doctrine. Certainly any semblance of good employee relations policy would seem likely to avoid

---

[34] Harless v. First National Bank in Fairmont, 246 S.E. 2d 270 (W.Va. 1978).

[35] Tameny v. Atlantic Richfield Co., 610 P.2d 1330 (Cal. 1980).

[36] McNulty v. Borden, Inc., 474 F.Supp. 1111 (E.D. Pa. 1979).

[37] Michigan compiled annotated, Sect. 15.36–15.369.

[38] U.S.C. 2302(b)(8) (1981 Supp.).

[39] Agis v. Howard Johnson Co, 355 N.E. 2d 315 (Mass. 1976).

malice and bad faith. In actual situations, however, the employer can become involved without obvious intent or malice.

The leading case in the malice and bad faith areas, Monge v. Beebe Rubber Co., involves an employee who was discharged for refusing to date her supervisor. The court states that this was a breach of the contract of employment at will because it was motivated by malice and bad faith and therefore not in the best interest of the economic system and the public good.[40]

The language in the Monge case is similar to that used in public policy exceptions. The use of the terms *malice and bad faith,* however, is adopted by some courts when they want to go further than the public policy exception. They hold that a breach of contract had occurred, defining the contract as developed by the employment relationship. Relying heavily on the Monge case, one court found malice and bad faith when an employee with 25 years of service was discharged before a customer placed a $5-million order for which the employee would have received a large sales commission.[41] Over 19 state courts have adopted the Monge decision in one form or another.

The farthest that any court has gone in finding bad faith was in the case of an employee of 18 years' experience who was falsely accused of violating the employer's work rules and employer's personnel policies. The court said that termination of a long-term employee without just cause offends an implied-in-law covenant of good faith and fair dealing. The California court took the position that an employer must establish just cause when discharging a long-term employee; failure to do so will result in punitive damages (damages that compensate above actual loss are punishment for evil behavior).[42]

The bad faith exception has been adopted by many states. If they go as far as the California court in the Cleary case, enforcement of the just-cause provisions of labor agreements by arbitration will be replaced by litigation. Bringing an action for punitive damages is much more rewarding than asking an arbitrator for reinstatement with back pay.

One employee in California discovered this when he was reinstated through the arbitration process and in a separate action the court allowed punitive damages after the arbitration award.[43] The malice and bad faith public policy exception has been accepted in Alabama, California, Connecticut, Idaho, Illinois, Indiana, Kansas, Maryland, Massachusetts, Michigan, New Hampshire, New Jersey,

[40] Monge v. Beebe Rubber Co., 316 A.2d 549 (N.H. 1974).

[41] Fortune v. Nat'l Cash Register Co., 364 N.E. 2d 1251 (Mass. 1977).

[42] Cleary v. American Airlines, Inc., 168 Cal. Rptr. 722 (Cal. App. 1980).

[43] Alcorn v. Anbro Engineering, Inc., 468 P.2d 216 (Cal. 1970).

Oregon, Pennsylvania, and West Virginia. This wide acceptance will certainly encourage employees in other states to seek claims for relief where there is any resemblance of a wrongful discharge.[44]

Implied Contract

The personnel administrator who takes pride in good employee relations would consider the foregoing exceptions as something that could not happen personally. In many companies that have positive personnel policies, the common law exception of public policy, whistle blowing, malice, and bad faith is academic, but this would not be necessarily so with the implied contract exception. Positive personnel administration could increase the exposure to the implied contract exception by aggressive recruiting and promotion that results in promises being made at the time of hiring, handbooks to sell the company as a place of continuous employment, and salaries quoted as annual salaries, which may imply a contract of employment for one year.

The personnel administrator is the most vulnerable where in the interest of selling the company or promoting good employee relations certain promises are made. In determining whether such a promise is implied contract of continuous employment, the courts look at the surrounding circumstances at the time of hiring to determine whether a promise was in fact made. In one instance a fixed annual salary for a long period was taken to establish the period of employment.[45]

In cases of a promise being an implied contract, the employee must show some reliance on the promise. One example might be a long-distance move where the employee left a secure job with a competitor and at a later date was discharged without cause or where there was a reliance on a promise of a better opportunity, which never materialized. Promises of this kind are not uncommon when an aggressive employment manager is operating in a tight labor market. The reason that the job does not materialize or employee is laid off may be legitimate, but the employee is still emotionally and financially harmed.[46] In this situation the courts often allow punitive damages.

In one case an employer makes promises of eventual promotion. In relying on that promise, the employee does not take another job offer; for some legitimate reason the promotion never takes place. In an early California case

---

[44] Some courts call it "outrageous conduct" where the alleged "strip search" of an employee suspected of theft held sufficient for the jury to find "outrageous conduct." Bodewig v. K-Mart, Inc., 635 P.2d 657 (Ore. 1981).

[45] Delzell v. Pipe, 294 S.W. 2d 690 (Tenn. 1956).

[46] O'Neil v. ARA Services, Inc., 457 F.Supp. 182 (E.D. Penn. 1978). Also Rowe v. Noren Pattern and Foundry Co., 283 N.W. 2d 713 (Mich. 1979).

the court allowed recovery in this situation.[47]

Communication to the employees is one of the earmarks of every good personnel department. High quality of performance can get the personnel administrator into trouble if not properly done. Statements made at the time of hiring are sometimes held to be an implied contract.

Where an employee's salary was fixed at hiring as an annual salary, the court may interpret this as a contract of employment for one year if the employee shows that the statement was interpreted to mean one year's employment.[48] A promise made at hiring, which is relied on by the employee, is usually held a contract even though the interviewer had no authority to make it. In one case the interviewer said that the employee had a job for life. The court allowed damages.[49]

The Supreme Court has given indirect approval to the concept that a promise at the time of employment is a contract wherein they permit an action in state courts for a breach of contract when a promise was made at the time of hiring.[50]

A common practice in operating during a strike is to hire a new work force and then as part of the settlement agreement to end the strike replace the new work force with the previous employees who went on strike. Under the law, when an employee goes on economic strike, that employee does not have a right to his/her old job, but only to the next vacancy when it occurs, unless the strike is over an unfair labor practice in which the striking employees must be rehired.

In the Belknap case the employer replaced the strikers and promised permanent employment to the new employees. In order to get the strike settled he agreed to rehire the strikers and terminate the new employees. The replaced employees brought a breach of contract action and misrepresentation claim in the state court stating that they relied on the hiring promise of permanent employment. The employer argued that the National Labor Relations Act prevented this type of action as it preempts action in state courts. The Supreme Court disagreed stating that this is a contract action that can be brought in state courts and that the employer could have protected himself by making the promise of employment conditional on the strike settlement.

---

[47] Chinn v. China Nat'l Aviation Corp., 291 P.2d 91 (Cal. 1955).

[48] Lanier v. Alenco, 459 F.2d 689 (5th Cir. 1972). A South Dakota statute states that when a salary is quoted as an annual salary, it is a contract for employment for one year. [*South Dakota Codified Laws,* Sect. 60(1), (3)].

[49] Doody v. John Sextron Co., 411 F.2d 1119 (1st Cir. 1969).

[50] Belknap Inc. v. Hale 103 Sup. Ct. 3172 (1983).

HANDBOOKS AND POLICY MANUALS AS IMPLIED CONTRACTS

Certain statements made in an employee handbook or a policy manual have been held to be an implied contract. The Michigan court has gone as far as any court can where it held that guidelines and the supervisor's manual were an expressed contract.[51] The clauses that were especially troublesome were where the supervisor's manual stated that an employee could be discharged only for just cause and "could work until 65 as long as he did his job."

In a companion case the employee testified that he was promised at the time of hiring he could work for the company "as long as I did my job." The court said that was a contract that changed the at-will doctrine.[52]

Where the handbook lists benefits, some courts will refuse to find an implied contract but will state that it is bad faith not to pay the benefits.

In one situation the handbook stated than an employee would be discharged only for just cause. The employee signed the application, which stated that employment would be subject to the *Handbook on Personnel Policy*. Eight years later he was discharged. The court held that it was a contract; just cause had to be shown as stated in the handbook.[53] In Gates v. Life Insurance of Montana, 638 P.2d 1063 (Mont. 1982) the court refused to find the handbook an implied contract but held that it would be bad faith by the employers if the benefits stated in the handbook were not paid.

A similar result was reached when a supervisor's and office personnel policy stated that separation pay would be paid if an employee were permanently terminated. (No statement was made as to the reason for termination.) The court held that this was an implied contract because personnel policies constituted an offer; when an employee accepted the job, the contract was complete.[54]

If the policy exists but it is not properly communicated to the employees, some courts will still hold that it is an implied contract. In one case the employee knew about a severance pay plan in the company policy manual from other employees who read it. The court held this to be an implied contract.[55] This is contrary to the law

---

[51] Toussaint v. Blue Cross and Blue Shield of Michigan, 292 N.W. 2d 880 (Mich. 1980).

[52] Ebling v. Masco Corp., 292 N.W.2d 801 (Mich. 1980).

[53] Weiner v. McGraw-Hill, 443 N.E 2d 441 (N.Y. 1982).

[54] Hercules Power Co. v. Brookfield, 53 S.E. 2d 804 (VA 1949).

[55] Hinkeldey v. Cities Service Oil Co., 470 S.W. 494 (Mo. 1971).

in other areas, where in discrimination cases the courts require the policy to be clearly communicated before a discharge is justified for violating the policy. One of the strongest positions taken by any court on a handbook being implied contract is where a loan officer in a bank was in default on this personal loan and had approved 56 out of 57 loans in violation of the loan policy. The discharge was held to be a breach of contract as the employer failed to follow the discharge procedure outlined in the handbook.[56]

In a section entitled "Performance Review" the handbook stated:

Everyone wants to know "where he stands." Our performance evaluation program is designed to help you to determine where you are, where you are going, and how to get there. Factual and objective appraisals of you and your work performance should serve as aids to your future advancement.

A section entitled "Job Security" reads:

Employment in the banking industry is very stable. It does not fluctuate up and down sharply in good times and bad, as do many other types of employment. We have no seasonal layoffs and we never hire a lot of people when business is booming only to release them when things are not as active.

The job security offered by the *Pine River State Bank* is one reason why so many of our employees have five or more years of service. In return for this, Management expects job security from you. That is, the security that you will perform the duties of your position with diligence, cooperation, dependability, and a sense of responsibility.

The Section entitled "Disciplinary Policy" reads:

In the interest of fairness to all employees the Company establishes reasonable standards of conduct for all employees to follow in their employment at *Pine River State Bank*. These standards are not intended to place unreasonable restrictions on you but are considered necessary for us to conduct our business in an orderly and efficient manner.

If an employee has violated a company policy, the following procedure will apply:

1. An oral reprimand by the immediate supervisor for the first offense, with a written notice sent to the Executive Vice President.

2. A written reprimand for the second offense.

3. A written reprimand and a meeting with the Executive Vice President and possible suspension from work without pay for five days.

4. Discharge from employment for an employee whose conduct does not improve as a result of the previous action taken.

In no instance will a person be discharged from employment without review of the facts by the Executive Officer.

The court did not feel that the job security provisions of the handbook were an offer of employment, nor did they put a lot of weight on the performance appraisal section. It was considered a general statement of policy that did not constitute an offer of permanent employment, but what made the discharge wrongful is that this policy was not followed. The Court found that the disciplinary policy was an offer of a unilateral contract for procedures to be

---

[56] Pine River State Bank v. Richard F. Mettille Sr., 333 N.W. 2d 622 (Minn. 1983).

followed in job terminination and when those procedures were not followed the jury could find a breach of contract.[57]

Those jurisdictions that hold that a handbook is a contract are saying that the provisions in the handbook limit the employer's right to terminate at will and termination must be for a good cause.

Not all courts will agree with these decisions that handbooks and policy manuals are implied contracts.

Several Indiana courts have held that a handbook does not create a contract that will interfere with the employer's right to discharge. In McQueenery v. Glenn, 400 N.E.2d 806 (Ind. App. 1980), cert. denied, 449 U.S. 1125 (1981), the court held that there was no expressed or implied promise that employment would be continued for a definite period. In Shaw v. S.S. Kresge Co., 328 N.E. 2d 775 (Ind. App. 1975) the court stated

that because no promise is made by the employer, the handbook provisions were unenforceable because they lacked a mutuality of obligation. In Louisiana and Kansas the handbook would be held not an implied contract, an example, where the employer wins the case but incurred heavy litigation costs because of loose language in the handbook.[58]

Handbooks are contracts in some jurisdictions and not in others. Often the specific wording will cause the court to find a contract even where in the past they failed to find an implied contract in other cases.

The employer should word handbooks carefully to prevent litigation. Some employers put a disclaimer in the handbook; this may prevent the handbook from being interpreted as an implied contract but such a disclaimer may also destroy the employee relations effect of the handbook.

VOLUNTARY QUIT AS CONSTRUCTIVE DISCHARGE

Often an employer will give a sigh of relief when a problem employee turns in a resignation. There is a secure feeling that since the employee voluntarily quit there can be no possible complaint by the employee of wrongful discharge. This false feeling of security disappears when a constructive discharge claim is filed. Where an employee quits because of unreasonable working conditions caused by the employer's acts or failure to act, the court will consider it a constructive discharge rather than a voluntary quit.

[57] In Osterkamp v. Alkota Mfg. Co. 332 N.W. 2d 275 (S.D. 1983) the court reached the same result, stating it was a breach of contract when the progressive discipline procedure in the handbook was not followed. In Southwest Gas Corp. v. Ahmad, 688 F2d (Nev. 1983) the court reached the same result when a handbook was not followed.

[58] Simmon v. Westinghouse Electric Corp., 311 S.2d 38 (La. 1975); Johnson v. Nat'l Beef Packing Co., 551 P.2d 77 (Kan. 1976).

The law of constructive discharge was developed by the courts from National Labor Relations Board cases where the employer would harass an employee for union activity in violation of Section 8(a)(3) of the Labor Management Relations Act (LMRA). In the leading case, the employer continually threatened the employee with discharge but did not actually discharge her. The supervisor would, for example, tell the employee that he was keeping a detailed record of her work and would wave a black notebook in her face. When two errors were discovered in her work, the supervisor threatened that one more error would result in discharge. The supervisor gave instructions to others to make it as hard as possible so that she would quit. In this case an unlawful motive was clearly established and constructive discharge was found.[59]

Where the LMRA is alleged to have been violated, the courts will require the presence of or, implied unlawful motive to get rid of the employee.

The constructive discharge doctrine developed in National Labor Relations Board cases was later applied to other situations. In these cases, however, the courts dropped the unlawful motive requirement and required only a deliberate attempt to make working conditions intolerable. In constructive discharge involving statutes, the courts defined deliberate attempt as employer's conduct that made the job so unattractive and unpleasant that resignation would be foreseeable by the employer. Because the resignation was foreseeable, the court implied unlawful intent to discharge.[60]

This concept has been extended by the Fifth Circuit Court in a ruling where all that is necessary to establish constructive discharge is that conditions created by the employer, whether intentionally or unintentionally, are such that a reasonable person would consider them intolerable. The court refused to listen to the employer's argument that the actions were not intentional. An interesting point in this case is that the court ruled that failure to comply with the Equal Pay Act was not considered an unreasonable condition sufficient to support a finding of constructive discharge.[61]

Where there was discrimination for religious belief, the same court five years previously found constructive discharge. An employee was required to attend a staff meeting where in addition to business matters, a prayer and short religious talks were given. When the employee objected, the employer told her to "close her ears" during this part of the staff meeting. The employee contended that mandatory attendance was the same as discharge. The supervisor stated that she was not being

---

[59] NLRB v. Tennessee Packers, Inc., Frosty Morn Division, 339 F.2d 203 (6th Cir. 1964).

[60] Mueller v. U.S. Steel, 509 F.2d 923 (10th Cir. 1975).

[61] Bourque v. Powell Electrical Mfg., 617 F.2d 61 (5th Cir. 1980).

fired but had to attend the staff meetings. The court stated that this was constructive discharge as the employer made a deliberate effort to make the employee's working conditions intolerable. Further the employer made no attempt to accommodate the employee's religious objections.[62]

An improper transfer or demotion could lead to a constructive discharge claim. In demotion or transfer cases the court will look at the comparison between the old job and transferred job as to salary, fringe benefits, working conditions, and blow to the employee's prestige. However, the blow to prestige must be severe and caused by a substantial change in jobs.[63]

In one case of constructive discharge caused by a transfer, the college took away teaching duties of a professor and assigned nonprofessional work.[64]

Often personnel administrators will use hard-sell tactics to get an employee to quit, like talking the employee into early retirement because at his age a transfer would be a waste of time.[65] A personnel director told an employee that others were trying to get him fired and it would be best to resign because it would look better on his record.[66]

One technique used by personnel practitioners is to give an employee an opportunity to resign before being fired. This practice gives the employee the best of both worlds. For the purpose of applying for another job the person resigned; if for unemployment compensation eligibility or possible wrongful discharge lawsuit, it will be alleged to be a constructive discharge, an allegation that is very difficult to defend. In the courts, constructive discharge allegations are much more difficult to defend than when the employer discharges without subterfuge. Only under rare circumstances should this option be offered if the employer wants to avoid exposure to employee claims for monetary awards. The employee either quit or was discharged.

These cases show that in order to have constructive discharge the employer must create intolerable conditions. Whether intent must be shown depends on whether action is based on some other statute or a violation of the

---

[62] Young v. Southwestern Savings & Loan Assn., 509 F.2d 140 (5th Cir. 1975). In a similar situation the employer took away teaching duties and assigned nonprofessional work, held constructive discharge. Lincoln v. Board of Regents of the University of Georgia, 697 F.2d 928 (11 Cir. 1983).

[63] Frazer v. KFC Nat'l Management, 491 F.Supp. 1099 (M.D. Ga 1980 aff'd 636 F2d 313 (5th Cir. 1981)) and Meyer v. Brown & Root Construction Co. 661 F.2d 369 (5th Cir. 1981).

[64] Lincoln v. Board of Regents of the University System of Georgia, 697 F.2d 928 (11th Cir. 1983).

[65] Toussaint v. Ford Motor Co., 581 F.2d 812 (10th Cir. 1978).

[66] Velasquez v. City of Colorado Springs, Federal District Court Colo. (1980) 23 FEP cases 621 (BNA Reports).

Labor Management Relations Act. The employer who deliberately creates intolerable conditions or permits unpleasant and unattractive conditions to exist is exposed to litigation to the same extent as in a discharge in violation of a statute or where there may be an exception to the common law of employment at will.

PREVENTING WRONGFUL DISCHARGE LITIGATION

In view of recent developments in discharge cases, exposure to litigation is increasing. The large awards for punitive damages can only encourage the employee to make claims for relief. However, the employer that adopts a policy of no discharges because of the danger of being sued will unnecessarily increase labor costs by retaining marginal employees.

If a discharge is decided on by the supervisor, the personnel practitioner must take action and defend it with all available evidence to establish a legitimate reason. One can rely on an abundance of authority to defend a position provided that the proper precautions are taken before the discharge. If a manager decides to discharge, the manager will do so. The task of the personnel administrator is to advise that it be done in a way that will result in the least exposure to litigation; therefore, the personnel administrator must be notified well in advance of the discharge date.

At-will employees still exist and should be considered when no other reasons are judicially weak, but fewer and fewer courts are adhering to the old common-law doctrine. Some courts have openly repudiated the public policy exception. When an employee brought a civil action for discharge for filing a worker's compensation claim, the court declined to hear it even though is was a criminal offense under the statute to discharge for filing a claim.[67]

Courts in the state of Washington take the position that all the common-law exceptions remain an open question. They adopted the terminable-at-will doctrine for an employee with 18 years of service even though he showed an understanding of steady employment and had a satisfactory work performance record.[68]

Some courts have rejected all public exceptions, regardless of the facts or harshness of the employer's action, stating that there must be a written contractual relationship.[69]

Another example where some jurisdictions take an opposite view is where an employee was wrong-

---

[67] Christy v. Petrus, 295 S.W.2d 122 (Mo. 1956).

[68] Roberts v. Atlantic Richfield Co., 568 P.2d 764 (Wash. 1977).

[69] Murphy v. American Home Products 448 N.E. 2d 86 (N.Y. 1983).

fully demoted and then discharged because of refusal to continue falsifying certain medical records as instructed by employer. The court rejected public policy exception as being vague and said that discharge can be for "good reason, a wrong reason or no reason."[70]

Even in whistle-blower cases where the jurisdiction has adopted the public policy exception, courts may conclude that the employee is in no position to assert the exception to the common law. When a salesman of tubular steel products complained that the product sold was not safety-tested, the employee was discharged for complaining, even though the product was found unsafe. The court held that the employee was only responsible for selling the product, not for its safety and there was no violation of public policy.[71]

A Just-Cause Policy Is Recommended

A study of wrongful discharge cases indicates that the employer's policy must be carefully considered when discharge occurs. The development of legal doctrines that make an exception to the common law

employment-at-will doctrine encourages employees to file previously unthinkable claims for relief. The vague definition of public policy by the courts gives the employee free access to the courts and discourages the employer from discharging anyone except in extreme cases. Employees will file lawsuits in almost any discharge case where just cause is not clearly evident. The first question that the court will ask is the reason for the discharge. If none can be shown, the reason alleged by the employee could be an exception to the at-will doctrine.

Seldom will a wrongful discharge suit succeed when the employer adopts a just-cause termination policy and communicates to the employee the exact conditions that will cause severe disciplinary action or discharge.[72] Where just cause is shown, the courts have supported the discharge rather than relying on the common law exceptions.

In a New Jersey case the court said that even where public policy is violated, the employer may discharge if there is a legitimate reason.[73] In another case the federal court of appeals said that

---

[70] Hinrich's v. Tranquilaire Hospital, 352 So.2d 1130 (Ala. 1977).

[71] Geary v. United States Steel Corp., 319 A.2d 174 (Pa. 1974).

[72] Communication in this context is best described by a situation where an employer had to get 100 percent participation in order to have a group life insurance program. One employee would not sign; the supervisor talked to him, but could not convince him; the plant manager tried without success. They reported to the president that they could not put the program in. The president talked to the employee and said, "sign up or you are fired." The employee signed. The supervisor and plant manager were bewildered. They asked the employee why he signed when the president talked to him but refused when they tried to get him to do so. The employee's reply was, "Nobody explained it to me before."

[73] Cited in Note 29, Reuther v. Fowler and Williams.

the sole reason must be malice and bad faith.[74] In worker's compensation cases, where the courts are the most aggressive in holding wrongful discharge for filing a claim, if some other just cause can be found, the court will disregard the common law exception. When an employee filed a worker's compensation claim and was excessively absent because of the work-related injury, the court said that discharge was not because of the filing of a claim but for excessive absenteeism.[75] In a similar situation where the employee was excessively absent due to a work-related injury, the court said that the discharge was due to unwillingness and inability to work, not for filing a worker's compensation claim.[76]

In view of these cases, employers should seriously consider establishing a just-cause policy. A just-cause policy for discharges will usually be judicially accepted if it contains the following elements:

1. The employee must be clearly and unequivocally forewarned of the disciplinary consequences. This can be satisfied by a progressive discipline program: if it is a more serious offense, one violation could result in discharge; if an employee assaults the supervisor, it would not be necessary to allow another opportunity. This element can be satisfied if it is clearly understood that the employee can only dispute committing the act; once that is determined, the penalty is at the sole discretion of the employer.

2. The offense must be job-related; outside activities are seldom a just cause. If an employee's personal habits are contrary to good social behavior and what others consider wild, and this affects job performance, the employer does not allege immoral habits but that the employee is too tired to perform job duties when reporting to work.

3. Management must conduct a fair, unbiased investigation to determine the facts before making a decision. This is sometimes difficult for the immediate supervisor. For this reason it is advisable to have at least two management representatives investigate and take part in the decision.

4. After the investigation, management must as objectively as possible determine whether there is sufficient evidence to justify the discharge. Court cases indicate that management too often fails to investigate whether the rules have been uniformly applied. This is a primary

---

[74] Perks v. Firestone Tire & Rubber, 611 F.2d 1363 (3rd Cir. 1979).

[75] Mitchell v. St. Louis County, 575 S.W.2d 813 (Mo. App. 1978).

[76] Rodriquez v. Civil Service Com., 582 S.W. 2d 354 (Mo. App. 1979).

reason why employers lose wrongful discharge cases. Often discrimination charges by employee or retaliation claims influence management decisions. Management simply wants to get rid of the employee. When retaliation or discrimination is found, although just cause may also be present, the courts will usually find for the employee. One court went so far as to say that only a reasonable belief of an unlawful practice by the employer entitled the employee to protection.[77] Retaliation allegations are difficult to defend if there exists one thread of evidence that they occurred.

If some or all of these policies are practiced in discharge cases, just cause would easily be established and discharge litigation would be avoided. An almost certain defense would be to put a statement in a handbook or manual that employee would acknowledge that it was read and understood. The statement would read as follows:

In consideration of my employment, I agree to conform to the rules and policies of ABC Company and its successors. I understand that my employment and compensation can be terminated without cause at the sole discretion of either the company or myself for whatever reason that company or myself may determine. I understand that no other company employee other than an officer of the company, which the board of directors may designate, has authority to enter into any agreement for employment for any specific period of time or to make any agreement contrary to the above statement of policy.

A similar statement has been enforced by several courts.[78] This eliminates all possible problems as to the exception of the at-will doctrine. This type of statement has been extended to promotions at sole discretion of the employer.[79] The use of this type of policy statement, however, may have serious repercussions on recruiting efforts or the company's public and employee relations image. By this statement in a handbook the employer may be admitting that the employment-at-will doctrine has been eliminated, which is not the case in all jurisdictions. The exceptions to the doctrine discussed in this chapter should not be interpreted to mean that the doctrine has been eliminated and policies should be drafted accordingly.

Another less controversial method to protect against wrongful discharge is to adopt a complaint procedure that will allow the employee to air dissatisfactions but continue working while the problem is being processed. Complaint procedures in nonunion companies are not widely used. The management seldom wants to give up a right unless they have to. The courts in discharge cases are more active in modifying the employ-

---

[77] Berg v. La Crosse Cooler, 612 F.2d 1041 (7th Cir. 1980).

[78] Novosel v. Sears, Roebuck & Co., 495 F.Supp. 344 (Mich. 1980). Whittaker v. Care-More, Inc., 621 S.W.2d 395 (Tenn. 1981). Crain v. Burroughs Corp. 560 F.Supp. 849 (D.C. Cal. 1983).

[79] Summers v. Sears, Roebuck & Co., 549 F.Supp. 1157 (E.D. Mich. 1982).

ment-at-will doctrine with non-union employees than with union employees who have a formal complaint procedure unless the non-union employees also have a formal complaint procedure.

Recommended Procedures When Terminating An Employee

These procedures are helpful to prevent litigation in termination:

1. One should conduct an exit interview with the discharged employee. This exit interview should be different from the traditional unsuccessful exit interview, which had as its objective controlling turnover when the employee would voluntary quit. This interview should be structured so the employee leaves the company on the best possible terms. It should be a public relations or mutual understanding type of interview.

2. At the exit interview when the employee is discharged, the interview should be structured so as not to allow an emotional buildup. When the employee walks in the door, the discharge statement should be made, with explanations prepared. However, it is not advisable to show insensitivity to the decision. It is a traumatic experience.

3. Timing of the discharge is important. Why is it always on Friday? That spoils the weekend. Why is it late in the afternoon? Why isn't it first thing in the morning so employee has a chance to think of what to tell the spouse or family.

4. To eliminate the possibility of an implied contract or promise at the time of hire, the job offer should be in writing and the terms clearly stated. If one quotes an annual salary, this could mean employment for one year in some states. After the terms are stated, the following is suggested to be inserted in the job offer in nonlegal terminology.

This job offer contains the entire agreement and understanding by and between __ABC__ Company and _____ with respect to the terms and conditions of employment. No representations, promises, agreements, or understandings, written or oral, not stated above shall be binding. No change, additions, or modifications of this letter shall be binding unless it is in writing and signed by the parties to this letter.

Many lawsuits are started because the employee is mad at the company. Time spent in preparing for the discharge interview will pay off with less lawsuits. Lawsuits are expensive even when one wins.

SUMMARY AND CONCLUSIONS

The employer's right to discharge at will is the law. However, the courts in some jurisdictions have made exceptions to the common law principle that all employees are employed at the will of the employer. The exceptions, although not adopted in all states, are summarized as follows:

1. Discharge is contrary to the public policy where it is retaliation for exercising a right under a statute where an employee refuses to disobey the law or blowing the whistle on the employer when the law is being violated.

2. There is an implied contract of employment such as a handbook or supervisor's manual or broken promises upon which the employee relied.

3. Malice and bad faith that was expressed in the discharge.

In addition to common law exceptions there are statutory restrictions on discharge such as:

1. discharge for coerced or collective activity as defined by the National Labor Relations Act,

2. discharge in violation of anti-discrimination laws, and

3. discharge for garnishments, refusals to take polygraph tests (in certain states), avoiding health insurance or pension benefits under the Federal Employee Retirement Income Security Act of 1974 (ERISA).

The employer that believes that employment at will is a management right is challenging the discharged employee to test the doctrine and is exposed to litigation. The employer who modifies the discharge policy and procedures to protect against some exceptions to common-law employment at will, has considerably less exposure. The policy should not be such as to prevent the employer from discharging an employee or from taking advantage of what is left of the at-will doctrine, but just-cause policies along with other procedures should not be ignored when doing so. The law makes one thing clear: the day has passed when a supervisor or a manager in an emotional state can walk up to an employee and say, "you are fired," and not be exposed to litigation.

CHAPTER XVII

CONTROL OF UNEMPLOYMENT COMPENSATION COSTS AND WORKER'S COMPENSATION CLAIMS

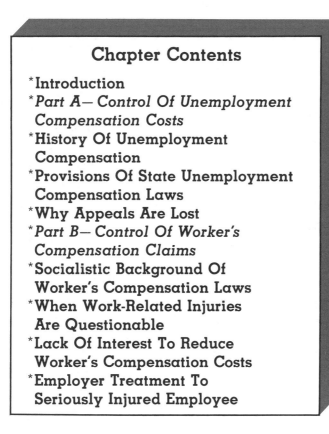

Chapter Contents

Chapter Contents (continued)

INTRODUCTION

Worker's and unemployment compensation laws have two provisions in common: they are state-administered and the benefits inure to the employee without any employee contributions (except in two states where unemployment compensation is contributory). The similarity between the two benefits ceases at this point, and it becomes necessary to consider the statutes separately. Because both benefit plans are state laws, this chapter does not attempt to discuss all the provisions of all the states except where a certain provision or legal theory is generally adopted by all jurisdictions.

One similarity for all states is reviewing cost control procedures which is something most employers in all the states have not done enough of in the last 15 years. As the costs of worker's and unemployment compensation increase, the interest in cost control rises.[1] After discussing the general provisions and intent of these two laws, this chapter details separate management procedures for each law that is effective in controlling the costs in worker's and unemployment compensation. It is the intent of this chapter to show that by recognizing the problems and doing something about them there can be considerable reduction of worker's compensation costs and unemployment compensation taxes.

Because the control of costs must be approached differently for each statute, this chapter is divided into two parts. Part A considers unemployment compensation and Part B worker's compensation.

---

[1] As it was once said "He who sits on a red hot stove, will rise again."

PART A— CONTROL OF UNEMPLOYMENT COMPENSATION COSTS

HISTORY OF UNEMPLOYMENT COMPENSATION

Unemployment compensation insurance is by no means a new idea. Many trade unions at the beginning of the 19th century provided aid for their members forced into temporary idleness. This type of benefit was found in England, Germany, Austria, Belgium, Norway, Sweden, and Denmark by the middle of the 19th century. The first public unemployment compensation insurance appeared in 1898, when the city of Ghent passed a local ordinance that supplemented the benefits provided by the trade unions. In 1911 England established the first compulsory unemployment compensation system.

In the United States, as in European countries, the beginnings of unemployment compensation are found in trade union benefit plans. Such plans appeared in the 1830s, the first probably established by a New York printers' local in 1831. From this period to 1937, unemployment compensation was provided either by trade unions, by joint plans arising from agreement between employers and unions, or by private voluntary plans established by individual employers for their workers.

At the beginning of the 20th century there was a movement to establish a public compulsory unemployment compensation plan; as early as 1916 a bill was introduced in the Massachusetts legislature. More than 20 other states followed. It was not until 1932 that the first state (Wisconsin) passed a statewide compulsory plan. Some states hesitated to pass unemployment compensation legislation as it would put them at a competitive disadvantage over other states that would not pass it.

This competitive concern of the various states caused pressure for legislation on the federal level. The argument whether the states or the federal government should do it delayed action by both federal and state legislative bodies. By 1934 the federal concept had won half the battle; unemployment compensation was included in the Social Security Act. The unemployment compensation section of the act provides that the federal government would set certain minimum standards but leave it to the states to decide which type of plan best suited their needs. However, if a state had no plan or if the state law was not in compliance with the federal law, the employers would still be taxed but the tax would not be returned to the states for unemployment compensation benefits. (Needless to say, all 50 states passed laws.)

The system is financed by two taxes, one levied by the federal government and one by the state. The tax levied by the federal government[2] against which a credit is given for state taxes paid for a reduction in taxes earned through experience ratings.[3] The states levy a tax that is used to finance the benefits. The tax levied by the states varies according to the needs. Various states have a minimum experience rating of zero to over 8 percent to a certain maximum earning level. The employer only is taxed. Two states, Alabama and New Jersey, require employee contributions.

PROVISIONS OF STATE UNEMPLOYMENT COMPENSATION LAWS

Although the federal government requires certain conformity provisions before the employer as taxpayer is granted tax credits under the Internal Revenue code, the states have considerable flexibility to design their own program. To ensure that the unemployment compensation payments are in keeping with the intent of the federal law, it is necessary for the states to establish eligibility requirements, benefit amounts, and reasons why an unemployed individual initially should be denied benefits or be disqualified from receiving further benefits.

In developing rules to determine the right to receive benefits, states have generally followed the principle that unemployment compensation is intended to provide temporary financial assistance to persons who are out of work through no fault of their own. In order to carry out the main intent of the act, state laws require eligible claimants to remain available for work and to be seeking work actively or face the loss of benefits. This requirement is loosely administered in many states.

Constitutional Restrictions Of State Laws

Although the federal law permitted the various states to pass their unemployment compensation statutes, they are limited in what they can do by the U.S. Constitution. Where one state denied benefits when an employee voluntary quit for religious reasons, the Supreme Court held that this was a

---

[2] Presently 3.5 percent of the first $7,000 of earnings for each employee in a calendar year. It will be increased to 6.2% in 1985. Cost per employee in 1983 is estimated at $98 and $140 in 1985.

[3] Credit of 2.7 percent is allowed, leaving 0.8 percent to be paid to federal government, which is used to pay administration costs in the various states. This credit will increase to 5.4 percent in 1985.

violation of the First Amendment.[4] The Supreme Court also struck down a Utah statute that denied benefits to pregnant women without regard to physical capacity to continue working. The Court found this a violation of the Fourteenth Amendment.[5] When another state gave unemployment compensation benefits to strikers, the court held that it was not a violation of any clause in the Constitution and it was within the authority of the state to do so.[6] However, in Brown v. A.J. Gerard Mfg. Co. ____ F2d ____ (11th Cir. 1983) the circuit court held that unemployment compensation could not be deducted from a Title VII back pay award.

Benefit Levels

One way to instill an incentive to return to work is to establish benefit levels that pay only a portion of the wages that an employee would have received if fully employed.

There is great diversity among the 50 states on the benefit levels paid. Some states have the absolute minimum and maximum based on employee's weekly earnings; others determine the minimum and maximum on the average statewide annual wage. The minimum benefit requires a certain level of earnings; if an employee earns below a level, no benefits are paid. For those who are marginally attached to the labor market, such as part-time workers or intermittent workers, usually the minimum amount is paid. The minimum amount paid varies from $5.00 per week (Hawaii) to $35 (Indiana).[7] Each state establishes a maximum amount, which may be a specified dollar amount or a percentage of the average statewide wage (from 50 percent to 66⅔ percent). This maximum amount ranges from $90 per week (several states have this level) to $222 (Alaska).

The state sets a limit on the total amounts that an employee can receive in one year; this limitation is in accord with the underlying concept expressed by Congress that unemployment compensation is designed to provide assistance while workers are unemployed and seeking another job or waiting to be called back from a layoff. The period of assistance should be of short duration under this concept. This period varies from 26 weeks to 39 weeks, 26 being the most prevalent.

Other benefit provisions in the various states allow benefits for partially unemployed (36 states) or some provide for nonworking dependent allowance (13 states).

---

[4] Thomas v. Review Board of Indiana Employment Security Div., 101 S.Ct. 1425 (1981).

[5] Turner v. Department of Employment and Security of Utah, 423 U.S. 44 (1975).

[6] New York Telephone Co. v. New York State Department of Labor, 440 U.S. 519 (1979).

[7] All benefit level figures are as of 1983. Each year some state legislatures change these levels. From 1969 to 1975 benefits increased 52 percent compared to 39 percent in wages and 47 percent in the cost of living for the same period.

Disqualification Provisions

All states have provisions seeking to carry out the intent of the law that benefits should be paid only to unemployed workers who are out of work through no fault of their own. The laws of the various states, in order to carry out this principle, have disqualification provisions such as voluntary quit without good cause, misconduct that results in discharge, refusal to accept suitable work offers without good cause, receipt of other payments while unemployed, involvement in labor dispute, and fraud.

Each state has certain procedures to be followed for obtaining facts involved in a disputed claim. The state agency set up for payment of compensation claims makes a determination whether the claimant is disqualified; the employer or claimant may appeal and request a hearing. The decision of the hearing referee as to disqualification may be appealed to a higher reviewing authority within the department. Subsequent appeals then may be carried to the state courts unless a constitutional question is involved which the federal courts decide.

Although all the disqualifying provisions are often subject to dispute, the most common is the discharge for misconduct. Misconduct that results in discharge for the purposes of the law and is accepted in all jurisdictions is defined as the willful or wanton and substantial disregard of employer's interest.[8]

When it is determined that a claimant is disqualified from benefits, some states merely postpone the benefits for a period of time while other states deny benefits for the entire period of unemployment.

Effect Of The Economy On Administration Of Benefits

A review of the state provisions for eligibility, duration, and disqualification reflects a broad spectrum in the various states. This is the result of the state legislature enacting provisions that are appropriate to the state's needs. The states periodically modify these provisions when warranted by economic conditions. These state laws clearly indicate that unemployment compensation laws are not static but are constantly changing. A downturn in the economy will cause a tightening of eligibility and disqualification provisions. As the funds are depleted by the unemployed, there is a tendency to save the available funds for the more legitimate claims. This is an administrative or legislative determination. The employer should not wait for an economic downturn to protect the funds for legitimate claims but should insist that the funds be protected regardless of economic conditions.

Policy And Programs To Reduce Costs

Most states allow the amount of tax that the employer pays to be experienced-rated, with a minimum and maximum that must be paid.

---

[8] This definition was stated in Boyton Cab v. Neubeck, 296 N.W. 636 (Wis. 1941) and is one of those rare decisions where every other state adopted it.

This allows the employer who is at or near the minimum to protect the low experience rating by paying into the fund the amount of benefits paid out. Where the employer has this opportunity it becomes extremely advantageous to keep the benefits charged to the account to lowest possible amount. This will not happen without some affirmative action through claim control programs and personnel policies. Some suggested policies and programs are:

1. Plan manpower needs to avoid layoffs. Often overtime is cheaper than hiring additional employees when one considers the cost of hiring and training a new employee plus fringe benefit costs, (approximately 35 percent of wages) as well as unemployment compensation costs.

2. Where possible, train or hire employees who have several skills. This allows lateral or upward transfers that not only save unemployment costs but also give flexibility in work assignments.

3. Have one person responsible for the entire program, who by practice and training becomes knowledgeable in unemployment compensation rules and appeal procedures. Some employers have one person responsible for the employee's work relationship, another for the taxes, and a third for accounting procedures. This is a mistake. The control of unemployment compensation costs require that the person who makes initial decisions or works with supervisors on employment decisions affecting costs should be responsible for the charges to the account as well as the employment decisions and appeal procedure.

4. Have the person responsible for the program audit all charges to the account such as quarterly reports. Often wrong charges to the account are found and can be corrected by a mere protest by the employer representative who is familiar with the employees and their activities.

5. When in doubt about a determination as to whether the claimant is entitled to benefits, appeal it. Over half of all initial benefit determinations appealed by the employer are reversed by the appeal procedure. (Sometimes in the interest of good employee relations, appeals to wrongful determinations are not made.)

6. Hold exit interviews for all terminations where possible and to attempt a mutual agreement on the reason for termination. In unemployment compensation matters employees often have a short memory between termination and the interview with the unemployment compensation representative who determines whether benefits are to be paid.

If these procedures are followed, there will be a substantial savings in unemployment costs before the appeal procedure has to be used. If used, the employer's position can be adequately defended.

WHY APPEALS ARE LOST

The procedure for appealing a determination for benefits by the governmental agency is, at its best, a quasi-judicial proceeding. All the appeal tribunal (Some states do not have an appeal tribunal, but they have a single person who makes the determination. This person is called a referee.) really wants to know is the first-hand facts that caused the separation from employment. Most cases are lost before appeal tribunals because:

1. Witnesses do not have actual knowledge of the facts. Whenever possible the supervisor should testify on what happened. A statement by the personnel practitioner who does not have first-hand information is less effective. Usually hearsay evidence can be admitted, but conclusions and findings of fact can not rely solely on hearsay evidence. Some direct evidence is needed to establish the facts.

2. Proper documentation of facts was not available at the hearing. Often employees forget what really happened, so they testify to facts that give the best case. By the time they get to a hearing they have a fair knowledge of what favorable facts are. Often it is difficult to get a supervisor to document warnings, statements, or other action taken when dealing with the employee before termination. The best way to present the case is to have the supervisor attend the hearing where the employee forgets everything the supervisor did but remembers everything not done.

3. Employer fails to give a clear reason for termination. Since the employee's and employer's reason for termination is often different, the employer's reason must have strong supporting circumstances to refute the employee's statement. Often the employer gives one reason for termination when giving reference checks, another for unemployment compensation, and a third for a grievance procedure. The employer should decide on the reason for termination based on facts and not change it to fit a specific situation. The legal structure to pay unemployment compensation benefits only where employees are out of work through fault of their own is available to the employer; all the practitioner must do is use it properly.

PART B– CONTROL OF WORKER'S COMPENSATION CLAIMS

SOCIALISTIC BACKGROUND OF WORKER'S COMPENSATION LAWS

Worker's compensation, like unemployment compensation, is not a new concept. Many people mistakenly think it is a 20th century innovation, but the purpose and intent can be traced as far back to the time of Henry I (about 1100). These laws provided that if a person is on a mission for another or is sent for by another and death occurs in the course of the mission, that sender or creater of the mission is responsible for the death. Likewise in early German law a provision held masters liable for the death of their servants, and a money payment had to be made for injury.

The present worker's compensation system had its origin in the German law, where in 1838 the German state of Prussia passed a law making the railroads liable for injuries to their employees, as well as passengers, other than acts of God or negligence on the part of the injured employee. The first modern worker's compensation was adopted in Germany in 1884; it required compulsory insurance for industrial accidents. The reason for pressure to pass such a law was a socialist movement supporting it. Iron Chancellor Otto Von Bismark wanted to head off the socialist movement and pushed the law through the Reichstag. The soundest movement for taking care of injured, started in the 1900s, was the philosophical belief that misfortunes, disabilities, and accidents of individuals are social rather than individual in origin and the state has a duty to care for the injured. Compulsory worker's compensation was first passed in this country 25 years later than in Germany (Wisconsin 1911). The German compensation system was studied by the various states but not completely adopted.

Most states rejected the employee contribution component of the German plan, but the socialistic philosophy of taking care of the injured can be found in almost all state statutes and the court interpretation. (In 1949 the last state, Mississippi, passed a worker's compensation law.) It is important to remember the socialistic or welfare origin of worker's compensation laws when receiving court interpretations of state worker's compensation statutes.

Purpose And Intent Of Worker's Compensation

Before worker's compensation laws were passed, the employer had three main defenses to liability for injury: contributory negligence of the injured worker, assumption of risk when the injured accepted employment, and the negligent act of co-workers (called the fellow servant rule under common law). The intent of worker's compensation statutes of the various states was to eliminate much of the controversy and legal strife inherent in these common-law defenses.

State statutes did not forget the socialist womb from which worker's compensation was born under the English and German philosophical belief that it is the duty of the state to care for the injured worker. Most state laws specify or imply that the intent is to relieve the hardships caused by occupational injuries or diseases by providing for the payment of medical expenses and some portion of wages while incapacitated, with benefits to dependents in the event of death.

Most state's statutes have four basic objectives:

1. To provide benefits regardless of fault or financial condition of the employer.

2. To reduce delays caused by litigation and controversy over responsibility for the injury, thereby reducing attorney's fees.

3. To relieve public charities of the financial drain caused by occupational injuries or diseases. The legislative bodies reason that the employer is in a better position to pay for the social ill caused by occupational injury by passing the cost to the consumer than the government is through taxation (an astute political decision).

4. To encourage employer interest in reducing accidents by making the employer liable for all costs.[9]

Basically these objectives have been accomplished by most state laws with the exception of attorney's fees. Some state statutes permit injured employees to seek their own attorneys at the employer's expense in disputes over the degree of disability and whether the injury occurred during the course of employment.[10]

Federal Restrictions Of Worker's Compensation Statutes

Because worker's compensation laws are state laws, the federal courts are restricted in their interpretation only to constitutional questions or conflicts with the fed-

---

[9] The cost must be excessive in relation to other costs before this arouses employer interests beyond moral considerations. In Minnesota, where costs are high, employer interests are not only aroused in safety programs but also in the political arena. The 1983 Minnesota Legislature passed a unique Worker's Compensation Law (Chapter 290—1983 *Minnesota Session Laws*) that gives the labor commissionor the power to create an incentive for employees to return to work by a two-tier system of benefits and to control insurance and medical abuses. The affect of this statute on costs will be closely watched by other states.

[10] Some employers buy insurance for worker's compensation liability while others are self-insured; in either situation, it is the employer's cost.

eral laws. One such conflict occurred when some state laws prohibited employers from reducing pension benefits by the amount of worker's compensation payments that pension plan participants would otherwise receive. New Jersey, Michigan, and Wisconsin among others had such a statute. The Supreme Court in holding the New Jersey statute invalid stated that the Employee Retirement Income Security Act (ERISA) permits private companies creating the pension plans to control the level of benefits without interference and the New Jersey state statute prohibiting the offset of pension benefits for worker's compensation payment is invalid because ERISA preempts the state law.[11]

The Problem Degree Of Disability

Under the worker's compensation statutes are two areas subject to dispute. One is the degree of permanent partial disability or temporary total disability caused by the injury. The permanent partial usually results in a lump-sum payment or payment for the disability even after optimum recovery. The temporary total usually involves benefits only while off work. Although both are basically a medical question, there are liberal doctors and conservative doctors in terms of their evaluation of a patient's condition, this often creates a problem for the employer's cost control program.

WHEN WORK-RELATED INJURIES ARE QUESTIONABLE

The duration of temporary disability and extent of permanent disability are medical questions often disputed and subject to litigation. Conflicting medical testimony must be decided by worker's compensation appeals courts or the state supreme court. Although the employer has little control over the medical testimony, the evidence of the employee's activity or facts other than physical condition can often aid the doctor in making a more accurate diagnosis of the injured employee's physical or mental condition. Employer participation is important if payments of

benefits are to be paid only for legitimate physical conditions.

Another area of dispute in worker's compensation cases is whether the injury was work-related. This is left to worker's compensation appeal courts and review courts to determine whether the injury occurred while serving the employer interests.

Being fully aware of social origin of worker's compensation, the courts in most jurisdictions have interpreted worker's compensation in favor of the employee when deciding work-related injury issues. If the employee testifies

---

[11] Buczynski v. General Motors, 101 S.Ct. 1895 (1981).

that the injury occurred in the course of employment, it is accepted by the courts unless the employer can offer strong evidence otherwise. In some cases the course of employment or acting on behalf of the employer is extended almost to infinity. The Michigan Compensation Appeals in Domenico Signorelli v. G.K.N. Automotive Components (Mich. App. 1982) held that an overseas employee who died while having sexual intercourse with his secretary died in the course of employment, as one can't expect an overseas employee to "stare at the walls of his hotel after work hours." Drowning in a boat accident at an employer-sponsored outing has been held an activity in the course of employment.[12]

In some jurisdictions injury while fighting on the job has been held a course of employment when no personal animosity is involved.[13]

Other situations where being work-related is questionable are:

1. Travel to and from work normally is not considered in the course of employment unless engaged in performing a duty incidental to the job. Dropping off the mail on the way home is considered in the course of employment. In one case an employee was hit in the face by two muggers after dropping off the mail; the court held that she was exposed to the "perils of the street" and it was work related.[14]

2. Is the accident traceable to the job? Where an employee got up from a chair and had a muscle tear in her leg, court said that it was not traceable to the job;[15] on the other hand if she had slipped, the result may have been different and worker's compensation would probably have been paid.

3. Horseplay or other misconduct is held to be compensable in some jurisdictions but not in others.

4. Fifteen states hold that mental stress is work-related; other states require a physical trauma before mental stress is compensable.[16]

5. Use of company auto for personal errands is usually held not compensable. Most courts look only at whether the interests of the employer are being served, not whether employee was clocked out for pay

---

[12] Tietz v. Hasting Lumber Mart, Inc., 210 N.W.2d 236 (Minn. 1973). However, in another state this would be held recreational activity, not in the course of employment. Smith v. Union Bleachery/Cone Mills, 280 S.E.2d 52 (S.C. 1981).

[13] Jolly v. Jesco, Inc., 135 N.W.2d 746 (Minn. 1965).

[14] Wayne Adams Buick, Inc., v. Ference, 421 N.E.2d 733 (Ind. 1981).

[15] Richmond Memorial Hospital v. Crane, 278 S.E.2d 877 (Va. 1981).

[16] In Lockwood v. Ind. School Dist. #877, 312 N.W.2d 924 (Minn. 1981) the court said that a high school principal who was mentally stressed because of his job could not claim that it was work-related when there was no evidence of physical trauma.

purposes or the employer's equipment was being used.

6. The employee who disobeys a work rule and injury results. Usually this is not covered under the legal theory that at the time of the accident the employee was "outside the scope of employment"; some courts are bending the theory and finding this compensable.[17]

LACK OF INTEREST TO REDUCE WORKER'S COMPENSATION COSTS

When an employee is injured on the job, the doctor, lawyer, insurance carrier, and employer are involved in the treatment of the injured employee and successful return of the employee to work: the doctor to treat the injury, the lawyer to protect the legal rights of the employee, the insurance carrier (or employer's insurance department, if self-insured) to compensate for the loss of wages and give assurance that the medical bills will be paid, and the employer to coordinate the activities of the others involved and provide back-to-work procedures. In order for the injured employee to receive the proper attention, it requires a real concern for the employee by everyone involved; it is the employer's responsibility to see that others perform their functions properly.

The employer is concerned not only that the employee receives the best attention but that unnecessary costs are not incurred in the process of returning the employee to work. The problem in keeping the costs at a minimum is that the others who are involved have no interest in cost control; often abuses occur. The law has a social origin, and courts interpret in favor of the employee. Where abuses result in unnecessary costs that could be corrected by the law, there is little interest in correcting them. Since there are more employees than employers, legislative changes that adversely affect abuses by the employee are not politically advisable. The doctors have little interest in cost caused by abuses as their concern is with the patient-doctor relationship established when the employee became injured. When the employee does not want to return to work, although physically able, the doctor through a medical opinion will sometimes grant the employee's wish; as a result employers often get a "patient's" opinion rather than a medical opinion on the employee's physical condition.

---

[17] Hoyle v. Isenhour Brick & Tile Co., 293 S.E.2d 196 (N.C. 1982). An employee was killed while driving a forklift truck in violation of work rules; this was compensable because he was acting on behalf of the employer. However, in Brown v. Arrowhead Tree Service, 322 N.W.2d 28 (Minn. 1983), the court ruled when a work rule was violated the employee left the scope of employment and injury was not compensable.

Many insurance carriers have no real interest in premium costs control. Experience-rated premiums have add-on administration costs, usually a percentage of the premium. There is seldom a direct percentage relationship between premiums and administration costs; as premium costs increase, so do profits through administration charges.

The lawyer who represents the injured employee has a duty to protect that person's rights under the law. Because the fee is somewhat related to the amount of the award, there is little interest in preventing employee abuse by the lawyer.

Who is left to control costs through abuses? The lonely employer is. If the employer does not do something about the abuses, nobody will. Some feel that because the employee was injured working on the employer's behalf, any program to deny the employee all possible benefits is poor employee relations. Spending money on an employee who is abusing the system is not treating the legitimately injured employee fairly. As costs increase, there is a tendency to keep the benefits lower, the other employees are being denied higher benefits level by the abuse of a few.

EMPLOYER TREATMENT OF SERIOUSLY INJURED EMPLOYEE

When an employee is seriously injured, it is a traumatic experience. Employees react differently. Sometimes they are mad at the company, sometimes at another employee; others are not mad at anybody but are concerned about their finances. Sometimes they are worried about their ability to work again or pursue a favorite hobby. Whatever the concern, the employer should find out and relieve the injured as much as possible of the worry. Maybe the employee wants to be left alone; then direct contact after initial approach is not advisable. By working through others the same results can be accomplished. The employer should be certain that the best possible medical care is being provided, that if other financial assistance is necessary, it should be obtained. The employee should have assurance that if not able to return to the old job, the employer will try to accommodate by finding other jobs or rehabilitation training for other vocations.[18]

---

[18] This concern should not imply a guilt complex on the employer as this would have a chilling effect on anything that the employer does for the benefit of the employee. Avoiding a guilt complex is especially important when informing the next of kin of an occupational death, if emotional and legal consequences are to be avoided.

For the seriously injured employee, some suggested employer practices are:

1. To visit the hospital and assess how or through whom the employee can best be relieved of any worry.

2. To contact the family; if the injured wants to be left alone, to offer help indirectly through someone else if such help is needed.

3. To keep in touch with the employee, to show interest in the recovery progress, and to assure the employee of return-ing to the job. Accommoda-tion, rehabilitation, possible job vacancies, etc., should be discussed.

4. To avoid any implication that it will be necessary to obtain legal counsel at the early stage of recovery. One should explain the worker's compen-sation law and company em-ployee benefits. If a lawyer becomes involved, one should establish a relationship with the employee's lawyer that the company is aware of the law and will keep the matter as nonlegal as possible.[19]

EMPLOYER POSTURE WHERE INJURED EMPLOYEE BECOMES A PLANT LAWYER

Some employees decide either before or after an injury to take advantage of the liberal social in-terpretation of worker's compensa-tion laws and turn their injury into a method to earn a livelihood with-out working. This type of employee becomes a worker's compensation expert, and often knows more than the practitioner about worker's compensation laws and their loop-holes. He/she is quick to take advantage of the employer and in-surance carrier's compliancy or the employer's fear of adverse em-ployee relations. The plant lawyer uses every loophole to accomplish the objective of being paid for not working. Whether insurance car-rier, doctor, or employer, all con-cerned are challenged by the "plant lawyer."

Almost every facility has a plant lawyer who causes about 90 percent of unnecessary worker's compensation costs. The plant lawyer is also being watched by other employees who are consider-ing joining the profession if it proves lucrative. When the plant lawyer does certain things that allow the employer to suspect the

---

[19] Sometimes a lawyer becomes involved in a probable third-party product-liability lawsuit against the manufacture of the machine that caused the injury. The employer should not aid in such a lawsuit until the worker's compensation case is closed, as often cooperation in the third-party suit can adversely affect the employer's worker's compensa-tion case.

employee might be a member of that "noble profession," then something should be done about it. Some indications that the injured might be a plant lawyer are:

1. Vague claims. The employee cannot remember how the injury occurred, which machine was involved, what day or what department, or exactly what the employee was doing.

2. The Monday morning accident, especially if the weather was pleasant over the weekend. The employee slipped on a piece of paper upon arriving at the work site on Monday morning (or the parking lot) and hurt the knee. Investigation often reveals that a Sunday afternoon touch football game, skiing, or fixing the roof was the real cause.

3. The delayed claim. "It happened two or three weeks ago, but I didn't think that it was serious; now it is getting worse, so I reported it." (Often the person talked to another plant lawyer.)

4. An injury that is medically difficult to determine as to the degree of disability usually has a long recovery period; back problems are most common, but tendonitis runs a close second.

RECOMMENDATIONS TO CHALLENGE THE PLANT LAWYER EFFECTIVELY

There is no one method to challenge the plant lawyer successfully. What works one time may not work another. However, one thing is certain; if nothing is done, the objective of getting paid for not working will be accomplished and others will join. Some of the following recommendations will prove effective at least some of the time:

1. Once it has become certain that the employee is a plant lawyer, one should challenge every move and suspect every action taken.

2. The employer should question the medical opinion. The plant lawyers often can convince the doctor of any physical condition when it comes to returning to work. If a medical opinion is suspect, the employee should be sent to another doctor or to several doctors until the medical opinion correlates with the apparent physical condition, activities of the employee, or other circumstances. If the employee refuses to go to other doctors, compensation benefits should be stopped and a written demand made to return to work. If the insurance carrier refuses to

stop compensation, legal action should be started against the insurance carrier to show cause why the employee should not be submitted to further medical examination or be returned to work.[20]

3. The employer shouldn't be overanxious to return the employee to the old job but try to accommodate to a lesser-paying job. This technique heals a lot of backs when the employee is fabricating the back condition. Often the plant lawyer wants to return to work to have the opportunity to aggravate the condition and thus continue the compensation benefits for another period. The firm should never let the plant lawyer return to a job that he says he can do when medical opinion is to the contrary.

4. After trying various methods to convert the plant lawyer, it is advisable to terminate the employee medically. Often the employer waits too long to do this, either because of the request of the insurance carrier or an unwillingness to admit defeat. It is better to bite the bullet early.[21] By this time the plant lawyer has become a marginal worker, if

not one before injury, and to prolong the contest is wasting good money on wages after spending bad money on attempting to return the employee to work.

Company policies or legal restrictions may prevent the employer from using all of these recommendations, but some may work. Where they do not, the employer should continue the challenge by trying others.

Employer's Relationship With Doctor

To challenge the plant lawyer successfully, the employer must have the cooperation of the doctor or doctors involved. This is sometimes difficult due to the conflict of interest with the patient-doctor relationship. It is important that an employer-doctor relationship be established if the unnecessary costs caused by the plant lawyer are to be eliminated. The doctor has often aided the plant lawyer in continuing to be paid for not working when physically able to do so. Instances of no-work slips without seeing the doctor, diagnosis of a condition over the telephone, or light-work slips that do not define light work are not uncommon and could be eliminated

---

[20] In some states this may be prohibited by the worker's compensation statute. However, several state statutes allow such an action.

[21] It took the author seven years to get an employee with a back injury to return to work and prevent a permanent total. It would have been more economical to pay the permanent total than pay wages for marginal work.

by an employer-doctor relationship. To establish the employer-doctor relationship, the following program is suggested:

1. The employer should inform the doctor of the physical requirements of certain job categories. This can be done by the doctor's visit to the plant site. If this is not possible, send an accurate job description of the physically demanding jobs. Often bad medical opinions are caused by the doctor not being informed.

2. If a medical opinion is suspect as unreasonable, the employer should challenge it by sending the employee to another doctor. If the employee refuses, after informing the employee, the employer should stop the weekly compensation benefits and require that the employee return to work.

3. The employer should establish sound back-to-work procedures that are based on the physical condition of the employee and not whether it is an occupational or nonoccupational injury. A double standard of back-to-work procedures confuses the doctor on what the employer really wants. Make-work policy must be based on the physical ability of the employee to perform the job, not the cause of the injury to protect a safety record.

4. The employer should make every effort to keep the doctor informed about the employee's medical history and activities off the job after the injury such as type of preemployment physicals, and physical requirements of the job. If the employer makes a real effort to establish a relationship with the doctor, the plant lawyer can be controlled. If the doctor seems to cooperate with the plant lawyer, the employer should use another doctor. Without an accurate medical opinion about the employee's physical condition, the plant lawyer cannot be put out of business.

Relationships With Insurance Carrier

The proper relationship with the insurance carrier is extremely important especially for small companies who do not have large legal staffs, personnel practitioners, and security department to investigate doubtful claims.[22] If the carrier does the proper job, it can make a real contribution in controlling the plant lawyer.

Many times the insurance carrier, when trying to get a new account, will stress the effectiveness of its lost control department (safety engineering). An employer in considering the selection of a carrier should emphasize how effective the carrier's claim control department

---

[22] If the employer is self-insured, the insurance carrier as used herein should be interpreted to mean the consulting organization or whoever is responsible for claim control.

is. All too often the insurance carrier's play-dead attitude in claim abuse is what the plant lawyer is seeking in order to survive. A common practice of the plant lawyer is alleging that he or she slipped on the steps when going to the locker-room before reporting to work and injured the back. The evening paper reports that the softball team that employee was playing for won the city championship Sunday afternoon. However, there were three injuries during the game, but the names were not given. This is reported to the insurance carrier. The investigator tells the safety director that the injury probably happened while playing ball but in view of the social welfare attitude of the courts the case would be difficult to win; thus it would be wise to not contest it. Everybody is satisfied. The employee is paid compensation for a back that was injured playing ball. The insurance company is satisfied as it saves investigation and litigation costs that have been included in the premium rate. The safety director is satisfied because it is not a reflection on the company's safety program but is an uncontrollable accident.

To develop an effective relationship with insurance carrier for claim control it is suggested that:

1. When injuries are first reported to a state commission and insurance company, the employer "flags" all doubtful claims and demands that they be thoroughly investigated. In a 1980 survey by the National Institute for Occupational Safety and Health it was reported that nationally only 10 percent of worker's compensation claims are contested. Considerably more than 10 percent of the claims should be investigated as to whether the injury occurred in the course of employment and the degree of disability alleged.

When investigating a doubtful claim, the employer's representative should take an active part in the investigation to be assured that all pertinent facts are given to the insurance carrier and the carrier makes a thorough investigation.

2. Contested claims should not be settled by the insurance carrier unless the employer approves. Settlements often have employee relations consequences; sometimes it may be advisable to litigate although economically the case should be settled. Many lawsuits are tried on other than economic basis.

3. Approximately 10 percent of all disputed claims should be disputed beyond the investigation stage. The employer should stay with the case to judge the quality of legal service being provided and avoid compliancy on the part of the insurance carrier and their attorneys.[23]

---

[23] The author once had an insurance company attorney drop in at 11 A.M. to prepare for a case that was to be argued at 1:30 that day. It is needless to ask who won.

Even though the chances of winning might be slim, forcing a disputed claim to hearing and having the plant lawyer testify to something different than known to be a fact by other employees has a sobering effect on other employees becoming plant lawyers. Periodically, to keep the profession from growing, plant lawyers must be exposed to their fellow employees.

SAFETY PROGRAMS ARE IMPORTANT IN COST CONTROL

This analysis of cost control in worker's compensation purposely ignored the role that safety programs play in reducing worker's compensation costs. A good safety program is, of course, a contributing factor to reducing costs. However, it has few legal implications except where the Occupational Safety and Health Act seeks to force compliance. The safety program should be separate from claim control; the safety director should be not responsible for claim control. With responsibility for both, there is always a tendency to let up on claim control to protect the safety record. Hidden compensation costs are compromised in order to protect a safety record that cannot be covered up. Such techniques are helpful in performance appraisals and at bonus time, especially if hidden costs are never exposed.

SUMMARY AND CONCLUSIONS

Although unemployment and worker's compensation laws are designed to favor the employee in order to cure social ills, this does not mean that costs cannot be controlled. Concerned employers can prevent abuses by forcing the administering agency to carry out the purpose and intent of the law. Failure of the employer to correct abuses or to allow payments of benefits to those employees who choose to become plant lawyers is not giving fair treatment to other employees who are denied higher benefits for legitimate claims. Employer compliancy is one of the main causes of high costs in worker's and unemployment compensation. It takes a little time and effort to control these costs but the rewards are great. Most staff functions are overhead burdens on the cost of doing business. Seldom is there an opportunity to show where a program can objectively measure the staff contribution in dollars on the organization's income statement. Worker's compensation and unemployment compensation are two programs that afford this opportunity.[24]

Costs of these two benefits are unlikely to decrease through legislative action. Only an effort on the part of the employer in claim control will prevent these two benefits from being prohibitive. No other persons are interested in controlling the cost of these two benefits. If employers do not do it through political pressure and claim control, nobody will.

---

[24] For several years the author had an undisclosed personal goal to save his employer four times his annual salary. Savings in worker's compensation and unemployment compensation were two areas that greatly contributed to achieving this goal. Undisclosed goals of this nature afford job satisfaction when one attains them and do little harm if one fails.

CHAPTER XVIII

DIRECTION OF LEGAL RESTRICTIONS ON THE PERSONNEL FUNCTION IN THE 1980s

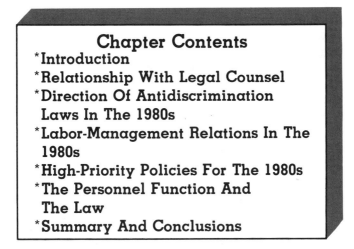

Chapter Contents
*Introduction
*Relationship With Legal Counsel
*Direction Of Antidiscrimination Laws In The 1980s
*Labor-Management Relations In The 1980s
*High-Priority Policies For The 1980s
*The Personnel Function And The Law
*Summary And Conclusions

INTRODUCTION

This book has discussed the legal restrictions on the personnel function. It is evident by court decisions that the law has not interfered with personnel administration in carrying its function, but it has caused the personnel practitioner to eliminate many subjective practices that did not contribute to organizational goals. The changes that the laws forced on the personnel function in the 1970s will not stop in the 1980s, but as the laws mature through court interpretation there will be fewer gray areas and the employer and employees alike will become more sophisticated in using the law to accomplish their objectives. Policies and guidelines adopted in the 1970s will also have to become more refined. Their modification to fit management policies and goals will not be as difficult as in the 1970s. The personnel function is gradually becoming accustomed to working with the law. Management resistance to the new laws experienced in the 1970s will fade; the second stage of getting along will be the menu of the day. Management in the 1980s will develop a painless way to economically live with the requirements of the law in making employment decisions.

The personnel practitioner in the 1980s must be alert to how employees will use their rights developed in the 1970s and advise management on how to minimize litigation and still not interfere with organizational goals.

RELATIONSHIP WITH LEGAL COUNSEL

The economic use of legal counsel will depend on the degree that the personnel practitioner accepts responsibility of understanding the basic principles of personnel law, not to the extent of becoming a lawyer, but to recognize an exposure to litigation. The personnel practitioner does not have to be a lawyer to go to the library and look up a volume of the *Federal Reporters* (___F2d___). The volume will give a summary of a case's facts and conclusion in lay language that will contain enough information to enable the reader to determine whether there is an exposure to litigation in making an employment decision. If further information is needed, advice of legal counsel would be necessary.

The personnel practitioner who refuses to take the first step in understanding the law will become obsolete in the 1980s. One might say that whenever there is a question, call legal counsel, but it is not always that easy: the employee is waiting outside the office for an answer and legal counsel is in court or busy with a client.

The personnel practitioner in the 1980s must have enough knowledge of the law not only to keep legal costs and damages at a minimum but to be able to carry out the personnel function as economically as before employee rights legislation. The legal counsel, to be of service to the personnel practitioner, must be more discrete in giving legal advice in the 1980s. Counsel must do a better job of distinguishing between opinion on policy and legal advice. There may be many policies with which legal counsel does not agree with but are still legal. "On advice of counsel" must be legal advice and not policy advice on personnel matters unless specifically requested.

The personnel legal counsel of the 1980s must say no[1] less often and assess the exposure to taking a certain action to keep the wheels turning. Saying that a particular employment decision is not legal is easy and safe because the exposure of being proven wrong by a lawsuit is almost eliminated if followed and it does not take much research. An employment decision must be made. One with the least legal exposure should be forthcoming from the legal counsel.[2] There is a duty on the personnel practitioner to demand useful legal advice of how to do something, not that it can't be legally accomplished. If such demand is made without success, then a change in legal counsel should be considered.[3]

The legal counsel of the 1980s must be aware of personnel practitioner problems and understand that although there may not be the best evidence to discharge an employee to prevent a wrongful discharge lawsuit, the manager is going to discharge the employee regardless of the legal advice. The task of legal counsel is to advise on the best way to do it.

Managers are not going to let the law or courts run the operation; the job of the legal counsel and personnel practitioner is to advise the most legal way to do it.[4] The personnel practitioner must insist on legal advice that tells how to do it, not that one can not do it, if economic effective use of legal counsel is to be accomplished.

DIRECTION OF ANTIDISCRIMINATION LAWS IN THE 1980s

In the early 1970s most discrimination cases dealt with race. Many of the basic principles that apply to sex, age, and religion were developed in racial cases. There is considerable maturity in the law in

---

[1] When this author was a corporate legal counsel and was called to give opinion on problem, the answer was "no it could not be legally done." The practitioner then reminded me of a directive I had written while a personnel executive two years previous directing the requested action. This author's answer was, "then I was in personnel, now I am legal counsel and I say you can't legally do it."

[2] As the author's superior once said in mild reprimand, "Mismanagement is better than no management at all."

[3] This is sometimes difficult where there is in-house counsel. The best effort is probably to complain to the supervisor, who uses best political judgment on how to correct the situation.

[4] The author once was legal counsel to manager who always got in trouble with the law. When asked why he did things that tested the law, he replied "you are smart enough to get me out of it."

racial discrimination. Employers know what is required to validate a test, what is meant by the labor market area, what is required for a prima facie case, what are acceptable recruiting practices, that the law permits the employer to hire the best-qualified applicant, and that there is no obligation to maximize the hiring of minorities. These principles were developed in racial discrimination cases. But what happens with sex and age? Do all employees and employers know their obligations and rights? Statistics of cases filed from 1980 to 1983 clearly say no.

Age And Sex Issues To Predominate Discrimination Problems In The 1980s

In the early 1970s budgets of the regulatory agencies were used to resolve the immediate problem of racial discrimination. Age and sex cases were brushed aside. In disputes under ADEA, the Department of Labor until 1979 was the enforcement agency, with a small budget; in the case of sex, the EEOC was too busy with racial problems. Many of the women's rights groups were using their resources and energy in getting the Equal Rights Amendment to the Constitution passed. These conditions that prevented active enforcement of age and sex cases in the 1970s are not present in the 1980s.

The older worker no longer has a stigma of suing the employer. In the past persons in lower-level jobs were bringing discrimination lawsuits that consisted mostly of younger workers who were not protected by ADEA. As the stigma of suing the employer diminishes, middle- and upper-level management, almost all over 40, will use the ADEA by hiring an attorney and going directly into court. Their financial resources will permit this, rather than depending on a governmental agency. This makes the employer extremely vulnerable to age discrimination litigation.

Few employers have a measurement of performance that will pass judicial review. What other reason is there to terminate an employee of 30 years' service except performance or policy violation (which is rare with middle and upper management)? If performance is the reason for discharge, the measurement must be objective and uniformly applied to the extent that a jury will accept. Age cases also have a practical problem in that one does not see many young people on the jury. Furthermore can anyone imagine going before the U.S. Supreme Court and arguing that an employee is too old to perform the job, without very convincing evidence? Since the enforcement of ADEA is relatively new, there is still time for the employer to establish policies and procedures to prevent litigation that will not result in bad law. Bad policies and decisions are the major cause of bad law.

In sex discrimination problems, members of women's group are active in correcting discrimination similar to what occurred in the racial discrimination area in the early 1970s. Over one-third of all law students are women.[5] Women are not only accepted in great numbers by law firms; to the surprise of some male attorneys, they are good or are becoming good trial lawyers. Because of influx of women into the legal profession, women employees are more comfortable in going to a woman lawyer with their problems; as with all young lawyers they are anxious to take the case. The employer of the 1980s must prepare for an increase in sex discrimination cases and establish policies and procedures that will prevent litigation in areas such as a sexual harassment, a training procedure that includes females, and integration of job categories to deal with the com-

parable worth concept, as in World War II. Sex discrimination will continue to be a major problem in the 1980s.

Other Discrimination Areas Playing A Lesser Role

It appears that religious and nationality cases will maintain the level of enforcement experienced in the 1970s. However, the alien worker may become a problem, depending on congressional determination of dealing with illegal aliens and rights given to legal aliens by the courts.[6]

Handicap discrimination will be an increasing problem in states with handicap discrimination laws. There is also a good possibility that Congress will pass a handicap discrimination law. The handicap problem is easily solvable if a reasonable effort at accommodation is made and the fact that handicapped workers properly placed are as valuable as nonhandicapped workers is accepted by employers.

---

[5] When the author first went to law school there was one woman in his class of 125 students and when asked what she was doing in law school her reply was "to marry a lawyer" and she did in her junior year and never returned.

[6] The Immigration Reform and Control Act of 1983 (S.525) is being considered by the 98th Congress.

LABOR-MANAGEMENT RELATIONS IN THE 1980s

There will be little increase in unionization in the 1980s. The previous peak level of 30 percent unionization of the work force will not be reached in the 1980s.[7] The 20 percent to 25 percent level is more realistic.[8] The heavy concentration of union membership in the auto, steel, aerospace, entertainment, mining, construction, transportation, communications, and manufacturing industries will continue.

Minorities and women will play a greater role in union affairs. This will cause unions to become more active in enforcing antidiscrimination and safety laws. When the governmental enforcement agencies relax their enforcement activities, they will be prodded by the unions and other special interest groups through litigation and in the political area.

The biggest change in the 1980s in the labor-management area will occur with nonunion employees. They will become more aware of their rights under the National Labor Relations Act. The realization by employees that it is not necessary to belong to a union to obtain protection under the act will cause problems for the nonunion employer who believes that there must be a union for employees to have protection under the act. When employees refuse work because of a dispute over wages or working conditions, the first reaction of many nonunion employers is to discharge them. These employers all too soon find that this is a legal concerted activity protected under NLRA. It is a strike in the same sense as if called by the union when negotiations break down.

The employer who considers refusal to work as a strike and does not want to discuss the problems with the dissenting workers should not discharge them but hire replacements, as is sometimes the practice when a union is involved. The employer in the 1980s that wants to stay nonunion must be alert to the rights and liabilities of union members. The nonunion employer should always ask the question when making an employment decision, whether the same decision could be made if unionized. If the answer is no, then an effort

---

[7] Jack Fiorito and Charles Greer, "Determinants of U.S. Unionism, Past Research and Future Needs," *Industrial Relations*, 21, no. 1 (Winter, 1982). William J. Usery, Jr. and Douglas Henne, "The American Labor Movement in the 80s," *Employee Relations Law Journal*, 7, no. 2 (Autumn, 1981).

[8] Joseph Krislov and J. Silver, "Union Bargaining Power in the 1980s," *Proceedings of the 1981 Spring Meeting, Industrial Relations Association* (Madison: University of Wisconsin, 1981).

must be made to sell the decision to the employees.[9]

The 1980s will see a growing problem with nonunion workers, not that they will obtain a union to represent them, but by collective action they will represent themselves in seeking remedies to their dissatisfactions under the National Labor Relations Act. The employer must not depend on the lack of remedy when making employment decisions involving nonunion employees. They have the same remedies as a union worker except those rights provided in a labor agreement that either supplement or grant additional rights that the law fails to provide.

Growth Of Employee Rights

In the 1980s employee rights will continue to grow through court interpretation and legislation. The areas most vulnerable are employee benefits and discharge for cause. The thinking that an employee has a property right in a job and an equity in the benefits connected with the job has only begun to be recognized by the law. Unless the employer's policies and practices take specific measures to change it, the growth of employee rights in these areas will be phenomenal.

The California courts seem to be leading the way. A determination by the California court was that employees have a vested right in vacation pay that accrues when they begin work. The employer's policy that requires one-year service for vacation time was declared null and void. This could start a trend in all benefit areas that would eliminate all eligibility requirements for benefits.[10]

In the area of discharge, most students of the subject believe that only a small percentage of wrongful discharge cases are ever brought to court. As more awards for punitive damages are made, there will be more wrongful discharge litigation.[11] The 1980s will see almost a complete erosion of the employment-at-will doctrine as courts continue to find an exception to the doctrine where the facts are strong enough. The California court in Cleary v. American Airlines, 168 Cal. Rpts. 722 (1980) allowed recovery when a discharge was held to be a breach of public trust. The vague definition of public policy or public trust permits almost any set of facts to

---

[9] The author was once asked by a nonunion employer how he could reduce wages for night shift workers. The answer "very carefully because if there was a union it would have to be negotiated." A discussion with the employees stating the reason and an adjustment period would certainly be necessary to keep that facility nonunion.

[10] Suastez v. Plastic Press-Up Co., 647 P.2d 122 (1982).

[11] Frederick Brown, "Limiting Your Risks in the New Russian Roulette, Discharging Employees," *Employee Relations Law Journal,* 380 (Winter 1982/1983).

allow the exception to the common-law doctrine of employment at will. The just-cause requirement found only in labor agreements and groups protected by discrimination clauses in statutes will spread to unprotected groups as the social pressures continue to advocate a property right to work.

The access to the courts in discharge cases will make arbitration under the labor agreement less attractive. More and more employees will seek the lucrative awards of punitive damages rather than reinstatement and back pay under arbitration awards.

Leave-of-absence policies that are based solely on whether the supervisor can release the worker as the work load permits will cause problems in the 1980s. Antidiscrimination laws, and retaliation allegations will play an important role in removing this discretion from the supervisor. A black female employee, pregnant with an artificial leg and Vietnam veteran, may in the supervisor's opinion be needed on the job in July and denied leave of absence to see her dying mother in New York but the blond blue-eyed male may not, in the supervisor's opinion, be needed in August and is allowed to see his dying mother in Sweden. The employer in these situations must be objective as to what constitutes a business need in order to defend a discrimination, sexual harassment or retaliation charges over the denial of leave of absence.

In the 1980s the supervisor's judgment will have a decreasing value unless backed by objective data. The leave-of-absence policies, promotion, hiring, and wage increases that allow supervisor judgment constitute a potential hazard to discrimination charges; unless better criteria are established, the supervisor's decision could be a high litigation area.

Worker's Compensation And Unemployment Compensation In The 1980s

Worker's compensation and unemployment compensation will demand increasing attention in the 1980s. The increase in benefits tends to increase the abuse. Studies show that when it becomes more profitable not to work than to work, there is little incentive to return to work.[12] There are no reliable data on the extent of abuse. When half the bus drivers of the Metropolitan Transit Company (Minneapolis and St. Paul) collected worker's compensation in 1981, there is certainly a basis to conclude that abuse is a suspect. The exposure to abuse and high costs will continue in both unemployment and worker's compensation areas in the 1980s.

Although the state legislatures may give some relief, the ultimate solution to lower costs is in the employer's hands. The return to the original purposes of these two laws should be a must for the employers in the 1980s. Nobody disputes the benefit level if an employee who is out of work

---

[12] "Worker's Compensation Reform—Get the Employees Back on the Job," (Minneapolis: Minnesota Citizens League Worker's Compensation Committee Report, 1982).

through no fault of one's own and makes a continuing effort to seek work. Nobody disputes that a worker disabled from an industrial injury should not receive a livable benefit. However, the requirement that the employee must be disabled from an industrial accident is often overlooked. As the benefits in-crease, more abuse is likely unless the employer does something. In the 1980s more of the employer's attention will be directed to the areas of worker's compensation and unemployment compensation. Efforts will increase due to increasing costs and rewards to be obtained from an effective program.

HIGH-PRIORITY POLICIES FOR THE 1980s

This book has an abundance of recommendations and suggestions either to prevent litigation or defend lawsuits. If all were adopted, the personnel practitioner would do nothing else but write and administer policy changes. It would be unrealistic to expect that such recommendations would fit all organizations and all situations. It is, therefore, appropriate at this time to recommend four of the most important policies and procedures that will prevent litigation and not interfere with the objectives of the organization to make a profit or perform a service. They are:

1. measurement of performance
2. uniform policy administration
3. adoption of a termination policy
4. development of criteria to determine a qualified worker for employment and promotion

Measurement Of Performance

If there is only one opportunity to change procedures in the 1980s, the measurement of performance will reap the highest rewards. In every law mentioned in this book an almost absolute defense to alleged violations would be poor performance. Poor performance is often stated as an affirmative defense but fails when scrutinized by the courts. In some categories, measurement is easy, in others more difficult; but any human endeavor can be measured. In some job categories the measurement may not be as accurate as the courts would like, but any degree of objectivity is better than a completely subjective measurement. In reviewing the large number of cases cited in this book, the author failed to find any court decision where employer's defenses of poor performance objectively measured was not accepted by the courts. Unfortunately too few employers have a valid procedure to measure performance; for this reason the defense is not used or fails.

Uniform Policy Administration

In the 1980s uniform administration of policies and procedures is essential if litigation under the antidiscrimination laws is to be avoided. In the areas of leaves of absence, vacation, merit pay, absenteeism, etc., policies were often different between departments or job categories and in some cases between nonexempt and exempt employees. Because of the external audit caused by antidiscrimination laws and the demand for information by employees when filing a complaint for an alleged violation of the law, information about practices in other parts of the company cannot be kept from the employees. The word *discrimination* became so popular in the 1970s that any different treatment of one employee from another becomes discrimination and a potential lawsuit, and the demand for information about company practices.

Forcing an employee through a policy door never was a good employee relations practice; their individual problems often didn't fit the policy door. It still is a poor practice, but due to the new laws of the 1970s more policy doors are needed in the 1980s. They should be as wide as possible to accommodate most situations and still be uniform enough to serve as a defense in lawsuits.

Adoption Of Termination Policy

This is the third most important policy to be adopted. The day is gone when the supervisor while in an emotional state and with shakey hands goes to the work site and says "You're fired." Employers must adopt a just-cause policy for discharge before legislation and the courts do it for them. If adopted by the employer, the policy should coordinate with other policies and goals of the organization. If just-cause requirement is passed by legislatures, it will not fit any employer's procedures. If required by the courts, it will fit a certain set of facts and will result in case-by-case litigation.

The adoption of a just-cause policy by the employer should be a gradual program starting at certain job levels or job categories and expanding with experience. In a nonunion plant the blue-collar worker should have a just-cause policy. The policy in the beginning does not have to be any more than communication of the reasons for discharge and a procedure to determine the facts. Many employers feel that adoption of a just-cause policy would eliminate any defense that the common law employment-at-will doctrine affords. This is not necessarily true. The policy could adopt the exceptions to public policy, malice, and bad faith, but no implied a contract exists. Since the United States is the only industrialized country that does not have a legislative just-cause policy, it is essential that it is kept that way and employers adopt one of their own to suit their own needs and goals.

Employment And Promotion Of Best-Qualified Worker

In the early 1970s some employers believed that the new employment laws required them to hire or promote only qualified workers and they had lost their right to determine the best-qualified workers to hire or promote. No court decision ever said that this was the law; however, some regulatory agencies did. Court decisions such as Furnco and Burdine have cleared up the problem of the best-qualified worker. In the 1980s the employer will benefit from these landmark decisions.[13]

Since employers often fail to adopt a policy of qualified worker either through fear of not meeting affirmative action goals or litigation under Title VII, the 1980s will afford the opportunity for this group of employees to do so, and it therefore rates as a high priority procedure.

THE PERSONNEL FUNCTION AND THE LAW

The personnel function in the 1980s should be exciting. One can consider questions on the application blank that are meaningful, merit increases that reward performance, tests that will predict performance on the job, performance appraisals that will actually rate performance, criteria for discharge, and not having to defend supervisor's subjective judgment of hiring and promotion.

The personnel function can become one of the most important functions of management. By hiring qualified applicants the company will grow. Poor performance when objectively measured is always correctable and accordingly does not prevent growth. The work force will take an interest in the company growth and with high quality people, stock options, profit sharing, and other incentive plans will be easily sold to the board of directors as an effective means to accomplish organizational goals.

The passive personnel practitioner who looks at the function as one to put out fires and be available when needed will depart, no longer needed in the 1980s by either employer or the law.

SUMMARY AND CONCLUSIONS

The personnel practitioner of the 1980s must accept a dual responsibility. The traditional personnel functions of wage and salary adminstration, labor rela- tions, personnel records, training, EEOC compliance, performance evaluation and community services (fund drives, Chamber of Commerce, Employer Associations)

---

[13] Furnco Construction Co. v. Waters, 438 U.S. 567 (1978); Texas Department of Community Affairs v. Burdine, 450 U.S. 248 (1981).

must continue to be a responsible staff resource for operating and adminstrative management.

The second responsibility of the personnel practitioner, to develop policies and procedures that will minimize exposure to lawsuits, is new and the practitioner who does not accept it will be obsolete before the end of the decade. In a era when employee rights are on the increase, lawyers are more willing to accept cases of little merit under present law and employees are becoming better educated, the personnel practitioner must develop rapport with legal counsel. Failure to develop an economic way to use legal counsel will result in budgetary restrictions on seeking legal advice when it is needed. This legal advice must be "how to do it legally" and not that it can not be done.

Age and sex discrimination will be the biggest problem in the 1980s. The number of persons between 40 and 69 years of age is on the increase and the stigma of suing your employer is diminishing. Large awards in punitive damages for wrongful discharge and otherwise discriminating because of age will be an encouragement to the older employee and the fee-minded attorney.

In the sex area the number of female lawyers is rapidly increasing. There still exists "cause female lawyers" who will take a case not necessarily for a economic reason or because it is legally a sound case, but it is cause that they believe in. This type of motivation on the part of the female lawyer that has has created new concepts is best illustrated in the case of Roe v. Wade.[14] In that case Roe (whose real name is Norma McCorvey) became pregnant as a result of a gang rape and found that abortion was not legally possible in Texas and not economically possible anywhere else. Although the baby was given up for adoption, two female attorneys (Linda Coffee and Sarah P. Eddington) relatively new to the practice of law took a cause of what they felt was a social injustice of state law. As a result of their motivation to change things it is now unlawful for a state to prevent abortion in the first three months of pregnancy. Many attorneys like those who represented Norma McCorvey have taken up other causes that have increased employer exposure to sex discrimination cases. This will not change in the 1980s.

The nonunion employer should always be aware of the possibility of unionization. The continued adoption of personnel policies and procedures that eliminates the necessity for unions. This will be aided by the increasing role of the government to protect employee rights and do for employees what was the traditional function of the union. The result will be in little increase in unionization in the 1980s. The peak of 30 percent of the workforce being unionized will not again be reached unless employers "lower their guard." The biggest

---

[14] 410 U.S. 113 (1973).

change in the 1980s will be non-union employees exercising the rights they have had under the National Labor Relations Act for forty odd years. Better educated employees, and court interpretation of existing state and federal statutes will cause employees to test their rights in areas that were traditionally employer prerogatives. Restrictions on vacation eligibility policy as found in Suastez v. Plastic Press-Up Co., 647 P.2d 122 (Cal. Sup. Ct. (1982) is an example.

Wrongful discharge cases will be popular in the 1980s. The chipping away of the employment at will doctrine will continue, state by state until there is little left of the doctrine by 1990.[15]

Worker's compensation and unemployment compensation reform is long overdue. As the cost increases year by year it will be become a more important management goal. The personnel practitioner who fails to develop an expertise in these two areas will witness the responsibility going to some other staff function. Worker's compensation and unemployment compensation can be an important contribution by the personnel function to the organizational goals if an effort is made to reduce costs.

The neglect of the high priority items in the 1980s will result in a decline of the personnel function as an important and essential staff resource. Performance must be objectively measured if exposure to ligitation is to be miminized. Adoption of a termination policy are the messages that the courts are giving employers to avoid violation of employee rights and still maintain management prerogatives.

The workload of the personnel practitioner will increase in 1980s not only as a result of the demands of the law, but because more activities will be added.[16] The personnel job will be more work but also more exciting than what the author experienced over three and one-half decades ago.

---

[15] From November 1982 to November 1983 author's research shows that eight states have adopted either the implied contract or public policy exception to the employment at will doctrine.

[16] In a survey among personnel executives it was found that 80% of those surveyed increased the activities of the personnel department in 1982 and 1983. "ASPA-BNA Survey No. 46 Personnel Activities, Budgets and Staff 1982–1983." Bulletin to Management, May 26, 1983. Wash. D.C., Bureau of National Affairs Inc. 1983.

TABLE OF CASES

The cases listed below are all cited in this book, either in footnotes or within the body of the text.

INDEX

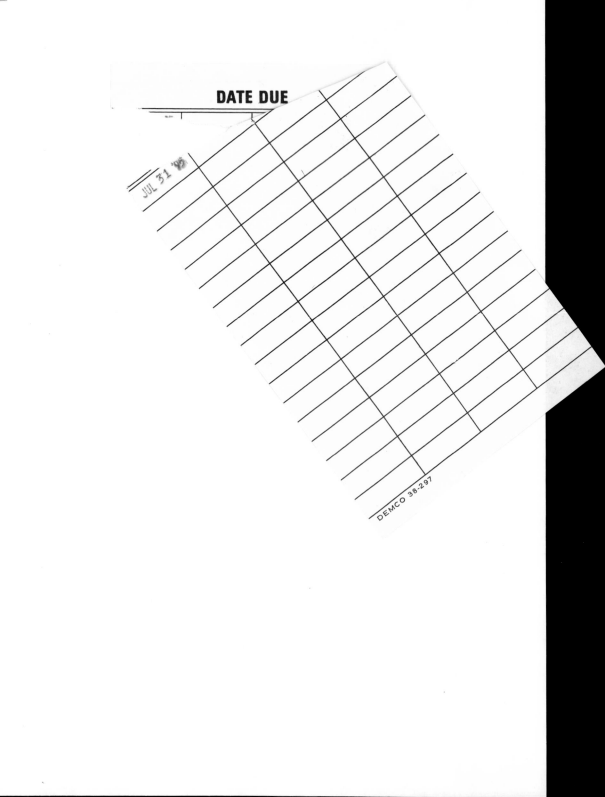

DATE DUE

JUL 31 '95

DEMCO 38-297